Tourism and Poverty Reduction

Over the past decade, there have been an increasing number of publications that have analysed and critiqued the potential of tourism to be a mechanism for poverty reduction in less economically developed countries (LEDCs). This book showcases work by established and emerging researchers that provides new thinking and tests previously made assumptions, providing an essential guide for students, practitioners and academics.

This book advances our understanding of the changes and ways forward in the field of sustainable tourism development. Four main themes are illustrated in the book: (1) development agency strategies and approaches; (2) governance and biodiversity conservation; (3) assessment of tourism impacts; and (4) value chain analysis and inter-sectoral linkages. Furthermore, the book shows that academic research findings can be used practically in destinations, and how practitioners can benefit from sharing their experiences with academic scholars.

This book was based on a special issue and various articles from the *Journal of Sustainable Tourism*.

Anna Spenceley is an international consultant working on innovative solutions in global sustainable tourism. She is Chair of the International Union for Conservation of Nature (IUCN) World Commission on Protected Areas (WCPA): Tourism and Protected Areas Specialist Group, and editor of *Responsible Tourism: Critical issues for Conservation and Development* (2010).

Dorothea Meyer is Senior Lecturer in Tourism, and leads the special interest research group *'Political Economy of Tourism for Development'*, at Sheffield Hallam University, UK. She specialises in the political economy of tourism development, and the role of tourism as an agent for poverty reduction in less economically developed countries.

Tourism and Poverty Reduction

Principles and impacts in developing countries

Edited by
Anna Spenceley and Dorothea Meyer

Routledge
Taylor & Francis Group

LONDON AND NEW YORK

First published 2016
by Routledge
2 Park Square, Milton Park, Abingdon, Oxon, OX14 4RN, UK

and by Routledge
711 Third Avenue, New York, NY 10017, USA

First issued in paperback 2017

Routledge is an imprint of the Taylor & Francis Group, an informa business

© 2016 Taylor & Francis

British Library Cataloguing in Publication Data
A catalogue record for this book is available from the British Library

ISBN 13: 978-1-138-29480-6 (pbk)
ISBN 13: 978-1-138-93608-9 (hbk)

Typeset in Times New Roman
by RefineCatch Limited, Bungay, Suffolk

Publisher's Note
The publisher accepts responsibility for any inconsistencies that may have arisen during the conversion of this book from journal articles to book chapters, namely the possible inclusion of journal terminology.

Disclaimer
Every effort has been made to contact copyright holders for their permission to reprint material in this book. The publishers would be grateful to hear from any copyright holder who is not here acknowledged and will undertake to rectify any errors or omissions in future editions of this book.

Contents

CONTENTS

Section 4: Value chain analysis and inter-sectoral linkages

Citation Information

The following chapters were originally published in the *Journal of Sustainable Tourism*, volume 20, issue 3 (April 2012). When citing this material, please use the original page numbering for each article, as follows:

Chapter 2
Tourism and development at work: 15 years of tourism and poverty reduction within the SNV Netherlands Development Organisation
John Hummel and Rene van der Duim
Journal of Sustainable Tourism, volume 20, issue 3 (April 2012) pp. 319–338

Chapter 3
Influenced and influential: the role of tour operators and development organisations in tourism and poverty reduction in Ecuador
Louise Mary Erskine and Dorothea Meyer
Journal of Sustainable Tourism, volume 20, issue 3 (April 2012) pp. 339–357

Chapter 5
Blessing or curse? The political economy of tourism development in Tanzania
Fred Nelson
Journal of Sustainable Tourism, volume 20, issue 3 (April 2012) pp. 359–375

Chapter 6
Tourism revenue sharing policy at Bwindi Impenetrable National Park, Uganda: a policy arrangements approach
Wilber Manyisa Ahebwa, Rene van der Duim and Chris Sandbrook
Journal of Sustainable Tourism, volume 20, issue 3 (April 2012) pp. 377–394

Chapter 8
The role of tourism employment in poverty reduction and community perceptions of conservation and tourism in southern Africa
Susan Lynne Snyman
Journal of Sustainable Tourism, volume 20, issue 3 (April 2012) pp. 395–416

Chapter 9
Tourism and poverty alleviation in Fiji: comparing the impacts of small- and large-scale tourism enterprises
Regina Scheyvens and Matt Russell
Journal of Sustainable Tourism, volume 20, issue 3 (April 2012) pp. 417–436

Chapter 10
A critical analysis of tourism, gender and poverty reduction
Hazel Tucker and Brenda Boonabaana
Journal of Sustainable Tourism, volume 20, issue 3 (April 2012) pp. 437–455

Chapter 12
Value chain approaches to assessing the impact of tourism on low-income households in developing countries
Jonathan Mitchell
Journal of Sustainable Tourism, volume 20, issue 3 (April 2012) pp. 457–475

Chapter 13
Tourism–agriculture linkages in rural South Africa: evidence from the accommodation sector
Christian M. Rogerson
Journal of Sustainable Tourism, volume 20, issue 3 (April 2012) pp. 477–495

Chapter 14
Social enterprises in tourism: an exploratory study of operational models and success factors
Janina von der Weppen and Janet Cochrane
Journal of Sustainable Tourism, volume 20, issue 3 (April 2012) pp. 497–511

The following chapter was originally published in the *Journal of Sustainable Tourism*, volume 19, issue 1 (January 2011). When citing this material, please use the original page numbering for each article, as follows:

Chapter 4
Community-based tourism enterprises: challenges and prospects for community participation; Khama Rhino Sanctuary Trust, Botswana
Lesego Senyana Stone and Tibabo Moren Stone
Journal of Sustainable Tourism, volume 19, issue 1 (January 2011) pp. 97–114

The following chapter was originally published in the *Journal of Sustainable Tourism*, volume 20, issue 1 (January 2012). When citing this material, please use the original page numbering for each article, as follows:

Chapter 7
Community-based cultural tourism: issues, threats and opportunities
Noel B. Salazar
Journal of Sustainable Tourism, volume 20, issue 1 (January 2012) pp. 9–22

The following chapter was originally published in the *Journal of Sustainable Tourism*, volume 23, issue 3 (March 2015). When citing this material, please use the original page numbering for each article, as follows:

Chapter 11

Can ecotourism deliver real economic, social, and environmental benefits? A study of the Osa Peninsula, Costa Rica
Carter A. Hunt, William H. Durham, Laura Driscoll and Martha Honey
Journal of Sustainable Tourism, volume 23, issue 3 (March 2015) pp. 339–357

For any permission-related enquiries please visit:
http://www.tandfonline.com/page/help/permissions

Notes on Contributors

Wilber Manyisa Ahebwa is a Senior Lecturer and Coordinator of External Relations in the Department of Forestry, Biodiversity and Tourism at Makerere University, Kampala, Uganda, and is the current Chair of ATLAS Africa. He is also the Coordinator of the East African Network for Sustainability, Senior Technical Advisor for the Uganda Tourism Association, and a Country Representative for the East Africa Tourism Platform. He holds a PhD in Tourism, Conservation and Development, an MSc in Tourism and Environment from Wageningen University, The Netherlands, and a Bachelor's degree in Tourism Management from Makerere University, Kampala, Uganda. His research interests are in sustainable tourism, tourism conservation and development; entrepreneurship in tourism; tourism business management; and tourism planning and policy analysis. He has published widely in the field of tourism conservation and development, and is a reviewer with a number of international journals. He is currently finalising a post-doctoral program (Enterprises and Biodiversity Conservation in Greater Virunga Landscape) at the University of Cambridge, UK.

Brenda Boonabaana is a Lecturer in the Tourism programme at Makerere University, Kampala, Uganda. She holds a PhD in Tourism from the University of Otago, Dunedin, New Zealand. Her research expertise is in tourism development and gender, with a special interest in the relationship between tourism, women's empowerment and poverty reduction in developing countries. She is a Fellow of African Women in Agricultural Research and Development (2015/2016), supported by the Bill and Melinda Gates Foundation and USAID. She recently published the article 'Negotiating gender and tourism work: Women's lived experiences in Uganda' in *Tourism and Hospitality Research.*

Janet Cochrane is an experienced consultant and researcher in the travel industry. She worked as a tour leader and travel writer in South East Asia during the 1980s, and then in nature-based tourism consultancy with international development agencies. After five years working with a UK-based outbound activity tour operator, she taught on, and later led, an MSc course in Responsible Tourism Management at Leeds Beckett University, UK, from 2004–2013. She now runs a social enterprise focusing on equestrian tourism in Yorkshire and does lecturing and consultancy work on outdoor and activity tourism, especially in rural and protected areas.

Laura Driscoll is a PhD student in Environmental Science, Policy and Management at the University of California, Berkeley, USA. She holds a BA and MA in Anthropological Sciences from Stanford University, California, USA. Her masters research explored the impacts of ecotourism on cultural identity and consumption patterns in communities near Peru's Bahuaja-Sonene National Park. Her current research interests include global dynamics of climate change, food systems, social-ecological interactions and environmental policy. Her dissertation examines how governance frameworks and private food safety standards in leafy greens production affect farmers' environmental practices, through a comparison of agricultural production sectors in California and the United Kingdom.

William H. Durham is a human ecologist who works on conservation and community development with the goal of helping local people find paths to healthy and sustainable futures. He is Professor in Human Biology and Senior Fellow in the Woods Institute for the Environment at Stanford University, California, USA. He serves as co-Director of the 'Osa-Golfito Initiative' for sustainability in Costa Rica and was co-founder of the Center for Responsible Travel (CREST), Washington D.C., USA, which he also co-Directed at the time of the research of this chapter.

Louise Mary Erskine is a consultant in corporate social responsibility with a particular focus on expert employee volunteering in developing countries. She has a PhD from Sheffield Hallam University, UK, in which she investigated the involvement of development organisations and tour operators in tourism poverty reduction projects in remote regions of Ecuador. Her research interests include corporate social responsibility, stakeholder relationships and sustainable livelihoods. She is a Special Advisor to the international development charity, Village by Village.

Martha Honey is co-founder and Executive Director of the Center for Responsible Travel (CREST), Washington D.C., USA. She has written and lectured widely on sustainable tourism issues. Her books include *Ecotourism and Sustainable Development: Who Owns Paradise?* (1999 and 2008) and *Ecotourism and Certification: Setting Standards in Practice* (2002). She is currently writing a book on coastal and cruise tourism. She was Executive Director of The International Ecotourism Society from 2003 to 2006. For 20 years Martha was a journalist based in East Africa and Central America. She holds a PhD in African History.

John Hummel has been working in tourism, poverty reduction, and sustainable development for over 20 years. He worked as a tourism adviser for SNV in several countries, the Himalayas and the Mekong between 1996 and 2011. He was knowledge network leader for SNV Asia for several years, coordinated the ST-EP partnership with UNWTO, and initiated and coordinated the development of manuals and lessons learned documents with UNWTO, ODI, and ICIMOD. He published articles on sustainable and pro-poor tourism, rural development, and value chain development. He is currently finalising his PhD on the rise and fall of tourism for poverty reduction in SNV.

Carter A. Hunt is an Assistant Professor of Recreation, Park and Tourism Management at Pennsylvania State University, USA. He obtained his MS and PhD degrees in Recreation, Park and Tourism Sciences from Texas A&M University, College Station, TX, USA, and also received three years of postdoctoral training in the Department of Anthropology at Stanford University, California, USA. In field-based research in Latin America, he leverages his background in environmental anthropology and an interest in political ecology to assess the impact of tourism on biodiversity conservation and sustainable community development in rural destination communities around parks and protected areas.

Dorothea Meyer is a Senior Lecturer at Sheffield Business School, Sheffield Hallam University, UK. She holds a PhD from the University of North London, UK, in Political Economy of Tourism Development. She has published widely in journals such as *Annals of Tourism Research, Journal of Sustainable Tourism, Current Issues in Tourism* and *Tourism Recreation Research*, and she currently leads the Special Interest Group of Tourism & Development at Sheffield Hallam University. Her research interests include the political economy of tourism development, tourism as a tool for poverty reduction, gendered power relations, and social network analysis.

Jonathan Mitchell has degrees in Geography from Bristol University, UK; Development Economics from the University of Cambridge, UK; and Planning from University College London, UK. He worked in the economic consultancy sector in the UK with Ove Arup for four years before an eleven-year sojourn in Southern Africa around the tumultuous period of the 1994 Elections in South Africa. He worked in Lesotho as a project economist for a water programme (1994–1996), then as the development economist for one of South Africa's new provinces (1996–2001), and finally led the local economic development portfolio for the EU (2001–2005). Returning to Europe he led the rural programme at the Overseas Development Institute for seven years, before joining Coffey International Development, a development consultancy, in 2012.

Fred Nelson is the founder and Executive Director of Maliasili Initiatives, an organisation which promotes sustainable natural resource management and conservation in Africa by focusing on strengthening leading local civil society organizations. He lived in Tanzania for more than a decade, working closely with pastoralist communities on wildlife, tourism, and livelihood issues. He has done applied research on community natural resource management across eastern and southern Africa, authoring the edited volume *Community Rights, Conservation and Contested Land: The Politics of Natural Resource Governance in Africa* (Routledge, 2012).

Christian M. Rogerson is a Professor in the School of Tourism and Hospitality, Faculty of Management at the University of Johannesburg, South Africa. His major research focus is the relations between tourism and development, with a specific interest in local and regional development, small enterprise development, and tourism space economies.

Matt Russell is a tutor and doctoral student in the Department of Sociology at Massey University, Palmerston North, New Zealand. He has worked with Regina Scheyvens on a number of pro-poor tourism projects in the capacity of research assistant. He has a particular interest in bridging the gap between sociological theorising and development practice.

Noel B. Salazar is a Research Professor in Anthropology at the University of Leuven, Belgium. He is the co-editor of *Tourism Imaginaries* (2014) and the *Anthropology of Tourism Book Series*, and author of *Envisioning Eden* (2010) and numerous peer-reviewed articles and book chapters on tourism. He sits on the editorial boards of, among others, *Annals of Tourism Research, Journal of Sustainable Tourism, Journal of Heritage Tourism*, and *International Journal of Tourism Anthropology*. In addition, he is on UNESCO's and UNWTO's official roster of consultants and an expert member of the ICOMOS International Cultural Tourism Committee and the UNESCO-UNITWIN Network 'Culture, Tourism and Development'.

Chris Sandbrook is a political ecologist with diverse research interests around a central theme of biodiversity conservation and its relationship with society. His current research activities include investigating trade-offs between ecosystem services at the landscape scale in developing countries, and investigating the role of values and evidence in shaping the decisions of conservationists and their organizations. He is particularly interested in the use of market-based mechanisms in conservation, including nature-based tourism, which he has studied in Uganda, Rwanda, Kenya, and Mozambique.

Regina Scheyvens is Head of Development Studies at Massey University, Palmerston North, New Zealand. Here she combines a passion for teaching about international development with research on tourism and development. Two books have emerged from this research, *Tourism for Development: Empowering Communities* (2002), and *Tourism and Poverty* (2011), along with articles on themes such as backpacker tourism, ecotourism, empowerment, and sustainable tourism. Her current research examines the contributions of multinational tourism resorts to community development in Fiji.

Susan Lynne Snyman has a PhD in Economics from the University of Cape Town, South Africa. The focus of her PhD research was on the socio-economic impact of high-end ecotourism in remote, rural communities adjacent to protected areas, based on over 1800 community surveys in six southern African countries. She joined Wilderness Safaris in 2008, bringing with her over a decade of experience in the ecotourism industry in southern Africa. She is currently Group Community Development and Culture Manager, as well as Regional Director of Children in the Wilderness. She is also Vice-Chair of the IUCN WCPA Tourism and Protected Areas Specialist Groups and Research Fellow at the Environmental Economics Policy Research Unit at UCT.

Anna Spenceley is a tourism consultant focusing on sustainable tourism based in South Africa. Her PhD led to the development of a Sustainable Nature-Based Tourism Assessment Toolkit. In particular, she works in areas of high biodiversity in developing countries, through her company STAND. She is Chair of the IUCN's World Commission on Protected Areas Tourism and Protected Areas Specialist Group, and a Senior Research Fellow with the University of Johannesburg, South Africa. She is also the editor of the book *Responsible Tourism: Critical issues for Conservation and Development* (Routledge, 2008), and co-editor of *Evolution and Innovation in Wildlife Conservation* (Routledge, 2009). She is on the editorial board of the *Journal of Sustainable Tourism*.

Lesego Senyana Stone is a Research Scholar at the Okavango Research Institute, University of Botswana, Maun, Botswana. Her research interests are in sustainable tourism development with specific reference to nature-based tourism, community-based tourism, and community participation in tourism.

Tibabo Moren Stone is a Research Scholar at the Okavango Research Institute, University of Botswana, Maun, Botswana. His research interests are in sustainable tourism development and conservation, especially nature-based tourism and ecotourism with a focus on protected areas and community-based tourism.

Hazel Tucker is an Associate Professor in the Department of Tourism at the University of Otago, New Zealand. She has a background in social anthropology and is the author of *Living with Tourism* (2003), and the co-editor of *Tourism and Postcolonialism* (2004) and *Commercial Homes in Tourism* (2009). Her recent journal article publications focus on tourism and emotion, tourism and world heritage, and gender issues in tourism. She sits on the editorial board of *Annals of Tourism Research,* and is co-Vice-President of the International Tourism Research Committee of the International Sociological Association.

Rene van der Duim currently works as a Professor at the Cultural Geography Group at Wageningen University, The Netherlands. His research interests are tourism, conservation, and development with a particular interest in Eastern Africa. He is a co-editor of *Actor-Network Theory and Tourism: Ordering, materiality and multiplicity* (2012), and *Institutional arrangements for Conservation, Development and Tourism in Eastern Africa* (2015), and has published his work in journals such as *Annals of Tourism Research*, *Journal of Sustainable Tourism*, *Tourist Studies*, *Tourism Geographies*, *Society & Natural Resources*, and *Conservation and Society*. He is also Chair of the European Association for Leisure and Tourism Education and Research, ATLAS.

Janina von der Weppen completed her MSc in Responsible Tourism Management at the School of Events, Tourism and Hospitality at Leeds Beckett University, UK, in 2010. She volunteered with a social enterprise in Indonesia, assisting with the development of its sustainable tourism operations, and wrote her MSc dissertation on social enterprises in tourism. She moved to Australia in 2011, and worked with a tourism and environmental management and advisory group, developing sustainability projects and training for tourism businesses.

Tourism and poverty reduction: principles and impacts in developing countries

Anna Spenceley and Dorothea Meyer

This chapter provides an introduction to this edited volume with an overview of chapters on *Tourism and Poverty Reduction*, and a synthesis of the main issues. Four main themes are illustrated in the book: (1) development agency strategies and approaches; (2) governance and biodiversity conservation; (3) assessment of tourism impacts; and (4) value chain analysis and inter-sectoral linkages. Key potential topics for future research and action are outlined including: (1) the use of new techniques measuring tourism impacts; (2) the roles of development agency governance and operational practices; (3) how inequitable power relations and weak governance can undermine efforts; (4) the importance of private sector business practices that contribute to poverty reduction; (5) the value of multidisciplinary quantitative and qualitative research tools; and (6) the need for linkages between academic research and practitioner interventions.

Introduction

Governments, development agencies and non-governmental organisations have increasingly sought to invest in initiatives that aim to reduce poverty through tourism development. They begin with an assumption that tourism can improve the livelihoods and incomes of the poor. However, what evidence is available to demonstrate that tourism does have this impact? What theoretical underpinnings is the relationship supported by? Furthermore, what conditions are required to maximize the local economic impact of a global industry, when the poor often have little power or understanding of how the system works?

This chapter introduces recent and new research into links and relationships between tourism and poverty in developing countries. It does this through collating and analysing the evolving evidence and debates coming from academics and practitioners working in this area. And it adds to that evidence and discussion by introducing the very diverse chapters in this book, which seek to address the questions posed in the opening paragraph.

A brief scan of the literature reveals that a large number of peer reviewed papers on the poverty reduction theme in developing countries have focused on case studies related to community based tourism (CBT) (e.g. Bramwell, 2010; Choi & Murray, 2010; Harrison & Schipani, 2007; Lapeyre, 2010; Lepper & Goebel, 2010; Matarrita-Cascante, Brennan, & Luloff, 2010; Mehta & Kellert, 1998; Saarinen, 2010; Stone & Stone, 2011; Wearing & McDonald, 2002). A general assumption seems to have prevailed that CBT offers considerable opportunities for marginal communities to participate in the tourism industry. Pearce (1992) suggests that CBT provides a mechanism for an equitable flow of benefits to all tourism stakeholders, through a system of local development control and consensus-based decision making. However, many papers have shown that this might not necessarily be the case and generally a rather pessimistic picture of tourism as a potential tool for poverty reduction has emerged (Dixey, 2008; Goodwin, 2006; Spenceley, 2008). For example, findings from southern Africa suggest that the majority of CBT managers have little understanding of how to operate a tourism business, with limitations in financial management, monitoring, market access, advertising, and communications (Spenceley, 2008). Some of the failings of CBT appear to have been caused by the development approach taken, which has been driven by "capacity building" or "empowerment" agendas; and by "collective" rather than "individual" benefits within communities, rather than focusing on a business approach (Spenceley, 2008). Häusler (2008) describes how funding proposals for CBT in South America and Asia frequently addressed issues of participation, gender, empowerment, and capacity building, but failed to include business plans, product development or marketing strategies. As they are often supported by donor agencies and non-governmental organisations and seldom managed and controlled by the community, Salazar (2012, see also chapter 7 in the book) suggests that "community-centered tourism" would be a more accurate description. Although there is an assumption that all parties have an equal opportunity to participate in the CBT planning process, Jamal and Getz (1995) indicate that power imbalances pose a barrier to this ideal. In addition, if communities do not have sufficient understanding of how the tourism industry functions, or how to attract tourists and manage them, then they are unlikely to benefit.

The second major strand of papers which stands out has focused on broader structural conditions and power relations between the global tourism industry and local communities. Again, a consensus seems to have emerged that these global structures prevent developmental impacts and poverty reduction on the ground as tourism development decisions are frequently made by trans-national corporations (TNCs) based in generating countries. Applying a dependency theory approach, Britton (1982) argues that the structural characteristics of "Third World" economies can detract from achieving economic and social development objectives, and "equally problematic is the organization of the international tourism industry itself" (1982, p. 336). The work of practitioners, in particular those working with the concept of pro-poor tourism (PPT), was criticised for supporting neo-liberal ideologies (Hall, 2007; Mowforth & Munt, 2009; Schilcher, 2007; Scheyvens, 2007, 2011). Hall and Brown (2006), for example, question the potential of PPT by asking "does PPT simply offer another route by which economic imperialism, through tourism, may extend its tentacles, or is it an appropriately liberating and remunerative option?" (2006, p. 13).

This book assesses some of the assumptions made in the academic and grey literature about the link between poverty reduction and tourism in developing countries. It updates the discussion on tourism and poverty reduction, collating together in one book new evidence and debate from prominent academics and practitioners. New perspectives that are presented include how development agencies are using tourism as a development agent, and how their abilities to create impacts are in certain circumstances possibly more limited than those initiated by the private sector. The connections between power relations and governance are also explored, and demonstrate that adopting rights-based approaches can be fruitful, but that state authorities can be resistant to relinquishing control. In relation to tourism impact studies and value chain analysis (VCA), quantitative analyses and data are used to demonstrate how the level of poverty is reduced in destinations where operators actively promote local employment and procurement, particularly among women.

At this stage it is important to remind the reader of past and current discussions evaluating tourism's potential to act as a tool for poverty reduction in developing countries.

What is the link between poverty and tourism?

It is estimated that approximately 20% of the world's population (1.4 billion people) are currently living in "extreme poverty" as they survive on under $1.25 per day (as defined by the United Nations; Chen & Ravallion, 2008; Wroughton, 2008). While the International Poverty Line (IPL) measures poverty largely in monetary terms, Sen (1999) shows that poverty is a multidimensional phenomenon and that it arises when people lack key capabilities, such as inadequate income, lack of access to education, poor health, insecurity, low self-confidence, a sense of powerlessness, and the absence of rights such as freedom of speech. Sen's broader approach focuses on the capability of the individual to function in society, which makes solutions to poverty far more complex than simply analysing financial impacts. Poverty is related to, but distinct from, inequality and vulnerability (Haughton & Khandker, 2009). Inequality focuses primarily on the distribution of economic factors (such as income or consumption) across the whole population, and it requires a comparative analysis within that society; vulnerability, on the other hand, is seen as the risk of falling into poverty in the future and is a key dimension of well-being since it affects individuals' behaviour in terms of investment, production patterns, coping strategies, and their perceptions of their own situation.

Tourism is a truly global industry and it generated an estimated US$919 billion in export earnings in 2010 (UNWTO, 2011a). Rich cultural and natural assets exist in some of the poorest regions of the world, and they offer great potential for travel itineraries. Tourism can provide one possible mechanism to re-distribute wealth from the rich to the poor. As tourists travel to impoverished regions of the world for a variety of reasons, they spend money on travel, accommodation, excursions, food, drinks, and shopping. In many tourism destinations, the poor have the potential to capture some of this spending through employment and, probably most importantly, through providing products and/or services that the tourism sector and tourists need.

Tourism is a highly significant foreign exchange earner for many of the poorest countries and it is currently estimated that approximately 40% of all international tourist arrivals accrue to developing countries (Scheyvens, 2011). International tourist arrivals have grown significantly faster in developing countries than they have in the EU or OECD countries (Organisation for Economic Co-operation and Development) (Meyer, 2010; Roe, Ashley, Page, & Meyer, 2004; Scheyvens, 2011). Even more striking is the dependence on this industry for many developing countries: in 2005, it accounted for 80% of total goods and services exports for Samoa, 70% for the Maldives, 56% for Sao Tome and Principe, and 43% for Vanuatu. Between 2000 and 2005, both annual international visitor arrivals and revenues for developing countries have grown significantly, by 8.2% and 12.0% respectively (Meyer, 2010; UNWTO, 2006).

The past two decades have seen an increasing volume of research, publications, and development agency interventions that have focused on how to increase the proportion of tourism expenditure that reaches impoverished people and their communities. The next section outlines some of the theoretical discussions and findings from practitioners that have emerged on tourism and poverty reduction during this time.

A short history of the theory and practice on tourism and poverty reduction

Since the development of mass tourism in the 1960s, no consensus seems to have emerged as to whether the tourism industry can contribute to poverty reduction or, in fact, might actually exacerbate the inequality gap between "hosts" and "guests", and between the "hosts" involved and those not involved in the tourism sector within destinations.

In the 1960s and 1970s discussions on the tourism industry's contributions to development and poverty reduction were analysed through a macro-economic lens and adopted a neo-liberal "trickle down" assumption. It was assumed that tourism not only generates jobs and foreign exchange earnings, but it can also bring socio-cultural change to traditional societies by demonstrating "modern" ways of life (Scheyvens, 2011). Tourism was regarded as "a catalyst for modernization, economic development and prosperity in emerging nations in the third world" (Williams, 1998, p. 1). Authors supporting this view were often based in an econometric tradition focusing on macro level development (for a detailed discussion, see Burns, 1999; Desforges, 2000; Friedmann, 1992; Harrison, 2003; Mowforth & Munt, 2009).

The 1980s and 1990s saw a new breed of papers that adopted a post-structuralist political economy approach, arguing that unless major structural reforms of the tourism industry take place, the sector is unlikely to aid poverty reduction or reduce inequality (e.g. Britton, 1982; Brohman, 1996; Bryden, 1973; Clancy, 1999; de Kadt, 1979; Wilkinson, 1987). A key focus here was on dependency debates, and tourism was frequently seen as supporting a new kind of colonialism, a view which is still prominent especially among African academics today (Akama, 2004; Manyara & Jones, 2007; Mbaiwa, 2005). Tourism was viewed as an industry dominated by Transnational Corporations (TNCs), which exploited the workers and resources of developing countries, commodified traditional cultures, entrenched inequality, and deepened poverty (Britton, 1982; Duffy, 2002; Pleumarom, 1994; Schilcher, 2007).

Also in the 1990s neo-liberalism became fully enshrined in the approaches taken by the development community, and it was supported by the economic prescriptions of the International Monetary Fund and World Bank. The Washington Consensus was a term coined in 1989 to describe ten economic policy prescriptions that were considered a "standard" reform package for countries in crisis (Williamson, 2004). It stressed the importance of economic rationalism and efficiency, market liberalisation, and a small role for the state (Öniş & Şenses, 2005; Scheyvens, 2011). In that context tourism was seen as a mechanism for impoverished and indebted countries to trade their way out of poverty (Brohman, 1996). Much of the work focused on grassroots development, empowerment, and CBT (Cole, 2006; Sofield, 2003; Timothy, 2007; Zhao & Ritchie, 2007).

Yet Scheyvens (2007, 2009) argues that tourism might not be effective as a tool for poverty reduction, and it might instead increase the dependency of the "south" on "northern" TNCs. Alternatives to mass tourism were proposed by several authors (e.g. de Kadt, 1990; Krippendorf, 1987; Smith & Eadington, 1992). Several studies warned that tourism can increase inequalities (Scheyvens, 2002, 2007), increase dependency on outward orientated growth (Brohman, 1996), exploit the workforce (Tourism Concern, 2004), lead to the displacement of communities (Akama, 1996, 2004; Mowforth & Munt, 2009) and contribute to conflict over scarce resources (Mbaiwa & Darkoh, 2009). A key concern has been that the global structures of the tourism industry made it impossible for developing countries to reap the benefits from tourism development (Scheyvens, 2009). Some authors claimed that "leakages" (i.e. monies that leave the destination to pay for imports necessary to sustain the industry or monies paid to TNCs in the "north" that never reach the destination) were exceptionally high in this industry (e.g. Britton, 1982; Oppermann & Chon, 1997).

Thus, negative trends were identified, and also some more positive ones. Some of the more positive evidence and arguments indicate that leakages were not necessarily higher in tourism than in other industries (Page, 1999; Roe et al., 2004), and that tourism can contribute to employment and income generation (Ashley & Mitchell, 2007), gender equality (Anker, 1998; Scheyvens, 2002), education and knowledge exchange (Ashley, Roe, & Goodwin, 2001), inter-sectoral linkages (Belisle, 1983, 1984; Meyer, 2007; Momsen, 1996; Torres 2002, 2003), entrepreneurship and small, medium and micro-enterprise (SMME) development (Kirsten & Rogerson, 2002), and nature conservation (Saarinen, 2009; Spenceley, 2008).

Further, Scheyvens (2011) argues that not all writers in the critical tradition are philo-sophically opposed to tourism and it was recognised that tourism could bring benefits if development took a form in which state governance focused on national interests (Clancy, 1999; Potter, 1993). These discussions were in line with the new attention paid to soft, green (Dann, 2002; Krippendorf, 1987; Müller, 1984) and later sustainable tourism (Butler, 1990; Neto, 2003; Sofield, 2003; Thomlinson & Getz, 1996).

At the beginning of the new millennium the neo-liberal orthodoxy was challenged by a renewed focus on the role of the state (Sofield, 2003). It became clear that inequalities between developed and developing countries were increasing and that the liberalisation of economies did not automatically lead to enhanced economic growth (Scheyvens, 2011). A "new poverty" agenda was now increasingly focusing on enhancing the role of the state and on the importance of strong institutions, governances, and more effectively targeting poverty and vulnerability. Furthermore, researchers became interested in detailed studies of systems, processes, places, and interactions between people in order to understand how power influences the actions of stakeholders and the link between tourism and poverty (e.g. Burns, 2004; Higgins-Desbiolles, 2006; Jafari, 2001; Schilcher, 2007; Teo, 2003). These studies have embraced the complexity of tourism and moved away from a reductionist approach that sees tourism either as a force for good or evil. Rather than viewing tourism simply as an industry aligned to neo-liberal thinking, tourism was perceived as a powerful social force which needs to be better understood in order to connect it more effectively to development agendas that go beyond purely economic considerations.

There has also been an attitude shift over the past decade among development agencies towards tourism, and its role in alleviating poverty. Whereas in the past donors, interna-tional non-governmental organisations (INGOs) and technical assistance organisations stayed clear of promoting tourism as a development agent, this has changed considerably since the UK Department for International Development (DfID) commissioned research into the possibilities for the tourism industry to contribute to poverty reduction (Bennett, Roe, & Ashley, 1999). It was realised that tourism could provide the opportunity for a shift to non-farm economic activities in peripheral areas struggling to keep agricultural production afloat and that are, because of their isolation, unsuitable for large-scale export-orientated manufacturing (Ashley & Maxwell, 2001; Farrington, Carney, Ashley, & Turton, 1999).

Weighing up all these arguments, it was suggested by Bennett et al. (1999) that the tourism sector actually had promising potential to contribute to poverty reduction in developing countries, for the following reasons:

- the market comes to the producers, thus providing additional sales opportunities in the destination;
- inter-sectoral linkages can be created, especially with agriculture, artisan production, and additional services, which are essential for livelihood diversification;
- tourism is generally labour intensive (although often less so than agriculture);
- tourism takes place in marginal areas; areas where the majority of the poor live;

- tourism generally employs a high level of females, young people, and unskilled or less-skilled individuals; a high percentage of the poorest in society fall into these categories;
- tourism has rather limited barriers to entry when compared to manufacturing or other export activities; and
- the tourism sector is already growing at a very high rate in many developing countries.

The research undertaken by the Pro-Poor Tourism (PPT) Partnership (e.g. Ashley, Roe, & Goodwin, 2000; Ashley et al., 2001) was influential for this new way of thinking about tourism. The UK-based Overseas Development Institute (ODI), for example, claims that the need and opportunity to harness markets for poverty reduction is particularly evident in tourism (Ashley & Mitchell, 2007; Mitchell & Ashley, 2009). Rather than just condemning tourism as a hedonistic, pleasure-seeking "white men's industry", practitioners and donors acknowledged that there was potential for it to reduce poverty. However, whether this could and would be achieved was a rather different undertaking altogether.

As a consequence, over the past 10 years, many of the most influential development organisations invested considerable funds into how the tourism industry could be harnessed more effectively as a tool for poverty reduction, and adopted the ideas of PPT. These organisations include DfID, Netherlands Development Organization (SNV), International Trade Centre (ITC), Development Bank of Southern Africa (DBSA), Kreditanstalt für Wiederaufbau (KfW), Gesellschaft für internationale Zusammenarbeit (GiZ), Asian Development Bank (ADB), US government Overseas Aid Program (USAID), Australian government Overseas Aid Program (AUSAID), New Zealand government Overseas Aid Program (NZAID), International Finance Corporation (IFC), and the World Bank.

Much recent work on tourism and poverty reduction has focused on four main themes: the strategies and approaches of development agencies; governance and biodiversity conservation; assessments of tourism's impacts; and VCA and inter-sectoral linkages. The first theme is the role of development agencies. These agencies have been important in providing both funding and technical assistance in developing countries for tourism and poverty reduction interventions. The interventions have varied from strategic international programs to individual initiatives in destinations. The donors have had the capacity to experiment with different approaches, and also to evaluate and document what works, and what does not. The second theme is governance and biodiversity conservation. These activities are important, and they are frequently linked together, because nature-based tourism often takes place in areas of high biodiversity in remote, rural destinations where the poor reside. However, it is difficult to establish the good governance required equitably to manage the access to charismatic wildlife and natural resources, the opportunities for tourism development, and the allocation of the ensuing benefits. The third theme is the assessment of tourism's impacts. Work that quantifies and assesses tourism's impacts on poverty reduction, particularly addressing the financial and social implications, are clearly important in determining whether there is a correlation between tourism and local economic development. The final theme addresses VCA and inter-sectoral linkages, which shifts focus from direct financial benefits (i.e. from employment or operating tourism businesses) to indirect benefits from enterprises that support tourism (i.e. from products and services needed for the industry to operate, such as food and beverages).

These four themes associated with recent research on tourism and poverty reduction continue to be very important, and thus they are the focus of this book and an overview of the chapters follows next.

Development agency strategies and approaches

The first set of chapters address the theme of intervention strategies used by development agencies in order to harness the potential of tourism as a poverty reduction tool in developing countries. Development agencies and practitioners have introduced a broad range of interventions in this field, ranging from providing seed funding for CBT (e.g. USAID) or for joint-ventures between private sector enterprises and communities (e.g. World Bank), to providing capacity building and technical support to impoverished communities (e.g. SNV, UN-WTO, GiZ), and supporting private sector approaches that provide greater local economic benefits (e.g. IFC, ITC, DfID). The tourism programs within these agencies are not always stand-alone, but are often incorporated within broader programs supporting economic development or biodiversity conservation. The extent to which the level of funding invested in such interventions has directly led to fewer people living in poverty is difficult to ascertain (see Hummel & van der Duim, 2015: chapter 2). Development agencies each have their own mechanisms and indicators for measuring the impact of their work, but these are not compiled collectively, and nor are they broadly disseminated.

The first chapters illustrate the conditions under which development agencies operate and the organisational processes that they employ, and are embedded in, to achieve poverty reduction impacts. Two chapters are in line with the post-structuralist discussions that focus on the power of actors and the role of processes and structures that restrict or enable agency. The chapters indicate that it is impossible to understand the "what" and "how many" if we do not know more about the "why" and "how". The third chapter provides a case study illustrating how CBT operations frequently struggle to find commercial success, and require long-term subsidisation by development agencies – and local stakeholders – before returning a profit.

Chapter 2, by Hummel and van der Duim (2015), discusses the changing approaches to tourism as a tool for poverty reduction by the Dutch development organisation SNV over the past 15 years. Hummel and van der Duim examine how and why tourism became an important part of SNV's work and how changing policy discourses influenced its operation. Until early 2011 SNV was seen by many as a frontrunner in developing projects and advisory services in sustainable tourism in developing countries. Before it ceased engaging with tourism in early 2011, SNV employed around 60 national and international tourism advisers in 25 countries. This chapter contributes to the recent surge in "aidnography", or ethnographic encounters with the international development sector (see Büscher, 2010; Mosse, 2005), by examining the way in which heterogeneous entities, such as people, concepts and ideas, interest, events, and objects, are tied together into material and conceptual orderings. The focus of this chapter is not on whether tourism and development worked, but on *how* it worked. The chapter does this by portraying the development and operation of five phases in SNV's involvement in tourism projects in developing countries, and it is thus congruent with post-structuralist concerns related to processes and power relations between agency and structure. Hummel and van der Duim argue that success in development depends on the stabilisation of a particular interpretation of events, and on the way in which tourism and development ideas are socially produced and sustained. They state that the success of SNV's work is determined by how SNV as an organisation itself defines success. They argue, however, that in their view SNV's achievements have been demonstrated in part through the satisfaction of their clients, the number of projects and partnerships, and the use of their work by other development agencies.

The chapter recalls how SNV reluctantly started with a small number of tourism projects in the 1990s but by the late 2000s it seems to have significantly influenced the international discussion on the relation between tourism and poverty reduction. Hummel and van der Duim argue that SNV attempted to stabilise the prevailing chaotic and ad-hoc practices by systematically validating ideas and practices for various stakeholders, including donors, politicians, scientists and their peers. As Hummel and van der Duim (2015) state, "this obviously leads to the question whether SNV's involvement in tourism over the last 15 years has been successful" (2015, p. 37). The chapter concludes that relations between tourism and development remain highly contested and require the continual production of "successes". While the chapter does not explicitly explain the successes of SNV, the authors argue that the organisation has left significant legacies on national policies and practices and it has also provided socio-economic benefits in remote areas. Subsequent papers on this subject should ideally complement this narrative with evaluations of the impacts that SNV has had on poverty reduction in destinations. Later in this volume, Salazar (2015: chapter 7) analyses a CBT program initiated by SNV in Tanzania, questioning the value of short-term interventions, and reflecting on the need for effective handover strategies to be created before programs end.

The third chapter, by Erskine and Meyer (2015), critically compares the approach and work of development agencies with that of private sector enterprises in Ecuador. It adds a theoretical dimension by using Giddens' structuration theory to compare the work of development organisations with that of initiatives implemented by the private sector. Erskine and Meyer assess key elements of Giddens' structuration theory by exploring what Giddens terms actor's "knowledgability", "reflexivity", and "institutionalised interactions", leading to a discussion of the duality of agency and structure. Giddens' (1979, 1984) work focuses on processes, and it treats structure as both a product of, and a constraint on, human action. It aims to bridge the gap between deterministic, objective, and static notions of structure, on the one hand, and voluntaristic, subjective, and dynamic views, on the other, by illustrating the duality of the two realms of social order and of the intersections between them.

The assumption of this chapter is that in order to assess the outcomes of poverty intervention strategies it is important to understand the duality, rather than the frequently discussed dualism, between agency and structure. The chapter deduces that development organisations are strongly influenced and confined by institutional structures, whereas the private sector can be more effective in altering traditional tourism industry structures.

By comparing three local socio-economic development projects in Ecuador, the chapter is able to show that this duality is evident in each of the projects. In PPT projects, the influential differences between development organisations and the private sector suggest that the power of structure outweighs the power of agency for the development organisations, and vice versa for the private sector. The majority of academic studies related to the use of tourism as a tool for poverty reduction focus on the negative impacts of structural dependency (e.g. Sofield, 2003; Schilcher, 2007), but this was generally dismissed by the majority of interviewees in this study, who argued that the structure of the international tourism industry means that these relationships are essential, and positive, for projects to contribute to livelihood improvements. The authors found that the private sector was, to an extent, gifted with more freedom than the development organisations, and that the private sector was more likely to alter patterns of behaviour and, as such, structure. Analysing the duality of structure and agency within PPT projects adds an important new theoretical dimension to academic discussions on the potential of tourism to contribute to poverty reduction.

Chapter 4, by Stone & Stone (2015) focuses on the CBT enterprise Khama Rhino Sanctuary Trust (KRST) in Botswana, which has received extensive support from donors over the years. The chapter describes how development agencies increasingly promoted community participation in rural development initiatives, since the 1972 United Nations Conference on Human Development. They note that although the objectives of CBT have been to ensure the empowerment, control, and economic benefits that reduce poverty, many CBT initiatives have failed – particularly in terms of generating economic benefits – due to their poor financial viability (Mitchell & Muckosy, 2008).

The KRST was initiated by community members, in order to generate revenue for the community based on use of its renewable resources, including through wildlife tourism. KRST provides camping, chalets, and dormitory facilities for tourists (78 beds), who are also offered game drives and opportunities to purchase local crafts. A series of interviews with relevant stakeholders revealed a variety of challenges, including a lack of communal sense of ownership; inadequate employment creation; dependence on external funding; and weak community participation. In relation to donor agencies, the KRST relies heavily on financial support from a suite of agencies: the African Development Foundation, Environmental Heritage Foundation of Botswana, the European Development Fund, and the Global Environment Facility (through the United Nations Development Program). Collectively these agencies provided BWP 745,774 to the KRST between 2003 and 2008 (c. USD 75,000). In certain years, the KRST had to call upon its board members for loans to pay employees, and tourism revenue was used to re-pay these. However, there are positive signs of improvement: following five years of deficit, the KRST made its first profit in 2008, with a surplus of BWP 887, 579 (c. USD 89,309). The KRST proposes to distribute funds to one of three villages each year. Stone and Stone's (2015) research supports findings by many others, particularly relating to the financial struggles that CBTs face (e.g. Dixey, 2008; Goodwin, 2008, 2009; Spenceley, 2008), and provides a valuable contribution to this body of knowledge.

Governance and biodiversity conservation

The second theme in this book is governance issues related to biodiversity conversation. This topic has seen fierce debates in the last two decades (van der Duim, Meyer, & Saarinen, 2011) due to changes in the approaches to conservation and development. There has been an increased shift from government to governance, growing discussion of the neo-liberalisation of nature conservation (Büscher, 2008), and an increased emphasis on the political processes of "land grabbing" (Cotula, Vermeulen, Leonard, & Keeley, 2009). Brockington, Sachedina, and Scholfield (2008) argue that in recent decades the political economy of conservation has been transformed from a predominantly state-led conservation model to one in which corporate interests are becoming increasingly important. Governance issues related to sustainable tourism development are also the subject of increasing discussion (Bramwell & Lane, 2011). The next three chapters in this section use a political economy approach to assess the processes and power relations between the various actors who determine the outcomes of policy choices for conservation areas and for the livelihoods of people living adjacent to them. The chapters also focus on biodiversity conservation and capacity building interventions in East African countries where wildlife resources are particularly important for tourism development.

Chapter 5, by Nelson (2015), analyses how tourism development in Tanzania is shaped by a highly centralised and weakly accountable state, a prevalence of informal rent-seeking interests, institutionalised corruption in government at all levels, and the intermingling of a developmentalist discourse built on foreign and private investment. Nelson shows that these factors limited the ability of local communities to capture tourism's value as a poverty reduction instrument. He illustrates the growing conflicts over land tenure, wildlife revenues, and access to tourism benefits in northern Tanzania. Nelson concludes that the development of explicitly rights-based approaches to tourism that emphasise tenure and devolved governance potentially would aid the implementation of poverty alleviation strategies. The emphasis of this chapter is on understanding the underlying political-economic dynamics that perpetuate these well documented and enduring conflicts (Homewood, Kristjanson, & Trench, 2009; Nelson, 2010; Snyder & Sulle, 2011). Through this analysis, Nelson shows the importance of contextualising tourism development and poverty reduction efforts within wider contests over market access, economic and political empowerment, and citizenship. He concludes that tourism is one component of a much wider, and increasingly well-documented, contemporary "land grab" in Tanzania, where local resources are re-centralised and expropriated. It is seen as essential that a rights-based approach to tourism development is used that recognises the critical and contested role of resource tenure and the centrality of governance in determining outcomes.

In chapter 6, Ahebwa, van der Duim, and Sandbrook (2015) provide a discussion of the development and implementation of tourism revenue sharing policies at Bwindi Impenetrable National Park in Uganda. They use a policy arrangements perspective to analyse the actors, resources, rules of the game, and discourses that are involved. They conclude that the Uganda Wildlife Authority (UWA) remains the most powerful actor, while the local communities they studied do not feel adequately compensated for the conservation costs. The governance capacity of this arrangement was found to be low and the policy arrangements were structurally incongruent. There were two very different discourse coalitions, and the relationships between actors lacked mutual trust, and the regulative instruments that were established were poorly known, understood, and accepted by the local residents. The distributional effects of the income from revenue sharing were much discussed in Bwindi, with two competing discourses emerging. First, there was an "official" discourse voiced by UWA and the International Gorilla Conservation Programme, which reflected the storylines of international and national conservation and which focused on linking conservation and development (Newmark & Hough, 2000). The second discourse was advocated by local communities and it challenged the way tourism revenue sharing was implemented. Ahebwa et al., conclude that tourism revenue sharing remains a statist policy arrangement, and they echo the findings of Nelson and Agrawal (2008), who found that there is a reduced likelihood of state institutions (the UWA in the case of Bwindi) relinquishing control over resources when they are highly valuable.

Returning to Tanzania, chapter 7 by Salazar (2015) describes an anthropological study of community tour guides who had received training through SNV's award winning Cultural Tourism Program (CTP). The program had intended to establish a Tanzania Cultural Tourism Organisation, but this failed to materialise as there was an inconsistent desire among community members to have tourists in their villages, inequitable distribution of revenues, and escalating conflicts over land and natural resources (Nelson, 2003, 2004). Salazar (2015) found that there were many problems with the experiences guides provided to tourists. These included language barriers, visits to Massai villages resembling "a human zoo" (p. 123), tensions between Maasai and Meru that were exacerbated by a lack of transparency regarding which tribe the guide was from, and guides from each tribe denigrating each other. Salazar suggests that although local participation is vital for sustainable development, this requires a shift of power from authorities to local actors, coupled with true consensus and tangible local control.

Assessments of tourism impacts

The third theme in this book is the assessment of tourism impacts. In their recent book on "Tourism and Poverty Reduction", Mitchell and Ashley (2010) state that the measurement of tourism's impacts span a plethora of fields, including anthropology, sociology, conservation, local economic development, PPT, sustainable livelihoods, and corporate social responsibility. These studies generally focus on understanding the extent to which tourism impacts on the lives of specific target groups, or on assisting in designing, modifying, and evaluating tourism interventions. They generally examine micro-level impacts (e.g. the impact of one tourism enterprise on one or two local communities) or niche tourism products (e.g. CBT; ecotourism). There is also a tendency for studies to be narrowly focused on economic impacts, rather than taking into account environmental, social, and cultural changes. This book contains four chapters on the measurement and assessment of tourism impacts.

The first of these chapters by Snyman (2015) concerns an extensive socio-economic impact analysis of wildlife tourism by Wilderness Safaris, a luxury safari company in Southern Africa. Snyman undertook nearly 200 staff interviews and over 600 local community interviews around six lodges in Malawi, Namibia and Botswana. This type of analysis is important because, rather than tackling only individual enterprises, it presents a larger-scale evaluation of an international business approach to tourism, and it offers substantial samples and data that give weight to the research findings. Wilderness Safaris is a specialist luxury safari operator with 59 safari camps and lodges in seven southern African countries, hosting over 25,000 guests each year (Wilderness Holdings Ltd, 2011). Snyman found that the salaries of around 300 employees at the camps were not only used to buy luxuries (e.g. mobile phones), but also to support their dependents. In fact, the employee salaries were found to support over 2,300 dependents in the communities around the lodges. This effectively lifts the dependents above the absolute poverty line of $1.25 per day. The majority of staff interviewed perceived that tourism reduced poverty in the local area (81%), compared with fewer community representatives who agreed with that perception (50%). One of the interesting aspects of Snyman's work is that a relatively high proportion of non-employees considered the link between tourism, poverty reduction and conservation as important. Snyman also found that with increasing income, the interviewees considered conservation as crucial, which supports work by others (e.g. Ellis, 1999; Ellis & Freeman, 2004). Although her work reflects the impact of one company, Wilderness Safaris, the extensive scale of the research (440 staff interviews and 1,403 community interviews across 40 villages) (Snyman, personal communication, 30 December, 2011) has generated data that can be used by the company and by others to monitor changes over time. Wilderness Holdings Ltd recently released an integrated sustainability report, which incorporates some of Snyman's data, and it also addresses the impacts on environment and culture in the destinations where they work (Wilderness Holdings Ltd, 2011).

Chapter 9, by Scheyvens and Russell (2015) compares the poverty impacts of small and large-scale tourism enterprises in Fiji. They identify that poverty in Fiji is largely due to the decline in agriculture, and that both small and large-scale tourism enterprises contribute positively to revenue generation, job creation and community development. Their survey included one large resort, one medium-sized resort, and four small scale operations. Interviews were conducted with staff at the enterprises and with representatives of the land-owning communities. They found that food procured by the large enterprises was almost entirely imported (99%), while smaller companies purchased the majority of their food locally (80–90%). The findings reveal that, while the country encourages the development of large foreign-owned resorts, indigenous businesses receive less support. Also, the participation by Fijians in the tourism sector is primarily through employment or as landlords, but they are rarely involved in tourism planning and development. Scheyvens and Russell note that there is considerable potential for improvement in local procurement and labour conditions for Fijians, which could increase the extent of poverty reduction. The comparative analysis approach of Scheyvens and Russell is particularly interesting because many case studies tend to look at individual and often small scale enterprises and their impacts. Other evaluations have looked at the economic impacts of large resorts (e.g. Akama & Kieti, 2007; Ashley, Goodwin, & McNab, 2005; Barrowclough, 2007; Mitchell & Faal, 2006; Torres & Momsen, 2004), but this study provides an interesting comparison of the impacts of different sized tourism enterprises in one destination.

The link between gender, tourism and poverty is often neglected in tourism research, and this is despite some PPT developments focussing on female empowerment and women's roles in tourism and enterprise development (Ferguson, 2010; Flacke-Neudorfer, 2007; Scheyvens, 2000; Tucker, 2007; UNWTO, 2011b). In chapter 10, Tucker and Boonabaana (2015) present a comparative analysis of gender role-enactment and empowerment in the rural township of Göreme in central Turkey, and in the parish of Mukono in South-Western Uganda. Tucker and Boonabaana found that in both destinations women seek their husband's permission to work in the tourism industry. In addition, women in both Göreme and Mukono wanted to align with local cultural expectations by fulfilling their household and marriage duties, and they were reluctant to step outside their usual roles. However, part-time and flexible tourism jobs do enable women to balance their childcare and other household responsibilities. Some of the women Tucker and Boonabaana interviewed also negotiate to secure the help of relatives, friends or paid-helpers for childcare and other household and gardening duties. While the salaries earned by women in Göreme had not replaced men's productive work at all, in Mukono women were major contributors to household incomes. In Mukono men were "replacing their 'household breadwinner' responsibilities with drinking, gaming and womanizing habits" (p. 185). Tucker and Boonabaana conclude that "it is crucial to consider the cultural specifics of gender relations in each particular tourism development context when exploring the relationships between gender, tourism and poverty reduction" (pp. 186–187).

The final chapter in this section, by Hunt, Durham, Driscoll, and Honey (2015), returns to the well established concept of *ecotourism*. They aim to rebut arguments that ecotourism does little to address poverty and that it frequently exacerbates the very inequalities it purports to address. Hunt et al., counter this criticism by analysing the economic, social and environmental benefits on the Osa Peninsula in Costa Rica. They test the hypothesis that ecotourism in this region is more effective at improving well-being for local residents, at enhancing their access to key resources and information, and at supporting biodiversity conservation than other locally available economic sectors.

They therefore take a different approach to Scheyvens and Russell (chapter 9 in this book) by not comparing the impacts of ecotourism to other types of tourism, but by looking at the benefits derived from tourism compared to other sectors (e.g. construction, transportation, artisanal gold mining, retail, small-scale and plantation agriculture including African oil palm and cattle). This approach is valuable as inter-sectoral comparisons have been neglected in the past and it is crucially important to understand the value of tourism compared to other sectors when local economic development decisions are made. Ecotourism is the most commonly found operating practice in their chosen study area, and thus the findings represent the impacts of this niche tourism type rather than more prominent large-scale tourism developments. In chapter 10, Hunt et al., employ an exploratory, multi-method, and interdisciplinary research approach structured around semi-structured interviews with local workers in various economic sectors.

Their findings indicate that tourism, or in this case ecotourism, offers the best currently available employment opportunities, double the earnings of other livelihoods, and other linked benefits such as English language training and the development of entrepreneurial skills. An important finding is that tourism employees were more likely to start their own business, whether in tourism or not, compared to residents not working in the tourism industry. This suggests that working in the tourism industry can create transferable skills and might spark entrepreneurial drive which is a highly important ingredient in fostering local economic development in general.

Hunt et al., argue that compared to other development opportunities available in the study area, ecotourism provides greater benefits for biodiversity conservation and community development. However, they also found that inter-sectoral linkages between tourism and other sectors are very high and that the direct and indirect economic activity generated by ecotourism is critical, for instance, for local shop owners, farmers, fishers, and road workers. The importance of inter-sectoral linkages will be further discussed by Rogerson (2015), chapter 13 in this book.

Value chain analysis and inter-sectoral linkages

The fourth theme in this book is that of the use of value-chain analysis (VCA) and consideration of inter-sectoral linkages, a theme that focuses mainly on economic aspects of tourism and poverty. There has been much recent interest in the mapping of the chain of goods and services that are provided for tourists, from their primary inputs to final consumption, and in consideration of how tourism supply chains traverse different economic sectors. Much of this research and publications has been generated by the ODI, SNV and the ITC, and it has explored how the poor are broadly incorporated within tourism economies. Traditionally studies tend only to consider financial benefits from tourism through activities directly related to tourism, such as from employees in hotels, tourist guides, or from artisans selling crafts to tourists. However, VCA expands the scope of research to explore indirect impacts too, such as from farmers who provide food, or from entrepreneurs providing transport, maintenance and other support services to the tourism industry. The three chapters in this section examine aspects of VCA and of other inter-sectoral linkages.

Mitchell's (2015) chapter on this theme describes how VCA tools have been used to measure tourism's impacts on poverty in destinations. As well as providing an overview of the development of the PPT agenda, Mitchell describes how an "action research" approach to VCA has been used to quantify the portion of tourism revenue captured by the poor in destinations. VCA has also been used to identify opportunities to enhance the economic benefits of tourism for the poor and to use this information in designing feasible interventions. Since the ODI has used VCA in 12 destinations in developing countries, a rich database of case studies now exists on the financial impacts of tourism for the poor, which is useful for comparing the pro-poor impacts of tourism in different destinations. The importance of this type of work is the detailed quantification of tourism's financial impacts, which can be linked to the design of practical interventions at a destination level. However, perhaps one of the main weaknesses of the VCA approach is its concentration on flows of money, and its lack of attention to environmental, socio-cultural, and political and governance aspects of sustainable development. Furthermore, it would perhaps be useful to have more researchers using this tool to understand how tourist destinations are linked into the global value chains in order to demystify very common assumptions about leakages and power relations between generating and receiving countries. Nevertheless, as the outcomes emerge of interventions designed using a VCA planning tool its true value will become clearer. Although Mitchell addresses destination-level evaluations, individual enterprises can also use supply chain analysis at a micro-level in order to map their own supply chains. For example, Ashley and Haysom (2008) describe how the South African tourist resort of Spier used this approach to understand their local spend, and to identify opportunities for improving local spending and enterprise development. This work in Spier led to interventions that not only created greater local employment and revenue retention from tourism, but also presented cost savings and greater profit margins for the resort.

In chapter 13, Rogerson (2015) considers inter-sectoral linkages between agriculture and tourism in South Africa using an extensive survey of the food supply chains of 80 luxury safari operations in South Africa. He highlights the tendency of high-end hotels to use imported foods rather than locally grown produce. This can be due to constraints in the availability of goods, as well as issues of reliability, quality, lack of local skills or capital, transport, health and safety concerns, prices and also the specialised nature of the foods desired by tourists. However, the enterprises that had interacted with the Fair Trade in Tourism South Africa certification programme increased the proportion of local goods they procured. Where proactive enterprises had attempted to develop food production projects within local communities, these had rarely succeeded. The reasons for the failures described by Rogerson included poor management, the organisational difficulties of running community farming projects, and lack of capacity within many local communities. A critical finding of his paper was recognising the failure of community initiatives to deliver food to the tourism sector, and the need for greater training, support and capacity building, coupled with improved communication and trust with the private sector. However, an additional reason why such initiatives faced difficulties was that there are often insufficient economies of scale for them to succeed. For example, a vegetable farm that only supplies one small-scale client (e.g. one lodge) might not be commercially viable (Rylance, Spenceley, Mitchell, & Leturque, 2009). Thus, linkages have to be forged between a number of tourism enterprises, and also with non-tourism retail outlets and fresh produce markets, in order to spread the commercial risk.

Considering a particular type of tourism enterprise, von der Weppen and Cochrane (2015) explore the impacts of "social enterprises" on local economic development in chapter 14. The difference between businesses that act in a socially responsible way, and social enterprises, is that the income from social enterprises is tied directly to their mission (Boschee & McClurg, 2003). Von der Weppen and Cochrane analysed 50 tourism enterprises from a sample that was shortlisted for three major international sustainable tourism awards: The Responsible Tourism Awards, the Geotourism Challenge, and the Tourism for Tomorrow Awards. Linkages between the tourism enterprises they studied and local communities related to employment and also to channelling operating expenses and profits into external projects. Von der Weppen and Cochrane found that when interviewed the senior representatives of the social enterprises demonstrated typical entrepreneur qualities, such as the identification of market opportunities, innovation and a determination to succeed, but they also showed additional characteristics of "passion and belief in people's capacity to contribute to economic and social development" (von der Weppen and Cochrane, 2015, p. 252). They also highlight how all of the social enterprises cooperated closely with their target populations. Sometimes this was done by placing community members on the management board, or by more informal approaches, such as through consulting with village elders. Von der Weppen and Cochrane (2015) emphasise that the ultimate success of social enterprises depends on balancing their mission with profitability, through the "integrative drivers of leadership, strategy and organisational culture, and through successful implementation of the mechanisms that operationalise the strategy" (p. 259).

Discussion

The chapters in this book have advanced our understanding of the changes and potential ways forward in this subject area. Six main topics arise from the papers: (1) the use of analytical techniques in measuring impacts; (2) the need for development agencies to analyse their operational practices, and to monitor and report on their impacts on poverty reduction; (3) how inequitable power relations and weak governance can undermine efforts; (4) the importance of the role of the private sector in using business practices that contribute to poverty reduction; (5) the value of using multidisciplinary research tools that use quantitative and qualitative data; and, finally, (6) how academic research findings need not be confined to university libraries, but can be interpreted and applied in destinations to make advances in practice, and, vice versa, how development organisations and practitioners can benefit from sharing their experiences with academics.

First, some contributions in this book indicate how analytical techniques to assess tourism's potential for poverty reduction have become much more sophisticated over recent years. There is no doubt that many of these studies were inspired by early PPT work (e.g. Ashley et al., 2001), and it is very refreshing to see that discussions have moved on and that approaches and impact analysis tools have considerably changed. From earlier rather loosely defined livelihood approaches to tourism it now seems that VCA has become a very prominent tool for impact analysis utilised by practitioners, and that its application can identify reasons for weak inter-sectoral linkages. As would have been expected of research related to the economic issues of poverty, the papers by practitioners still focus largely on quantitative impacts. However, several studies show that the scale and volume of data collection and analysis have moved up considerably from the early PPT studies conducted over a decade ago.

Second, some chapters highlight the very important influence of development agencies on the debates and techniques associated with tourism and poverty reduction. This illustrates a change in thinking, but it also exemplifies the need for development organisations to show accountable results. Several chapters provide a much needed discussion of the way in which development organisations are controlled and operate, and how ideologies, mantras and practices can change very quickly. In the future it would be interesting to learn more about the tangible impacts that SNV, CARE and social enterprises have had on reducing poverty. Most of all, it will be useful to learn more about how their operating practices have impacted on local communities by developing raised expectations of tourism as a tool for poverty reduction. What has become clear to us while assembling this book is that the question has maybe moved on from simply asking "how much?" to "how can it be improved?" Practical tools, such as the ITC's *Opportunity Study Guidelines* and training manuals, provide an example of how the theory of VCA can be applied within development agency intervention planning processes (e.g. Ashley, Mitchell, & Spenceley, 2009; Rylance et al., 2009; Spenceley, Ashley, & de Koch, 2009), as do the tools developed by the ODI.

Third, in explaining why tourism's poverty impacts are often perhaps less than expected, the role of, and issues within, power and governance re-occur in the discussions in many of the chapters in this book. These discussions included analysing the power of foreign direct investment and global capital; the power relations between international, national, and local stakeholders related to biodiversity conservation and revenue sharing; the role, power, and constraints of international development agencies; and also the inter-community and inter-household power dynamics. All relate to the links between tourism, poverty, and gender. Several chapters show that weak communication between actors, land tenure-issues, corruption, excessive bureaucracy, ad hoc policy changes, and the all important power dynamics between actors serve to minimise the tangible benefits to the poor from institutional and commercial systems that are fundamentally designed to uplift them. These findings are not particularly surprising to those who work in developing countries, but we need more research in this field to move away from purely economic impact studies. A further challenge lies not only in identifying such problems, but in creating mechanisms and drivers to change them. Such changes will only occur when there is sufficient political will within countries, but in some cases this can be catalysed by pressure from development agencies, the private sector, enlightened representatives of the public sector, and hopefully academic publications like this special issue.

Fourth, the focus on the private sector remains very strong, and there seems to be a consensus that the private sector can considerably contribute to poverty reduction if operating practices are changed. Several chapters show that tourism businesses can have extensive meaningful impacts on the livelihoods of the people they work with; and that smaller enterprises in destinations such as Fiji can often have a greater local economic impact than larger resorts. Analysing how social enterprises differ from private sector businesses illustrates that the drive and mission of an enterprise to benefit local people while balancing commercial profitability requirements, plays a fundamental part in guiding their interventions and success in poverty reduction. The studies on development agencies imply that practitioners seeking to work on tourism and poverty reduction in developing countries should continue their focus on work with the private sector in tourist destinations as well as in tourist generating countries. Although providing the national policy framework is important, it is the industry and its source markets that have the real power to make a difference to the livelihoods of poor people in practical terms. A challenge remains to mainstream mentalities and approaches towards poverty reduction within the private sector, so that it becomes the norm rather than the exception within the tourism industry.

Fifth, the book points to an increasing diversity in the research methodologies used to examine tourism and poverty reduction. Rather than just focusing on purely quantitative data that counts the financial impacts on a local community, this collection of papers illustrates how extremely diverse research on poverty and tourism can and should be. It is refreshing to see a number of studies focusing on a comparative analysis of organisations, businesses, and destinations. Of particular value is the increased emphasis on qualitative data to understand why things happen, or not, and how they can be improved. The combination of quantitative and qualitative research is important for fully understanding the relationships between tourism and poverty reduction. A further step will have been made when studies broaden to include multi-disciplinary approaches that consider the triple bottom line of sustainable development, and incorporate social and environmental considerations in addition to the economic perspective so frequently pursued by practitioners.

Sixth, and finally, several chapters highlight how academic research on tourism and poverty can be directly useful in assisting practitioners. The practical application of tourism research on poverty reduction is perhaps the most important aspect of this field. It may not be enough for academics to undertake research studies that measure impacts, or to evaluate power relationships and institutional systems. Mechanisms need to be found and tested that translate the lessons learned into a medium that can be understood and practically applied by practitioners, development agencies, governments, and the private sector. Practitioners, for example, can advance work in the field by understanding more about the motivation and drive that leads businesses to provide greater local economic benefits. If such communication between academia and practitioners does not take place, then it is likely that advances will be fragmented and slow to emerge. The dissemination of the key themes and findings of this collection of papers to broad stakeholder audiences working in developing countries might help to merge theory and practice and help to expedite poverty reduction through tourism.

References

Ahebwa, W.M., van der Duim, R., & Sandbrook, C. (2012). Tourism revenue sharing policy at Bwindi Impenetrable National Park, Uganda: A policy arrangements approach. *Journal of Sustainable Tourism, 20,* (in this issue).

Akama, J.S. (1996). Western environmental values and nature-based tourism in Kenya. *Tourism Management, 17*(8), 567–574.

Akama, J.S. (2004). Neocolonialism, dependency and external control of Kenya's tourism industry: A case study of wildlife safari tourism in Kenya. In C.M. Hall & H. Tucker (Eds.), *Tourism and Postcolonialism: Contested discourses, identities and representations* (pp. 140–152). London: Routledge.

Akama, J.S., & Kieti, D. (2007). Tourism and socio-economic development in developing countries: A case study of Mombasa resort in Kenya. *Journal of Sustainable Tourism, 15*(6), 735–748.

Anker, R. (1998). *Gender and job: Sex segregation of occupations in the world.* Geneva: International Labour Organization.

Ashley, C., Goodwin, H., & McNab, D. (2005). *Making tourism count for the local economy in the Dominican Republic: Ideas for good practice.* Pro-poor tourism partnership and Travel Foundation. Retrieved from http://www.odi.org.uk/resources/docs/1945.pdf

Ashley, C., & Haysom, G. (2008). The development impacts of tourism supply chains: Increasing impact on poverty and decreasing our ignorance. In A. Spenceley (Ed.), *Responsible tourism: Critical issues for conservation and development* (pp. 129–156). London: Earthscan.

Ashley, C., & Maxwell, S. (2001). Rethinking rural development. *Development Policy Review, 19*(4), 395–425.

Ashley, C., & Mitchell, J. (2007). *Assessing how tourism revenues reach the poor.* ODI Briefing Paper No 21. London: Overseas Development Institute.

Ashley, C., Mitchell, J., & Spenceley, A. (2009). *Opportunity Study Guidelines.* Geneva: International Trade Centre's Export-Led Poverty Reduction Program UNCTAD.

Ashley, C., Roe, D., & Goodwin, H. (2001). *Pro-poor tourism strategies: Making tourism work for the poor: a review of experience.* Pro-Poor Tourism report No. 1, April 2001. ODI/IIED/CRT. London: The Russell Press.

Barrowclough, D. (2007). Foreign investment in tourism and small island developing states. *Tourism Economics, 13*(4), 615–638.

Belisle, F.J. (1983). Tourism and food production in the Caribbean. *Annals of Tourism Research, 10* (4), 497–513.

Belisle, F.J. (1984). Tourism and food imports: The case of Jamaica. *Economic Development and Cultural Change, 32,* 819–842.

Bennett, O., Roe, D., & Ashley, C. (1999). *Sustainable tourism and poverty elimination: A report for the Department for International Development.* London: Deloitte and Touche, IIED and ODI.

Boschee, J., & McClurg, J. (2003). *Toward a better understanding of social entrepreneurship: Some important distinctions.* Retrieved from http://www.caledonia.org.uk/papers/social-Entrepreneurship.doc.

Bramwell, B. (2010). Participative planning and governance for sustainable tourism. *Tourism Recreation Research, 35,* 239–249.

Bramwell, B., & Lane, B. (2011). Critical research on the governance of tourism and sustainability. *Journal of Sustainable Tourism, 19*(4 & 5), 411–422.

Britton, S. (1982). The political economy of tourism in the Third World. *Annals of Tourism Research, 9*(3), 331–358.

Brockington, D., Sachedina, H., & Scholfield, K. (2008). Preserving the new Tanzania: Conservation and land use change. *International Journal of African Historical Studies, 41*(3), 557–579.

Brohman, J. (1996). New directions for tourism in Third World development. *Annals of Tourism Research, 23*(1), 48–70.

Bryden, J. (1973). *Tourism and development: A case study of the Commonwealth Caribbean*. Cambridge: Cambridge University Press.

Burns, P.M. (1999). Paradoxes in planning: Tourism elitism or brutalism. *Annals of Tourism Research, 26*(2), 329–348.

Burns, P.M. (2004). Tourism planning: a Third Way? *Annals of Tourism Research, 31*(1), 24–43.

Büscher, B. (2010). Anti-Politics as a political strategy: Neoliberalism and transfrontier conservation in Southern Africa. *Development and Change, 41*(1), 29–51.

Butler, R. (1990). Alternative Tourism: pious hope or Trojan horse? *Journal of Travel Research, 28*(3), 40–45.

Chen, S., & Ravallion, M. (2008). *The developing world is poorer than we thought, but no less successful in the fight against poverty.* The World Bank Development Research Group. Washington D. C.: World Bank Publications.

Choi, H.C., & Murray, I. (2010). Resident attitudes toward sustainable community tourism. *Journal of Sustainable Tourism, 18*(4), 575–594.

Clancy, M. (1999). Tourism and development: Evidence from Mexico. *Annals of Tourism Research, 26*(1), 1–20.

Cochrane, J., & von der Weppen, J. (2012). Social enterprises in tourism: An exploratory study of operational models and success factors, *Journal of Sustainable Tourism,* (in this issue).

Cole, S. (2006). Information and empowerment: The keys to achieving sustainable tourism. *Journal of Sustainable Tourism, 14*(6), 629–644.

Cotula, L., Vermeulen, S., Leonard, J., & Keeley, J. (2009). *Land grab or development opportunity? Agricultural investment and international land deals in Africa.* London/Rome: FAO, IIED and IFAD.

Dann, G. (2002). Tourism and development. In V. Desai, & R. Potter (Eds.), *The companion to development studies* (pp. 236–239). London: Arnold.

De Kadt, E. (Ed.). (1979). *Tourism: Passport to development?* New York: Oxford University Press.

De Kadt, E. (1990). *Making the alternative sustainable: Lessons from development for tourism.* Discussion Paper No 272. Sussex: Institute of Development Studies.

Desforges, L. (2000). State tourism institutions and neo-liberal development: A case study of Peru. *Tourism Geographies, 2*(2), 177–192.

Dixey, L. (2008). The unsustainability of community tourism donor projects: Lessons from Zambia. In A. Spenceley (Ed.), *Responsible tourism: Critical issues for conservation and development.* (pp. 323–341). London: Earthscan.

Duffy, R. (2002). *A Trip too far.* London: Earthscan.

Ellis, F. (1999). *Rural livelihood diversity in developing countries: Evidence and policy implications.* ODI Natural Resource Perspectives No. 40. London: Overseas Development Institute.

Ellis, F., & Freeman, H.A. (2004). Rural livelihoods and poverty reduction strategies in four African countries. *The Journal of Development Studies, 40*(4), 1–30.

Erskine, L.M., & Meyer, D. (2012). Influenced and influential: The role of tour operators and development organisations in tourism and poverty reduction in Ecuador. *Journal of Sustainable Tourism,* 20, (in this issue).

Farrington, J., Carney, D., Ashley, C., & Turton, C. (1999). *Sustainable livelihoods in practice: Early applications of concepts in rural areas.* Natural Resource Perspectives No 42. London: Overseas Development Institute.

Ferguson, L. (2010). Interrogating gender in development policy and practice: The World Bank, tourism and microentreprise in Honduras. *International Feminist Journal of Politics, 12*(1), 3–24.

Flacke-Neudorfer, C. (2007). Tourism, gender and development in the third world: A case study for Northern Laos. *Tourism and Hospitality Planning and Development, 4*(2), 135–148.

Friedmann, J. (1992). *Empowerment: The politics of alternative development.* Cambridge: Blackwell.

Giddens, A. (1979). *Central problems in social theory: Action, structure and contradiction in social analysis.* London: Macmillan.

Giddens, A. (1984). *The constitution of society: Outline of the theory of structuration.* Cambridge: Polity Press.

Goodwin, H. (2006). *Community-based tourism: Failing to deliver?* Brighton: Institute of Development Studies.

Goodwin, H. (2008). Tourism, local economic development and poverty reduction. *Applied Research in Economic Development, 5*(3), 55–63.

Goodwin, H. (2009). Reflections on 10 years of pro-poor tourism. *Journal of Policy Research on Tourism, Leisure and Events, 1*(1), 90–94.

Hall, C. (Ed.). (2007). *Pro-poor tourism: Who benefits? Perspectives on tourism and poverty reduction. Current themes in tourism.* Clevedon: Channel View Publications.

Hall, D., & Brown, F. (Eds.). (2006). *Tourism and welfare: Ethics, responsibility and sustained well-being.* Wallingford: CABI.

Harrison, D. (2003). Themes in Pacific Island tourism. In D. Harrison (Ed.), *Pacific Island Tourism* (pp. 1–23). New York: Cognizant Communication Corporation.

Harrison, D., & Schipani, S. (2007). Lao Tourism and poverty alleviation: Community-based tourism and the private sector. *Current Issues in Tourism, 10*(2 & 3), 194–230.

Haughton, J., & Khandker, S. (2009). *Handbook on poverty and inequality.* Washington D.C.: World Bank Publications.

Häusler, N. (2008). Community based tourism – what works and what does not work? Drawing on experiences in South America and Asia. Presentation at the 2nd International Conference on Responsible Tourism in Destinations, 21–24 March, Kerala, India.

Higgins-Desbiolles, F. (2006). More than an 'industry': The forgotten power of tourism as a social force. *Tourism Management, 27*(6), 1192–1208.

Homewood, K., Kristjanson, P., & Trench, P.C. (2009). *Staying Maasai? Livelihoods, conservation, and development in East African rangelands.* New York: Springer.

Hummel, J., & van der Duim, R. (2012) Tourism and development at work: 15 years of tourism and poverty reduction within the SNV Netherlands Development Organisation. *Journal of Sustainable Tourism,* 20, (in this issue).

Jafari, J. (2001). The scientification of tourism. In V.L. Smith & M. Brent (Eds.), *Hosts and guests revisited: Tourism issues of the 21st century* (pp. 28–41). New York: Cognizant Communication.

Jamal, T.B., & Getz, D. (1995). Collaboration theory and community tourism planning. *Annals of Tourism Research, 22*(1), 186–204.

Kirsten M., & Rogerson, C.M. (2002). Development of SMMEs in South Africa. *Development Southern Africa,* 19, 29–59.

Krippendorf, J. (1987). *The holidaymakers.* Oxford: Butterworth-Heinemann.

Lapeyre, R. (2010). Community based tourism as a sustainable solution to maximize impacts locally? The Tsiseb Conservancy case, Namibia. *Development Southern Africa, 27*(5), 757–772.

Lepper, C.M., & Goebel, J.S. (2010). Community-based natural resource management, poverty alleviation and livelihood diversification: A case study from northern Botswana. *Development Southern Africa, 27*(5), 725–740.

Manyara, G., & Jones, E. (2007). Community-based enterprise development in Kenya: An exploration of their potential as avenues of poverty reduction. *Journal of Sustainable Tourism, 15*(6), 628–644.

Matarrita-Cascante, D., Brennan, M.A., & Luloff, A.E. (2010). Community agency and sustainable tourism development: The case of La Fortuna, Costa Rica. *Journal of Sustainable Tourism, 18*(6), 735–756.

Mbaiwa, J.E. (2005). Enclave tourism and its socio-economic impacts in the Okavango Delta, Botswana. *Tourism Management, 26*(2), 157–172.

Mbaiwa, J.E., & Darkoh, M. (2009). The socio-economic impacts of tourism in the Okavango Delta, Botswana. In J. Saarinen, F. Becker, H. Manwa & D. Wilson, (Eds.), *Sustainable tourism in southern Africa: Local communities and natural resources in transition* (pp. 210–230). Clevedon: Channel View.

Mehta, J.N., & Kellert, S.R. (1998). Local attitudes towards community-based conservation policy and programmes in Nepal: A case study in the Makalu-Barun Conservation Area. *Environmental Conservation,* 25, 320–333.

Meyer, D. (2007). Pro-poor tourism: From leakages to linkages. A conceptual framework for creating linkages between the accommodation sector and 'poor' neighbouring communities. *Current Issues in Tourism, 10*(6), 558–583.

Meyer, D. (2010). Pro-poor tourism: Can tourism contribute to poverty reduction in less economically developed countries? In S. Cole & N. Morgan (Eds.), *Tourism and inequality: Problems and prospects* (pp. 164–182). London: CABI.

Mitchell, J. (2012). Value chain approaches to assessing the impact of tourism on low-income households in developing countries. *Journal of Sustainable Tourism*, 20, (in this issue).

Mitchell, J., & Ashley, C. (2009). *Value Chain Analysis and poverty reduction at scale.* ODI Working Paper 49. London: Overseas Development Institute.

Mitchell, J., & Ashley, C. (2010). *Tourism and poverty reduction: Pathways to prosperity.* London: Earthscan.

Mitchell, J., & Faal, J. (2006). *The Gambian tourist value chain and prospects for pro-poor tourism.* Draft report. Retrieved from http://www.odi.org.uk/resources/docs/3802.pdf.

Mitchell, J., & Muckosy, P. (2008). *A misguided quest: Community-based tourism in Latin America.* London: Overseas Development Institute.

Momsen, J. (1996). *Linkages between tourism and agriculture in the Caribbean.* Paper presented at the International Geographical Union Conference (IGU), August, The Hague.

Mosse D. (2005). *Cultivating development: An ethnography of aid policy and practice.* London: Pluto Books.

Mowforth, M., & Munt, I. (2009). *Tourism and sustainability: Development and new tourism in the Third World.* (3rd ed.). London: Routledge.

Müller, B. (1984). Fremdenverkehr, Dezentralisierung und regionale Partizipation in Mexiko. *Geographische Rundschau*, 36, 20–24.

Nelson, F. (2003). *Community-based tourism in northern Tanzania: Increasing opportunities, escalating conflicts and an uncertain future.* Paper presented at the Community Tourism: Options for the Future Conference, Arusha, Tanzania.

Nelson, F. (2004). *The evolution and impacts of community-based ecotourism in northern Tanzania.* London: International Institute for Environment and Development.

Nelson, F. (Ed.). (2010). *Community rights, conservation and contested land: The politics of natural resource governance in Africa.* London: Earthscan.

Nelson, F. (2012) Blessing or curse? The political economy of tourism development in Tanzania. *Journal of Sustainable Tourism*, 20, (in this issue).

Nelson, F., & Agrawal, A. (2008). Patronage or participation? Community-based natural resource management reform in sub-Saharan Africa. *Development and Change*, 39(4), 557–585.

Neto, F. (2003). A new approach to sustainable tourism development: Moving beyond environmental protection. *Natural Resources Forum*, 27(3), 212–222.

Newmark, W., & Hough, J. (2000). Conserving wildlife in Africa: Integrated conservation and development projects and beyond. *BioScience*, 50(7), 585–592.

Öniş, Z., & Şenses, F. (2005). Rethinking the emerging post-Washington consensus. *Development and Change*, 36(2), 263–290.

Oppermann, M., & Chon, K.S. (1997). *Tourism in developing countries.* London: International Thompson Business Press.

Page, S. (1999). *Tourism and development: The evidence from Mauritius, South Africa and Zimbabwe.* ODI Working Paper. London: Overseas Development Institute.

Pearce, D.G. (1992). Alternative tourism: Concepts, classifications, and questions. In V.L. Smith & W.R. Eadington (Eds.), *Tourism alternatives: Potentials and problems in the development of tourism* (pp. 15–30). Philadelphia, PA: University of Pennsylvania Press.

Pleumarom, A. (1994). The political economy of tourism. *The Ecologist*, 24(4), 142–148.

Potter, R. (1993). Basic needs and development in small island states of the Eastern Caribbean. In D. G. Lockhart, D. Drakakis-Smith & J. Schembri (Eds.), *The development process in small island states* (pp. 92–116). London: Routledge.

Roe, D., Ashley, C., Page, S., & Meyer, D. (2004). *Tourism and the poor: Analysing and interpreting tourism statistics from a poverty perspective.* PPT Working Paper No. 16. London: ODI/ IIED/CRT.

Rogerson, C. (2012). Tourism-agriculture linkages in rural South Africa: Evidence from the accommodation sector. *Journal of Sustainable Tourism*, 20, (in this issue).

Rylance, A., Spenceley, A., Mitchell, J., & Leturque, H. (2009). *Training module for agriculture.* Geneva: International Trade Centre.

Saarinen, J. (2009). Conclusion and critical issues in tourism and sustainability in southern Africa. In J. Saarinen, F. Becker, H. Manwa & D. Wilson (Eds.), *Sustainable tourism in southern Africa: Local communities and natural resources in Transition* (pp. 269–286). Clevedon: Channel View.

Saarinen, J. (2010). Local tourism awareness: Community views in Katutura and King Nehale Conservancy, Namibia. *Development Southern Africa, 27*(5), 713–724.

Salazar, N.B. (2012). Community-based cultural tourism: Issues, threats and opportunities. *Journal of Sustainable Tourism, 20*(1), 9–22.

Scheyvens, R. (2000). Promoting Women's Empowerment through involvement in ecotourism: Experiences from the Third World. *Journal of Sustainable Tourism, 8*(3), 232–249.

Scheyvens, R. (2002). *Tourism for development: Empowering communities.* London: Prentice Hall.

Scheyvens, R. (2007). Exploring the tourism–poverty nexus. *Current Issues in Tourism, 10*(2 & 3), 231–254.

Scheyvens, R. (2009). Pro-poor tourism: Is there value beyond the rhetoric? *Tourism Recreation Research*, 34, 191–196.

Scheyvens, R. (2011) *Tourism and poverty.* New York: Routledge.

Scheyvens, R., & Russell, M. (2012). Tourism and poverty alleviation in Fiji: Comparing the impacts of small and large-scale tourism enterprises. *Journal of Sustainable Tourism*, 20, (in this issue).

Schilcher, D. (2007). Growth versus equity: The continuum of pro-poor tourism and neoliberal governance. *Current Issues in Tourism, 10*(2 & 3), 166–193.

Sen, A. (1999). *Development as freedom.* Oxford: Oxford University Press.

Smith, V.L., & Eadington, W.R. (1992). *Tourism alternatives: Potentials and problems in the development of tourism.* Philadelphia: University of Pennsylvania Press.

Snyder, K.A., & Sulle, E.B. (2011). Tourism in Maasai communities: A chance to improve livelihoods? *Journal of Sustainable Tourism, 19*(8), 935–951.

Snyman, S. (2012). The role of tourism employment in poverty reduction and community perceptions of conservation and tourism in southern Africa. *Journal of Sustainable Tourism*, 20, (in this issue).

Sofield, T. (2003). *Empowerment for sustainable tourism development.* Oxford: Elsevier.

Spenceley, A. (2008). Local impacts of community-based tourism in Southern Africa. In A. Spenceley, (Ed.), *Responsible tourism: Critical issues for conservation and development* (pp. 285–303). London: Earthscan.

Spenceley, A., Ashley, C., & de Koch, M. (2009). *Tourism and local development: An introductory guide, core training manual.* Geneva: International Trade Centre.

Stone, L.S., & Stone, T.M. (2011). Community-based tourism enterprises: Challenges and prospects for community participation; Khama Rhino Sanctuary Trust, Botswana. *Journal of Sustainable Tourism, 19*(1), 97–114.

Teo, P. (2003). Striking a balance for sustainable tourism: implications of the discourse on globalization. *Journal of Sustainable Tourism, 10*(6), 459–474.

Thomlinson, E., & Getz, D. (1996). The question of scale in ecotourism: Case study of two small ecotour operators in the Mundo Maya region of Central America. *Journal of Sustainable Tourism, 4*(4), 183–200.

Timothy, D.J. (2007). Empowerment and stakeholder participation in tourism destination communities. In A. Church & V.T. Coles (Eds.), *Tourism, power and space* (pp. 203–216). London: Routledge.

Torres, R. (2002). Toward a better understanding of tourism and agriculture linkages in the Yucatan: Tourist food consumption and preferences. *Tourism Geographies*, 4, 282–306.

Torres, R. (2003). Linkages between tourism and agriculture in Mexico. *Annals of Tourism Research, 30*(3) 546–566.

Torres, R., & Momsen, J.H. (2004). Challenges and potential for linking tourism and agriculture to achieve pro-poor tourism objectives. *Progress in Development Studies, 4*(4), 294–318.

Tourism Concern (2004). Holidays from hell. *TSSA Journal*, July/August. London: Transport Salaried Staffs Association.

Tucker, H. (2007). Undoing shame: Tourism and women's work in Turkey. *Journal of Tourism and Cultural Change, 5*(2), 87–105.

Tucker, H., & Boonabaana, B. (2012). A critical analysis of tourism, gender and poverty reduction. *Journal of Sustainable Tourism*, 20, (in this issue).

United Nations World Tourism Organization (UNWTO) (2006). *Tourism and least developed countries: A sustainable opportunity to reduce poverty.* Madrid: United Nations World Tourism Organization.

United Nations World Tourism Organisation (UNWTO) (2011a) *UNWTO tourism highlights, 2011 Edition.* Retrieved from http://mkt.unwto.org/sites/all/files/docpdf/unwtohighlights11enlr_1.pdf

United Nations World Tourism Organization (UNWTOb) (2011) *Global report on women in tourism 2010.* Madrid: United Nations World Tourism Organization.

van der Duim, R., Meyer, D., & Saarinen, J. (2011). Introduction: New alliances. In R. van der Duim, D. Meyer, J. Jaarinen & K. Zellmer (Eds.), *New alliances for tourism, conservation and development in eastern and southern Africa.* Delft: Eburon.

Wearing, S., & McDonald, M. (2002). The development of community-based tourism: Re-thinking the relationship between tour operators and development agents as intermediaries in rural and isolated area communities. *Journal of Sustainable Tourism, 10*(3), 191–206.

Wilderness Holdings Ltd (2011). *Wilderness integrated annual report 2011.* Retrieved from http://www.wilderness-group.com/system/assets/94/original/Integrated%20Annual%20Report%20 2011.pdf?1311953120

Wilkinson, P.F. (1987). Tourism in small island nations: A fragile dependency. *Leisure Studies, 6*(2), 127–146.

Williams, S. (1998). *Tourism geography.* London: Routledge.

Williamson, J. (2004). *A short history of the Washington Consensus,* Paper presented at Forum Barcelona 2004 conference "From the Washington Consensus towards a new Global Governance", Barcelona, 24–25. September 2004.

Wroughton, L. (2008). More people living below poverty line – World Bank, *Reuters,* Tuesday Aug 26, 2008. Retrieved from http://www.reuters.com/article/2008/08/26/idUSN26384266 on 28 December 2011.

Zhao, W., & Ritchie, J.R. (2007). Tourism and poverty alleviation: An integrative research framework. *Current Issues in Tourism, 10*(2 & 3), 119–143.

Tourism and development at work: 15 years of tourism and poverty reduction within the SNV Netherlands Development Organisation

John Hummel and Rene van der Duim

Cultural Geography, Wageningen University, Netherlands

Over the last 20 years, international development agencies like SNV Netherlands Development Organisation have hesitantly become involved in tourism. This paper explains the complex and rarely researched political and technical issues behind the working practices, drivers and beliefs of an aid agency seeking to alleviate poverty via tourism development. Based on insiders' commentaries and documentary sources, it presents five phases of the conceptual and material ordering of tourism within SNV. The phases took SNV from opposition to tourism work, through Community-Based Tourism (CBT), expansion, links to Millennium Development Goals, working in partnership with the private sector and an overall increasing need to deliver defined short term results – to closure. It explains how and why tourism became an important part of development work and how changing policy discourses and practices of international and national organisations influence the way tourism is practised as part of development work. It shows that SNV itself stimulated strong international debates about tourism and development. It concludes that relations between tourism and development remain highly contested and require the continual production of "success". SNV is now gradually closing its poverty reduction through tourism work. The paper reflects on lessons that might be learned from the SNV story.

Introduction

Although the relationship between tourism and development has been a field of fierce debate for 50 years (Ashley & Goodwin, 2007; Ashley & Harrison, 2007; Britton, 1982; de Kadt, 1979; Harrison, 2010; Hawkins & Mann, 2007; Lea, 1988; Mowforth & Munt, 2003; Scheyvens, 2007, 2009, 2011; Sharpley, 2009; Sharpley & Telfer, 2002; Smith & Eadington, 1992; Telfer, 2009; Telfer & Sharpley, 2008; van der Duim, 2008), international development organisations like Germany's GTZ, USAID and the SNV Netherlands Development Organisation entered this field only in the last two decades. Influenced by pre- and post-Rio discussions on sustainable development, these organisations embraced tourism, first reluctantly and then enthusiastically, as a tool for development and poverty reduction (see Goodwin, 2008, 2009; Harrison & Schipani, 2009; Hawkins & Mann, 2007; Scheyvens, 2007, 2011; van der Duim, 2008). Whereas in the 1980s and early 1990s, attention was focused on alternative, community-based and small-scale tourism, at the turn of the new century "pro-poor tourism" became the focus of concern (Goodwin, 2008).

Pro-poor tourism seeks to harness the tourism industry as a whole in contributing to poverty reduction. Especially, the UK Department for International Development (DFID), the International Institute for Environment and Development (IIED), the International Centre for Responsible Tourism (ICRT), the Overseas Development Institute (ODI) and, later, the UN World Tourism Organization (UNWTO) have developed and promoted the idea of pro-poor tourism (see Mitchell, in press).

SNV Netherlands Development Organisation embraced the notion of pro-poor tourism and until 2011 was a frontrunner in developing tourism projects and advisory services: in 2010, the organisation had 60 national and international tourism advisers in 25 countries. In the last 15 years, the ideas and practices of SNV were clearly influenced by the changing discourses and practices of international and national donor and development organisations. In turn, the ideas and practices of advisers and managers in the organisation itself stimulated and influenced national and international debates on the relation between tourism and development.

SNV tourism advisers and staff have put into circulation a number of concepts and tools that function as mobilising metaphors (e.g. "local participation", "partnerships", "value chain", "inclusive business"), which could mean many things to many people. This allowed the development initiative to win and retain the support of a range of actors with very different interests and agendas (Mosse, 2004, p. 650). This ambiguity and lack of conceptual precision conceals ideological differences: it allowed compromising and enrolling different interests, building coalitions, distributing agency and the multiplication of criteria of success within development initiatives (Mosse, 2004, p. 663).

Following some of the ideas of Mosse (2004, 2005, 2007), this paper examines how heterogeneous entities – people, concepts and ideas, interests, events (conferences, workshops, training courses) and objects (country and project offices, departments, strategy documents, manuals and toolboxes, websites, subsidy agreements, reporting formats) – were tied together by translation into material and conceptual orderings of tourism within SNV. It therefore contributes to the recent surge in "aidnography" (see Büscher, 2010; Mosse, 2004, 2005, 2007), which in tourism is exemplified by the World Bank's study on tourism (Hawkins & Mann, 2007). Our focus is not primarily on whether tourism and development worked, but on *how* it worked. In other words, the issue is not whether linking tourism and development within SNV was successful, but how the organisation defined and produced success. As Mosse (2005, p. 232) argues:

> In order to work, policy models and programme designs have to be *transformed* into practice. They have to be translated into the different logic of the intentions, goals and ambitions of the many people and institutions they bring together. ... Failures arise from inadequacy of translation and interpretation: from the inability to recruit local interest, or to connect actions/events to policy or to sustain politically viable models and representations.

From this perspective, success in development depends on the stabilisation of a particular interpretation of events, and the way in which (in this case) tourism and development ideas are socially produced and sustained. Since success is fragile and failure a political problem, hegemony has to be worked out and not imposed; it is "a terrain of struggle" (Li, 1999, p. 316).

After introducing our methodology, we present the related tourism and development discourses of the last 60 years and explain how they were included in SNV's work. We portray five phases of how tourism and development was dealt with within SNV, and discuss the conceptual and key ordering processes at stake and the extent to which successes were produced and sustained. We conclude that although SNV has seen the successful enrolment of actors for some time now, the recent phasing out of the SNV tourism development sector shows that this process is transient. The paper explains the complex and rarely researched political and technical world behind the working practices, drivers and beliefs of aid agencies seeking to alleviate poverty via tourism development.

Methodology

This paper is a historical account. It presents the case of one development organisation and its relations to development theories, development institutions and individuals in tourism and development. In development, historical accounts often tend towards a compartmentalisation of bounded, successive periods characterised by specific theoretical hegemonies, articulating one uni-linear development path, and mapped to particular events and processes (Khotari, 2005). Although this paper reviews tourism and development within these development chronologies, it goes beyond a singular record of the past. It introduces and highlights individuals, institutions and ideologies, influenced by theories and practices, converging and diverging over time and space, shaping "pro-poor" and "sustainable tourism" in and around SNV over the last 15 years. The account explores the relationship between personal experience, ideas and institutions of development, highlighting their interconnected relationships (Khotari, 2005).

The paper is based on the involvement of the first author within SNV as a tourism development adviser and draws on his 15 years of work and discussions with SNV colleagues and partner organisations. Practices and experiences were recorded in notebooks, proposals, plans, field reports and progress reports. The second source of information was SNV documents – strategy documents, annual reports, publications, workshop reports, evaluations, etc. – gathered in 2009 and 2010 from SNV's archives in various countries in Asia and at SNV headquarters in The Hague. The third source of information included 10 semi-structured interviews with SNV advisers and staff members involved in pro-poor sustainable tourism development. Some of them have read the paper to validate our findings, as well as – if necessary – to object to what was written (Latour, 2000, in Mosse, 2007).

Tourism, development and poverty reduction

The relationship between tourism and development has been conceptualised in a variety of ways. The early liberal approach to tourism embodied the logic of the modernisation paradigm. In the 1950s and 1960s, tourism was identified as a potential modernisation strategy that could help newly independent and "Third World" countries to earn foreign exchange. Tourism was promoted as a development strategy to transfer technology, increase employment and GDP, attract foreign capital and promote a modern way of life based on western values (see Scheyvens, 2007; Sharpley & Telfer, 2002; Telfer, 2009). The World Bank led the way in the 1970s, financing infrastructure projects and providing credit for foreign investment; however, it closed its Tourism Projects Department in 1979, leaving tourism to the private sector (Harrison, 2008; Hawkins & Mann, 2007).

The neoliberal agenda of the 1980s stressed the role of the free market and a minimal role for the state. However, to strengthen tourism as an export industry, international organisations like the European Union and the World Bank (through its International Finance Corporation; IFC) invested in infrastructure and product, market and strategy developments. Structural adjustment programmes, inspired by the World Bank and the IMF, highlighted the strategic importance of the private sector in the development of tourism. These programmes reduced the role of governments to providing investment incentives that would stimulate the participation of private companies in the tourism sector (see Harrison, 2008; Hawkins & Mann, 2007; Sharpley & Telfer, 2002).

At the end of 1970s, the World Bank and UNESCO organised the first international seminar on tourism and development. This initiated a body of research on the impacts of tourism development (Hawkins & Mann, 2007) and linked tourism to the dependency paradigm, arguing that tourism might add to the inequalities between developed and developing countries (Britton, 1982; Hardy, Beeton, & Pearson, 2002; Hawkins & Mann, 2007). Many social scientists, influenced by political economy and structuralist schools of thought, soon started to argue that poor people and non-western countries were typically excluded from or disadvantaged by what tourism can offer (Scheyvens, 2007). In the Netherlands, several organisations were established, including Tourism and the Third World (1984) and the Retour Foundation (1986). These organisations studied tourism and development impacts, and tried to encourage Dutch development agencies like SNV to become critically involved in tourism development (de Man, 1996).

Alternative approaches to tourism development emerged as a result of the pre- and post-Rio discussions on sustainable development. Informed by a number of schools of thought, they embraced ideas about local participation, equity, gender sensitivity and empowerment and therefore focused on grassroots development (Scheyvens, 2007). Similar to trends in development theory, whereby scholars became dissatisfied with existing development philosophies, tourism analysts became disillusioned with mass tourism and abandoned it in favour of community-based tourism (CBT) and small-scale and locally owned developments. This led to the rapid expansion of alternative forms of tourism (Hardy et al., 2002; Sharpley & Telfer, 2002). In the 1980s and 1990s, ecotourism dominated the development agenda (Boo, 1990, 1992; Hummel, 1994; van der Duim, 1993; Ziffer, 1989). However, in the 1990s increased attention was paid to the equity dimensions of sustainable development, which led to new interest in the community as a critical element in achieving development goals and diversifying communities' livelihood options (Hardy et al., 2002). This also sparked a new interest in the relation between tourism development and pro-poor strategies (Hall, 2007). As we elaborate below, around that time tourism entered SNV and other development organisations. In countries where SNV supported rural development projects, local NGOs and governments asked for SNV's assistance in "sustainable tourism development". In response to this, SNV supported development initiatives in small-scale tourism in Tanzania and Albania.

In the last 10 years, the focus has been on poverty reduction (see Goodwin, 2008, 2009). At the end of the 1990s, the UK DFID commissioned an overview study of the activities of development organisations in the field of tourism and development (Bennett, Ashley, & Roe, 1999). The DFID concluded that earlier concepts like "sustainable tourism" and "community-based tourism" had not sufficiently addressed poverty reduction. Therefore, a more explicit concept was framed, namely "pro-poor tourism". In 2002, the pro-poor tourism concept was endorsed at the Johannesburg World Summit on Sustainable Development (WSSD), and the UNWTO launched the Sustainable Tourism Eliminating Poverty Initiative (ST-EP). The UNWTO invited UN agencies, governments, donor agencies, NGOs and other stakeholders to unite in a concerted effort to use the socio-economic benefits that derive from tourism in actively combating poverty throughout the world (UNWTO, 2002a, 2002b, 2004). SNV became one of the leading partners in this effort (SNV, 2004, 2006; UNWTO, 2002a, 2004).

The concept of pro-poor tourism is now seen as an overall approach specifically focused on unlocking opportunities for the poor within tourism. An essential aspect is that tourism is not necessarily just small-scale and alternative, as previously proposed in alternative approaches. Instead, pro-poor tourism seeks to harness the tourism industry as a whole to contribute to development aims (Goodwin, 2008; Meyer, 2007; van de Mosselaer & van der Duim, in press). The concept pays specific attention to obstacles that constrain greater participation in tourism by the poor. Pro-poor tourism initiatives aim to establish a direct link between tourism and poverty reduction, and emphasise the voices and needs of the poor in tourism development. The poor become the focus of concern (Zhao & Ritchie, 2007). The benefits that can accrue to the poor in destination areas have become a popular and appealing moral focus (Harrison, 2008).

In the wake of the 2002 WSSD, the market once again became central to the development debate, as did partnerships (van Tulder & Fortanier, 2009). As Meyer (2009, p. 199) summarises:

> Amongst the development community there seems to be a consensus today that the private sector can play a considerable role in the fight against poverty by helping to speed up economic development through its core business activities in the workplace, the market place, along the supply chain, through their social investment and philanthropic activities, and through their engagement in public policy dialogue and advocacy.

However, far less attention has been paid to the private sector's "economic multipliers and impacts along local and global value chains to contribute to local economic development and poverty reduction in destinations in developing countries" (Meyer, 2009, p. 199).

Pro-poor tourism includes a variety of approaches (thus amalgamating various development paradigms), all of which have contributed in some way to the growth of interest in pro-poor tourism (Scheyvens, 2007; Telfer & Sharpley, 2008). Liberal/neoliberal, critical and alternative development approaches have contributed in different ways to the growth of interest in tourism and poverty reduction, although it has been particularly influenced by neoliberal and alternative development thinking (Scheyvens, 2007, 2011). These approaches seem to have recently converged at least partly around such concepts as "value chain development", a strong market-orientation, an engaged, "socially responsible" private sector, and multi-level and multi-stakeholder collaboration (cf. Ashley, 2006a, 2006b; Ashley & Goodwin, 2007; Ashley & Haysom, 2006; Ashley & Mitchell, 2005, 2007, 2008; Ashley, Roe, & Goodwin, 2001; Kremer, van Lieshout, & Went, 2009; Mitchell & Ashley, 2007, 2009, 2010; Spenceley & Meyer, in press).

Fifteen years of tourism and poverty reduction within SNV

The history of tourism and poverty reduction within SNV embodies the shifting paradigms presented above. It also shows how shifting paradigms and concepts, as well as people (especially advisers and managers at SNV and partner organisations), subsidy agreements and the strategies of SNV departments in the field and at its headquarters, and many other things have been "ordering" pro-poor sustainable tourism practices within SNV through five emerging phases.

Phase 1: the end of opposition to tourism (pre-1995)

Tourism growth since the 1990s has been characterised by a pronounced geographical expansion. Along with increasing numbers of destinations, tourist arrivals increased significantly in many developing countries. Between 1990 and 2006, the growth rates in international arrivals and international tourism receipts for developing countries were 196% and 419%, respectively. Of the 30 countries with the largest poor populations, 10 saw a growth in international arrivals between 1990 and 2001 of over 200%. This rate of growth is significantly higher than that achieved by developed countries (Leijzer, 2007).

A combination of growth in tourism to developing countries since the early 1990s, growing global environmental concerns, and the efforts of international conservation organisations (e.g. the WWF, Conservation International and the IUCN) and local conservation and development NGOs, led to increased interest in developing forms of tourism that contributed to sustainable development and the start of, often small-scale, tourism development initiatives. Development agencies, however, hardly ever discussed tourism as a tool for development, and often regarded tourism development as "commercial", "private sector driven" or "elitist". The prevailing discourse reflected the dependency paradigm of the 1970s and 1980s, exemplified by an SNV memorandum on tourism (Loermans, 1995, p. 3):

> Despite the economic significance of tourism to the South, development target organizations have so far given it scant consideration. At best they had no opinion on the matter, but usually they were against it, on the grounds that only the elite benefited.

However, tourism gradually entered SNV's agenda through a number of events. First came a small number of tourism initiatives, instigated at the request of NGOs and SNV staff. The gradual shift from a critical tourism discourse to a more alternative/sustainable development discourse (cf. Scheyvens, 2007), in which tourism was increasingly seen as a tool for local development and environmental conservation, resulted in local requests for assistance. One request came from the Maasai around Arusha in northern Tanzania. SNV supported several economic development initiatives with these Maasai, but the initiatives were not very successful (Leijzer, personal communication, May 14, 2007). Continued requests from the Maasai for tourism development were initially not granted, as tourism was outside the regular development activities of SNV and it had no tourism experience.

However, an employee based in Tanzania, working at SNV's Department International Dimension (DID; set up to link development activities in SNV countries with organisations in the Netherlands), allocated a small budget to start a tourism activity with the Maasai. As SNV was not involved in tourism initiatives, the project was subcontracted to a small Dutch sustainable tourism advocacy NGO, the Retour Foundation. This NGO had been successful in advocating tourism development and the marketing of small-scale CBT in the Netherlands. Links with Dutch tour operators were quickly established. Overland trucks brought tourists to the project, resulting in revenue of US$10,000 in the first year (Leijzer, personal communication, May 14, 2007; de Man, personal communication, May 21, 2007; van der Duim, Peters, & Wearing, 2005). Requests from other countries, for example Albania, followed.

At that time, SNV advisers directly supported "groups of poor, disadvantaged and oppressed people" through a "process approach". Target groups were involved in problem identification and analysis, choice of approach to solving problems and the pace of implementation (Verhoeven, 2002). These groups kept requesting support for tourism development. SNV country directors and staff decided to explore ways in which tourism could promote local development and poverty reduction in their respective countries. This resulted in a tourism feasibility study being carried out in Albania in 1994, an investigation of tourism development potential in Botswana, and SNV Zimbabwe's small-scale involvement in the Campfire programme in 1995 (Loermans, 1995).

Second, DID was instrumental on a practical and operational level in developing these initial tourism initiatives. DID's main task was to facilitate the raising of awareness in the Netherlands of development cooperation. It also offered SNV target groups in the South direct access to Northern (mainly Dutch) networks of information, contacts and finance (Verhoeven, 2002). It received requests (e.g. from SNV Tanzania) to create linkages between local tourism projects and potential tour operators, and allocated some of its own budget to launch the small-scale tourism initiative with the Maasai.

Third, an internal memorandum (Loermans, 1995) opened up discussion about the role of tourism in development assistance within SNV. This led to the first Memorandum on Tourism, which reflected the growing interest in tourism and development among academics and NGOs/development organisations in the Netherlands. For example, Oxfam Novib had started CBT initiatives in the Philippines, Indonesia and Thailand (de Man, 1996; Westerlaken, 1998 in van Wijk, 2009). The Memorandum on Tourism also addressed the changes in SNV's environment. It reflects how tourism became a part of SNV, albeit not comfortably:

> Although many have debated this subject before us, tourism is a new subject for SNV. Until recently we were one of the few in Dutch development circles to broach the issue. We had a scoop when we presented the results of a modest study in a single field area to the press. From the PR point of view this was important, but in the Policy Department we weren't entirely comfortable with it. We felt that, as an organization, we didn't have enough experience and weren't really sure where we wanted to go. In short, we lacked both a policy and a long-term vision. (Loermans, 1995, p. 27)

The memorandum led to a wider discussion on tourism development within SNV, and provided the first ideas towards policy development (SNV Nepal, BDB, & BBA, 2000). It conceptualised tourism and development in terms of "local participation", "target groups", "community empowerment" and "host–guest relationships" – all elements of the "process approach". It also resonated with the emerging alternative development approach by referring to "sustainable" and "small-scale development". The discourse at DID and SNV headquarters seemed highly influenced by critical and alternative development approaches. The previously critical development discourse was slowly replaced by one that included both critical and alternative development discourses. The SNV Memorandum on Tourism both reflects this duality and opened the doors for tourism development work:

> A more positive attitude to tourism has gradually come about even within SNV. Some seven field areas have indicated that they are investigating the subject of tourism or plan to do so. The impression is that we can no longer oppose tourism. (Loermans, 1995, p. 4)

Thus, the first Memorandum on Tourism resulted from the changing discourse, the tourism activities of other development organisations in the Netherlands, the initial involvement of DID in Tanzania, subsequent Dutch media attention and the response within SNV to this initiative. The memorandum heralded SNV's entry into tourism development for poverty reduction. SNV was involved in tourism, and could no longer "oppose" it.

Phase 2: a modest but promising start in tourism (1995–1999)

In 1990–1995, tourism projects increasingly became part of rural development and/or conservation programmes in a small number of countries. Examples are the Cultural Tourism Project in Tanzania (SNV, 1999), the Sustainable Tourism project in the Shala Valley in Albania (Glastra, 1995; Hummel, 1996), a tourism component in the Community-based National Resource Management project in Botswana (Rozemeijer, 2001) and tourism initiatives in the integrated rural tourism projects in Nepal (Hummel, 1999a, 2002, 2004). These projects had active support from SNV country managements. For the first time, tourism advisers were hired by SNV itself; SNV acquired in-house tourism expertise, establishing it as an advisory organisation involved in tourism development for poverty reduction.

The processes of conceptual and material ordering in this phase are clearly illustrated by four related events and developments. First, tourism was embedded in SNV by linking it to the corporate strategy for 1996–2000 (SNV, 1996). SNV reformulated its commitments to technical assistance as its core business. It defined four "product groups", namely capacity-building, project implementation, mediation and service provision to Northern organisations (SNV, 2000; Verhoeven, 2002). The tourism projects became integrated into the product groups' "capacity development" and "project implementation". Here, SNV focused on "sustainable regional development". A tourism officer was appointed at the Services and Mediation Bureau (Bureau Diensten en Bemiddeling; BDB), the successor to DID. This bureau served as an intermediary between North and South, facilitated knowledge exchange and maintained strategic forms of cooperation in the Netherlands. The tourism officer supplied information, facilitated workshops, developed networks, contributed to policy development and provided marketing support and public relations (Mulder, 2000). Through BDB, SNV showed that it had a role to play in linking the tourism industry, development agencies and universities in the Netherlands. As a consequence, the isolated SNV tourism projects linked up with BDB to share experiences and lessons learned in their projects.

Second, the small-scale tourism projects in Tanzania, Albania and, soon afterwards, Botswana, and the tourism advisers employed in these projects, which were supported by SNV country directors and staff and BDB, entrenched tourism as a part of SNV. Tourism entered the organisation as the projects had close links with the themes of natural resource management (NRM) and private sector development (PSD). These themes, along with the theme of local governance, had been identified as SNV priorities in its 1998 strategy paper, which narrowed down the earlier identified "sustainable regional development" (SNV, 1996, 2000).

Third, among the tourism advisers, the need arose to share:

> [. . .] experiences in order to attain better concepts and strategies of tourism development which serves local poor groups and individuals. At the same time there was a need at SNV policy level to gain insight into how tourism could contribute to the economic structural development of poor people in marginalized areas. (Hummel, 1999b, p. 12)

To address this need, the BDB tourism officer, the policy officer for economic development of the Policy Affairs Bureau (BBA) of SNV The Hague and the tourism adviser at SNV Nepal organised the first "SNV tourism advisers" meeting. In 1999, advisers from Bolivia, Laos, Nepal, Tanzania and Vietnam, and representatives of the BDB and BBA departments at SNV headquarters, met in Nepal. Just as Loermans' memorandum of 1995 demarcated the first phase, the Nepal meeting defined the progress made in the second phase. It was the first time that SNV advisers had tried to "elevate tourism within SNV to the next level" (Stoer, personal communication, May 29, 2007). At the meeting, strategies, guidelines and checklists on sustainable tourism development were shared. It was a turning point; Stoer considers it as pioneering knowledge management at SNV. The event created a "critical mass" and "momentum" (Stoer, personal communication, May 29, 2007). The results were recorded in a joint workshop document (SNV Nepal, BDB, & BBA, 2000).

Fourth, SNV's work in tourism became nationally and internationally recognised. In 1999, the Cultural Tourism Project in Tanzania – a community tourism project consisting of several tour/village modules – received the TO DO award (SNV/Caalders & Cottrell,

2001). These results generated recognition both outside and within the organisation (see e.g. SNV Annual Reports of 1998 and 1999; SNV, n.d.).

This phase embedded tourism within SNV, reaffirmed by SNV's "commitment to tourism programmes in the regions" (SNV, n.d., our translation, SNV Annual Report, 1999, p. 11). However, although the request for a policy document from the advisers gathered in Nepal was not fulfilled, it did result in 2001 in a sustainable tourism background paper (SNV/Caalders & Cottrell, 2001), which led to increasing recognition by other organisations of the role of SNV as a development actor in tourism for poverty reduction. Success was embodied in a few advisers and tourism officers, and embedded in projects, the first development results in projects, an award, documentation and commitments recorded in annual reports. However, SNV's main donor agency – the Netherlands Ministry of Foreign Affairs – did not acknowledge the development of the tourism sector as being part of Dutch development aid (Bennett et al., 1999).

Phase 3: projects phasing out, countries phasing in (2000–2004)

> At the beginning of the 1990s, SNV was one of the first development organizations to start advising communities on developing tourism projects. Although at the time it was seen as an almost revolutionary step, it is now impossible to imagine sustainable tourism not being part of the work of SNV and many other development organizations. (Leijzer in SNV/Caalders & Cottrell, 2001)

In 2002, the WSSD in Johannesburg and the Quebec Ecotourism Summit clearly illustrated the increased interest in tourism, development and poverty reduction. The concept of pro-poor tourism, as suggested by Bennett et al. (1999) and Goodwin (2008), had been endorsed. During the WSSD, the UNWTO launched ST-EP. The aim of the initiative was to use seven mechanisms to enhance the local economic impact of tourism and benefit the poor (UNWTO, 2004). This clearly reflected the importance given to development approaches by the UNWTO. The international development discourse shifted to tourism and poverty reduction, to a need for partnerships and to an increasing emphasis on the private sector's role.

In addition to ST-EP, other initiatives, documents (see e.g. Ashley et al., 2001; Roe & Urquhart, 2001) and websites supported the move towards the potential role of tourism in poverty reduction. Especially the documents on the Pro-Poor Tourism Partnership website became very influential in debates on tourism and poverty reduction (Goodwin, 2008), gradually influencing discourses within SNV.

However, the first years of the new century saw an attempt to consolidate the position of tourism within SNV (Leijzer, personal communication, May 14, 2007). Internal changes influenced how tourism related to poverty reduction was conceptualised and materialised.

First, in 2002, after a process lasting several years, SNV became a fully independent NGO, uncoupled from the Netherlands Ministry of Foreign Affairs. Apart from a larger degree of independence from the ministry, this also implied that government subsidies would be more dependent on the organisation's results and effectiveness (Brinkman & Hoek, 2005). SNV also changed from an organisation involved in project implementation into an advisory services organisation (SNV, 2000), supplying "advisory services" to meso-level, governmental and non-governmental organisations in developing countries, "demand-driven" and establishing "a stronger knowledge function" and a "stronger regional outreach". In 2000, SNV defined its mission as providing capacity-building support to meso-level organisations and local capacity builders with the aim of improving governance and reducing poverty

(SNV, 2000, 2002). Technical assistance was replaced by notions of capacity development and institutional development, government-to-government agreements and budget support to enhance the national ownership of development processes, while societal interaction with and consensus on effective development was encouraged by, for example, poverty reduction planning processes (Ubels & van de Gronden, 2004).

This discursive change reflected a broader reorientation in the 1990s of the "development industry", which switched from project implementation to larger scale programmatic approaches. Underlying this change was a new view on the nature of development, as an expansion of people's capabilities or a widening of their choices, as exemplified by, for instance, Sen's *Development as Freedom* (1999). Similarly, the World Bank's report of 2000/2001 (World Bank, 2000) presented the multi-dimensional nature of poverty and the importance of such factors as governance and social institutions. This report clearly influenced the strategic choices of SNV (Ubels & van de Gronden, 2004). It also changed the language in which tourism was conceptualised: SNV programmes became "portfolios", "implementers" became "change facilitators" and SNV advisers no longer worked only with community-based organisations, but also with a wider group of "clients", such as national governments, destination management organisations, knowledge and training institutes, and tourism business associations (SNV Asia, 2005).

Second, and related to the first, during these years, projects were phased out as they reached the end of their project cycles (e.g. the Cultural Tourism Project in Tanzania: see Salazar, 2012), and tourism as a subsector was phased in, especially in several Asian countries. SNV's decision to opt for three broad thematic areas (local governance, natural resource management and conservation, and private sector development) led to some countries viewing tourism as a part of natural resource management, and to others including tourism in private sector development (Allcock, 2003; SNV/Caalders & Cottrell, 2001). At the time, tourism was still referred to within SNV as "cultural tourism" (in SNV Annual Report 2000), "ecotourism" (in SNV Annual Report 2001), "community-based tourism" (in SNV Annual Report 2002) or "tourism for rural poverty reduction" (in SNV Annual Report 2003; SNV/Caalders & Cottrell, 2001). This shows that although the "pro-poor tourism" development concept had already entered SNV (Ashley et al., 2001; Goodwin, 2005; Hummel, 2002, 2004; Saville, 2001), the alternative/sustainable development approach was still prevalent within the organisation.

Third, and most importantly, tourism became a "practice area". Ever since the corporate plan of 1996, SNV had tried to focus its development efforts in a few themes or sectors. The broad themes needed to be narrowed down to more specific ones (SNV, 2000, p. 15). In 2003, two workshops identified "sustainable tourism" as an SNV development sector. The SNV Annual Report 2004 states (p. 10):

> In the course of 2004, SNV has further defined its fields of work into practice areas. We moved from three large container themes to four corporate fields of expertise and four regional fields of expertise, with underlying products and services. (SNV, n.d.)

Tourism became a "corporate field". The ordering of "pro-poor sustainable tourism" as an emerging "practice area" was supported by documents: a background document on sustainable tourism within SNV (SNV/Caalders & Cottrell, 2001); an internal memorandum to include "Tourism: Pro-poor, Sustainable and Networked" as part of SNV's corporate identity (Nass, 2001); publications on tourism initiatives in Botswana (Rozemeijer, 2001) and Asia (Allcock, 2003); and a reference guide on sustainable tourism development. Some of these were referred to in UNWTO ST-EP publications of 2002 and 2004 (UNWTO, 2002a, 2002a, 2004). All reflected the wish to enhance SNV's role in knowledge development and brokering. The documents were shared and discussed with a wide network of contacts in other development and conservation organisations. During the World Ecotourism Summit (2002), a meeting between SNV and the UNWTO laid the foundation for a memorandum of understanding. The memorandum was signed in 2004, demarcating the next phase.

The third phase had a strong focus on human development and capacity strengthening, combined with elements of a pragmatic pro-poor tourism development perspective. However, this perspective was not yet clearly embedded in SNV. Despite this, the role of SNV was increasingly recognised by other donor agencies in Asia through project linkages (e.g. the Mekong Tourism Development Project of the Asian Development Bank in Cambodia, Laos and Vietnam; see Harrison & Schipani, 2009) and donor funding (e.g. in the DFID/UNDP/SNV Tourism for Rural Poverty Alleviation Programme). Moreover, within SNV the tourism practice area was considered a high achiever, clearly helping fulfil the "success" criteria set by the Dutch subsidy agreement, expressed as numbers of "clients" and "advisory services", in a "recognised role in the sector", through "working in a regional context", and by a "diversified funding base" (Leijzer, 2007).

Phase 4: tourism as a rapidly growing practice area (2004–2007)

The fourth phase was characterised by a large increase in the number of tourism advisers in SNV. Pro-poor sustainable tourism as a practice area became firmly institutionalised within SNV. When tourism was selected as a corporate practice area, other SNV countries eagerly studied the possibility of including tourism in their country's portfolios. The number of tourism advisers jumped from 10 working in six countries in 2000, to over 40 in 26 countries at the end of 2005. This process of institutionalisation was supported by three developments: (1) the incorporation of the Millennium Development Goals (MDGs) and, closely related, an increased and more explicit focus on development impacts in SNV's work; (2) the partnership with the UNWTO; and (3) the focus of SNV on the concept of "pro-poor tourism" and the consequences of pro-poor tourism as an intervention strategy.

First, MDGs were integrated as the leading framework in SNV's work (see www.undp.org/mdg). With the adoption of MDGs in 2000, and the reaffirmation of the declaration and MDGs during the UN World Summit in 2005, the focus of capacity development in development organisations began to shift. The introduction of MDGs as points of reference resulted in a stronger focus on impacts, reinforcing a result-oriented approach to development, one that looked beyond input–output relationships to the assessment of intervention impacts (Yocarini, 2007). Only in 2004 and beyond was impact measurement taken up (SNV Annual Report of 2003; SNV, n.d.). The SNV strategy paper 2007–2015 noted:

> Capacity development services are more effective in contributing to poverty reduction and the promotion of good governance if they are context sensitive, evidence based, offered to (groups of) clients that have the potential to make a difference to the lives of poor people, and are explicitly focused on impact. (SNV, 2007, p. 12)

As a consequence, MDGs were included in the tourism sector strategies (see e.g. SNV Asia, 2005) and impact assessments were included in tourism case studies (Yocarini, 2007). However, a framework for impact measurement within SNV was developed only in 2007, and measuring impact was still not part of SNV's overall annual reporting.

Second, the international significance of SNV's role in tourism development debate increased, illustrated by, for instance, the signing of a memorandum of understanding between the UNWTO and SNV (SNV, 2006). This reflected pressure from the Netherlands

Ministry of Foreign Affairs to establish partnerships, in turn reflecting the outcomes of the WSSD and the increasing influence of the MDGs. From 2005–2007, SNV contributed substantially to the financing of advisory services and technical assistance (Scheyvens, 2007). Closer collaboration with ODI, the Asian Development Bank, the Pacific Asia Travel Association (PATA) and other international organisations reflected SNV's shift from an inward to a more outward looking attitude.

Third, the pro-poor tourism development debate strongly influenced SNV. In the previous phase, SNV's work already had direct relations with the pro-poor tourism initiative (Ashley et al., 2001; Goodwin, 2005; Saville, 2001), and in 2001 the term "pro-poor sustainable tourism" (PPST) was mentioned for the first time in the SNV background paper (SNV/Caalders & Cottrell, 2001). However, the importance of the concept increased significantly as a result of the evaluation of the pro-poor sustainable tourism subsector in Asia by Goodwin, Ashley and Roe from the Pro-Poor Tourism Partnership at the end 2005 and beginning of 2006. The evaluation concluded that SNV had a clear and specific advisory role in tourism development for poverty reduction, but asserted that the organisation needed to focus more on poverty impact and ways to better measure this impact (Goodwin, 2006, 2008).

The work by ODI and Ashley in Africa (Ashley, 2006b) and Asia (Ashley, 2006a) showed the importance of out-of-pocket expenditure (see also Mitchell, Keane, & Laidlaw, 2009) and supply chains in tourism destinations (see especially Ashley, 2006a), and of policy approaches to boosting pro-poor impact, notably good destination development and management. Through such studies, both the concept of pro-poor tourism and the attempt to measure success in terms of impacts on "the poor" began to guide the work of SNV tourism advisers.

Phase 5: impacts through partnerships (2007–2010)

> SNV can look back on an important year in which it concluded its 2002–2006 subsidy agreement underlining the importance of building capacity in developing countries. In 2006 we achieved concrete gains in developing human capacities within institutional settings. We also succeeded in jump-starting our programme for the next decade. (in SNV Annual Report, 2006; SNV, n.d. p. 3)

In 2006 and 2007, SNV again went through internal changes, which also defined the role of tourism within SNV. Discussions and negotiations involving a wide range of SNV advisers and managers, clients, partners and development experts resulted in a new corporate strategy: "Local impact, Global presence" (SNV, 2007). Based on this strategy, the Dutch government awarded the organisation a second subsidy agreement for nine years (2007–2015). Compared to the previous phase, the emphasis in this agreement clearly shifted to impact measurement and partnerships. The work of SNV tourism advisers increasingly reflected the post-WSSD focus on partnerships, the private sector, value chains and "inclusive business". In its advisory work, SNV emphasised the socio-economic impacts of tourism and result measurement through a value chain approach. As Laumans (personal communication, June 6, 2008) explained for SNV East and Southern Africa (but also reflecting SNV's work in other regions):

> The focus has to be on mainstream tourism, not on community-based tourism. With mainstream tourism we mean that tourism development should be considered an inclusive business, in which the poor will benefit from investments from the private sector. Governments will have to play their role to assure that the poor are not forgotten. This will include, for instance, a legislative environment that favours PPT development. And there is also still a huge amount of work to

do in terms of changing the mind-set of the public and the private sector towards a pro-poor development in tourism.

Although not explicitly mentioned in the SNV strategy 2007–2015, in the period 2007–2009, sustainable tourism was chosen as a development subsector in four of the five SNV regions. The aim was to create an impact in terms of "production, income and employment". In 2009, all regions included tourism for poverty reduction as a development sector for the period 2010–2012.

In 2008, SNV signed a second memorandum of understanding with the UNWTO and the ST-EP Foundation covering a further three-year period, aiming to support 21 programmes in Latin America, Africa, the Balkans and Asia. All programmes explicitly addressed the expected contribution to impact measurement, policy and strategy formulation, and knowledge development and management. By renewing its UNWTO partnership, and intensifying processes of sharing and learning between tourism advisers and clients in SNV countries and regions, SNV aimed to strengthen its clients' ability to enhance local socio-economic impacts from tourism, through services in sustainable destination development and management, business development services, policy and strategy development, and the development of market linkages (SNV Asia, 2008). SNV thus adhered to the emerging development agenda, which is "more one of investments and business models than of subsidies and philanthropy" (van Tulder & Fortanier, 2009, p. 211).

In this period, SNV tourism advisers also tried to address the increasing pressure to measure and quantify tangible results in terms of poverty reduction. SNV worked closely with ODI and Action of Enterprise, which conducted several of SNV's studies on pro-poor value chain analysis. Although this emphasis on value chain analysis has been welcomed as a step towards understanding tourism's diverse poverty reducing impacts (Meyer, 2011), it has faced (and still faces) important methodological and conceptual problems (see also van de Mosselaer & van der Duim, in press). Evidence has not been fully convincing or consistent due to the diversity of the methods used, the ambiguous ways of defining poverty and its indicators, and the problem of attribution (see Mitchell & Ashley, 2010 for an overview, and Mitchell, in press). It showed that attributing observed changes to any particular cause – such as a development intervention by SNV (or any other development organisation) – is fraught with difficulties. It also showed that the tourism value chain is affected by the practices of many stakeholders and events, literally all round the world, which obviously creates significant obstacles to producing evidence on pro-poor tourism impacts (see Ashley & Mitchell, 2008).

In addition to value chain analysis, and as part of the strategy changes in 2007, SNV developed a "Managing for Results" policy framework to explicitly measure SNV's development impact. The attention shifted to "emphasize what is to be achieved instead of what is to be done". Managing for Results implied that "SNV management asks the right questions and promotes result orientation throughout the organization; and result orientation becomes part of SNV culture" (SNV, 2007, p. 3). In the same year, SNV Asia requested ODI (Ashley & Mitchell, 2007) to support the organisation with an input paper for the SNV/IFC conference on "Measuring and Enhancing Impact through Pro-Poor Interventions in Tourism Value Chains", which was held in Cambodia in December 2007 (Ashley & Mitchell, 2008). Discussions resulted in the further development of the pro-poor tourism value chain approach (Mitchell & Ashley, 2009), and also revealed the difficulties in finding indicators to identify the poverty reduction impact of tourism.

Although SNV shifted its development approaches, it had still not managed to measure its development impact in a convincing manner. The tourism development programmes had not yet resulted in clearly presented net benefits for poorer households in SNV countries (see Goodwin, 2008). SNV's way of measuring development impact had changed from counting the numbers of beneficiaries in CBT projects, via more general outcome indicators based on capacity-building (numbers of people trained), to an alignment with the Donor Committee for Enterprise Development (DCED) standards. These standards are a common approach to impact measurement, with eight control points and corresponding compliance criteria, using three "universal impact indicators" across programmes: scale (number of target enterprises that realise a financial benefit), net additional income created, and net additional jobs created (DCED, 2009, p. 3). As a result, SNV identified beneficiaries in terms of numbers of jobs and increases in the income of the poor. Although crucial for justifying development interventions, it also became clear that assessing these impacts requires a considerable investment in terms of both time and financial resources (Hummel, Gujadhur, & Ritsma, in press).

In early 2011, however, even before development impacts in tourism could be presented, SNV decided to focus on those sectors that have a high probability and visibility of impacts as well as a clear alignment with donor agency priorities (Hummel et al., in press). Due to the economic crisis – and fuelled by the national and international debates on the future of development cooperation sparked by a report of the Netherlands Scientific Council for Government Policy (van Lieshout, Went, & Kremer, 2010) – in 2011, Dutch development organisations were confronted with serious budget cuts by the Dutch government (see Schulpen, 2010). As a consequence, Dutch development organisations once again had to "refocus" their development involvement, and "reorganise" their working arrangements. Almost all Dutch development organisations (e.g. ICCO, Cordaid, Agrittera, the IUCN-NL, SNV) either slashed or cancelled their tourism-related programmes.

For SNV, this closed a period in which it had been rather influential nationally and internationally in conceptualising and implementing the relation between tourism and development. SNV prioritised agriculture, water and sanitation, and renewable energy; it is phasing out forestry, education, health and tourism.

Conclusion

This paper presented a particular and arguable reconstruction of the ways in which in the last 15 years, SNV and its alliances materially and conceptually ordered tourism in their development practices, as well as the way in which success was produced and measured (Mosse, 2004, 2005). It showed how the organisation reluctantly started with a few tourism projects and advisers in the 1990s, and grew into a global player with 60 tourism advisers in 25 countries, especially by identifying "pro-poor sustainable tourism" as an "emerging practice area" in the organisation in 2004. During those 15 years, SNV's tourism advisers put into circulation a number of concepts and tools (e.g. "local participation", "community-based tourism", "pro-poor sustainable tourism", "inclusive business", "multi-stakeholder approaches" and "value chain analysis and development"), which were influenced by ever-shifting development paradigms and debates both within and outside the Netherlands. These debates were reflected in the subsidy agreements that SNV had to regularly negotiate with the Netherlands Ministry of Foreign Affairs. Changes in development discourses and policies were translated into SNV's objectives and practices; the ways in which success was measured were also subject to change several times. Involvement in tourism was first disallowed, then accepted and then phased out as a development practice.

SNV only got involved in tourism when the development paradigm shifted from the critical and neoliberal development paradigms of the 1970s and 1980s, to the alternative/sustainable development paradigm of the 1990s. SNV's work on tourism then increasingly influenced the international discussion on the links between tourism and poverty reduction (see e.g. Mitchell & Ashley, 2007, 2009, 2010). Mobilising metaphors – such as "pro-poor sustainable tourism", "multi-stakeholder approaches" and "value chain analysis and development" – allowed SNV and its associates to enrol and work with various interests and actors, and thus obtain further funding and support. The resulting and related material techniques used, including subsidy agreements, internal and external documents, toolboxes, websites, partnerships with organisations and, of course, "clients" (intermediary organisations, local, regional/national governmental bodies, the "poor") were sustained and supported by distinct processes of conceptual ordering.

In that sense, our history in five phases should not be seen as an account of eras in which coherent ideas and practices shaped the realities on the ground. Through efforts to create particular, fractional and fragile conceptual and material orderings, SNV attempted to stabilise chaotic practices and to validate and fit together their ideas and practices for various publics (donor managers, politicians, professionals, scientists, colleagues in other countries, civil servants, clients, etc.). Although these ideas were sometimes ignored or resisted by some, others "consumed" or tactically used them. The workings of SNV implied not only putting concepts and tools into practice, but also – and even more importantly – transforming these concepts and tools into the different logic of the intentions, goals and ambitions of the many people and institutions they have brought together (or failed to tie into their networks).

Was SNV's involvement in tourism over the last 15 years successful? This paper's central question has been to seek *how* success was measured and produced. We argue that SNV created "success" predominantly through its international agenda setting, its increasing number of advisers, projects and partnerships, its expanding number of clients, its clients' satisfaction with SNV's work, international awards for specific tourism projects, references by other development agencies to SNV's tourism development initiatives, and the economic and non-economic effects of the tourism initiatives especially in remote parts of developing countries. Outside the Netherlands, SNV has stimulated and mobilised a great deal of support and has influenced the international debate on tourism and development through, for example, cooperation with the UNWTO, ODI and many national and regional tourism and non-tourism actors, especially in Asia (Mitchell & Ashley, 2007, 2009, 2010; UNWTO, 2002a, 2002b, 2004, 2010a, 2010b). The organisation left significant marks on national policies and practices and provided socio-economic benefits primarily in remoter areas of the countries it has supported. Its success is also evidenced by the numerous requests for assistance it received in the last 15 years from national and local governments, international development organisations and local private-sector companies.

However, SNV tourism advisers were not able to produce evidence of "success" in terms of quantifiable pro-poor impact beneficiary figures – such as numbers of jobs or increases in the income of the "poor" – in a timely and convincingly manner. The results of the attempts in recent years to measure these impacts based on value chain analysis and the DCED standards in the Managing for Results framework (the latter fitting neatly into the current and dominant development discourses) have not been convincing enough to mobilise those supporting actors within and outside SNV that could withstand the volatility of policymaking and, more importantly, the recent cuts in budgets within SNV and within DGIS, the SNV's main donor. The termination of SNV's tourism programme therefore also illustrates both the on-going struggle to demonstrate development impact and the consequences of not being able to definitely validate it.

The first lesson from this paper, therefore, is that development organisations should try to do a better job of assessing if and how tourism works for specific development projects. Despite the pioneering work of Ashley and Mitchell (see Ashley & Mitchell, 2008; Mitchell & Ashley, 2010; Mitchell, in press), the data that tourism contributes directly to poverty alleviation is still sporadic and often tokenistic (Scheyvens, 2011). Goodwin (2011) recently argued that we are still a long way from being able to provide policymakers with the evidence for informed decision-making that the benefits of tourism reach the poor. To improve the conceptual and methodological underpinning of research in this field, the gap between different disciplines, and between different disciplinary research and the work of practitioners, should be bridged.

Second, eventually development agencies need to become less dependent on only one single donor agency. Dependency on multiple donors instead of one, and including tourism within broader and politically more accepted themes, like rural development/agriculture and climate change, could make the tourism programmes of development agencies less vulnerable to political volatility and could foster the development relevance of tourism. However, integrating tourism into other sectors also creates a risk that tourism will not be seen as a separate field of expertise and will simply be implemented by advisers without specific knowledge and skills. Although most of the SNV tourism advisors have already found jobs elsewhere, some of the work continues in tourism programmes of other donor agencies like the EU, DFID and UNESCO, as commitments were already made earlier. Other work continues under similar programmes like the silk sector development programme in Laos, funded by the World Bank. Through these programmes, several international and national tourism advisers are still employed, especially in Asia.

Third, although 15 years of experience in pro-poor tourism has shown that it always takes time for pro-poor policies to mature and make a difference (see also Ahebwa, 2012), often short-termism in approach and project length has been, and increasingly is, the common modus operandi for agencies working in pro-poor tourism (and elsewhere). SNV faced a series of short-term (internal and external) policy changes that made it difficult to develop a consistent strategy on tourism and to measure the long-term success of agency work. Here again lies an important task for "aidnography": to unfold how development works. As this paper shows, it, at the very least, requires resilience, collaboration, a lot of compromises and, above all, time to be able to achieve and measure development results.

References

Ahebwa, W. (2012). *Tourism, livelihoods and biodiversity conservation: An assessment of tourism related policy interventions at Bwindi Impenetrable National Park (BINP), Uganda.* Doctoral dissertation, Wageningen University, The Netherlands.

Allcock, A. (2003). *Sustainable tourism development in Nepal, Vietnam and Lao PDR: Experiences of SNV and partner organizations.* The Hague: SNV.

Ashley, C. (2006a). *Participation by the poor in Luang Prabang tourism economy: Current earnings and opportunities for expansion*. Working Paper 273. London: ODI.

Ashley, C. (2006b). *How can governments boost the local economic impacts of tourism? Options and tools*. London: ODI and SNV.

Ashley, C., & Goodwin, H. (2007). *"Pro poor tourism": What's gone right and what's gone wrong?* ODI Opinion 80. London: ODI.

Ashley, C., & Harrison, D. (2007, June). *Mainstreaming pro-poor approaches in tourism: How did we get here and where are we now?* Paper presented at the ODI tourism event "Pathways to prosperity? Mainstreaming pro-poor approaches in tourism", London.

Ashley, C., & Haysom, G. (2006). From philanthropy to a different way of doing business: Strategies and challenges in integrating pro-poor approaches into tourism business. *Development Southern Africa, 23*(2), 265–280.

Ashley, C., & Mitchell, J. (2005). *Can tourism accelerate pro-poor growth in Africa?* ODI Opinion 60. London: ODI.

Ashley, C., & Mitchell, J. (2007, December). *Measuring and enhancing impact through pro poor interventions in tourism value chains: Diagnostics, baselines, monitoring and assessment*. Paper presented at the SNV/IFC workshop on Measuring and Enhancing Impact in Tourism Value Chains, Cambodia.

Ashley, C., & Mitchell, J. (2008). *Doing the right thing approximately not the wrong thing precisely: Challenges of monitoring impacts of pro-poor interventions in tourism value chains*. ODI Working Paper 291. London: ODI, SNV and IFC.

Ashley, C., Roe, D., & Goodwin, H. (2001). *Pro-poor tourism strategies: Making tourism work for the poor – a review of experience*. London: IIED, ICRT and ODI.

Bennett, J., Ashley, C., & Roe, D. (1999). *Sustainable tourism and poverty elimination: A report for the Department for International Development*. London: Deloite and Touche, IIED and ODI.

Boo, E. (1990). *Ecotourism: The potential and pitfalls* (Vol. 1). Washington, DC: WWF.

Boo, E. (1992). Tourism and the environment: Pitfalls and liabilities of ecotourism development. *WTO News* (9), 2–4.

Brinkman, I., & Hoek, A. (2005). *Bricks, mortar and capacity building, 1965–2005: 40 years of SNV Netherlands Development Organisation*. The Hague: SNV.

Britton, S. (1982). The political economy of tourism in the Third World. *Annals of Tourism Research, 9*(3), 331–358.

Büscher, B. (2010). Anti-politics as a political strategy: Neoliberalism and transfrontier conservation in Southern Africa. *Development and Change, 41*(1), 29–51.

DCED. (2009). Quantifying achievements in private sector development - control points and compliance criteria. Retrieved October 23, 2009, from http://www.enterprise-development.org/ (2009).

de Kadt, E. (1979). *Tourism: Passport to development?* Oxford: Oxford University Press.

de Man, F. (1996). Toerisme en ontwikkelingssamenwerking [Tourism and development cooperation]. *Derde Wereld, 15*(1), 8–16.

Glastra, R. (1995). *Developing sustainable tourism in the Shala Valley, Shkodra district: Report of a formulation mission to Albania*. The Hague: SNV.

Goodwin, H. (2005, May). *Pro-poor tourism: Principles, methodologies and mainstreaming*. Paper presented at the international conference on Pro-Poor Tourism Mechanisms and Mainstreaming, Universiti Teknologi Malaysia, Johor, Malaysia.

Goodwin, H. (2006). Pro poor sustainable tourism practice area evaluation report: PPST evaluation, Module C. Internal report SNV. The Hague: SNV.

Goodwin, H. (2008). Tourism, local economic development and poverty reduction. *Applied Research in Economic Development, 5*(3), 55–64.

Goodwin, H. (2009). Reflections on 10 years of pro-poor tourism. *Journal of Policy Research in Tourism, Leisure and Events, 1*(1), 90–94.

Goodwin, H. (2011). Tourism and poverty reduction. *Annals of Tourism Research, 38*(1), 339–340.

Hall, C. (2007). *Pro-poor tourism: Who benefits? Perspectives on tourism and poverty reduction*. Clevedon: Channel View Publications.

Hardy, A., Beeton, R.J.S., & Pearson, L. (2002). Sustainable tourism: An overview of the concept and its position in relation to conceptualisations of tourism. *Journal of Sustainable Tourism, 10*(6), 475–496.

Harrison, D. (2008). Pro-poor tourism: A critique. *Third World Quarterly, 29*(5), 851–868.

Harrison, D. (2010). Tourism and development: Looking back and looking ahead – more of the same?. In D. Pearce & R. Butler (Eds.), *Tourism research: A 20-20 vision* (pp. 40–52). Oxford: Goodfellow.

Harrison, D., & Schipani, S. (2009). Tourism in the Lao People's Democratic Republic. In M. Hitchcock, V. King & M. Parnwell (Eds.), *Tourism in Southeast Asia: Challenges and new directions* (pp. 165–188). Copenhagen: Nias Press.

Hawkins, D.E., & Mann, S. (2007). The World Bank's role in tourism development. *Annals of Tourism Research, 34*(2), 348–363.

Hummel, J. (1994). Ecotourism development in protected areas of developing countries. *World Leisure and Recreation, 36*(2), 17–23.

Hummel, J. (1996). *When are the tourists coming? Voortgangsrapportage Shala Valley Tourism Development Project* (Submitted to Novib). Tirana: SNV.

Hummel, J. (1999a). *SNV Nepal and sustainable tourism development: Background document.* Kathmandu: SNV Nepal.

Hummel, J. (1999b). Economic tourism benefits for local poor: Conclusions and recommendations of the international SNV sustainable tourism development workshop. *SNV/Nepal Newsletter* (3), 12–13.

Hummel, J. (2002, February–March). *Reinventing sustainable tourism: Correcting the existing? The role of SNV Netherlands development organisation in the development of pro-poor sustainable tourism.* Paper presented at the international conference on Tourism Development Community and Conservation, Bhundelkhand University, Jhansi, India.

Hummel, J. (2004). Pro-poor sustainable tourism. In K. Luger, C. Baumgartner & K. Wohler (Eds.), *Ferntourismus wohin? Der Globale Tourismus erobert den Horizont* (pp. 123–145). Innsbruck: Studien Verlag.

Hummel, J., Gujadhur, T., & Ritsma, N. (in press). Evolution of tourism approaches for poverty reduction impact in SNV Asia: Cases from Lao PDR, Bhutan and Vietnam. *Asia Pacific Journal of Tourism Research.*

Kothari, U. (2005). A radical history of development studies: Individuals, institutions and ideologies. In Kothari, U. (Ed.), *A radical history of development studies: Individuals, institutions and ideologies* (pp. 1–13). London: Zed Books.

Kremer, M., van Lieshout, P., & Went, R. (2009). Towards development policies based on lesson learning: An introduction. In M. Kremer, P. van Lieshout & R. Went (Eds.), *Doing good or doing better: Development policies in a globalised world* (pp. 15–26). Amsterdam: Amsterdam University Press.

Lea, J. (1988). *Tourism and development in the Third World.* London: Routledge.

Leijzer, M. (2007, December). *Using national tourism statistics for poverty reduction impact measurement.* Paper presented at the IFC/SNV conference on Poverty Alleviation through Tourism: Impact Measurement in Tourism Chain Development, Phnom Penh, Cambodia.

Li, T.M. (1999). Compromising power: Development, culture and rule in Indonesia. *Cultural Anthropology, 14*(3), 295–322.

Loermans, H. (1995). *Memorandum on tourism: "The true voyage of discovery is not in seeking out new lands but in seeing with new eyes".* The Hague: SNV.

Meyer, D. (2007). Pro-poor tourism – from leakages to linkages: A conceptual framework for creating linkages between accommodation sector and "poor" neighbouring communities. *Current Issues in Tourism, 10*(6), 558–583.

Meyer, D. (2009). Pro-poor tourism: Is there actually much rhetoric? and, if so, whose? *Tourism Recreation Research, 34*(2), 197–199.

Meyer, D. (2011). Pro-poor tourism: Can tourism contribute to poverty reduction in less economically developed countries?. In S. Cole & N. Morgan (Eds.), *Tourism and inequality: Problems and prospects* (pp. 164–182). Wallingford: CAB International.

Mitchell, J. (in press). Value chain approaches to assessing the impact of tourism on low-income households in develooping countries. *Journal of Sustainable Tourism, 20*(3).

Mitchell, J., & Ashley, C. (2007). *Can tourism offer pro-poor tourism pathways to prosperity: Examining evidence on the impact of tourism on poverty.* ODI Briefing Paper 22. London: ODI.

Mitchell, J., & Ashley, C. (2009). *Value chain analysis and poverty reduction at scale: Evidence from tourism is shifting mindsets.* ODI Briefing Paper 49. London: ODI.

Mitchell, J., & Ashley, C. (2010). *Tourism and poverty reduction: Pathways to prosperity.* Sterling, VA/London: Earthscan/ODI.

Mitchell, J., Keane, J., & Laidlaw, J. (2009). *Making success work for the poor: Package tourism in northern Tanzania*. London: ODI/SNV.

Mosse, D. (2004). Is good policy unimplementable? Reflections on the ethnography of aid policy and practice. *Development and Change, 35*(4), 639–671.

Mosse, D. (2005). *Cultivating development: An ethnography of aid policy and practice.* London: Pluto.

Mosse, D. (2007, June). *Notes on the ethnography of expertise and professionals in international development.* Paper presented at the Ethnografeast III conference on Ethnography and the Public Sphere, Lisbon, Portugal.

Mowforth, M., & Munt, I. (2003). *Tourism and sustainability: Development and new tourism in the Third World.* London: Routledge.

Mulder, A. (2000). *Duurzaam toerisme binnen ontwikkelingssamenwerking: Strategie voor duurzame ontwikkeling en empowerment. Initiatieven van de Nederlandse Ontwikkelingsorganisatie SNV op het terrein van duurzaam toerisme* [Sustainable tourism and development cooperation: Strategy for sustainable development and empowerment. Initiatives of SNV Netherlands Development Organisation in the field of sustainable tourism] (Master's thesis), Rijksuniversiteit Groningen, The Netherlands.

Nass, L. (2001). *SNV corporate identity "Tourism: pro-poor, sustainable and networked".* Unpublished document. The Hague: SNV.

Roe, D., & Urquhart, P. (2001). *Pro-poor tourism: Harnessing the world's largest industry for the world's poor.* London: IIED.

Rozemeijer, N. (2001). *Community-based tourism in Botswana: The SNV experience in 3 community tourism projects.* Gaborone: SNV Botswana.

Salazar, N.B. (2012). Community-based cultural tourism: Issues, threats, and opportunities. *Journal of Sustainable Tourism, 20*(1), 9–22.

Saville, N. (2001). *Practical strategies for pro-poor tourism: Case study of pro-poor tourism and SNV in Humla District, West Nepal.* PPT Working Paper No. 3. London; CRT, IIED and ODI.

Scheyvens, R. (2007). Exploring the tourism–poverty nexus. *Current Issues in Tourism, 10*(2&3), 231–254.

Scheyvens, R. (2009). Pro-poor tourism: Is there value beyond the rhetoric? *Tourism Recreation Research, 34*(2), 191–196.

Scheyvens, R. (2011). *Tourism and poverty.* New York: Routledge.

Schulpen, L. (2010). Oxfam Novib en ICCO grote verliezers van bezuinigingen [Oxfam Novib and ICCO big losers of cutbacks]. *Vice Versa on-line.* Retrieved May 13, 2011, from http://www.viceversaonline.nl/2010/12/oxfamnovib-en-icco-grote-verliezers-van-bezuinigingen/

Sen, A. (1999). *Development as freedom.* Oxford: Oxford University Press.

Sharpley, R. (2009). Tourism and development challenges in the least developed countries: The case of The Gambia. *Current Issues in Tourism, 12*(4), 337–358.

Sharpley, R., & Telfer, D.J. (2002). *Tourism and development: Concepts and issues.* Clevedon: Channel View Publications.

Smith, V.L., & Eadington, W.R. (1992). *Tourism alternatives: Potentials and problems in the development of tourism.* Philadelphia, PA: University of Pennsylvania Press.

SNV. (1996). *Corporate plan.* The Hague: SNV.

SNV. (1999). *Cultural tourism in Tanzania: Experiences of a tourism development project.* The Hague: SNV.

SNV. (2000). *Strategy paper.* The Hague: SNV.

SNV. (2002). *SNV's advisory practice: Emerging lines.* The Hague: SNV.

SNV. (2004). *Annual Report.* The Hague: SNV.

SNV. (2006). *SNV's strategy 2007–2015: A bird's eye view.* The Hague: SNV.

SNV. (2007). *Strategy Paper 2007–2015: Local impact, global presence.* The Hague: SNV.

SNV. (n.d.). *Annual Reports of 1998, 1999, 2003, 2004, 2006, 2009 and 2010.* The Hague: SNV Netherlands Development Organisation.

SNV Asia. (2005). *Pro-poor sustainable tourism in Asia strategy (2006–2008).* Hanoi: SNV Asia.

SNV Asia. (2008). *Sustainable poverty reduction: SNV Asia regional results and strategies 2007–2010.* Hanoi: SNV Asia.

SNV/Caalders, J., & Cottrell, S. (2001). *SNV and sustainable tourism: Background paper.* The Hague: SNV.

SNV Nepal, BDB, & BBA. (2000). *SNV and sustainable tourism development: Economic benefits for local poor.* The Hague: SNV.

Spenceley, A., & Meyer, D. (in press). Tourism and poverty reduction in less economically developed countries. *Journal of Sustainable Tourism, 20*(3).

Telfer, D.J. (2009). Development studies and tourism. In. J. Tazim & M. Robinson (Eds.), *The SAGE handbook of tourism studies* (pp. 147–163). London: Sage.

Telfer, D.J., & Sharpley, R. (2008). *Tourism development in the developing world*. London: Routledge.

Ubels, J., & van de Gronden, J. (2004). From theory to practice: Case studies in meso-level capacity-building. *Capacity.Org, 22*, 2–3.

UNWTO. (2002a). *Tourism and poverty alleviation*. Madrid: Author.

UNWTO. (2002b). *Contributions of the World Tourism Organization to the world summit on sustainable development*. Madrid: Author.

UNWTO. (2004). *Tourism and poverty alleviation: Recommendations for action*. Madrid: Author.

UNWTO. (2010a). *Joining Forces – Collaborative Processes for Sustainable and Competitive Tourism*. Madrid: UNWTO/SNV.

UNWTO. (2010b). *Manual on Tourism and Poverty Alleviation – Practical Steps for Destinations*. Madrid: UNWTO/SNV.

van de Mosselaer, F., & van der Duim, V.R. (in press). Tourism and the explicit concern with poverty reduction. In K. Bricker, R. Black & S. Cottrell (Eds.), *Ecotourism and sustainable tourism: Transitioning into the new millennium*. Burlington, MA: Jones & Bartlett.

van der Duim, V.R. (1993). Ecotoerisme, een nieuwe natuurbeschermer? [Ecotourism, a new way to conserve nature?] In *Paperboek Nederlands-Vlaamse Vrijetijdsstudiedagen* (pp. 24–33). Den Haag: VVS.

van der Duim, V.R. (2008). Exploring pro-poor tourism research: The state of the art. In H. De Haan & R. van der Duim (Eds.), *Landscape, leisure and tourism* (pp. 179–196). Delft: Eburon.

van der Duim, V.R., Peters, K., & Wearing, S. (2005). Planning host and guest interactions: Moving beyond the empty meeting rounds in African encounters. *Current Issues in Tourism, 8*(4), 286–305.

van Lieshout, P., Went, R., & Kremer, M. (2010). *Less pretension, more ambition: Development in times of globalization*. Amsterdam: Amsterdam University Press.

van Tulder, R., & Fortanier, F. (2009). Business and sustainable development: From passive involvement to active partnerships. In M. Kremer, P. van Lieshout & R. Went (Eds.), *Doing good or doing better: Development policies in a globalised world* (pp. 210–235). Amsterdam: Amsterdam University Press.

van Wijk, J. (2009). *Moving beyond heroes and winners: Institutional entrepreneurship in the outbound tour operations field in the Netherlands, 1980–2005*. (Doctoral dissertation), Vrije Universiteit, The Netherlands.

Verhoeven, D. (2002). *Aid – a changing necessity. SNV: From volunteers to advisors*. The Hague: SNV.

World Bank. (2000). *World development report 2000/2001: Attacking poverty*. New York: Oxford University Press.

Yocarini, L. (2007, July). *Capacity development for impact: Where is the evidence?* Paper presented at the AEGIS European conference on African Studies, Leiden.

Zhao, W., & Ritchie, J.R.B. (2007). Tourism and poverty alleviation: An integrative framework. *Current Issues in Tourism, 10*(2&3), 119–143.

Ziffer, K.A. (1989). *Ecotourism: the uneasy alliance*. Washington DC: Conservation International.

Influenced and influential: the role of tour operators and development organisations in tourism and poverty reduction in Ecuador

Louise Mary Erskine and Dorothea Meyer

Centre for Tourism, Hospitality and Events Research, Sheffield Business School, Sheffield Hallam University, Sheffield S1 1WB, United Kingdom

This paper uses a comparative analysis of three differently funded and managed tourism projects in Ecuador to examine the use of a theoretical dimension in the study of tourism as a tool for poverty reduction. The key elements of Giddens' structuration theory are tested by exploring actor's knowledgeability and reflexivity, and institutionalised interactions, leading to a discussion of the duality of agency and structure. Ninety-seven resident interviews, along with 28 expert stakeholders' interviews were carried out, shedding light on the dense web of relations, interactions and structures in which poverty reduction tourism projects operate. The key ways in which tourism projects initiated and funded by development organisations differ from private sector-funded projects are uncovered. Short-term development organisation funding was found to be a serious problem, as was the lack of collaborative partnerships between the private sector and development organisations. Contrasting ideologies were found at agency and private sector levels, but were less pronounced at community levels. The paper deduces that development organisations are strongly influenced, and confined, by institutional structures, whereas tour operators' freedom of action can be more effective in altering traditional tourism industry structures. All three projects demonstrate the duality of agency and structure to varying degrees.

Introduction

The development of tourism projects that could potentially contribute to poverty reduction in less economically developed countries (LEDCs) has brought forward new debates over the past decade. A number of recent studies analyse tourism's impacts on livelihoods and poverty reduction (e.g. Ashley, 2000; Goodwin & Roe, 2001; Spenceley, 2003; Murphy & Roe, 2004; Tao & Wall, 2009). Tourism impact studies, however, rarely link up to broader theoretical discussions, which are important in understanding the underlying reasons for the "counted" impacts (Meyer, 2009).

The academic community seems to have maintained a rather pessimistic view regarding tourism's value as a tool for poverty reduction and adopted a position which claims that major structural reforms are necessary to allow the tourism industry to aid poverty reduction and reduce inequality (e.g. Britton, 1982; Bryden, 1973; Brohman, 1996; Clancy, 1999; De Kadt, 1979; Scheyvens, 2007; Schilcher, 2007). A key concern has been that power relationships and the global structures of the tourism industry make it impossible for LEDCs to reap the benefits from tourism development (Mowforth & Munt, 1998; Scheyvens, 2009, 2011; Telfer, 2003).

While the private sector and governmental organisations appear keen to promote tourism as a viable development option in LEDCs, donors, (I)NGOs (international non-governmental organisations) and technical assistance organisations stayed clear of tourism until the early 1990s. When the UK Department for International Development (DfID) commissioned research into the possibilities of tourism contributing to poverty reduction (Bennett, Roe, & Ashley, 1999), it was realised that tourism could provide the opportunity for a shift to non-farm economic activities in peripheral areas struggling to keep agricultural production afloat which, due to their isolation, are unsuitable for large-scale export-orientated manufacturing (Ashley & Maxwell, 2001; Farrington, Carney, Ashley, & Turton, 1999). As a consequence, in the past 10 years, many of the most influential development organisations (e.g. DfID, SNV [Netherlands Development Organisation], ITC [International Trade Centre], GIZ, ADB [Asian Development Bank], IFC [International Finance Corporation], World Bank) funded activities geared to exploring tourism as a tool for poverty reduction (for a detailed discussion, see Scheyvens, 2011).

This paper emphasises the importance of the application of theory in discussing tourism's role in poverty reduction, focusing on power relations and actor involvement in three tourism development projects in Ecuador to understand the *duality* of agency and structure rather than their frequently perceived *dualism*, i.e., a focus on their inseparability, rather than seeing them as distinct and competing elements. This approach is in line with Murdoch (1997) and Bramwell and Meyer (2007), who argue that there is a growing recognition of the need to challenge binary oppositions, whether it is between subjective and objective, developed and undeveloped, or local and global. Given the interest of both the private sector and development organisations in tourism as a tool for poverty reduction, it is important to compare and contrast these very different arrangements and approaches to tourism within this context.

Theoretical conceptualisation

Much of the tourism literature in the 1980s identified the terms of international trade and the power of foreign investors as structures of dependency, which were viewed as inhibiting national development or at least threatening national control over the development process (e.g. Britton, 1982; Bryden, 1973; Turner & Ash, 1975). Clancy (1999) argues that early calls for encouraging tourism exports were based on modernisation assumptions. The economic benefits associated with tourism (i.e. employment creation, foreign exchange earnings, government revenues), the establishment of forward and backward linkages, and income and employment multipliers were emphasised by policymakers and academics alike (Lea, 1988; Pearce, 1989). However, Britton (1982) argued that tourism's economic benefits are often overstated and contended that destinations are frequently dependent on northern transnational corporations (TNCs), which control much of the transport, accommodation, and packaged tourism products.

This dependency paradigm gained prominence when it became apparent that tourism did not necessarily act as the development agent it was promised to be (Oppermann & Chon, 1997). The multiplier effects of tourism in developing countries were considerably less than expected, while the international orientation and organisation of mass tourism required high investment costs and led to a high dependency on foreign capital, skills and management personnel (Bryden, 1973; Müller, 1984; Östreich, 1977). The political economy approach to the study of tourism development in LEDCs traditionally focuses on the systemic causes of poverty and inequality within destinations, and between the "core" and the "periphery" (Cox, 1987; Meyer, 2010a, 2010b; Strange, 1994). The aim was to understand the structure and dynamics of tourism development with an emphasis on power relations resulting in uneven bargaining powers. Britton (1982), for example, argued that the enclave development pattern associated with tourism is supported by the organisational structure of the international tourism industry itself.

While the neo-colonial model did highlight many of the major structural inequalities between generating and receiving countries, it often failed to investigate the crucial aspects of *agency*, i.e., the power of individuals and/or groups of individuals to challenge, inform and transform these apparently deterministic structures. Bianchi (2002) argues that the neo-colonial model was fixated on an excessively deterministic relationship between the North and the South, and destinations in the South were portrayed as inert objects or sub-systems (Hills & Lundgren, 1977), unable to resist the hegemonic power of metropolitan tourist capital.

In essence, the study of tourism as a tool for poverty reduction has been rather one-sided and informed by a structuralist approach, which rejects the concept of human freedom by focusing instead on the way in which structures determine choices and behaviour. It also views the international tourism industry and the private sector as the key culprits in supporting these dependencies, while development agencies are often viewed as "untouchable" (Clarke, 1998; Hulme & Edwards, 1997; Lewis, 2002; Salamon, 1994). However, this dualistic thinking seems to be unhelpful as it unnecessarily polarises research and leads to a fractured *Weltanschauung* or worldview (Meyer, 2010a).

Structuration theory

In the late 1970s, the British sociologist Anthony Giddens developed the theory of structuration, which provided an account of the constitution of social life that departed from and challenged established theoretical positions and traditions (Cohen, 1989), alerting researchers to adopt dualistic thinking. Structuration theory examines the dualistic relationship between agency and structure: i.e. (1) how are actions of individual agents related to the structural features of society? and (2) how are structured features of actions reproduced to inform structure? It is argued that there is a *duality of agency and structure* rather than a *dualism*. Related to tourism development, this implies that perhaps structural inequalities within the tourism system do not automatically determine the outcome in terms of poverty reduction, but that agency is possibly equally important.

A concept central to structuration theory is the idea that social actors are *knowledgeable* and *reflexive*. Giddens (1984) argues that any study of the structural properties of social systems need to include reference to the knowledgeability and action of the relevant actors. The structural properties of patterns of actions and interactions become standardised (and over time even institutionalised) and, as such, while created by human actors, might simultaneously enable and constrain human action. Giddens (1984) maintains that structure has no existence independent of the knowledge that agents have about what they do in their day-to-day activity, and it is essential that the study of the actors' social world is an integral part of any social science research.

A second element of structuration theory is the notion of how individuals manage to organise themselves across *time* and *space* (Giddens & Pierson, 1998), and how the study of the contextualities of institutionalised patterns of interactions across time and space can shed light onto the occurrence of social reproduction. While the study of organisations and organisational change is inseparable from the analysis of time/space, rather limited attention has been given to the context, history and processes involved in tourism development projects in the past.

Giddens (1989, p. 256) argues that structure exists only in and through the activities of human agency and, as such, departs from the conceptualisation of structure as some given or external form. Similarly, agency does not refer to people's intentions in doing things but rather to the flow or pattern of people's actions. Giddens profoundly challenges the established notions of the dualism of structure and agency by arguing that "action, which has strongly routinized aspects, is both conditioned by existing cultural structures and also creates and re-creates those structures through the enactment process" (Walsham, 1993, p. 34). Structuration theory is a general theory of the social sciences which aims to break down the dualism between agency and structure by focusing not on a categorisation of rules and resources involved in a given social conduct but rather on the constitution and reconstitution of social practices. Giddens argues that structure is embedded in practice, or in a series of practices, in which it is recursively implicated (1976, 1984).

Giddens treats the three essential elements of structuration theory, i.e. (1) actors' knowledgeability and reflexivity, and (2) institutionalised patterns of interaction over time and space, leading to (3) a deeper investigation of the duality of agency and structure, as part of an overall orientation to social research. He suggests that structuration theory should be employed in a selective way in empirical work and should be seen more as "sensitizing devices than as providing detailed guidelines for research procedure" (1989, p. 294). Rather than just accounting for the impacts of tourism projects on poverty reduction, structuration theory provides a theoretical approach that helps to understand how actors are involved and interact in tourism development projects over time and space, how these interactions have evolved and potentially become institutionalised, what the implications of these interactions are and how actors deal with their intended and unintended consequences. Structuration theory aims to create a bridge between micro and macro levels of analysis by going beyond dualistic ways of thinking and proposing a form of social analysis that avoids the historical division between determinist and voluntarist views.

This paper links Giddens' structuration theory to the study of institutional theory, i.e. a focus on cultural influences on decision-making and formal structures, and contends that organisations, and the individuals involved in them, are suspended in a web of values, norms, rules, beliefs and taken-for-granted assumptions, which are at least partially of their own making (Edwards, 1993; Tandon, 2000). Berger and Luckmann (1967) argue that institutions are socially constructed templates for action, generated and maintained through ongoing interactions.

Giddens' thoughts are also closely related to Foucault's (1980) discussion of "power-knowledge" and reflexivity. Both authors acknowledge a double hermeneutic when aiming to understand a social world that is already interpreted by the actors who inhabit it. Based in post-structuralist tradition, Foucault concurs with Giddens that actors (or agency) are at least partially reflective and views social practices as ongoing streams of interactions, and as such, structures are not just constraining but also enabling. Similar to Giddens, Foucault argued that power is not tied to a particular individual or collective entity but that in order to understand power, "we must seek, rather, the pattern of the modifications which the relationships of force imply by the very nature of their process" (Foucault, 1978, p. 99).

Case study contexts

In 2009, tourism in Ecuador accounted for approximately 7.7% of GDP and employed 378,000 people (WTTC, 2009). Between 2007 and 2008, international tourist arrivals grew by 7.2% to just over 1 million visitors per annum, one of the highest growth rates in South America (UNWTO, 2009). Despite clear potential areas for growth on the mainland, the Galapagos Islands continue as the marketing focus of the Ministry for Tourism, and while the potential for rural tourism development is evident, adequate public sector investment is lacking. The need to maintain traditional rural industries and reduce the urban growth rate is recognised by the government and various international development organisations working in the country, including the United States Agency for International Development (USAID), SNV, the World Tourism Organisation (WTO) and the Rainforest Alliance. Each of these organisations is involved in some form of tourism initiative, either instigating projects or partly financing them. The World Bank (2000) made specific recommendations for Ecuador in order to address inequality and distributive justice, suggesting that "rural development programs should examine ways to promote the rural non-farm sector given the evidence suggesting the importance of this sector in reducing rural poverty, creating employment and decreasing migration to urban zones" (2000, p. 60). Although each of the three projects examined in this study has adopted a different approach, all three share a desire to combat rural poverty (see Figure 1).

The first project is an eco-lodge initiated and primarily funded by Tropic Ecological Adventures, an Ecuadorian tour operating business owned by a UK citizen, which also received small grants from USAID and GIZ to assist with initial construction of the lodge. The project is based around local excursions in the Yasuní Biosphere Reserve (part of the Huaorani territory) and was initiated based on the vision of Tropic's founder and a prominent community leader: to develop a sustainable tourism product that would aid in protecting the natural and cultural heritage of the region from oil companies, logging companies and exploitative tour operators. It aimed to attract high-end tourists and compete with other upmarket lodges in the Amazon. Through joint development and consent of the community, Tropic began operating tours in 1994 (although the lodge was not completed until 2007), while also commissioning extensive research to reveal the livelihood needs of the community to ensure that any tourism development project would meet these needs. Tropic plans to transfer ownership of the eco-lodge to the community when the community and Tropic can agree that the Huaorani people have the capacity to manage the operation. Although there is no indication yet as to when transferral will occur, the plan represents a unique way of assisting community development by a private sector tour operator.

The second project was initiated by CARE Ecuador and primarily funded by CARE UK, while receiving additional funding from the International Labour Organization (ILO) and DfID. The project is a "tourist trail" of different communities and small tourism businesses in northern Ecuador. It aimed to facilitate alliances between communities, private businesses and local governments to aid the development of responsible tourism and contribute to poverty reduction. CARE initiated the project to combat the negative effects of narcotics trading from Colombia, such as vulnerability and exposure to narcotics trading, migration, health and environmental problems, and a general sense of insecurity. CARE aimed to strengthen existing tourism ventures, and develop others, to provide residents with an alternative income that would deter locals from becoming involved in the illegal narcotics industry. With the diverse range of product offerings, including indigenous communities of Ecuador and marginalised Afro-Ecuadorian communities, along with numerous natural attractions, developing a responsible tourism network and trail was the most suitable and viable option, according to CARE Ecuador. The project differs significantly from the Tropic project in approach, yet the fundamental aim remains the same: both seek to contribute to the livelihoods of marginalised and vulnerable groups through the development of rural tourism.

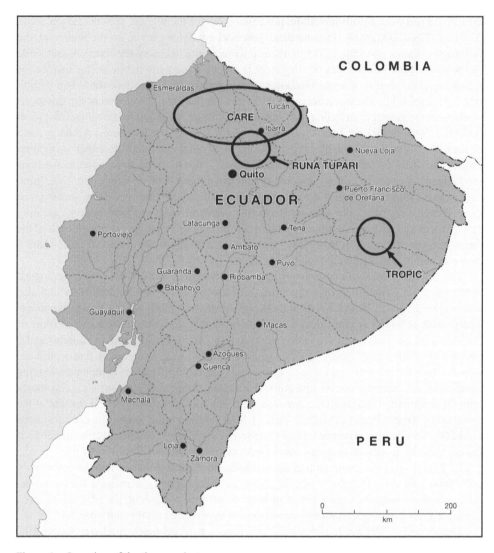

Figure 1. Location of the three projects.

The third is the Runa Tupari project, jointly initiated and funded by the local Ecuadorian farmers' organisation, Unión de Organizaciones Campesinas de Cotacachi [The Union of Rural Organisations of Cotacachi] (UNORCAC), and the Dutch development organisation, Agriterra. The project is based around home-stay tourism and local excursions in the Cotacachi region. Agriterra provided the majority of start-up funds, and UNORCAC and the Ministries for Tourism and Housing collectively contributed small grants for home-stay developments. The aim was to offer tourists an authentic experience, participating in daily activities, exchanging knowledge to appreciate the struggles of rural communities, while simultaneously contributing to livelihoods. Since the project's initiation in 2001, 16 home-stays have been funded. Agriterra officially withdrew after four years of funding and technical advice in 2005, and the project is now operated by UNORCAC.

These differently funded and operated tourism projects were all deemed appropriate for the context of the study, and each presented an interesting case study of the successes and

Table 1. Summary of the three projects.

Project details	Name of project		
	Huaorani Eco-lodge (Tropic project)	From the Snow to the Mangroves (CARE project)	Runa Tupari
Project initiator and operator	Tropic Ecological Adventures	CARE Ecuador	Agriterra/UNORCAC
Type of organisation operating project	Private sector tour operator	Development organisation	Development organisation/local NGO
Sources of funding	Tropic Ecological Adventures, USAID, GIZ	CARE UK, ILO, DfID	Agriterra, UNORCAC, and Ministries for Tourism and Housing
Classification of project	Private enterprise	Community project	Donor/NGO/community project
Main focus of project	Eco-lodge, excursions and cultural activities	Development of tourist trail, networking and capacity building	Home-stay development, excursions and cultural activities
Average number of tourists per year	200	400 (estimate)	700
Dates of project operations	1994–present (lodge opened in 2007)	2007–2010	2001–present (Agriterra involved until 2005)

failures of the fervent involvement of external organisations and the duality of structure and agency. Table 1 provides brief details of the projects, while Table 2 summarises the main livelihood benefits of each of the projects.

This paper investigates how the actions of individual agents are influenced by structural constraints, and how, in turn, these actions inform and transform structure. It does not seek to explore the poverty reduction impacts of these projects.

Methodology

While Giddens' structuration theory is increasingly used to study organisational phenomena, the applicability of Giddens' concepts is not without difficulties. Structuration theory is complex and not easily coupled with any specific research method, making it difficult to apply empirically. Although many studies carried out on tourism and livelihood impacts have traditionally employed quantitative methods (e.g. Ashley, 2000; Saville, 2001), this study primarily utilised a qualitative approach that enabled the collection of rich, in-depth data necessary to address the three key components of structuration theory (see Table 3).

Research was carried out from 2008 to 2010 in Ecuador and the UK. Two distinct sets of qualitative research exercises were conducted. Firstly, 97 community residents took part in ranking exercises and interviews, spread across the three projects. In line with purposive sampling, a relatively equal split of male and female respondents were questioned, aged between 19 and 64 with varying occupations, to gain a variety of perspectives. Due to time and financial constraints, it was not possible to access a representative proportion of the population of each community, although each respondent was selected based on his/her knowledge of the project in order to collect rich in-depth data. Community residents were questioned on the livelihood impacts of the projects, whether the projects impacted on their basic needs, their general views on the projects, and their views and expectations of the

Table 2.   Summary of the main livelihood benefits of the three projects.

Main benefits	Tropic project	CARE project	Runa Tupari project
To human capital	• Trained construction workers (transferable) • Trained lodge workers (skills in hygiene, maintenance) • Access to transport for emergency medical care	• Embroidery training (increase in sales) • Rise in disposable income (spent on further education) • Tourism training for communities not involved (improving knowledge to start a venture)	• Trained construction workers (transferable) • Rise in disposable income (spent on further education)
To social capital	• Formalising of women's group (empowerment) • Strengthening position of community (fight for land protection)	• Establishment of tourism action groups (community cohesion in working towards a common goal) • Empowerment for home-stay operators	• Building of relationships within communities through supply chain • Empowerment for home-stay operators
To physical capital	• Canoes for access to market • Plane for access to emergency medical care • Eco-lodge (ownership to be transferred) • Laundry facility (easier for washing clothes)	• Construction of prickly pear production plant (increased production and sales) • Influence on more frequent buses (easier access to market for communities) • Potential for road improvements (more bus routes)	• Home-stay construction (financial gain for families)
To financial capital	• Significant financial outputs for 22% of respondents • Money used to invest in houses, support families, save for college	• Significant financial outputs for 11% of respondents • Money used for education, food and clothing • None of the home-stay fee retained by CARE	• Significant financial outputs for 38% of respondents • Money used for education, food, clothing and investment in livestock • Effective local supply chain, which is spreading financial benefits
To natural capital	• Reduction in river pollution (health benefits) • Land protection (food and water access)	• Training in organic produce (higher sell rate for producers) • Acquisition of land for communal crops (more food for families and to sell)	• Cleaner surrounding environment (more attractive for tourists)

project operator. These themes were generic for each interviewee to enable comparisons of responses and, subsequently, the projects. Secondly, 28 semi-structured interviews were conducted with relevant experts, including representatives of the three project operating bodies ($n = 7$), tour operators ($n = 5$), development organisations ($n = 6$), local and national government ($n = 2$), tourism-specific organisations ($n = 5$), local tourism consultants

Table 3. Structuration theory and how it was investigated in this study.

Components of structuration theory	Methodology
Knowledgeable and reflexive actors	Semi-structured, in-depth interviews with residents, project managers and external observers, and industry and development experts
Institutionalised patterns of interaction across time and space	Semi-structured, in-depth interviews; participant and non-participant observation; analysis of scripts
Duality of agency and structure	Semi-structured, in-depth interviews, observation, and analysis of scripts

($n = 1$) and development think-tanks ($n = 2$). Interviewees were selected based on their knowledge of the three tourism projects and their involvement in private sector and/or tourism-related development projects. The interviews were guided by research themes focusing on the effects of institutional structures on development organisations/tourism companies, motivations to facilitate and fund pro-poor tourism projects, project contexts, power relationships within local and international actor networks surrounding the three projects, and changing structures and approaches within the tourism industry. Participant and non-participant observation was employed to examine contextual challenges facing the projects and project operators and to study the interactions between the host communities, the project operators, and tourists. Classic observational analysis was used to account for recurring patterns of interactions, and differences and similarities between the projects. Empirical evidence was supplemented with secondary data from reports, academic and practitioner literature, and organisation or company documents, while attendance at public events, both in the UK and in Ecuador, provided further information. The data were analysed using a systematic approach, guided by the study objectives.

Findings and discussion

The findings are based on Giddens' three key elements of structuration theory: (1) knowledgeable and reflexive actors, and (2) institutionalised patterns of interaction across time and space, leading to (3) a deeper investigation of the duality of agency and structure.

Knowledgeable and reflexive actors

Giddens (1984) argues that in order to understand how patterns of interaction can become standardised, it is essential to study the actors' knowledgeability. All three projects showed that local residents had a degree of awareness that they were able to exercise some control over the projects' development, while also being cognizant of their dependence on structures. It was generally agreed that communities may well be dependent on financial aid and technical expertise from external organisations, but the organisations were equally dependent on the communities. A respondent from the Tropic project argued that "we are in demand, so we control it to the extent we wish". Foucault argued that "power and knowledge indirectly imply one another; there is no power relation without the correlative constitution of a field of knowledge" (1987, p. 27). Power, however, does not necessarily need to be viewed as a negative, but can be a "productive and positive phenomenon" (Wearing & McDonald, 2002, p. 197), enabling positive changes to structures. If power can be exercised by all actors involved, then dependency can actually move between actors, constantly shifting and re-negotiating power relationships.

This argument of shifting power relationships encapsulates the concept of actors' knowledgeability. Stronza and Gordillo (2008) conclude from their study of tourism projects in the Amazon that the knowledge acquired by the community residents was invaluable in altering their relative "power", and that it provided residents with a "newly gained temerity to talk with donors, NGOs, and other sources of potential support for the community" (Stronza & Gordillo, 2008, p. 461). Similar views were also voiced by residents in each of the case study projects, and the importance of empowerment within localised social structures was expressed by respondents. The formalising of women's groups to sell arts and crafts within the Tropic project was cited as one example of empowerment, and the women discussed the sense of pride and ownership they had assumed over the venture, without which they had limited ways of asserting their independence in a male-dominated community. The formation of tourism action groups within the CARE project and home-stay operator groups within the Runa Tupari project demonstrated how these developments had strengthened the position of community members. The groups acted as a platform for some residents to voice opinions and concerns on project developments and to ensure that their needs and the needs of the communities were met. For instance, a home-stay owner in the Runa Tupari project stated that "now this is my business I go to meetings [public and open council] to be a representative and try to protect what we have". His views demonstrated a distinct causal link between a sense of empowerment and the knowledge that he was able to influence and partake in decision-making. Participation in decision-making and a desire to accomplish something as a community appeared to hold more prominence than tangible assets. While other livelihood outcomes were pivotal in how respondents viewed the overall success of the projects, for many, these aspects of social capital appeared to outweigh other outcomes, such as financial gain or physical assets. The tourism projects seemed to enable residents to achieve a sense of command and ownership of local development, and it was argued that "having a thing which we can all be part of will change the way we unite in the community, and I think that people can achieve more together than as one man" (CARE project community member). CARE's efforts to create a network of private businesses and local communities had also instilled residents with a sense of empowerment, as many believed the network had facilitated working relationships that empowered particularly local artisans who had the opportunity to sell their products. Runa Tupari project respondents expressed a different type of empowerment by emphasising the effects of interaction and cultural exchange with tourists. One resident stated that "I've learnt about different cultures because tourists come here and I ask questions about them and their country" (Runa Tupari project community member) and implied that such interaction aided residents in learning.

Respondents in the Tropic project were the most enthusiastic about the positive effects on social dynamics within the community and applauded Tropic's "open-door" policy. Tropic's efforts to be all-inclusive were palpable, and open workshops attended by a diverse mix of residents considerably strengthened the feeling of involvement and empowerment. Whereas the Runa Tupari and CARE projects both faced criticisms from certain residents about strengthening the position of existing "elites", the sense of community pride and ownership among the Huaorani was expressed by the majority. Scheyvens (1999) argues that tourism projects should only be viewed as "successful" if the community is able to acknowledge the existence and potential of empowerment. All three projects demonstrated this. Several respondents noted that the involvement of the respective project operators had taught them how to build and manage such relationships with organisations external to the community, an attribute which, they believed, could be applied in the future to relationships with other organisations. Although there were isolated criticisms from residents about specific beneficiaries of the projects, the majority stressed how the projects had resulted in improved unity within the communities. Thus, knowledge acquisition and increased confidence resulted in a new sense of power, potentially combating any future exploitation of the communities or the imposition of projects by development organisations which the communities do not agree with.

Tapper (2001) and Goodwin and Francis (2003) discuss the growing demand for "ethical" holidays, and the knowledge that adopting responsible practices could exploit the changing structure of the market was a key factor for Tropic. Expert private sector interviewees argued that a culmination of consumer and industry pressure and the potential to increase profits were driving the private sector to adjust their practices in order to satisfy this growing demand. The Millennium Development Goals (MDGs), which were drawn up during the UN Millennium Summit in 2000 as a response to the key development challenges across the globe, are a clear motivator and mandate for CARE and Runa Tupari. Tropic, however, contribute to poverty reduction primarily based on a mix of market demands and their own operating ideologies (see also, Ashley, 2005; Poultney & Spenceley, 2001). Tropic's efforts to gain assistance from various development organisations and the nature of their product offering demonstrated their awareness to utilise structural opportunities, whereas the Runa Tupari and CARE projects appeared far more constrained by their own institutional structures, in terms of increased monitoring and reporting and the pressure to achieve the MDG targets. A representative of CARE stated that "the MDGs are more pressure when you work with local governments . . . CARE has to fit into this framework".

Institutionalised patterns of interaction across time and space

A key element in structuration theory is how the contextualities of institutionalised patterns of interactions across time and space can shed light on the occurrence of social reproduction. Interactions refer to actual arrangements of people, objects and events in the minute-by-minute flow of social life's unfolding (Ranson, Hinings, & Greenwood, 1980).

Institutionalised patterns of interaction between actors and within organisational structures differed substantially between the three projects. CARE recognised that their actions were heavily influenced by international agendas and targets, such as the MDGs, which had a profound effect on increased monitoring and reporting procedures. In addition, their Ecuador project was subject to short-term funding of three years due to project quotas. Ebrahim (2003) claims that development organisations frequently need to focus on "short-term functional accountability at the expense of longer-term strategic processes" (Ebrahim, 2003, p. 813) in order to report outputs and outcomes (see also Brown & Moore, 2001; Buckland, 1998). CARE Ecuador was only able to secure one year's funding for its three-year project from CARE UK, which resulted in a suspension of the project in 2008 before CARE obtained additional funding from DfID. This break in funding and operations led to a lack of trust by the community in CARE's abilities and commitment and thus to uncertainty about the project's future. Although activities have now recommenced, the break in project operations epitomises some of the bureaucratic and financial issues associated with tourism projects initiated by development organisations and the confining institutional structures in which they must operate.

The CARE project manager discussed the time taken away from project operations to submit proposals for funding; a process described as "lengthy and bureaucratic" but part of the routine. A representative of CARE UK argued that "sometimes you really need medium to long term [funding], but you run out of resources before you can finish". This demonstrates the inextricable link between agency and structure, whereby agency is restricted by its need to perform institutionalised practice. Several interviewees suggested that short-term funding forces development organisations to produce a multitude of evidence to show that they are achieving poverty reduction outputs, which is required to ensure the continuity of donor funding. The CARE project was only allocated seed-funding for a total of three years, despite being described as "a vast and challenging project" by the CARE Ecuador project manager. The project suffered directly from internationally determined project funding structures and lacked a sustained focus locally. This was confirmed by a prominent UK academic, who claimed that development organisations seem to have relatively easy access to funding for projects, but "whether it's spent well is another matter ... sometimes they just fill a quota". He argued that project targets for development organisations are unrealistically high, and the result is a host of semi-functional projects that do not have sufficient levels of funding and support required to stabilise them – or, as a representative of the Latin American Tourism Association (LATA), argues, "we [Latin America] have a smattering of village projects but nobody is going there, which creates a hostile environment".

This implies that development organisations seem far more prone to institutionalised types of behaviour (e.g. Borren, 2000; Clarke, 1998; Lewis, 2002; Tandon, 2000), and it is questioned whether the "development industry" is becoming too closely knitted "in terms of interests, values, methods, priorities and other factors" (Hulme & Edwards, 1997, p. 3). Despite stark criticisms and a plethora of failing tourism projects, the pattern of developing short-term projects appears embedded in the culture of development organisations.

Similar concerns were raised about the Runa Tupari project. The project, now operated by UNORCAC, suffers from an over-supply of home-stays, limited demand, a lack of product development and marketing channels, and a distinct lack of transparency and utilisation of the community fund. It was argued that Agriterra's attempt to capacitate the organisation was not as successful as planned. Agriterra admitted that they were concerned about the lack of development and innovation, but also realised that the project was technically no longer their responsibility and believed that the timescale of their involvement with Runa Tupari was appropriate, stating that "instead of worrying about donors they should start worrying about the market and about clients and how to generate business". While the short-term involvement of Agriterra resulted in insufficient capacity building, this common approach among development organisations aims to ensure that projects do not become overly dependent on their assistance (Borren, 2000; Novelli & Gebhardt, 2007).

Despite criticisms of development organisations emanating from residents and expert interviewees alike, 74% of community respondents still maintained that they would favour assistance from a development organisation rather than the private sector. Respondents argued that development organisations "need to care about what the community needs and wants; it is what they do" (Runa Tupari community resident). Conversely, a lack of community control and understanding of community needs were some of the reasons cited for preferring not to collaborate with a private tour operator. Development organisations seem to be idolised, and residents' comments reflect this. Yet, while residents seem to have positive sentiments towards development organisations, comparing respondents' interpretations of impacts across the three projects suggested that the Tropic project "out-performed" the CARE and Runa Tupari projects in terms of livelihood contributions.

Networks surrounding the two development organisation projects, particularly the CARE project, were often based on "cooperation agreements", which equated to the signing of "token agreements". CARE Ecuador, for example, had cooperation agreements with

UNWTO-ST-EP, the Rainforest Alliance, USAID, and the Ecuadorian Ministry of Tourism, yet these organisations clearly indicated that they had doubts over the potential success of the CARE project. USAID, for example, declined an application for additional funding as they believed the project was unlikely to sustain itself following CARE's withdrawal. It was evident that despite being well networked with powerful institutions at the macro level, CARE Ecuador was relatively isolated from such institutions at the destination level. Such institutional structures and patterns of interaction, described by some respondents as "cliques", seem to reduce the power of CARE Ecuador as agency. This was in stark contrast to the Tropic project, which had strong links to several organisations such as USAID, the Rainforest Alliance, and the Ecuadorian Sustainable Tourism Alliance (ESTA), enabling Tropic to break the confines of traditional institutionalised patterns of tourism networks that rarely display such collaboration between the private sector and development organisations. CARE Ecuador also appeared to suffer a loss of power in terms of adhering to CARE International's mandates, such as the strong focus on working with marginalised groups. This predated that the CARE project had to incorporate certain communities that were not easily accessible for tourists, thus making it harder for CARE to attract tourists to these sites due to their isolated locations. A representative of CARE recognised that working to international mandates can make on-the-ground projects difficult to operate and manage, and one prominent international thinker in the field of tourism criticised development organisations, claiming that "a lot of the problems they have are problems they created for themselves; they do [get] caught up in their own procedures". Despite being primarily funded by the head office of CARE International and not by an external organisation, this still resulted in a loss of power for CARE Ecuador and the projects they operate. Several interviewees recognised that working with large-scale organisations has its disadvantages, and a representative of ESTA claimed that "there's always the giant bureaucratic NGO's like USAID and TNC [The Nature Conservancy] and RA [Rainforest Alliance]; thousands of fiery hoops that you have to jump through to get things rolling, just even to get things started". This suggests that such organisations have the power to influence smaller organisations to work within their own institutional structures. The Tropic project demonstrated the highest level of network connectedness in terms of technical knowledge exchange, cooperative agreements and financial grants. Many of the actors were connected to each other independently of the project, meaning that the network was exceptionally dense. Dredge (2006) asserts that dense networks suggest higher levels of cohesion and reciprocity, whereas sparse networks demonstrate a lack of cooperation and isolation, lending itself to little innovation or support. However, Tropic stated that receiving funding and technical assistance from their network partners led to the dictation of terms and conditions, and a loss of power. Tropic argued that the amount of report writing and monitoring required placed a strain on their working relationships, as these bureaucracies reduced the time available for the Huaorani eco-lodge. Although these networks represent routinised patterns of collaborating with large-scale institutions, the existence of such collaboration challenges the ordinary patterns of institutional divisions between development organisations and the private sector.

The Runa Tupari network was the least complex of the three projects, which meant that on the one hand, they have fewer parties to appease yet, on the other hand, the level of technical expertise and advice available to them is limited. Furthermore, the majority of organisations with which they are connected are not linked to one another independently of the project, which meant that these network members did not necessarily share the same objectives. While Runa Tupari coped well by working with local organisations and individuals, the lack of technical knowledge and funding available to them has become an issue, threatening improvement of the product and the enhancement of livelihood outputs.

In stark contrast, the main funder of the project, Agriterra, was the most well-connected organisation at the macro level, displaying strong working relationships with numerous powerful institutions such as SNV, the International Federation of Agricultural Producers (IFAP), and the UN Food and Agricultural Organization (FAO). Other than SNV, however, the level of tourism expertise within this dense network was lacking, and it appeared that the network had little benefit for the operation and outputs of the project at the micro level. The smaller network, however, meant that the loss of power felt by Tropic due to the demands of their collaborators was not so evident within the Runa Tupari project.

Duality of agency and structure

Structuration theory departs from the conceptualisation of structure as some given or external form and contends that structure exists only in and through the activities of human agents: structure is embedded in practice in which it is recursively implicated (Giddens, 1976, 1984). The element of power is essential for understanding the duality of agency and structure. The first relates to the power of agency to alter structural barriers in the tourism industry. A prominent tourism consultant in Ecuador claimed that Tropic "has the potential to change the way the industry works . . . but nobody wants to support them enough because they are 'evil' just because they are private sector". Despite this assertion, Tropic did manage to procure small grants from USAID and GIZ, and technical expertise from the Rainforest Alliance. According to a representative from Tropic, the company seeks to be an industry leader in pioneering a form of alternative tourism that merges private sector profits with poverty reduction. As a self-proclaimed agent of "change" Tropic represents a palpable shift from the acceptance of tourism structures to the recognition that ownership structures of tourism businesses can be transformed by agency. Tropic's attempt to alter structures is implicit in their "ultimate goal" to transfer the ownership of the lodge to the community; a strategy generally associated with development organisations after seed-funding ceases. The main reason for transferring ownership to the local community is to provide the community with a regular source of income that can be designated to further community development such as health and education improvements. Tropic was founded through an individual's desire to contribute to the livelihoods of communities while allowing tourists access to unique experiences. This ideology resonates throughout the company and the personnel. The duality of structure and agency is therefore clearly evident. While Tropic is bound by contracts to their international buyers, they are simultaneously seeking to alter the way in which their international buyers market such projects. A representative of Tropic claimed that "I think it's us that's led the way and helped demonstrate [to the UK buyers] what a sustainable CBT [community-based tourism] project is". This was confirmed by a representative of *Journey Latin America*, who confessed that Tropic was going beyond what was asked of them and attempting to market themselves as a "benchmark" for a new form of tourism. Thus, Tropic is confined by certain structures, yet is also able to influence and alter them.

The co-evolvement of human action and institutional structures was perhaps most evident in the Runa Tupari project. Agriterra did not previously use tourism as a strategy to achieve their objectives, and the Runa Tupari project was pioneering for the organisation. Since then, Agriterra have initiated and funded several tourism projects across the world and the Runa Tupari project was promoted as a framework for the use of tourism to complement, rather than replace, the agricultural industry. Tourism is now an inherent part of achieving Agriterra's objective: this project altered the structure and focus of the organisation.

The power of agency was also apparent in the CARE project in respect of amalgamating community tourism ventures with local small-scale tourism businesses as part of a tourism trail. Community residents admitted that without CARE's input, the prospect of these two actor groups working together was limited. The manner in which CARE encouraged local SMEs to source produce and staff locally has had a profound effect on how the communities now view their relationship with the commercial sector. For example, a lodge and orchard owner involved in the project stated that CARE's involvement encouraged him to source occasional labour from the local village. He recognised that "in a weekend they can earn $30 or $40, which is double what they can usually earn in a week [working in farming]". This has changed the attitudes of some local residents, who now view the lodge owner as a provider of more permanent, well-paid jobs. Some residents, however, remained cynical, questioning why CARE was assisting businesses rather than focusing all of their efforts on community development issues, as such reinforcing the prevailing idea that the private sector and development organisations are "two different animals" (A. Drumm, personal communication, March 5, 2010). Despite such cynicisms, CARE's approach to bridging the gap between community development and private enterprises goes some way to confirming theories proffered by proponents of pro-poor tourism, that creating linkages between the private sector and communities is pivotal in tourism development in LEDCs (e.g. Ashley, 2005; Meyer, 2007). This demonstrates the power of agency to promote a change of structure represented in a shift from community-based tourism as an alternative to mainstream tourism, to the recognition that tourism requires the assistance and input of the private sector if it aims to contribute to poverty reduction.

Conclusion

Giddens' (1976, 1984) work on structuration as an attempt to develop a process-oriented theory that treats structure as both a product of and a constraint on human action draws simultaneously on ideas of functionalism and phenomenology. It aims to bridge the gap between deterministic, objective and static notions of structure on the one hand, and volun-taristic, subjective and dynamic views on the other by illustrating the duality of two realms of social order and the intersections between them.

The paper has shown that this duality is evident in each of the three projects. In pro-poor tourism projects, the lucid influential differences between development organisations and the private sector suggests that the power of structure outweighs the power of agency for development organisations, and vice versa for the private sector.

While the majority of academic studies related to the use of tourism as a tool for poverty reduction focus on the negative impacts of structural dependency (e.g. Chok, Macbeth, & Warren, 2007; Schilcher, 2007; Sofield, 2003), this was generally dismissed by the majority of interviewees, who argued that the structure of the international tourism industry meant that these relationships were essential, and positive, for projects to contribute to livelihood improvements. A representative of LATA explains that "they will always have a dependence because it's a link in the chain ... without the tour operators and that access to markets, they're not going to have anybody interested, so it's a necessary dependence". This correlates to the concept of institutionalised patterns of interactions across time and space and recognises the contextualities of rural tourism projects in LEDCs, which have few resources to market themselves directly to consumers and must utilise the structures of the international tourism industry.

The power of the private sector is, to an extent, gifted with more freedom than that of development organisations. The actions of Tropic are not confined to working within funding cycles or particular strategic objectives established by a head office in another country, in contrast to the CARE project. It seems that private tourism companies such as Tropic adopt a pro-poor approach for a combination of reasons: firstly, it makes business sense in order to gain a competitive advantage, gain accreditation for marketing purposes and warrant charging higher prices; secondly, it is a response to industry and consumer pressure to act more responsibly and be accountable; and thirdly, because they are motivated by the ideologies of the company. Agency engagement, as in the case of Tropic, is able to alter patterns of behaviour and, as such, structure.

There is growing recognition that to make a development organisation project success-ful, the private sector has to be involved (Fadeeva, 2004; Zhao & Brent Ritchie, 2007), and that "establishing links with the private sector is probably the best way to help ensure that initiatives are commercially successful" (van der Duim & Caalders, 2008, p. 109). However, a representative of a development think-tank declared that "most donor projects working in tourism avoid the private sector quite deliberately ... they run away from the people who might actually make the projects work". Another interviewee refers to this as "the stigma of the tour operator"; they are viewed as profit-hungry with little social conscience. Altering these institutional barriers, which inadvertently dictate that collaboration between these two actor groups is difficult, requires further empirical evidence to prove that jointly initiated projects can be both lucrative and beneficial to communities.

This is mirrored by Poultney and Spenceley (2001), who argue that the collaborative tourism partnership between Wilderness Safaris and local communities has acted as a catalyst for change over time, and that "the contact between the community and tour operators generates ideas and opportunities, which quite often fall outside the competence of the private tour operator" (Poultney & Spenceley, 2001, p. 31). In line with Poultney and Spenceley's findings, the Tropic project discussed in this study shows that the willingness of agency to embrace change, including collaborative partnerships between communities, conservationists and the private sector, represents a new era of structural change, and the evolvement of these in line with the increasing power of agencies.

Despite providing evidence to suggest that agency has far greater power in influencing structure than frequently assumed, Giddens' (1976) argument that structure is a constraint on human action is equally applicable. All three projects were confined by bureaucratic pro-cedures due to their embeddedness in extensive networks, processes that shifted resources from the actual project to the maintenance of these relationships. While these networks have clearly been invaluable in providing funding and technical expertise, it seems that bureau-cracy, form-filling and lengthy procedures associated within certain institutional structures were detrimental to the projects, and their subsequent outputs.

This paper sought to compare development organisations and tour operators and show that tour operators have equal, if not more, propensity to contribute to poverty reduction through their role as agents who are capable of altering traditional institutionalised struc-tures. There is, however, recognition by Tropic themselves that "private operators have a long way to go". Although tour operators are not obligated to deliver livelihood benefits to communities, unlike development organisations, the ideology of a company can clearly have a profound impact, as the Tropic example has shown. The power of structure and the power of agency are clearly entwined and fluctuate depending on the context. Analysing the duality of structure and agency within pro-poor tourism projects adds a new theoretical dimension to academic discussions on the potential of tourism to contribute to poverty re-duction. Whereas previous studies focused either on the theoretical structural constraints of using tourism in this manner or on micro-level impact studies, this paper has sought to place pro-poor tourism within a renewed discussion of structuration theory. We are very aware that this paper leaves many open questions: we encourage, therefore, longitudinal studies into causal links between tourism and institutional structures and resulting livelihood outputs.

References

Ashley, C. (2000). *The impacts of tourism on rural livelihoods: Experience in Namibia* (Working Paper No. 128). London: Overseas Development Institute (ODI).

Ashley, C. (2005). *Facilitating pro-poor tourism with the private sector: Lessons learned from "pro-poor tourism pilots in Southern Africa"* (Working Paper No. 257). London: Overseas Development Institute (ODI).

Ashley, C., & Maxwell, S. (2001). Rethinking rural development. *Development Policy Review, 19*(4), 395–425.

Bennett, O., Roe, D., & Ashley, C. (1999). *Sustainable tourism and poverty elimination: A report for the department of international development.* London: Deloitte and Touch, IIED and ODI.

Berger, P. L., & Luckmann, T. (1967). *The social construction of reality.* New York, NY: Doubleday.

Bianchi, R.V. (2002). Towards a political economy of global tourism. In R. Sharpley & D.J. Telfer (Eds.), *Tourism and development – Concepts and issues* (pp. 265–299).. Clevedon: Channel View Publications.

Borren, S. (2000). Development agencies: Global or solo players? *Development in Practice, 10*(3–4), 408–419.

Bramwell, B., & Meyer, D. (2007). Power and tourism policy relations in transition. *Annals of Tourism Research, 34*(3), 766–788.

Britton, S. (1982). The political economy of tourism in the third world. *Annals of Tourism Research, 9*(3), 331–358.

Brohman, J. (1996). New directions for tourism in Third World development. *Annals of Tourism Research, 23*(1), 48–70.

Brown, L.D., & Moore, M.H. (2001). Accountability, strategy, and international nongovernmental organisations. *Nonprofit and Voluntary Sector Quarterly, 30*(3), 569–587.

Bryden, J. (1973). *Tourism and development: A case study of the Commonwealth Caribbean.* Cambridge: Cambridge University Press.

Buckland, J. (1998). Social capital and sustainability of NGO intermediated development projects in Bangladesh. *Community Development Journal, 33*(3), 236–248.

Chok, S., Macbeth, J., & Warren, C. (2007). Tourism as a tool for poverty alleviation: A critical analysis of "pro-poor tourism" and implications for sustainability. *Current Issues in Tourism, 10*(2–3), 144–165.

Clancy, M. (1999). Tourism and development: Evidence from Mexico. *Annals of Tourism Research, 26*(1), 1–20.

Clarke, G. (1998). Non-governmental organisations (NGOs) and politics in the developing world. *Political Studies, 46*(1), 36–52.

Cohen, I.J. (1989). *Structuration theory: Anthony Giddens and the constitution of social life.* New York, NY: St Martin's Press.

Cox, R. (1987). *Production, power and world order: Social forces in the making of history.* New York, NY: Columbia University Press.

De Kadt, E. (Ed.). (1979). *Tourism: Passport to development?* New York, NY: Oxford University Press.

Dredge, D. (2006). Networks, conflicts and collaborative communities. *Journal of Sustainable Tourism, 14*(6), 562–581.

Ebrahim, A. (2003). Accountability in practice: Mechanisms for NGOs. *World Development, 31*(5), 813–829.

Edwards, M. (1993). Does the doormat influence the boot? Critical thoughts on UK NGOs and international advocacy. *Development in Practice, 3*(3), 163–175.

Fadeeva, Z. (2004). Translation of sustainability ideas in tourism networks: Some roles of cross-sectoral networks in change towards sustainable development. *Journal of Cleaner Production, 13*, 175–189.

Farrington, J., Carney, D., Ashley, C., & Turton, C. (1999). *Sustainable livelihoods in practice: Early applications of concepts in rural areas* (Natural Resource Perspectives No. 42). London: Overseas Development Institute (ODI).

Foucault, M. (1978). *The history of sexuality. Volume I: An introduction.* New York, NY: Vintage Books.

Foucault, M. (1980). Two lectures. In C. Gordon (Eds.), *Power/knowledge: Selected interview and other writings 1972–1977* (pp. 78–108). New York, NY: Pantheon Books.

Foucault, M. (1987). *Discipline and punish.* London: Penguin.

Giddens, A. (1976). *New rules of sociological method.* London: Hutchinson.

Giddens, A. (1984). *The constitution of society: Outline of the theory of structuration.* Cambridge: Polity Press.

Giddens, A. (1989). A reply to my critics. In D. Held and J.B. Thompson (Eds.), *Social theory of modern societies: Anthony Giddens and his critics* (pp. 249–305). Cambridge: Cambridge University Press.

Giddens, A., & Pierson, C. (1998). *Conversations with Anthony Giddens: Making sense of modernity.* Cambridge: Polity Press.

Goodwin, H., & Francis, J. (2003). Ethical and responsible tourism: Consumer trends in the UK. *Journal of Vacation Marketing, 9*(3), 271–284.

Goodwin, H., & Roe, D. (2001). Tourism, livelihoods and protected areas: Opportunities for fair trade tourism in and around national parks. *International Journal of Tourism Research, 3*(5), 377–391.

Hills, T. L., & Lundgren, J. (1977). The impact of tourism in the Caribbean. *Annals of Tourism Research, 4*(5), 248–267.

Hulme, D., & Edwards, M. (1997). NGOs, states and donors: An overview. In D. Hulme & M. Edwards (Eds.), *NGOs, states and donors: Too close for comfort?* (pp. 3–22). London: Macmillan Press.

Lea, J. (1988). Tourism and development ethics in the Third World. *Annals of Tourism Research, 20*, 701–715.

Lewis, D. (2002). Non-governmental organisations: Questions of performance and accountability. In V. Desai & R.B. Potter (Eds.), *The companion to development studies* (pp. 519–523). London: Arnold.

Meyer, D. (2007). Pro-poor tourism: From leakages to linkages. A conceptual framework for creating linkages between the accommodation sector and "poor" neighbouring communities. *Current Issues in Tourism, 10*(6), 558–583.

Meyer, D. (2009). Pro-poor tourism – is there value beyond the rhetoric? *Tourism Recreation Research, 34*(2), 191–196.

Meyer, D. (2010a). The emergence of the semi-periphery in tourism investment in East Africa. In J. Mosedale (Ed.), *Political economy of tourism – a critical perspective* (pp. 157–174). Oxford: Routledge.

Meyer, D. (2010b). Pro-poor tourism: Can tourism contribute to poverty reduction in less economically developed countries? In S. Cole & N. Morgan (Eds.), *Tourism and inequality: Problems and prospects* (pp. 164–182). London: CABI.

Mowforth, M., & Munt, I. (1998). *Tourism and sustainability: New tourism in the third world.* London: Routledge.

Müller, B. (1984). Fremdenverkehr, Dezentralisierung und Regionale Partizipation in Mexiko. *Geographische Rundschau, 36*(1), 20–24.

Murdoch, J. (1997). Towards a geography of heterogeneous associations. *Progress in Human Geography, 21*, 321–337.

Murphy, C., & Roe, D. (2004). Livelihoods and tourism in communal area conservancies. In S.A. Lond (Eds.) *Livelihoods and CBNRM in Namibia: The findings of the WILD project* (pp. 119–138). Windhoek: Ministry for Environment and Tourism.

Novelli, M., & Gebhardt, K. (2007). Community based tourism in Namibia: "Reality show" or "window dressing"? *Current Issues in Tourism, 10*(5), 443–479.

Oppermann, M., & Chon, K.S. (1997). *Tourism in developing countries.* London: International Thompson Business Press.

Östreich, H. (1977). Gambia – Zur Sozio-ökonomischen Problematik des Ferntourismus in Einem Westafrikanischen Entwicklungsland. *Geographische Zeitschrift, 65*, 302–308.

Pearce, D. (1989). *Tourism development* (2nd ed). Harlow: Longman.

Poultney, C., & Spenceley, A. (2001). *Wilderness Safaris South Africa: Rocktail Bay and Ndumu lodge* (PPT Working Paper No. 1). London: ODI/IIED/CRT.

Ranson, S., Hinings, B., & Greenwood, R. (1980). The structuring of organizational structures. *Administrative Science Quarterly, 25*, 1–17.

Salamon, L.M. (1994). The rise of the nonprofit sector. *Foreign Affairs, 73*(4), 109–122.

Saville, N.M. (2001). *Practical strategies for pro-poor tourism: Case study of pro-poor tourism and SNV in Humla District, West Nepal* (Working Paper No. 3). London: PPT Partnership.

Scheyvens, R. (1999). Ecotourism and the empowerment of local communities. *Tourism Management, 20*(2), 245–249.

Scheyvens, R. (2007). Exploring the poverty-tourism nexus. *Current Issues in Tourism, 10*(2–3), 231–254.

Scheyvens, R. (2009). Pro-poor tourism: Is there value beyond the rhetoric? *Tourism Recreation Research, 34*(2), 191–196.

Scheyvens, R. (2011). *Tourism and poverty.* Oxford: Routledge.

Schilcher, D. (2007). Growth versus equity: The continuum of pro-poor tourism and neoliberal governance. *Current Issues in Tourism, 10*(2–3), 166–193.

Sofield, T. (2003). *Empowerment for sustainable tourism development.* Oxford: Elsevier.

Spenceley, A. (2003). *Tourism, local livelihoods, and the private sector in South Africa: Case studies on the growing role of the private sector in natural resources management,* Sustainable Livelihoods in Southern Africa Research, Paper No. 8. Brighton: Institute of Development Studies.

Strange, S. (1994). *States and markets* (2nd ed). London: Pinter.

Stronza, A., & Gordillo, J. (2008). Community views of ecotourism. *Annals of Tourism Research, 35*(2), 448–468.

Tandon, R. (2000). Riding high or nosediving: Development NGOs in the new millennium. *Development in Practice, 10*(3–4), 319–329.

Tao, T.C.H., & Wall, G. (2009). Tourism as a sustainable livelihood strategy. *Tourism Management, 30*(1), 90–98.

Tapper, R. (2001). Tourism and socio-economic development: UK tour operators' business approaches in the context of the new international agenda. *International Journal of Tourism Research, 3*, 351–366.

Telfer, D.J. (2003). *Development issues in destination communities: Tourism and host communities.* Cambridge, MA: CABI.

Turner, L., & Ash, J. (1975). *The golden hordes: International tourism and the pleasure periphery.* London: Constable.

UNWTO. (2009). *Tourism highlights.* Madrid: Author.

van der Duim, R., & Caalders, J. (2008). Tourism chains and pro-poor tourism development: An actor-network analysis of a pilot project in Costa Rica. *Current Issues in Tourism, 11*(2), 109–125.

Walsham, G. (1993). *Interpreting information systems in organizations.* Cambridge: Wiley.

Wearing, S., & McDonald, M. (2002). The development of community-based tourism: Re-thinking the relationship between tour operators and development agents as intermediaries in rural and isolated area communities. *Journal of Sustainable Tourism, 10*(3), 191–206.

World Bank. (2000). *Ecuador gender review: Issues and recommendations.* Washington, DC: World Bank Group.

WTTC. (2009). *Travel and tourism economic impact: Ecuador.* London: Author.

Zhao, W., & Ritchie, J.R.B. (2007). Tourism and poverty alleviation: An integrative research framework. *Current Issues in Tourism, 10*(2–3), 119–143.

Community-based tourism enterprises: challenges and prospects for community participation; Khama Rhino Sanctuary Trust, Botswana

Lesego Senyana Stone[a] and Tibabo Moren Stone[b]

[a] Harry Oppenheimer Okavango Research Centre, University of Botswana, Maun, Botswana;
[b] Department of Environmental Sciences, University of Botswana, Gaborone, Botswana

This study assesses community participation in a community-based tourism enterprise in Botswana, the Khama Rhino Sanctuary Trust, founded in 1992. Data were collected using structured and semi-structured questionnaires, interviews with key stakeholders and community focus group discussions. Results indicate that although Community-Based Natural Resource Management is popular in many southern African nations, communities still face challenges and constraints which hinder their participation in community-based enterprises. While some other studies in Botswana indicate the value of community-based tourism, 95% of adult residents in the Khama Rhino Sanctuary Trust area did not know who owned the Trust, and 98% had never been to the Trust's lands. There was community disappointment about loss of cattle grazing and other land-related benefits, lack of communication with the community, lack of benefits, the low numbers employed and the slow progress of the project which did not record a profit until 2008. But the Trust now has over 25% of the rhinos in Botswana and has seen visitor numbers rise from 1820 in 1996 to over 21,000 in 2008. Suggestions for the future include appointment of a community liaison officer, training for local people in tourism and management and use of single-community rather than multi-community trusts.

Introduction

In Botswana, tourism is the second-largest economic sector after diamonds (Mbaiwa, 2004a; Mmopelwa & Blignaut, 2006), contributing 9.7% to the country's gross domestic product (World Travel and Tourism Council, 2007). It is the second-largest export sector and accounts for 23,226 jobs, 4.2% of total employment (World Travel and Tourism Council, 2007). Botswana's 1990 tourism policy encourages the conservation of natural resources and focuses on providing local communities, mainly from rural areas, with direct and indirect benefits from tourism and promoting employment, development and services in those rural areas. More importantly, the policy encourages communities to appreciate their resources (Government of Botswana, 1990) and calls for local communities to get a share of the profits made from the tourism sector.

In order to involve local communities in the tourism sector, Botswana officially adopted Community-Based Natural Resource Management (CBNRM) in 1989. The programme was initiated by the Botswana Government and the US Agency for International Development through a joint Natural Resource Management Project, housed by the Department of Wildlife and National Parks (DWNP; Gujadhur, 2000; National CBNRM Forum, 2005). The CBNRM policy came into effect in 2007. CBNRM devolves authority and decision-making to community level by promoting bottom-up approaches to development. This approach was chosen because of the failure of top-down approaches to development, to promote long-term sustainability and to offer communities the opportunities to become actively involved (Government of Botswana, 2007). As with the tourism policy of 1990, this policy promotes the involvement of local communities in the conservation of natural resources while deriving economic benefits from them (Gujadhur, 2000). It gives communities the responsibility to manage their resources and an opportunity to economically benefit from wildlife resources in their localities (Mbaiwa, 2008).

Building upon research on community-based tourism (CBT) enterprises, this paper determines the challenges and prospects for community participation at the Khama Rhino Sanctuary Trust (KRST; www.khamarhinosanctuary.com/about.htm). It examines the barriers and challenges to community participation at the KRST and makes suggestions about ways of addressing identified challenges and constraints.

Community participation in tourism

The 1972 United Nations Conference on the Human Environment led to a shift towards integrated resource management, calling for more participation by rural communities in rural development projects and for communities to have greater control in decision-making and benefits flowing to them (Hall & Lew, 1998). Aid agencies such as the US Agency for International Development, World Bank and UN have promoted community participation since then. This approach involves local people in decision-making, programme implementation, sharing the benefits of development and evaluating programmes (Catley, 1999). Community participation further gained status in 1987 with the concepts of sustainability and sustainable development, put forward by the World Commission on Environment and Development's Brundtland Report (Hall, 2000). Since the 1980s, the tourism literature has called for the inclusion and involvement of local communities in tourism; local residents are seen as a key resource in sustaining the product (Hardy, Beeton, & Pearson, 2002). The 1992 Rio Summit introduced Agenda 21, a blueprint for action by host communities, which calls for tourism–community interactions which are essential for sustainable development strategies. Adopted by 178 countries at Rio (Ritchie & Brent, n.d.), Agenda 21 promotes rural community participation to maximise the rural community's ability to control and manage its resources (Van Rooyen, 2004).

The participation of rural communities in tourism ventures has been a main focus in the developing world for 30 years. According to Li (2006), western scholars believe active local participation in decision-making is a prerequisite if benefits are to reach communities. However, this has been difficult to practise in many developing countries because of various constraints. Community participation is, however, advocated for environmental reasons as well as for more sustainable development (Van Rooyen, 2004). Unless local residents are empowered and participate fully in decision-making and ownership of tourism developments, tourism will not reflect their values and will less likely generate sustainable outcomes (Lea, 1988). Similar views were expressed in the World Tourism Leaders' Meeting on the Social Impacts of Tourism, which supported the increased involvement of communities in the planning, implementation, monitoring and evaluation of tourism policies, programmes and projects (World Tourism Organisation, 1997).

According to Tosun (2000), community participation in development paves the way for the implementation of principles of sustainable tourism development and creates better opportunities for local people to gain more benefits from tourism developments taking place in their localities. Indeed, "without benefits in proportion to the effort involved, communities are unlikely to participate" (Murphree, 1999, p. 6). Those benefits need not always be financial. Often the intangible benefit of skills development, increased confidence, growing trust and ownership of the project may be of greater value to the community (Clarke, 2002).

Community participation is believed to lessen opposition to development, minimise negative impacts and revitalise economies (Hardy et al., 2002). It helps local people to accept tourism ventures and tourism to be sustainable (Inskeep, 1994; Wahab, 1997), even though community attitudes may change over time from enthusiasm to euphoria, depending on how communities perceive tourism in a given area (Little, 1996). Many researchers believe that when local communities are involved in decision-making, benefits can be realised and the traditional lifestyles and values of the communities can be respected (Li, 2006). Success, however, relies on communities having a sense of project ownership (Scheyvens, 2002).

The political legitimacy of communities may be enhanced if their participation means that they have a greater share of decision-making about issues that affect them, leading to a building of the knowledge, insights and capabilities of involved stakeholders and the sharing of ideas (Bramwell & Sharman, 2000). Dialogue between the different stakeholders should be encouraged.

According to Wahab (1997), there are three differences in the tourism development process between developed and developing nations. Firstly, owing to other pressing needs, such as the lack of clean water, food and shelter, local communities devote less attention to tourism development and planning. Secondly, the lack of democracy in many developing nations leads to the dominance of the ruling class in the development process. And thirdly, there is no system in place to allow local people who are directly affected to determine their social input to development thinking, as tourism is thought to be an industry of national concern. According to Tosun (2000, p. 615), "community participation, as an ideal type, involves a shift in power from those who have had major decision-making to those who traditionally have not had such a role". Genuine participation ensures that the powerless can develop, create and systematise their own roles and define their vernacular forms of conservation and management (Ghimire & Pimbert, 1997).

The aim of CBT ventures then is to ensure that members of local communities have a high degree of control over activities taking place in their localities and a significant proportion of the economic benefits (Scheyvens, 2002). This contrasts with most tourism ventures which are controlled wholly by outside operators whose primary motive is to make profits. For local people to maximise their benefits and have some control over tourism occurring in their regions, Akama (1996) suggests alternative tourism initiatives which aim to empower local people. Local communities need empowerment to help decide what tourism facilities and wildlife conservation programmes they want in their communities and how tourism costs and benefits are to be shared among different stakeholders (Akama, 1996). Ideally, community participation involves designing development so that the intended beneficiaries are at the forefront and participate, by mobilising their own resources, making their own decisions and defining their own needs and how to meet them (Stone, 1989). Furthermore, it is a useful public education tool, educating local people about their rights, laws and political good sense (Tosun, 2000).

Although CBT has been promoted since the 1970s (Goodwin, 2006), often as a form of pro-poor tourism, studies indicate that many CBT projects have failed, usually because of lack of financial viability (Mitchell & Muckosy, 2008). Tourism is said to be pro-poor if it results in increased net benefits flowing to the poor (Mitchell & Faal, 2008). In his assessment of CBT, Goodwin (2006) states that only a few projects have generated enough benefits to provide incentives for conservation and contribute to local poverty reduction. In a survey of 200 CBT projects across the Americas, Mitchell and Muckosy (2008) discovered that accommodation offered by CBT projects had an occupancy rate of only 5%, and in Ecuador, the Siecoya CBT project generated only $200 for the community fund after nine years in operation, despite hefty subsidies from an oil extraction company. Mitchell and Muckosy (2008) attributed this lack of financial viability to poor market access and poor governance.

Furthermore it has been discovered that tourism practitioners working with communities know little about commercial tourism markets and run projects without bringing in business expertise and private sector partners (Ashley & Goodwin, 2007); this ultimately leads to project failure in many cases. Poor market access and governance are brought about by the long-held belief that poor people, those living below $1 per day, cannot participate successfully in commercial markets, resulting in the exclusion of communities in decision-making processes. According to Goodwin (2009), although the poor can benefit from ecotourism and CBT, there is rarely any connection with the mainstream industry, and they remain small in scale and often lack a market and commercial orientation (Goodwin, 2008).

An evaluation of CBT projects around the world carried out by the International Centre for Responsible Tourism at Leeds Metropolitan University, UK (Goodwin, 2006), found that CBT projects failed because of the following:

- There is a lack of understanding of the need for commercial activities. Local people must sell crafts, food, accommodation and wildlife or cultural experiences to tourists. This is the only way to ensure sustainable local income or conservation funds.
- There is a lack of engagement with the private sector, including travel agents, tour operators and hoteliers. The earlier this engagement takes place and the closer the partnership is, the more likely the project is to succeed.
- Location is critical. For poor people to benefit, tourists must stay in or near to these communities. Very few communities have tourism assets which are sufficiently strong to attract tourists – they rely on selling complementary goods and services. Tourists need to be close by for this to happen.
- CBT projects do not always provide appropriate tourism facilities for generating income. Too many CBT initiatives rely on building lodges, which are capital intensive and need considerable maintenance, or walking trails from which it can be difficult to secure revenue.
- Protected areas increasingly rely on money from tourists to pay for conservation initia-tives. Local communities often have to compete with conservation projects for revenues.

Study area

In the early 1980s the black and white rhino was on the brink of local extinction despite having been granted protection status in 1922 (Dow, 2009). This situation came about because of illegal poaching. The government of Botswana, with the help of donor agencies, especially the Natal Parks Board, decided to reintroduce them in the Chobe and Moremi game reserve in the 1960s. However, owing to lack of monitoring and security, poachers killed nearly all the reintroduced animals. There was a need to establish a protected area,

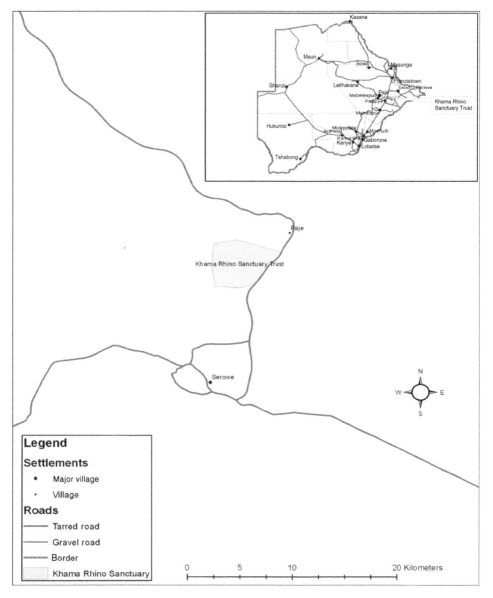

Figure 1. Map showing the location of the KRST in Botswana. Source: Harry Oppenheimer Okavango Research Centre, 2007.

which would offer security to try and increase the number of rhinos in the country (Chief Warden's Project Proposal, 2004).

The KRST, set up in 1992, is located in the Central District of Botswana on 4300 hectares of the Kalahari sandveld (Figure 1). The idea was initiated by community members in Serowe in 1989. The KRST is a community-based wildlife project, established, among other things, to "generate revenue for the local community from tourism and other uses of the Sanctuary's renewable resources" (Sebele, 2005). It is located around Serwe Pan, a large grass-covered depression with many natural water holes, chosen because of its suitability for white rhinos and other grazing animals. The area was formerly used for communal grazing: farmers had to be relocated for the project. Only one of the farmers had a borehole and was therefore compensated for that and was also given land on which to continue his farming activities; the other farmers without boreholes were not given any form of compensation.

The Trust is an initiative of three villages of Serowe, Paje and Mabeleapudi. Serowe, the biggest village in the district, had a population of 42,444 during the 2001 census; Paje had 2088; and Mabeleapudi had 1780 (Central Statistics Office, 2002). The Sanctuary is located 25 kilometres north of Serowe along the Serowe–Orapa road, 11 kilometres north-east of Mabeleapudi and 7 kilometres east of Paje village (Grossman and Associates, n.d.). The KRST is governed by a Board of Trustees appointed from the three villages. The board members are elected at the village *kgotla*s, and their membership is renewed every two years. As there is no non-governmental organisation or intermediary providing operational support, board members are solely elected by the community with no influence from any external donors. The project focuses on the conservation of the rhino species and also aims to provide local communities with economic benefits from tourism and other natural resources.

The KRST has attracted an increasing number of tourists, and besides rhinos, many other species of animals are found in abundance. Some settled in the area naturally: others were translocated into the area. Animals found include the following: zebras, blue wildebeests, giraffes, elands, springboks, impalas, gemsboks, kudu, steenboks, duikers, red hartebeests, waterbucks, warthogs, leopards, ostriches, African wild cats, caracals, small spotted genets, black-backed jackals, bat-eared foxes and brown hyenas. The KRST also has over 130 bird species.

The Sanctuary offers accommodation in camping sites and chalets and also offers game drives and night drives. There is a curio shop which sells arts and crafts bought by the KRST from a local project in Serowe and a San project in a neighbouring village, which is outside the project (personal interview with the Chief Warden, 13 September 2004). Arts and crafts are sourced from the neighbouring village because the local villages could not supply the quantity or variety of artefacts needed.

Methodology

Data collection from primary and secondary sources took place between July and October 2004 and was updated in September 2009. Primary data collection tools used included interviews with key stakeholders using both structured and semi-structured questionnaires. The interviews collected information on how community-based KRST is; benefits and losses derived by the community from the Trust; how benefits, if any, are distributed among the community; problems or losses the community has encountered since the inception of the KRST; and the level of interaction and community participation, if any, between the Trust and the community.

Informal face-to-face interviews were also held with the Chief Warden of the Sanctuary to get more information on why and how the project was set up, the daily operations of the enterprise and its performance and to get his views on how the community is involved and allowed to participate in the project. The interview method was chosen in order to increase the response rate, ensure respondents understood the questions asked and ensure effective information gathering.

Focus group discussions were also held in each of the three villages, to get the community's perceptions on the benefits of the KRST and to ascertain their level of community participation in the tourism enterprise.

Secondary sources of data collection included journals, published books, unpublished reports and newsletters, government policy documents and the Internet to get information on CBT. Audited financial reports, project proposals written by the Chief Warden and the management plan for the KRST were consulted to learn more about the KRST's performance and its mandate.

A case study approach was used to provide an "in-depth, detailed analysis" (Casley & Curry, 1981, pp. 61–63) and facilitated a detailed study of the KRST. Key decision-makers were interviewed, including chiefs from the three villages, all board members of the KRST and chairpersons of the village development committee (VDC) in each village. Two focus group discussions, each comprising 10 participants, were also held in each of the three villages, one comprising adults in the village and the other comprising the youth. Participants above the age of 30 were considered elders (these individuals would have been 19 years and older when the project started operating). This ensured that views about the CBT at the KRST from both groups in the society were obtained. The focus groups for elders included some of the relocated farmers, past board members and residents of the village since 1989 (the assumption was that they would have knowledge about the situation in their villages before and after the tourism initiative).

For the youth focus groups in Serowe, a local youth officer helped identify respondents. The first 10 available individuals were selected for the discussion. In Paje and Mabeleapudi the researcher was assisted by the VDC to identify youth to be included in the study. Active members of the society were targeted, including those involved in development issues (some had campaigned to be the KRST board members; others were members of the village youth development committee). Participants were aged between 19 and 30 (these participants would have been of school age or between the ages of 7 and 18 when the project started). The assumption was that they would have a better understanding of what was going on in their villages.

Focus group discussions were chosen because they allowed more in-depth views and comments to be given by respondents as opposed to individual questioning. Some disadvantages remained: the groups may not have represented the whole community, and more outspoken individuals may have dominated the discussions. However, this is one of the best methods to use when conducting qualitative research. All interviews and discussions were carried out by the researcher. For participants who spoke and understood English, the medium of communication was English, but for the rest the discussions and interviews took place in Setswana. Responses were then translated into English during the write-up of the research report.

The data collected were analysed using descriptions and classification. Descriptions refer to the portrayal of data in a form that can be easily interpreted (Kitchin & Tate, 2000). This involved a written account of the key points in the focus group discussions and interviews held with the management of the KRST. Descriptions generate "a more thorough and comprehensive description of the subject matter" (Kitchin & Tate, 2000, p. 233). Classification involved the breaking down of data into constituent parts and then placing them into similar categories or classes (Kitchin & Tate, 2000). For this research, data were classified into responses given and categorised into subheadings.

Results and discussion

The results indicated that there are a number of constraints and challenges in place, making it difficult for the community to get involved in the running and management of the KRST. These include the lack of communal sense of ownership; inadequate employment creation and dependence on external funding; lack of information, community participation and involvement in the KRST; loss of benefits; and an imbalance in board representation. These are discussed in detail below.

Lack of communal sense of ownership

For maximum community participation to occur there should be a communal sense of ownership of the project among community members (Scheyvens, 1999). At the KRST this is lacking, with 95% of adult and 50% of youth respondents not knowing who owns the enterprise. Adult respondents stated that the enterprise is owned by the Khama family, a prominent family in Serowe, which the first president of Botswana, whose son is now the fourth president, belongs to. Perhaps locals associate the Khamas with this project because their name is in the project's name. The president is, however, only a patron of the KRST. Others stated that although the project was initially supposed to be community-owned, it is owned by a few individuals from Serowe, who seem to reap all the benefits from the project; while others stated that it is a parastatal. Only 5% of the adults knew that it is a community-based project owned by the three villages. However, 50% of the youth knew who owned the KRST, although some stated that it is owned by the Mabeleapudi and Paje communities only.

It is surprising that even some residents from Paje, the village closest to the Sanctuary, did not know who owns the project. Most remarkable of all is the fact that some of the farmers who were relocated from the area did not know the owner of the project. Owing to this lack of communal sense of ownership, it is not surprising to hear some respondents say that the project uses the name of the community for the benefit of a few individuals, at the expense of the whole community.

Of all the adults interviewed, 98% had never been to the KRST compared with 25% of the youth. The 2% of adults who had visited the KRST did so during their membership on the board. The youths who had visited (75%) the Sanctuary had done so on school tours. Non-visitation by adults can be attributed to the lack of involvement, information and participation. It can then be deduced that had it not been for their membership of the board, almost none of the adults might ever the Sanctuary.

The lack of communal sense of ownership can perhaps be attributed to the dominance of certain individuals in the running of the KRST. According to Scheyvens (2002, p. 9), "elites often dominate community-based development efforts and monopolise the benefits of tourism". Walpole and Goodwin (2000, p. 527) also assert this and state that "the existence of local economic elites constrains the distribution of benefits", and at a village level, it is mostly elites who benefit from ecotourism, while at the national level, the central government gains more because it controls "fees and revenues from national parks". Respondents' assertions that certain prominent families from Serowe dominate the project can, therefore, be attributed to this power dominance by the rich over the poor within the society. The families identified by respondents are said to be part of the Board of Trustees and were instrumental in setting up the project, and according to respondents most goods are sourced from their businesses. Elite domination has been reported in other CBT projects in Botswana. According to Mbaiwa (2004b), with the Okavango Community Trust (OCT), only the board members and the elite and the influential in the village technical committees get high sitting allowances, while the rest of the members get nothing. Mbaiwa (2004b) further states that the OCT has become such a powerful village institution that it has lost touch with the general membership. The community has been left out; only a minority benefits from funds accrued, despite the original intentions of the Trust to distribute benefits widely.

"Power governs the interaction of individuals, organisations and agencies influencing, or trying to influence, the formulation of tourism policy and the manner in which it is implemented" (Hall, 1994, p. 52). Inequalities in power may also hinder the participation of various stakeholders in the community and in the wider society. Resource allocation, policy ideas and institutional practices in the society can limit the influence that some people may have in tourism planning (Bramwell & Sharman, 2000). When the interests and attitudes of local community members are not taken into consideration, the views of the more powerful participants may prevail (Bramwell & Sharman, 2000), a feature at the KRST revealed by this research. This may lead to a low sense of community-based project ownership, leading to resentment of tourism enterprises in the locality.

Local people can only have pride about the KRST if they have a sense of ownership of the project (Grossman and Associates, n.d.; Scheyvens, 2002). CBT should be run in a transparent manner with all stakeholders represented if it is to represent the interests of the community and reflect true ownership (Mearns, 2003).

Inadequate employment creation and dependence on external funds

In 2004 the KRST employed 26 permanent staff members, with 23 from the three member villages and 3 from southern Botswana (personal interview with the Chief Warden, 13 September 2004). Of the 26 employees, five were from Serowe, 15 from Paje and three from Mabeleapudi. Employee numbers were the same since project inception, attributed to high operational costs and a rise in inflation (as told by the Chief Warden, personal interview, 13 September 2004). Revenue from tourism activities at the KRST only covers operational costs and staff salaries. The failure of the project to make money and employ more people may make it lose the support of the community, which expects more benefits in jobs and income. Very few individuals get direct financial gains from the Sanctuary; many groups in the society get little advantage.

In a former cattle-farming community, people can only accept tourism if they see benefits exceeding costs and see rapid progress. Employee numbers since 2009 have risen to 48 (41 full time, seven casual) with 15 from Serowe, 10 from Paje, 16 from Mabeleapudi and seven from other parts of Botswana. Non-local employment could raise questions for some in the community. However, no explanation was given for this, but vacancies are advertised at the local *kgotlas*[1], post offices and local shops. In recruiting staff, preference is given to residents from the three participating villages; however, outsiders may be recruited if qualified.

The KRST appears too financially dependent on external donors including the African Development Foundation, Environmental Heritage Foundation of Botswana, European Development Fund, EU and Global Environmental Facility (implemented by the United Nations Development Programme). These organisations have enabled capital-intensive projects to be realised and jobs to be created. But the reliance on external donors makes the economical viability of the project questionable and financially dependent. The Sanctuary also gets assistance from the DWNP and the Botswana Defence Force for security and to guard against poaching (personal communication with the Chief Warden, 2004). Being a community project, one would assume that the community would be responsible for the provision of security, through the employment of community patrol guides/community policing, as is the norm in other community projects.

Table 1. Donor funds sourced by the KRST between 2003 and 2008.

Year	Donor funds (in pula)
2003	117,380
2004	43,763
2005	8013
2006	46,325
2007	293,536
2008	236,757

Source: Deloitte and Touche audit reports for the KRST (2003–2008).

Although the Chief Warden stated that the reliance on external donors has been reduced, the KRST has recently obtained funds to employ a consultant to develop a marketing strategy. The audit report also indicates that the enterprise still gets a substantial amount from donors (see Table 1). For example, KRST has been awarded funds from the Community Conservation Fund to relocate some elands to the Sanctuary.

Lack of information, community participation and involvement

The results indicate that community participation is hampered because people do not have any information about the KRST. The management does not get information about the KRST across to the local people. Although the board meets regularly, results indicate that *kgotla* meetings are only held once a year to give an annual report to community members and every two years to elect board members. Owing to this limited interaction between the community and the KRST, the community's voice is seldom heard. Respondents stated that their village representatives on the board never call *kgotla* meetings to brief them on the developments taking place at the Sanctuary. Furthermore, the community is not being educated about the initiative and is not being involved in the monitoring and evaluation of the tourism project. As a result of this lack of interaction between the KRST management and the community, the community does not get information which may be essential to its development as well as to improve its livelihoods. The interview with the Paje village chief revealed that the KRST provides an avenue for locals to sell their products at the KRST main entrance; however, none have taken up this initiative. However, it was apparent from group discussions with the community members that they have no knowledge of this; hence they have not taken up this initiative. However, if there were dual communication between the KRST and the community, this would probably not be the case. The selling of products at the main entrance can be a viable venture for the poor as indicated by studies in other countries such as South Africa, where women craft sellers in Kwazulu Natal are given sites within the parks, and Zimbabwe, where local communities have demanded for a market at the entrance to the Gonarezhou National Park (Mahony & van Zyl, 2002).

The board members interviewed indicated that they do not involve the community in decision-making processes, because newsletters are produced quarterly and the Sanctuary office is open for everyone. The offices are, however, located in Serowe; accessibility is an issue for many, especially the poor. In 2003, the poverty rate in rural areas in Botswana was estimated to be 36.1%, while in the urban areas it was 15.5% (Thurlow, 2007).

Although the quarterly newsletters are a good idea, they are written in English. Only a minority may therefore have access to the newsletter. There is a strong case for them to also

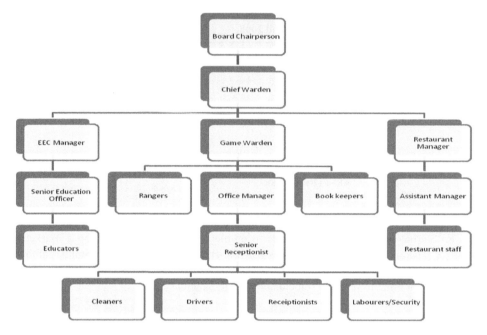

Figure 2.   Organisational structure of the KRST. Source: KRST, 2009.

be printed in Setswana, with *kgotla* meetings held regularly to accommodate those who are illiterate.

Participation comes in various forms and has different meanings to different people. It can range from selective consultation, as at the KRST, to complete self-mobilisation by local groups and activists (Neefjes, 2001). On the basis of the results obtained in this case study, we deduce that the local people are passive participants. In tourism development, communities that are passive participants in tourism ventures receive a few low-paying jobs at a tourist resort while having no control over the nature of development and no involvement whatsoever in the running of the tourism enterprise (Scheyvens, 2002). Passive participation occurs where people are "told what is to happen and act out predetermined roles" (Pretty, 2000). This seems to be the case at the KRST, where the community is not involved in any decision-making regarding the running of their supposedly owned enterprises. Furthermore, results indicate that although the community legally owns this project, its members are not practically involved: the word "ownership" is an irony to them. They are not actively involved in the day-to-day decision-making and do not reap benefits from the venture.

The KRST organisational structure (Figure 2) attests to this lack of community involvement and participation. The board should be accountable to the community members, and therefore they should appear at the top of the structure. The Chief Warden manages and has control of the enterprise and is accountable to the board chairperson.

Study results indicate that instead of participating in tourism development and becoming empowered, community involvement in tourism has not been strengthened but has led to the disempowerment of most in the society. This is clearly shown by the displacement of people from the land which they used to graze their cattle on, as well as the loss of access to natural resources they previously had access to. Although there has been a cash contribution of P4000.00 (7 Botswana pula = 1 US dollar) in 2004 to build a house for orphans in Paje, since inception no other funds have been used for community development purposes. The KRST has no benefits distribution plan; however, the board has made a decision that every year, depending on the profits made, it will provide financial assistance to one of the villages. To that end, according to the Chief Warden, the Mabeleapudi VDC was given P54,000.00 in 2009 to build a village community hall.

Loss of benefits

The results from focus group discussions with community members in the three villages indicate that residents have lost a number of valuable natural resources, now found and located within the KRST, the most important of which is their communal land. In this regard, the community believes it has incurred more costs than benefits. However, recent studies on the CBNRM indicate that the sustainability of projects whose costs outweigh benefits is small, as such projects have a higher risk of failure (Mbaiwa, 2004a; Murphree, 1999; Stone, 2006). Communities tend to support projects with more socio-economic benefits than costs. Residents feel the project has impoverished them by taking away their grazing land, leading to the production of poor-quality livestock, which only fetches low prices. The community members also indicated that they have lost access to resources such as wild fruits, which they used to gather and sell, thatching grass as well as roofing poles.

The losses, which they feel are enhanced by the lack of participation and involvement, further enhance the circle of poverty and defeat the goal of community-based initiatives, which is to eradicate poverty in the rural areas. Many people are not sharing in the benefits of tourism; most are disillusioned and are not interested in the initiative. According to Mander and Steytler (as cited in Scheyvens, 2002, p. 61), "it is desirable to design initiatives in such a way that benefits and costs are equitably distributed throughout the community from the outset to promote community cohesion".

In the Khwai Village, another community which promotes CBT in the Ngamiland District of Botswana, Mbaiwa's (2008) study indicates that the community of the Khwai Village, which was relocated to pave way for the development of the Moremi Game Reserve and consequently moved to the fringes of the reserve, is also very resentful because of the loss of access to a number of veld product resources. The community believes that the DWNP denies them access to resources that previously belonged to them (Mbaiwa, 2008). In Khwai, problems were also exacerbated by wildlife predation of livestock and crop damage and more so by the inadequate compensation, which is deemed to be low and taking a long time to be paid out. However, the introduction of CBT in Khwai has facilitated the participation of the community in the sustainable management of natural resources, especially on land and wildlife resources, and has also changed people's attitudes so that the hostility between the locals and the DWNP has now subsided.

Evidence shows that if conservation projects do not bring about livelihood security, then poverty and environmental degradation may intensify in areas around parks and nature reserves. In countries such as India and Kenya, rural conflicts have led to attacks on park guards, poisoning of animals and burning of forests (Pimbert & Pretty, 1995). In Kenya, the Masai hunted the black rhino until it was near extinction, not for its valuable horn but because they believed that the tourists' desire to see the animal had resulted in them losing their land to the Amboseli National Park (Koch, 1994). Similar problems have been reported worldwide (Pimbert & Pretty, 1995).

Imbalance in board representation

The KRST is governed by a board which is made up of 10 members, with one member coming from Paje, one from Mabeleapudi and eight from Serowe, thereby making it non-representative. This imbalance is attributed to the differences in the population sizes of the three villages (personal interview with the Chief Warden, 13 September 2004). In determining the figures, no ratio was used; the decision was just made arbitrarily. This imbalance has resulted in residents of Paje and Mabeleapudi perceiving that Serowe residents have an unfair advantage over them, and according to them this can be explained by the number of services sought from Serowe. Through focus group discussions, it was found that food as well as petrol and diesel are bought from Serowe, while minor services such as welding, thatching grass and roofing poles are sought from Paje residents.

Although locals acknowledge the importance of sourcing products from the community, there is a belief that Serowe villagers benefit more from the enterprise than the residents of the other villages (Sebele, 2005).

Prospects for CBT at KRST

Reintroduction of the rhino species

Despite the challenges outlined above, the KRST has been an ecological success in the reintroduction of the rhino species, a species on the brink of extinction in Botswana. In 2004, 27 of the 56 rhinos in Botswana were located at the KRST (Chief Warden's Project Proposal, 2004). The Sanctuary started with only four rhinos, which were translocated from northern Botswana in 1993, with the help of the Natal Parks Board (South Africa). Fourteen rhinos were translocated to the Sanctuary between 1993 and 1999, some donated from South Africa. In 2004, the KRST had the single black rhino in the country, a donation from the Zimbabwe Rhino Programme (Chief Warden's Project Proposal, 2004; see Figure 3).

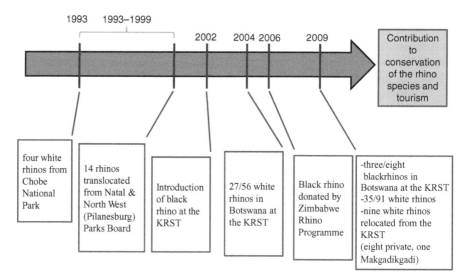

Figure 3.   KRST's success: reintroduction of the rhino species. Source: Modified from Discover Botswana, 2009.

Currently the KRST has 35 white and three black rhinos. Furthermore, nine white rhinos have been translocated from the KRST, eight to private game reserves and one to Makgadikgadi Pan National Park (Dow, 2009).

Increase in tourists' numbers and revenue generated

Although the KRST started operating in 1992, tourists' records have only been kept since 1996. Visitor numbers have grown from 1820 in 1996 to over 21,000 in 2008. The KRST makes money from activities such as guided game drives, rhino and giraffe trails, bird-watching and nature walks and the provision of accommodation (see Table 2).

The KRST has 78 beds, with 18 at camping sites, 28 in chalets and 32 available at some times of year in the Environmental Education Centre dormitories. The main feature of each camping site is a large Mokongwa tree (*Schinziophyton rautanenii*) which provides both character and shade. There is also a fireplace, a braai stand[2] with a grill and a tap with a bird bath. All the campsites are served by two communal ablution blocks. There are two 24-bed student dormitories and accommodation for up to eight teachers or supervisors. There is also a self-catered camping area with running water and a small ablution block at the Education Centre. The Chief Warden states that at project inception the occupancy rates were as low as 10% but that they had risen to around 65% by the year 2008.

For park entry fees, the enterprise has local, Botswana resident and non-resident charges. The intention of this is to allow community members to make use of its facilities. However, for all other activities offered as well as accommodation, the prices are the same for all visitors, including community members. Table 3 shows the fees charged by the enterprise.

Over the years, according to the Chief Warden, the KRST could not make enough money to meet all operational costs (see Table 4). The problem was so intense that in certain years the enterprise was forced to get loans from a few board members to pay the employees, and the money made through the provision of tourism facilities was then be used to pay off these loans. The project reached the break-even point after 16 years, with the year 2008 being the first year in which the project was able to make a profit, with a surplus of P887,579. With profits made, the enterprise has now made a commitment to distribute funds to one of the three villages every year.

Table 2.   Number of tourists who visited the KRST over the past six years.

Year	Day visitors	Campers	Chalets	EEC dormitory	EEC campers	EEC day	**Total**
2003	4719	4755	2255	112	0	215	**12,056**
2004	6511	4513	3243	16	82		**14,365**
2005	5185	5493	2590	400		137	**13,805**
2006	4648	5986	3131	527	205	549	**15,046**
2007	4949	7083	3643	777	887	366	**17,705**
2008	5923	7867	4381	779	761	1880	**21,591**
2009 (up to September)	4324	7157	3585	379	0	1331	**16,776**

Note: EEC, Environmental Education Centre.
Source: The Khama Rhino Sanctuary Trust, 2009.

Table 3. Fees charged by the KRST for the provision of tourism activities and facilities.

		Citizens	Residents	Non-residents
Parks fees	Adults	P15.00	P26.00	P33.00
	Children aged 6–12	P7.00	P13.00	P17.00
Camping	Adults	P40.00	P48.00	P53.00
	Children aged 6–12	P20.00	P24.00	P27.00
Chalets	Two rooms	P366.00	P366.00	P366.00
	Four rooms	P399.00	P399.00	P399.00
	Six rooms	P512.00	P512.00	P512.00
Hall rental	P800.00/day	P800.00/day	P800.00/day	P800.00/day
Dormitories	Students – six rooms	P366.00	P366.00	P366.00
	Teachers – two rooms	P366.00	P366.00	P366.00
Game drives	P333.00/four people	P333.00/ four people	P333.00/ four people	P333.00/ four people
Night drives	P484.00/ four people	P484.00/ four people	P484.00/ four people	P484.00/ four people
Guided drives	Hiring a guide but using own vehicle	P115.00/guide	P115.00/guide	P115.00/guide
Nature walk	Adults	P133.00	P133.00	P133.00
Rhino tracking	Adults	P200.00	P200.00	P200.00
Giraffe tracking	Adults	P173.00	P173.00	P173.00

Source: KRST (2009).

Table 4. Revenue made by the enterprise between 2003 and 2008.

Year	2003	2004	2005	2006	2007	2008
Income (in pula)	835,988	1,015,476	962,308	1304,756	2,417,304	3,097,935
Sanctuary expenditure	581,091	780,229	784,221	1038,903	1440,991	2474,252
Administration expenditure	296,573	360,680	280,927	504,732	1083,657	1044,807
Fair movement on biological assets					1205, 998	1308,703
Deficit for the year	41,676	125,434	102,840	238,879	1313,342	
Transfer of recognised portion of donor funds	117,380	43,763	8,013			
Adjustments made in donor funds – prior year amortised grant				46,325	293,536	236,757
Surplus for the year						887,579

Source: Deloitte and Touche audit reports for the KRST (2003–2008).

Conclusions

Although the project has experienced problems in involving the community, tourist numbers are now increasing, and since 2008, profits are being made. It would therefore be premature to say that CBT is not useful for rural communities and unfair to generalise that CBT projects are a failure. Studies in Botswana indicate that CBT has been a much-needed and important development tool in many communities (Mbaiwa, 2004a, 2004b, 2008; Mbaiwa & Sakuze, 2009). According to Mbaiwa and Stronza (2010), critics of the CBNRM make their arguments in isolation of the political, social and economic contexts of a particular project; therefore to avoid missing other key aspects of the CBNRM, particularly its achievements, projects need to be dealt with on an individual basis.

Mbaiwa's (2004a) study indicates that single-village trusts such as those of the Khwai and Sankuyo villages tend to do well in terms of benefits and the participation of community members. On the other hand, multiple-village trusts such as the OCT tend to experience problems (Mbaiwa, 2004b). The same is being experienced by the KRST which is also a multiple-village trust. Perhaps it is important to encourage communities to form single-village trusts to ensure success, as it is easier to get people from one area together to discuss trust issues and to ensure their participation in the trust.

To ensure maximum community participation, the community should be well informed and educated about its trust. The management should be transparent and accountable in its dealings: community members should have access to all business records at any time. Communities require training on their rights and responsibilities and should be fully conversant with their constitution and entitlements. For the benefit of the business enterprise, communities should hire the best candidates, on the basis of experience and qualifications and not place of residence; and hence the process of hiring might be discriminatory by placing more emphasis on community members, excluding other citizens who might be more beneficial to the enterprise. For community participation to be effective at the KRST, dialogue between the different stakeholders should be encouraged and facilitated by the employment of a liaison officer who can act as a broker between the community and the management.

Notes

1. A *kgotla* is a traditional meeting place for Tswana communities, where issues affecting the community are discussed and disputes are settled. The *kgotla* meeting is usually led by a *Kgosi* (chief) with the help of his advisors.
2. A metal grilling/barbeque stand, common in southern Africa, pronounced brr-eye.

References

Akama, J. (1996). Western environmental values and nature-based tourism in Kenya. *Tourism Management, 17*(8), 567–574.

Ashley, C., & Goodwin, H. (2007). *"Pro poor tourism": What's gone right and what's gone wrong?* London: Overseas Development Institute.

Bramwell, B., & Sharman, A. (2000). Approaches to sustainable tourism planning and community participation: The case of the Hope Valley. In D. Hall & G. Richards (Eds.), *Tourism and sustainable community development* (pp. 17–35). London: Routledge.

Casley, D.J., & Curry, D.A. (1981). *Data collection in developing countries*. Oxford: Claredon Press.

Catley, A. (1999). *Methods on the move; a review of veterinary uses of participatory approaches and methods focusing on experiences in Dryland Africa*. London: International Institute for Environment and Development.

Central Statistics Office. (2002). *2001 population and housing census; population of towns, villages and associated localities.* Gaborone, Botswana: Government Printer.

Chief Warden's project proposal. (2004). Unpublished report.

Clarke, V. (2002). *Differing understanding of "tourism and communities" within South Africa's tourism policy framework* (Unpublished M.Sc. dissertation). School of Leisure and Food Management, Sheffield Hallam University, Sheffield, UK.

Dow, P. (2009). Khama Rhino Sanctuary. *Discover Botswana, 9,* 78–81.

Ghimire, B., & Pimbert, M.P. (1997). Social change and conservation: An overview of issues and concepts. In B.K. Ghimire & M.P. Pimbert (Eds.), *Social change and conservation* (pp. 1–45). London: Earthscan.

Goodwin, H. (2006). *Community-based tourism failing to deliver? ID 21 Insights* (Issue no. 62). London: Department for International Development.

Goodwin, H. (2008). Tourism, local economic development and poverty reduction. *Applied Research in Economic Development, 5*(3), 55–64.

Goodwin, H. (2009). Reflections on 10 years of pro-poor tourism. *Journal of Policy Research on Tourism, Leisure and Events, 1*(1), 90–94.

Government of Botswana. (1990). *Tourism Policy: Government paper no. 2 of 1990.* Gaborone, Botswana: Government Printer.

Government of Botswana. (2007). *Community-based natural resource management policy.* Gaborone, Botswana: Government Printer.

Grossman and Associates. (n.d.). *Management and development plan for the Khama Rhino Sanctuary Trust.* Chicago, IL: Author.

Gujadhur, T. (2000). *Organisations and their approaches in community based natural resource management in Botswana, Namibia, Zambia and Zimbabwe.* Gaborone, Botswana: SNV/IUCN CBNRM Support Programme.

Hall, C.M. (1994). *Tourism and politics: Policy, power, and place.* Chichester, UK: John Wiley.

Hall, C.M. (2000). *Tourism planning: Policies, processes and relationships.* Harlow, UK: Prentice Hall.

Hall, C.M., & Lew, A.A. (1998). *Sustainable tourism: A geographical perspective.* Harlow, UK: Longman.

Hardy, A., Beeton, R., & Pearson, L. (2002). Sustainable tourism: An overview of the concept and its position in relation to conceptualisations of tourism. *Journal of Sustainable Tourism, 10*(6), 475–496.

Inskeep, E. (1994). *National and regional tourism planning.* London: Routledge and World Tourism Organization.

Kitchin, R., & Tate, N.J. (2000). *Conducting research in human geography: Theory, methodology and practice.* Harlow, UK: Prentice Hall.

Koch, E. (1994). *Reality or rhetoric? Ecotourism and rural reconstruction in South Africa* (UN-RISD/GEM Discussion Paper). Geneva: The United Nations Research Institute for Social Development.

Lea, J. (1988). *Tourism development in the Third World.* London: Routledge.

Li, W. (2006). Community decision-making participation in development. *Tourism Management, 33*(1), 132–143.

Little, P.D. (1996). The link between local participation and improved conservation: A review of issues and experiences. In D. Western, R.M. Wright, & S.C. Strumm (Eds.), *Natural connections: Perspectives in community-based conservation* (pp. 347–372). Washington, DC: Island.

Mahony, K., & van Zyl, J. (2002). The impacts of tourism investment on rural communities: Three case studies in South Africa. *Development Southern Africa, 19*(1), 83–103.

Mbaiwa, J.E. (2004a). The socio-economic benefits and challenges of a community-based safari hunting tourism in the Okavango Delta, Botswana. *Journal of Tourism Studies, 15*(2), 37–50.

Mbaiwa, J.E. (2004b). The success and sustainability of community-based natural resource management on the Okavango Delta, Botswana. *South African Geographical Journal, 86*(1), 44–53.

Mbaiwa, J.E. (2008). Local community attitudes towards wildlife conservation and community-based natural resources management in Ngamiland District, Botswana. In B. Schuster & O.T. Thakadu (Eds.), *Natural resources management and people.* Gaborone, Botswana: International Union for Conservation of Nature.

Mbaiwa, J.E., & Sakuze, L.K. (2009). Cultural tourism and livelihood diversification: The case of Gcwihaba Caves and XaiXai Village in the Okavango delta, Botswana. *Journal of Tourism and Cultural Change, 7*(1), 61–75.

Mbaiwa, J.E., & Stronza, A.L. (2010). The effects of tourism development on rural livelihoods in the Okavango Delta, Botswana. *Journal of Sustainable Tourism, 18*(5), 635–656.

Mearns, K. (2003). Community-based tourism: The key to empowering the Sankuyo community in Botswana. *Africa Insight, 33*(2), 29–32.

Mitchell, J., & Faal, J. (2008). *The Gambian tourist value chain and prospects for pro-poor tourism.* London: Overseas Development Institute.

Mitchell, J., & Muckosy, P. (2008). *A misguided quest: Community-based tourism in Latin America.* London: Overseas Development Institute.

Mmopelwa, G., & Blignaut, J.N. (2006). The Okavango Delta: The value of tourist. *South African Journal of Economic and Management Sciences, 9*, 113–127.

Murphree, M.W. (1999). *Congruent objectives, competing interests and strategic compromise: Concepts and processes in the evolution of Zimbabwe's CAMPFIRE programme.* Manchester: Manchester Institute for Development Policy and Management.

National CBNRM Forum. (2005, April 11–12). *The way forward for CBNRM in Botswana.* A Discussion Paper for the National CBNRM Forum, Gaborone, Botswana.

Neefjes, K. (2001). Learning from participatory environmental impact assessment of community-centred development: The Oxfam experience. In B. Vira & R. Jeffery (Eds.), *Analytical issues in participatory natural resource management.* Basingstoke, UK: Palgrave.

Pimbert, M.P., & Pretty, J.N. (1995). *Parks, people and professionals: Putting 'participation' into protected area management.* Geneva: United Nations Institute for Social Development.

Pretty, J. (2000). Conservation, participation and power: Protected-area planning in the coastal zone of Belize. *Journal of Planning Education and Research, 19*, 401–408.

Ritchie, B., & Brent, J. (n.d.). *Commentary – Local Agenda 21 and community participation in tourism policy and planning: Future or fallacy.* Retrieved from http://divcom.otago.ac.nz:800/tourism/current-issues/homepage.htm

Scheyvens, R. (1999). Eco-tourism and the empowerment of local communities. *Tourism Management, 20*, 245–249.

Scheyvens, R. (2002). *Tourism for development: Empowering communities.* Harlow, UK: Prentice Hall.

Sebele, L.S. (2005). *The social impacts of community-based tourism: A case study of Khama Rhino Sanctuary Trust in the central district, Botswana* (Unpublished master's dissertation). University of the Witwatersrand, Johannesburg, South Africa.

Stone, L. (1989). Cultural cross-roads of community participation in development: A case from Nepal. *Human Organisation, 48*(3), 206–213.

Stone, T.M. (2006). *Community-based natural resources management (CBNRM) and tourism: The Nata bird sanctuary project* (Unpublished master's dissertation). University of the Witwatersrand, Johannesburg, South Africa.

Thurlow, J. (2007). *Is HIV/AIDS undermining Botswana's "success story"? Implications for development strategy.* Washington, DC: International Food Policy Research Institute.

Tosun, C. (2000). Limits to community participation in the tourism development process in developing countries. *Tourism Management, 21*(6), 613–633.

Van Rooyen, J.C. (2004). *Rural community participation on tourism-based developments: The case of the Mbila community in Maputaland, Kwazulu-Natal* (Unpublished master's dissertation). University of Pretoria, Pretoria, South Africa.

Wahab, S. (1997). Sustainable tourism in the developing world. In S. Wahad & J. Pilgram (Eds.), *Tourism, development and growth.* London: Routledge.

Walpole, M.J., & Goodwin, H.J. (2000). Local economic impacts of dragon tourism in Indonesia. *Annals of Tourism Research, 27*, 559–576.

World Tourism Organisation. (1997). *World tourism leaders meeting: The social impacts of tourism final report.* Madrid: Author.

World Travel and Tourism Council. (2007). *Botswana: The impact of travel and tourism on jobs and the economy.* London: Author.

Blessing or curse? The political economy of tourism development in Tanzania

Fred Nelson

Maliasili Initiatives, Underhill, Vermont, USA

This paper analyses how tourism development in Tanzania is shaped in fundamental ways by the political–economic forces governing many post-colonial African states. Politics in Tanzania are characterized by a highly centralized and weakly accountable state, a prevalence of informal rent-seeking interests, institutionalized corruption in government at all levels and the intermingling of a developmentalist discourse built on foreign and private investment with the patronage and accumulative rent-seeking interests of political elites. Natural resources including land, forests and wildlife are central to these political processes, as is tourism as a major source of foreign exchange and investment. The resultant limitations on local communities and ordinary citizens to be able to create tourism enterprises that capture tourism's value as a poverty alleviation instrument are largely a function of the wider political economy, and the dependence of tourism on state-owned and controlled resources such as national parks and wildlife. Illustrations of growing conflicts over land tenure, wildlife revenues and access to tourism benefits in northern Tanzania are given. The development of explicitly rights-based approaches to tourism that emphasize tenure and devolved governance would aid the implementation of poverty alleviation strategies, as would research into the political economy of tourism and its governance.

Introduction

Few nations can boast Tanzania's potential as a site for environmentally sustainable and economically beneficial tourism development. The country's tourism assets – Serengeti, Ngorongoro Crater, Mount Kilimanjaro, as well as the Swahili Coast and Zanzibar – are among the most recognizable and attractive destinations found anywhere in the tropics. Tourism has grown rapidly since the economic doldrums of the 1980s to become a pillar of macroeconomic growth and investment, in a country long lauded as a bastion of political stability and regional leadership. Tourism's role in Tanzania's economic revival over the past two decades is unquestionably important in a developmental sense, since the country, despite its considerable natural resource wealth and stable political climate, remains one of the poorest countries in Africa. Tanzania's national economic policies, such as the cross-cutting National Strategy for Growth and the Reduction of Poverty (United Republic of Tanzania [URT], 2010), place considerable emphasis on opening up more economic opportunities from tourism at both national and local scale, echoing the earlier call of then-President Benjamin Mkapa for "a heightened onslaught on poverty, using the weapon of tourism" (URT, 2002).

While Tanzania's tourism industry itself thrives based on the blessing of the country's natural and cultural assets, and tourism's role in development policies becomes increasingly mainstreamed, the country is also establishing itself as an emblematic case of the contradictions and tensions that constrain sustainable tourism development in Africa (e.g. Honey, 2008). While national policymakers extol the potential of tourism, local communities living alongside leading tourism sites proclaim that "tourism is a curse to us" (Renton, 2009). Similarly, a recent feature article in a prominent international travel magazine entitled "Last Days of the Masai" (sic) (Hammer, 2010) examines the ongoing role of tourism in undermining the livelihoods and land rights of Maasai communities in northern Tanzania (see also Snyder & Sulle, 2011).

The contested nature of tourism development in Tanzania and its links to contemporary struggles over land rights, wildlife conservation policy and models of foreign investment are well documented (Charnley, 2005; Homewood, Kristjanson, & Trench, 2009; Honey, 2008; Nelson, 2004, 2010; Snyder & Sulle, 2011). What is less widely explored and understood are the underlying political–economic dynamics that underlie and perpetuate these enduring conflicts. Struggles over tourism development, in Tanzania and throughout much of contemporary sub-Saharan Africa, are to a large degree simply windows into wider contests over market access, economic and political empowerment, and citizenship. In Africa, the political character of the post-colonial state shapes these struggles in fundamental ways. Contextualizing efforts to link tourism development and poverty reduction within these wider political–economic systems is central to understanding the outcomes observed, and to developing appropriate strategies that can effectively address these challenges.

This paper frames the conflicts surrounding tourism development and poverty reduction in Tanzania by describing this context and interpreting the conflicts that revolve around tourism in relation to contemporary political dynamics in Tanzania and, by extension, many other parts of sub-Saharan Africa, where similar conflicts over land and natural resource rights and access are increasing (Alden Wily, 2011). The paper aims to integrate the established narratives of conflicts between local communities, private investors, the state and wildlife conservation interests, which often revolve around tourism development, with scholarship on the African state, using Tanzania as a case example. This political–economic interpretation of tourism development patterns in Tanzania is then used to develop practical suggestions for addressing the enduring and often-increasing challenges related to using tourism to advance poverty reduction objectives.

Methods and structure

This paper is synthetic and draws on the author's experiences as a field practitioner, facilitator and researcher in northern Tanzania for more than a decade (see Nelson, 2004, 2008; Nelson, Nshala, & Rodgers, 2007; Ngoitiko, Sinandei, Meitaya, & Nelson, 2010). The paper also draws on the findings from a recent multi-author research project on the politics of natural resource governance across eastern and southern Africa, which aims to improve the understanding of land and natural resource management outcomes through political–economic analysis (Nelson, 2010).

The paper is structured as follows. The next section provides an overview of literature on African political economy and governance in relation to development policy outcomes, including an overview of politics and development in contemporary Tanzania. This is then also related to the way that political–economic factors shape tourism development outcomes specifically. The following section provides a summary of recent conflicts in northern Tanzania revolving around land rights, tourism investments, government policy decisions and the underlying political factors that contribute to these ongoing tensions. The discussion section describes some key implications and suggestions for the development of more empowering forms of sustainable tourism that address existing constraints and challenges.

Politics and development in Africa

The rich body of scholarship on African polities continues to evolve in the light of both enduring democratic deficits and new reformative efforts across the region (Diamond & Plattner, 2010). While it is well beyond the scope of this paper to cover all the debates and shifts within this sub-field, this section does attempt a concise overview of the salient characteristics of African states and their implications for an understanding of tourism development outcomes.

The normative challenges of governance in African states are well documented. Nearly all African states – with the exception of a number of island nations and the southern African trio of South Africa, Botswana and Namibia – regularly fall in the bottom half of Transparency International's annual Corruption Perceptions Index, with many African nations clustered near the bottom of the index (Transparency International, 2011). Similarly, the six categories of governance indicators used by the World Bank's "Governance Matters" database generally place African countries, aggregated as a region, with the Middle East and South Asia at the bottom of global rankings (World Bank, 2010). The post-colonial political history of Africa has been dominated by single-party rule, presidents-for-life, coups and military rule; the combination of unaccountable government decisionmakers and the civil strife and violence resulting from competition for control of the state have combined to do immeasurable harm to Africa's developmental trajectory over the past 50 years (van de Walle, 2001).

Since the 1990s, electoral multi-party democracy has largely replaced military or authoritarian rule across most of the sub-continent, driven by both spreading influence and demand from African civil society and international support for "good governance" in the post-Cold War global political order (Bratton & van de Walle, 1997). Despite the prevalence of elections, democratic politics remain highly constrained through restrictions on political parties, eligibility rules, the selection and oversight of electoral commissions and other measures for incumbents to shape electoral outcomes. More fundamentally, the constitutional orders of African states – dealing with critical issues such as separation of powers, citizens' rights and freedoms, and mechanisms for accountability of government to its citizens – remain relatively unaltered by the reforms of the past two decades. As Prempeh (2010) notes, "Africa's post-1990 transitions have at best injected a few (but non-trivial) democratizing reforms into an old order that remains in key respects unreconstructed".

Several characteristics of African states are most fundamental to their functioning and the forms of corruption and unaccountable governance that they give rise to. Among the most important of these is the concentration of discretionary authority in the executive branch of government. This concentration of unchecked authority is rooted in the history of European colonial governance, which served to centralize unaccountable political authority and control over lands and resources, in ways that lacked historic precedent across most of Africa. The concentration of executive, legislative and judicial authority also occurred at the scale of local governance, by co-opting local traditional leaders of one form or another and elevating them to the status of "decentralized despots" whose authority derived from the colonial state, to use Mamdani's (1996) characterization. The high stakes attached to the executive branch have made the presidency the prized possession in African politics, conferring virtually unfettered control of the state and national resources to its holder in what Szeftel (1998) calls "a winner-take-all game" (see also Ake, 1996).

A second core characteristic of African politics, which is related to the centralization of discretionary authority in the hands of the executive, but which also has wider social and historic roots, is the informal or "personalized" nature of governance (Hyden, 2006). Personalized forms of governance rely on relationships between and decisions made by individuals and groups of people, in contrast to impersonal governance characterized by the rule of law (North, Wallis, & Weingast, 2009). The relative prevalence of informal relations in African politics, and conversely the relative weakness of the rule of law, is central to understanding the ubiquity of corruption, which is simply the informal bargaining over governance decisions and resources rather than adhering to the edicts of formal rules and regulations (Chabal & Daloz, 1999; Hyden, 2006; Kelsall, 2008; Szeftel, 1998).

High levels of corruption, coupled with centralized discretionary authority, result in the state serving the private interests – for dispensing patronage and personal enrichment – of those in power. Ake (1996) describes this as follows: "Instead of being a public force, the state in Africa tends to be privatized, that is, appropriated to the service of private interests by the dominant faction of the elite". African states driven by informal political interests and with weak or limited mechanisms for popular accountability tend to be geared more towards the creation of private rents than the production of public goods, which inherently undermines the pursuit of collective, national economic development (Bates, 1981).

Where public office holders widely use their positions to pursue private accumulative or patronage aims, the distinction between private business and public office is blurred to the point of indistinction. Indeed, as Szeftel (1998) says, politics in Africa is in essence "a means of entry into business", particularly in the context of post-colonial and/or post-socialist states where lands, natural resources and numerous productive enterprises are or were owned by the state, and where independent industrial production is limited. Lands and natural resources play a particularly important role in agrarian African societies as the main sources of wealth and commerce; controlling rights and access to land and resources is critical for elites both to exploit those rents and to maintain political authority over rural populations. Land tenure is consequently one of the most pivotal and politically contested issues across sub-Saharan Africa, with struggles over land playing a central role in wider efforts to democratize political orders and social relations (Alden Wily, 2011; Boone, 2007).

There are a range of fundamental implications for tourism development patterns and processes that emanate from these political–economic dynamics. Firstly, tourism development itself is often a part and parcel of elite patronage or accumulative interests; political elites and their allies are often significant investors or shareholders in tourism properties and developments. This is partly because elites have privileged access to and control over land and other state-held assets; the ability of political elites to privately acquire highly valued lands through public institutions is well documented, for example in Kenya and Tanzania (Alden Wily, 2011; Chachage & Mbunda, 2009). Similarly, the allocation of wildlife use rights through trophy-hunting concessions is, in countries such as Zambia and Tanzania, closely tied to public officials' patronage interests, with politicians significantly invested in the sector (Gibson, 1999; Nelson & Agrawal, 2008). Secondly, the existing political–economic order in most African countries creates substantial barriers to ordinary citizens' entry into tourism markets; this is particularly the case for the rural communities which potentially have the most to gain as the prospective proprietors of the natural assets prized by the various forms of eco- or wildlife tourism that predominate in eastern and southern Africa. Weaknesses in land and natural resource tenure and property rights limit the ability of rural communities to capitalize on these assets, and, as the case of Tanzania will describe, state interests often actively compete with or displace local initiatives to capture tourism revenues.

Tanzania

Tanzania is distinguished and rightly lauded within sub-Saharan Africa for never having experienced a violent or irregular change of government since independence in 1961. Similar to many other African nations, Tanzania adopted a single-party state in the 1960s and the ruling party (Tanganyika African National Union [TANU] before 1977 and Chama Cha Mapinduzi [CCM] thereafter following a merger between mainland and Zanzibari ruling parties) was largely fused with government administration in the 1960s and 1970s. In the 1980s, the socialist policies of independence leader and founding President Julius Nyerere were effectively abandoned following a period of economic collapse, and replaced with the adoption of a structural adjustment reform package with the International Monetary Fund. This initial move towards liberalization of the formerly state-dominated economy was followed in 1992 with constitutional reforms liberalizing political organization, including multi-party electoral competition.

Despite its history of peaceful political transitions and general stability, Tanzania nevertheless exhibits many of the core characteristics of neighbouring countries with more violent contemporary histories, with Tanzania's divergent experience perhaps best attributed to the exceptional personal ethos of President Nyerere, which focused on national unity and eschewed personal capital accumulation. Beyond these personal qualities – important as they have been to Tanzania – Nyerere steered Tanzania down a road of political evolution, similar to other African nations, by heavily concentrating power in the hands of the executive branch; severely restricting civil society, organized labour and other forms of independent social organization; abolishing elected local government for much of the 1970s; and placing control over productive resources and economic activity in the hands of the state (Coulson, 1982).

Since the 1990s, Tanzania has often been presented as a reformist "success story" by international development agencies, and compared to the state of economic collapse that prevailed in the 1980s, this narrative does hold some truth. Developmentally, though, Tanzania has increasingly come to be an emblematic African case of "growth without prosperity" (cf. Lewis, 2010), as gross domestic product has increased at upwards of 5% annually during the decade since 2000 without making significant headway in reducing poverty (Policy Forum, 2009). This has been particularly pronounced in the rural areas where the majority of Tanzanians live and where lack of market access, vulnerability to climatic changes and resource shortages, increasing food and fuel prices and other pressures all have worked to undermine or limit poverty reduction efforts. As is described below, the challenges that face efforts to better link tourism development with rural communities living in resource-rich areas are emblematic of the institutional struggles over market and resource rights and access that constrain the rural economy.

The political and economic liberalization that has taken place since the 1980s has created much greater flows of investment and revived economic activity in many sectors, but this has also contributed to increased levels of corruption, rent seeking and a political system that increasingly relies on patronage in the absence of any guiding ideology that enjoys popular legitimacy, as was the case in the 1960s and 1970s. Kelsall (2002) describes the process of liberalization as follows:

Generally speaking, economic liberalisation increased the desire and ability of members of the political elite to enrich themselves ... lucrative areas were to be found in land grabbing, urban real estate, and the exploitation of tax loopholes. Divestiture of parastatals also introduced a spoils character into Tanzanian politics, as politicians positioned themselves to receive kickbacks or to become part-owners of the newly privatised companies.

While corruption increased in the post-structural adjustment period of the late 1980s and early 1990s, it has become deeply institutionalized since then. The fourth phase government of President Jakaya Kikwete has witnessed the revelation of a series of major corruption scandals involving the systematic misuse or embezzlement of hundreds of millions of dollars in public funds (see Cooksey and Kelsall [2011] for a thorough summary of these). One of the most notorious of these, the so-called Richmond scandal involving the leasing of emergency power generators during a national electricity crisis, led to the unprecedented resignation of the Prime Minister in 2008 following a parliamentary enquiry.

Contemporary Tanzania thus features many of the political–economic characteristics of African states more generally: public resources are widely and systematically used for private accumulative or patronage purposes (i.e. to enrich public officials or to build alliances which enable these officials to maintain power); power is heavily concentrated in the hands of the executive branch, with limited authority held or exercised by the legislature or the judiciary; and numerous restrictions on the freedom of association limit the agency of the media and civil society organizations (Cooksey & Kelsall, 2011; Lawson & Rakner, 2005). Tanzanians are becoming more aggressive in challenging the current political order, with unprecedented opposition gains in parliament in the 2010 general election and a new constitutional reform movement – drawing inspiration in part from neighbouring Kenya's new 2010 constitution – but the reformist road will undoubtedly be long and heavily contested.

Tanzania's political dynamics and characteristics shape policy outcomes in critical ways. For tourism, the most important sectors are land and, particularly in Tanzania's case, wildlife. Both have been subject to extensive reform efforts since the 1990s, with the ostensive aim in both sectors to generally decentralize management; in the case of land, to strengthen local and customary tenure and security of property rights; and in the case of wildlife, to devolve user rights and access to benefits to support local development and generate incentives for conservation (Nelson et al., 2007). Implementing such reforms has proven challenging, inevitably. In the case of land, resistance among political elites to strengthening local customary ownership limited the degree of authority the state was originally willing to surrender under the 1999 Land Act and Village Land Act (Shivji, 1998; Sundet, 1997), and for practical purposes, contemporary land policy emphasizes allocating land to commercial investments rather than providing security to rural smallholders (Kamata, 2008).

The wildlife sector has been riddled with contradictory trajectories, with new legislation passed in 2009 serving to reconsolidate central discretionary authority over wildlife, quite in contrast to the policy reforms of a decade earlier (Nelson & Blomley, 2010). A key consideration in the wildlife sector has been the interests of policymakers and affiliated elites and business people in controlling wildlife's high commercial value, for example through the acquisition and allocation of trophy-hunting concessions (Nelson & Agrawal, 2008). Such interests conflict directly with proposals to devolve authority over lands and wildlife to local communities and thus have shaped the somewhat perverse wildlife governance outcomes of the past decade (Baldus & Cauldwell, 2004).

The importance to public officials of maintaining central control over wildlife, and land used by wildlife, is central to these policy contradictions. Cooksey and Kelsall (2011) describe the informal "system" of use and allocation of wildlife that lies at the heart of governance in the sector:

> Fishing and hunting licensing and regulation are other sources of major natural resource rents that are captured by officials and private actors . . . Tourist hunting is effectively coordinated and rents allocated by an informal network of private actors, politicians and government officials. At stake are substantial rents accruing from ivory and trophy poaching, hunting bloc allocation, and earnings from up-market hunting safaris.

In general, as one of Tanzania's most important economic sectors and sources of investment, tourism provides critical opportunities for capturing rents and distributing patronage, which motivates a range of political interests with stakes in controlling the sector's development. In addition to the consumptive uses of wildlife mentioned above, allocating land for lodges and other tourism developments in national parks or game reserves is a potentially lucrative source of income and patronage resources for those in power.[1]

The next section explores some of the conflicts revolving around land, wildlife and tourism development that arise within this political–economic context, and the implications such outcomes have for tourism as a poverty reduction strategy.

Tourism development and local communities in northern Tanzania

During the past 20 years, Tanzania has become one of sub-Saharan Africa's most popular and rapidly growing tourism destinations. Home to the Serengeti National Park, Mount Kilimanjaro, Ngorongoro Crater and Selous Game Reserve (all World Heritage Sites), Tanzania possesses unmatched wildlife populations and wilderness scenery, with around 30% of the country's total land area set aside in exclusive state-protected areas (Brockington, Sachedina, & Scholfield, 2008). Although Tanzania's tourism assets have been well known for decades, by 1990, tourism generated only $60 million in gross annual revenue. The socialist policies adopted in Tanzania during the late 1960s stymied private sector investment and trade, limiting the development of the tourism industry even as neighbouring Kenya became the African leader in the wildlife safari industry (Honey, 2008).

Following Tanzania's shift to more liberal economic policies, the tourism industry boomed, growing at more than 10% annually during the 1990s (The World Bank Group/Multilateral Investment Guarantee Agency [MIGA], 2002; Figure 1). The tourism sector's growth was driven by the popularity of the northern circuit (Figure 2), which includes Kilimanjaro, the Serengeti and Ngorongoro, as well as Tarangire and Lake Manyara National Parks. The wildlife of the northern parks is unquestionably the lynchpin of the tourism industry, with half of all visitors to Tanzania visiting Ngorongoro Crater, and the northern circuit generating an estimated $600 million out of total receipts now worth over $1 billion annually (Mitchell, Keane, & Laidlaw, 2008).

While there is little question that wildlife tourism has risen to become one of Tanzania's most important industries and economic sectors at the national, macro-economic scale, with continued high prospects for further growth given the right set of policy and marketing measures, a number of more complex and contentious issues surround the issue of tourism's environmental and socio-economic impacts and sustainability. These issues centre on the way that tourism influences ongoing contests over land and resource rights, access to and control over markets and revenues, and natural resource governance.

Land tenure security and access to natural resources have long been among the primary socio-economic concerns for the pastoralist Maasai communities that inhabit northern-central Tanzania, coexisting with the large populations of wildlife that have made this

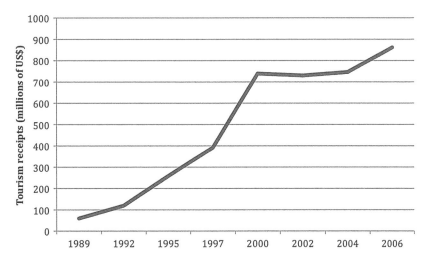

Figure 1. Tourism receipts in Tanzania, 1989–2006. Source: based on data from Honey, 2008.

region the centre of the country's tourism industry (Homewood et al., 2009; Snyder & Sulle, 2011). The history of land loss faced by the pastoralists of northern Tanzania is a long one, including the colonial establishment of new boundaries delimiting human movements across traditional lands, the loss of large areas to East Africa's first national parks set aside for wildlife in the late 1950s and the large-scale reconfigurations of land rights and settlement patterns that were attempted by the socialist government during the 1970s (Hodgson, 2001; Neumann, 1998; Shivji, 1998). In the 1970s and 1980s, pastoralists

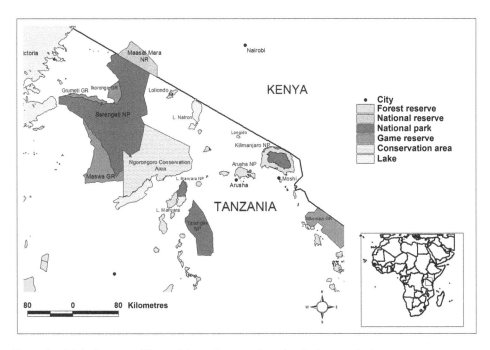

Figure 2. Main features of Tanzania's northern tourism circuit. Source: Author.

became particularly vulnerable to land alienations made throughout their territory for the establishment of commercial farms in areas such as Monduli and Simanjiro districts, as both local elites and foreign investors scrambled to enclose valuable territories in the aftermath of liberalization (Shivji, 1998). By this time, pastoralists' lands were already circumscribed by a growing number of wildlife-protected areas – national parks and game reserves – as well as these private land alienations (Igoe & Brockington, 1999). During the 1980s, the Loliondo area, which lies to the east of Serengeti National Park (Figure 2), had pending applications for individual allocations of land holdings that in total comprised more than the entire land area in Loliondo (Ojalammi, 2006). Today, pastoralists in this region continue to face pressure on their ever-contracting land area, but the main source of continuing pressure and insecurity comes from the interconnected forces of wildlife conservation and tourism investment.

The Ngorongoro Conservation Area (NCA), the country's single most important tourism attraction, has long been the site of conflict between local livelihood interests and wildlife conservation and tourism development interests. Originally established explicitly to cater to the economic and social interests of the Maasai as a part of the settlement which established Serengeti National Park in 1959, NCA's parastatal management has over the years consistently prioritized the interests of wildlife conservation over the resident communities (Homewood & Rodgers, 1991), even while promoting more and more commercial tourism developments within its boundaries (Charnley, 2005; Honey, 2008). Recently, conflicts have intensified as various government leaders have suggested that the resident population in NCA, which today comprises over 60,000 people, should be relocated in order to safeguard the area's wildlife and tourism assets (Juma, 2010). Such statements, along with earlier removals in 2007/2008 of a limited (several hundred) number of ostensive immigrants to the NCA (as distinguished from traditional residents), have heightened tension over land rights and livelihood security in the area (Olenasha, 2006).

As the NCA has seen its ability to generate revenue from tourism growth rise, it has also taken on new expansionist ambitions. The NCA launched a plan in 2008 to extend its boundaries more than 50 km to the north, to include Lake Natron, which has itself grown in popularity as a tourism destination as a result of its stark scenery, dominated by the active volcano, Oldoinyo Lengai, and the presence of more than two million flamingos that breed only in the lake's alkaline waters. The land surrounding Lake Natron is not enclosed within any protected conservation area, but is under the authority of a range of local villages (also predominantly Maasai). The plan to extend the NCA to cover Lake Natron and Oldoinyo Lengai was presented as a way to protect the area's unique natural features, but it encountered pronounced resistance from local communities that stood to lose many of their rights to manage the area and its resources (M. Ngoitiko, Coordinator, Pastoral Women's Council, personal communication, 24 July 2008). This includes not only restrictions on livestock rearing and agricultural activities should NCA expand to cover their lands, but also the ability to levy charges on tourists accessing the area, which villages in Lake Natron are able to do as a result of rights held under land and local government legislation (Snyder & Sulle, 2011), but which communities in the NCA are prohibited from doing under the NCA system of governance. As a result of local opposition to the planned extension, the plan was shelved, at least temporarily, by 2009 (see Ubwani, 2011).

To the north of NCA and the west of Lake Natron, the communities of the Loliondo area are facing even more pronounced challenges to their land and resource rights as a result of recent conflicts that revolve around wildlife, tourism and land use. As noted earlier, the Loliondo area, with some of the richest and most scenic pastoralist rangelands and wildlife habitats anywhere in East Africa, has long been the subject of land claims by outsiders attempting to circumvent local communities' customary rights (Ojalammi, 2006). In the 1980s, as Tanzania liberalized its economy and began to solicit foreign investment, land claims rapidly proliferated in many pastoralist areas, with urban elites or foreigners attempting to take advantage of legal changes at the time to "grab" choice pieces of land (Igoe & Brockington, 1999). Loliondo was the site of numerous such claims, some of which had a questionable procedural and legal basis. As the value of land in Loliondo has recently risen as a result of demand for tourism camps and lodges in the Serengeti, some of these land claims have been resurrected as new investment projects (e.g. Ihucha, 2008). Both Ololosokwan and Soit Sambu villages, located adjacent to Serengeti National Park's north-eastern border, now host land disputes where, in each village, an individual tourism investor claims to hold title over a piece of land that the village also claims that it retains rights over. In the case of Soit Sambu, the disputed property is over 12,000 acres and contains a range of key grazing and watering sites and a number of paths and cattle routes that connect villagers with their neighbours (Ngoitiko et al., 2010).

In addition to these disputed tourism investment properties, villagers in Loliondo face additional forms of land and resource alienation, which they continue to actively contest. The villages bordering Serengeti National Park have faced a number of boundary conflicts with the park, which they allege is a result of the park wanting to expand its boundaries to enclose additional choice sites for lodges or tourism camps (Ngoitiko et al., 2010). The villages also face a long-running dispute over land tenure and resource access rights with a tourist-hunting concession which the Ministry of Natural Resources and Tourism originally granted to a foreign company in 1992, and which is situated entirely on community lands (Honey, 2008). This dispute became violent in 2009, when government police units evicted a large number of Maasai households from their village lands in order to facilitate use of the area by the hunting concession holder (Perelman, 2010; Renton, 2009). These evictions occurred at the height of a major drought and led to a wide range of alleged human rights abuse charges being levelled at the government by the affected communities and Tanzanian civil society organizations (Ihucha, 2010). Negotiations over competing tenure and access rights to the entire Loliondo area between the central government and villages continue to the present, as do efforts to seek justice through national and international legal mechanisms. As elsewhere, the main source of conflict is to determine who will hold formal rights over land and resources, including the right to manage and benefit from commercial tourism activities based on wildlife and wilderness. Favoured investors – in the case of Loliondo, a Dubai-based senior military official – tend to be those with close ties to senior political elites and financial or other resources that can be used to purchase influence (Cooksey & Kelsall, 2011).

Beyond these direct territorial conflicts, the state has also established new regulations that limit the ability of local communities to generate revenue from tourism directly through joint venture agreements with private companies. Such agreements had proliferated in high-potential areas such as Loliondo, earning a few villages up to US$100,000 per annum, and many more villages more modest annual revenues which could be used by village govern-ments to improve social services (Nelson, 2004; Snyder & Sulle, 2011). Since 2000, the government, in the form of the Ministry of Natural Resources and Tourism, has introduced a range of restrictions on these agreements, partly due to the government's financial inter-ests in maintaining community lands with high-value wildlife and scenery for exclusive trophy-hunting concessions which the Ministry leases out to private companies (Nelson et al., 2007). In 2007, the Ministry introduced additional regulations specifically governing all tourism activities outside the core state-protected areas, including on community lands. These effectively required tourism companies to pay significant new fees to the government, displacing revenues which previously had been paid directly to rural communities and equating to a roughly 60% tax on these revenues (Snyder & Sulle, 2011). This new regulatory regime has significantly reduced the income from tourism of rural communities in a wide range of northern Tanzanian areas, including Loliondo.

The examples provided above are representative of more widespread conflicts between local communities and government tourism and natural resource management interventions which have occurred in Tanzania in recent years. Other documented examples include the western Serengeti (Perelman, 2010), community lands between Tarangire National Park and Lake Manyara (Igoe & Croucher, 2007), the West Kilimanjaro area (Benjaminsen & Svarstad, 2010; Nelson, 2004) and around Saadani National Park (Lara, 2010). In virtually all cases, the root tensions are largely driven by interconnected state-private interests pursuing expansionist or expropriative measures that serve to centralize access to lands and wildlife valued by tourism markets (including the trophy-hunting sub-component of the tourism industry). Objectives related to rural poverty reduction, while espoused in formal policy documents and government-donor projects, are effectively undermined by these overriding political–economic influences and interests.

Discussion

Even as contests surrounding the control over natural resources valued by expanding tourism investments increase, it is important to highlight that these conflicts are merely symptomatic of broader trends in natural resource governance in Tanzania. These wider dynamics relate to the increasing control of rural lands and resources by central government agencies and private companies or individuals, usually at the expense of local communities' collective rights of tenure and access. Indeed, as tourism's economic value grows, the industry increasingly takes centre stage in struggles over rights and revenues that are part and parcel of a wider set of contests over development policy, citizenship and the structure of the state itself.

State-protected areas in Tanzania have continued to increase during the past decade, even while official government policies espouse decentralization and strengthened local rights to benefit from wildlife (Nelson & Blomley, 2010). Brockington et al. (2008) document the continued large-scale expansion of wildlife-protected areas and the displacement of local resident communities across different parts of Tanzania. This process is largely driven by the increased influence of agencies such as Tanzania National Parks (TANAPA) as a result of their expanding tourism-generated coffers and by the interests of both government agencies and national political and government elites in centralizing the control over access to these areas (Honey, 2008; Nelson & Blomley, 2010). New tourist-hunting concessions have also been created, including those situated on community lands, leading to new conflicts over the use of land and wildlife in these areas (Dickinson, 2005).

All of these trends and developments – which notably contrast sharply with the narratives of decentralization that characterized much natural resource discourse in Tanzania and much of the developing world during the 1990s (see Nelson, 2010) – are best understood in the light of the private business and patronage interests that dominate the workings of government in the country.

While Tanzania's wildlife tourism industries are perhaps the most widespread and lucrative resource-based form of commerce, other forms of investment are contributing to similar territorial conflicts. For example, widespread concern has emerged surrounding the allocation of large areas of land (up to 250,000 hectares) for biofuel plantations (crops including sugarcane, palm oil and *Jatropha*; Sulle & Nelson, 2009). Large-scale agriculture projects are also raising alarm due to concerns about the displacement of local smallholders (e.g. Oakland Institute, 2011). The displacement of small-scale miners by large-scale foreign operations has been a source of major policy debate and tension in Tanzania since the initial large-scale mining concessions were established in the mid-1990s (Cooksey & Kelsall, 2011). Researchers in Tanzania highlight the growing concentration of land assets in the hands of political elites, through divested parastatal holdings and other privileged forms of access to state resources (Chachage & Mbunda, 2009). These debates over land and resource distribution are assuming centre stage in public debates about the country's development path and overall governance and leadership; in a recent parliamentary session, debate over land issues – particularly "land grabbing" by political elites – nearly led to rejection of the Ministry of Lands' annual budget by parliamentarians (Liganga, 2011).

Tourism is thus one component of a much wider and increasingly well-documented, contemporary "land grab" in Tanzania, and indeed in sub-Saharan Africa as a whole, which has recently attracted considerable attention from media, scholars and policymakers, with up to 70 million hectares leased or acquired in Africa since 2007 alone (Alden Wily, 2011). Land acquisition trends in Africa are being driven by the growing commercial value of African lands and resources for activities such as agricultural production, biofuels, the emerging carbon-forestry market and tourism (Deininger et al., 2011). A critical element of these land acquisitions is the enduring weakness of local land rights and tenure, and the ability of those in power to pursue accumulative interests without the constraints conferred by popular accountability. Alden Wily (2011) explains the pervasive sale or allocation of local communal lands and resources across much of sub-Saharan Africa as follows:

> ... governments are demonstratively reluctant to surrender their acquired position as majority landlords and controllers of most of the region's estate. This is for reasons which appear to stem as much from interwoven elite interests, and an unwillingness to deprive themselves of the ability to dispose of much of the country estate at will and at no cost, as from any genuine conviction that customary interests do not deserve legal force as property, the modern capitalized nature of society notwithstanding.

Thus, the present paradox facing efforts to direct tourism towards poverty reduction in African states derives from the fact that socially and environmentally beneficial forms of tourism depend largely on the ability of local groups of people to manage and regulate tourism activities within a framework of rights and governance that grants local communities sufficient authority and property rights to do so (Spenceley, 2008). Sustainable tourism is thus largely dependent on certain configurations of power, resource rights and governing authority that empower local groups of people, i.e. "the poor". Such power relations are, however, notably scarce across sub-Saharan Africa, and as current land acquisition and resource allocation trends indicate, perhaps becoming scarcer despite years of notional shifts towards decentralization (Nelson, 2010). As land and natural resource values rise, so do the incentives for elites and ruling regimes to extend or deepen control over these resources, as has occurred with wildlife in Tanzania over the course of the past decade (Brockington et al., 2008; Nelson & Blomley, 2010). Tourism is a leading source of such incentives to re-centralize and expropriate local resources, even as tourism is seen as a means to alleviate rural poverty and create positive local incentives for environmental conservation. This paradox arises largely from the political context of African states, where local customary property rights are weak, expropriation of resources is relatively feasible and public officials are frequently able to evade local citizens' efforts to claim their rights and demand accountability.

The foremost implication of this political–economic state of affairs with respect to developing forms of tourism that meaningfully empower rural communities is that efforts to link tourism with poverty reduction in African countries must take account of these political dynamics and design interventions accordingly. Specifically, this suggests the need for a rights-based approach to tourism development that recognizes the critical and contested role of resource tenure and the centrality of governance in determining outcomes, and incorporates these into operational strategies and interventions. Such rights-based approaches are becoming more widely mainstreamed in natural resource management and conservation efforts, in recognition of the critical role governance and tenure play in outcomes and the challenges that have faced past efforts to better link livelihoods and conservation (Campese, Sunderland, Greiber, & Oviedo, 2009). Such approaches could usefully be applied to tourism development strategies as well.

For example, the promotion of sustainable tourism could take note of similar debates around financing and tenure that are a prominent element of the development of global policies for reducing deforestation and forest degradation (REDD). Here, the concern is that financing for REDD – effectively, payments by wealthy northern countries with high levels of carbon dioxide emissions to tropical developing countries with high rates of deforestation – would undermine REDD's own objectives by creating incentives for governments to claim ownership over all forests in order to capture REDD financing, and despite governments' being unable to enforce such claims in practice (Sandbrook, Nelson, Adams, & Agrawal, 2010). Concerns around forest governance, local livelihoods and developing effective REDD policies have led to a growing focus on secure land and forest tenure as a critical enabling condition for REDD (Cotula & Mayers, 2009). This in turn has led to growing linkages between land and forest tenure debates and the development of REDD policies linked to climate change concerns, with the potential, for example, to address land reform as a part of "REDD readiness" efforts being funded by a range of bi-lateral and multi-lateral development agencies. Efforts to link tourism development with poverty reduction would similarly benefit from a clear conceptual understanding of the importance of tenure and property rights, the politically contested nature of land rights and natural resource governance, and mechanisms for supporting relevant reform measures.

A second practical issue that arises from this paper is that the local and national political dynamics that comprise the raw substance of negotiations over tourism's developmental trajectory and social and environmental impacts, in many cases, are relatively ignored as a subject of tourism-related scholarship. Again with reference to Tanzania, there are innumerable studies carried out by both foreign and national researchers on the local distribution of tourism revenues, the nature of community–private partnerships and local perceptions of tourism developments. As a result, local case studies of community-level experiences with tourism predominate in the sustainable tourism literature, while very little research attempts to lift the veil to examine the power relations underlying the observed outcomes, and to relate these to the ongoing evolutions of statehood and citizenship in Tanzania. Therefore, little is known about the critical "informal" political–economic dimensions of tourism development in Tanzania, or most other African countries, which are so influential in shaping both policy development and tourism outcomes on the ground, save that uncovered by intrepid journalists or rumoured on the blogosphere. In 2011, the *Journal of Sustainable Tourism* published a pioneering double issue on *Tourism Governance: Critical Perspectives on Governance and Sustainability* (Bramwell & Lane, 2011). But of the 13 papers in that collection, only one looked at the aspects of tourism governance in Africa, and then not in a way directly linked to national political power. This gap in the empirical understanding of what is actually occurring in the process of tourism development in Africa creates an important, albeit challenging, agenda for applied research.

Note

1. Unlike the allocation and ownership of trophy-hunting concessions, which has been subjected to a fairly high level of public scrutiny in recent years, little information is available with regard to senior public officials' links with major tourism developments in state-protected areas, beyond an abundance of web-based rumours and speculation. However, as far back as the mid-1990s, the government's Warioba Commission into corruption, commissioned by President Mkapa shortly after he assumed office in 1995, identified a range of specific instances of corruption in relation to the development of tourism lodges in such areas (Visram, 1997).

References

Ake, C. (1996). *Development and democracy in Africa*. Washington, DC: Brookings Institute.

Alden Wily, L. (2011). "The law is to blame": The vulnerable status of common property rights in sub-Saharan Africa. *Development and Change, 42*(3), 733–757.

Baldus, R.D., & Cauldwell, A.E. (2004). Tourist hunting and its role in development of wildlife management areas in Tanzania. *Game and Wildlife Science, 21*, 519–614.

Bates, R.H. (1981). *Markets and states in tropical Africa*. Berkeley: University of California Press.

Benjaminsen, T.A., & Svarstad, H. (2010). The death of an elephant: Conservation discourses versus practices in Africa. *Forum for Development Studies, 37*(3), 385–408.

Boone, C. (2007). Property and constitutional order: Land tenure reform and the future of the African state. *African Affairs, 106*, 557–586.

Bramwell, B., & Lane, B. (2011). Critical research on the governance of tourism and sustainability. *Journal of Sustainable Tourism, 19*(4–5), 411–422.

Bratton, M., & van de Walle, N. (1997). *Democratic experiments in Africa: Regime transitions in comparative perspective*. Cambridge: Cambridge University Press.

Brockington, D., Sachedina, H., & Scholfield, K. (2008). Preserving the new Tanzania: Conservation and land use change. *International Journal of African Historical Studies, 41*(3), 557–579.

Campese, J., Sunderland, T., Greiber, T., & Oviedo, G. (Eds.). (2009). *Rights-based approaches: Exploring issues and opportunities for conservation*. Bogor: CIFOR and IUCN.

Chabal, P., & Daloz, J.P. (1999). *Africa works: Disorder as political instrument*. Oxford: James Currey.

Chachage, C., & Mbunda, R. (2009). *The state of the then NAFCO, NARCO and absentee landlords' farms/ranches in Tanzania* (Unpublished Report). Dar es Salaam: Land Rights Research and Resources Institute (LARRI/HAKIARDHI).

Charnley, S. (2005). From nature tourism to ecotourism? The case of the Ngorongoro conservation area, Tanzania. *Human Organization, 64*, 75–88.

Cooksey, B., & Kelsall, T. (2011). *The political economy of the investment climate in Tanzania*. London: Africa Power and Politics Programme.

Cotula, L., & Mayers, J. (2009). *Tenure in REDD: Start-point or afterthought?* (Natural Resource Issues No. 15). London: International Institute for Environment and Development.

Coulson, A. (1982). *The political economy of Tanzania*. Oxford: Clarendon Press.

Deininger, K., Byerlee, D., Lindsay, J., Norton, A., Selod, H., & Stickler, M. (2011). *Rising global interest in farmland: Can it yield sustainable and equitable benefits?* Washington, DC: World Bank.

Diamond, L., & Plattner, M.F. (Eds.). (2010). *Democratization in Africa: Progress and retreat.* Baltimore, MD: The Johns Hopkins University Press.

Dickinson, D. (2005, April 14). Anger over hunting rights. *BBC News.* Retrieved from http://news.bbc.co.uk/2/hi/africa/4440375.stm

Gibson, C.C. (1999). *Politicians and poachers: The political economy of wildlife policy in Africa.* Cambridge: Cambridge University Press.

Hammer, J. (2010, November). Last days of the Masai? *Condé Nast Traveler.* Retrieved from http://www.concierge.com/cntraveler/articles/503114

Hodgson, D.L. (2001). *Once intrepid warriors: Gender, ethnicity and the cultural politics of Maasai development.* Bloomington: Indiana University Press.

Homewood, K.M., & Rodgers, W.A. (1991). *Maasailand ecology: Pastoralist development and wildlife conservation in Ngorongoro, Tanzania.* Cambridge: Cambridge University Press.

Homewood, K., Kristjanson, P., & Trench, P.C. (2009). *Staying Maasai? Livelihoods, conservation, and development in East African rangelands.* New York: Springer.

Honey, M. (2008). *Ecotourism and sustainable development: Who owns paradise?* (2nd ed.). Washington, DC: Island Press.

Hyden, G. (2006). *African politics in comparative perspective.* New York: Cambridge University Press.

Igoe, J., & Brockington, D. (1999). *Pastoral land tenure and community conservation: A case study from north-east Tanzania.* London: International Institute for Environment and Development.

Igoe, J., & Croucher, B. (2007). Conservation, commerce, and communities: The story of community-based wildlife management in Tanzania's northern tourist circuit. *Conservation and Society, 5*(4), 534–561.

Ihucha, A. (2008, December 20). Arusha villagers awaiting PM's land probe findings. *The Guardian,* p. 3.

Ihucha, A. (2010, August 16–22). United front to fight renewal of Emirates hunting contract. *The East African,* p. 3.

Juma, M. (2010, February 25). Relocate Ngorongoro Maasai-Bunge team. *AllAfrica.com.* Retrieved from http://allafrica.com/stories/201002250203.html

Kamata, N. (2008). *The mute plunder: Bioresources and dispossession in Tanzania.* Dar es Salaam: HAKIARDHI.

Kelsall, T. (2002). Shop windows and smoke-filled rooms: Governance and the re-politicisation of Tanzania. *Journal of Modern African Studies, 40*(4), 597–619.

Kelsall, T. (2008). Going with the grain in African development? *Development Policy Review, 26*(6), 627–655.

Lara, L.Y.R. (2010). *Analysis of the relation between land rights and environmental measures in protected areas in Tanzania: The case of Saadani National Park* (Unpublished MSc dissertation). University of Twente, Enschede, the Netherlands.

Lawson, A., & Rakner, L. (2005). *Understanding patterns of accountability in Tanzania.* Oxford: Oxford Policy Management, Chr. Michelsen Institute, and REPOA.

Lewis, P. (2010). Growth without prosperity in Africa. In L. Diamond & M.F. Plattner (Eds.), *Democracy in Africa: Progress and retreat* (pp. 88–102). Baltimore, MD: The Johns Hopkins University Press.

Liganga, L. (2011, August 16). PM rushes to the rescue of Sh48bn lands budget. *The Citizen.* Retrieved from http://www.thecitizen.co.tz/component/content/article/37-tanzania-top-news-story/13826-pm-rushes-to-the-rescue-of-sh48bn-lands-budget.html

Mamdani, M. (1996). *Citizen and subject: Contemporary Africa and the legacy of late colonialism.* Princeton, NJ: Princeton University Press.

Mitchell, J., Keane, J., & Laidlaw, J. (2008). *Making success work for the poor: Package tourism in northern Tanzania.* London: Overseas Development Institute and SNV.

Nelson, F. (2004). *The evolution and impacts of community-based ecotourism in northern Tanzania* (Drylands Issue Paper No. 131). London: International Institute for Environment and Development.

Nelson, F. (2008). Livelihoods, conservation, and community-based tourism in Tanzania: Potential and performance. In A. Spenceley (Ed.), *Responsible tourism: Critical issues for conservation and development* (pp. 305–321). London: Earthscan.

Nelson, F. (Ed.). (2010). *Community rights, conservation and contested land: The politics of natural resource governance in Africa*. London: Earthscan.

Nelson, F., & Agrawal, A. (2008). Patronage or participation? Community-based natural resource management reform in sub-Saharan Africa. *Development and Change, 39*(4), 557–585.

Nelson, F., & Blomley, T. (2010). Peasants' forest and the king's game? Institutional divergence and convergence in Tanzania's forestry and wildlife sectors. In F. Nelson (Ed.), *Community rights, conservation and contested land: The politics of natural resource governance in Africa* (pp. 79–105). London: Earthscan.

Nelson, F., Nshala, R., & Rodgers, W.A. (2007). The evolution and reform of Tanzanian wildlife management. *Conservation and Society, 5*(2), 232–261.

Neumann, R.P. (1998). *Imposing wilderness: Struggles over livelihood and nature preservation in Africa*. Berkeley: University of California Press.

Ngoitiko, M., Sinandei, M., Meitaya, P., & Nelson, F. (2010). Pastoral activists: Negotiating power imbalances in the Tanzanian Serengeti. In F. Nelson (Ed.), *Community rights, conservation and contested land: The politics of natural resource governance in Africa* (pp. 269–289). London: Earthscan.

North, D.C., Wallis, J.J., & Weingast, B.R. (2009). *Violence and social orders: A conceptual framework for interpreting recorded human history*. New York: Cambridge University Press.

Oakland Institute. (2011). *Understanding land deals in Africa: Agrisol Energy and Pharos Global Agriculture Fund's land deals in Tanzania*. Land Deal Brief. Retrieved from http://media.oaklandinstitute.org/sites/oaklandinstitute.org/files/OI_AgriSol_Brief.pdf

Ojalammi, S. (2006). *Contested lands: Land disputes in semi-arid parts of northern Tanzania* (Unpublished doctoral dissertation). University of Helsinki, Finland.

Olenasha, W. (2006). Parks without people: A case study of the Ngorongoro Conservation Area, Tanzania. In International Alliance of Indigenous and Tribal Peoples of Tropical Forests (Ed.), *Indigenous peoples' contributions to COP-8 of the Convention on Biological Diversity* (pp. 151–163). Retrieved from www.ffla.net/new/es/bibliografia-recomendada/doc_download/60-parks-without-people-a-case-study-of-the-ngorongoro-conservation-area-tanzania.html

Perelman, M. (2010, June 11). In the shadow of the Serengeti. *The Nation*. Retrieved from http://www.thenation.com/article/shadow-serengeti

Policy Forum. (2009). *Growth in Tanzania: Is it reducing poverty?* Dar es Salaam: Policy Forum and Twaweza. Retrieved from http://www.policyforum-tz.org/node/6939

Prempeh, H.K. (2010). Presidents untamed. In L. Diamond & M.F. Plattner (Eds.), *Democracy in Africa: Progress and retreat* (pp. 18–32). Baltimore, MD: The Johns Hopkins University Press.

Renton, A. (2009, September 6). Tourism is a curse to us. *The Observer*. Retrieved from http://www.guardian.co.uk/world/2009/sep/06/masai-tribesman-tanzania-tourism

Sandbrook, C., Nelson, F., Adams, W.M., & Agrawal, A. (2010). Carbon, forests and the REDD paradox. *Oryx, 44*(3), 330–334.

Shivji, I.G. (1998). *Not yet democracy: Reforming land tenure in Tanzania*. Dar es Salaam and London: IIED/HAKIARDHI/Faculty of Law, University of Dar es Salaam.

Snyder, K.A., & Sulle, E.B. (2011). Tourism in Maasai communities: A chance to improve livelihoods? *Journal of Sustainable Tourism, 19*(8), 935–951.

Spenceley, A. (Ed.). (2008). *Responsible tourism: Critical issues for conservation and development*. London: Earthscan.

Sulle, E., & Nelson, F. (2009). *Biofuels, land tenure, and rural livelihoods in Tanzania*. London: International Institute for Environment and Development.

Sundet, G. (1997). *The politics of land in Tanzania* (Unpublished PhD dissertation). University of Oxford, UK.

Szeftel, M. (1998). Misunderstanding African politics: Corruption and the governance agenda. *Review of African Political Economy, 76*, 221–240.

Transparency International. (2011). *Corruption perceptions index 2010 results*. Retrieved from http://www.transparency.org/policy_research/surveys_indices/cpi/2010/results

Ubwani, Z. (2011, August 31). Leaders' differences delay NCA plan. *AllAfrica.com*. Retrieved from http://allafrica.com/stories/201108310818.html

United Republic of Tanzania (URT). (2002). *Prudent exploitation of tourism potential for wealth creation and poverty reduction*. Keynote Address by the President of the United Republic of Tanzania, His Excellency Benjamin William Mkapa, at the Tanzania Tourism Investment Forum. Dar es Salaam: Government Printer.

United Republic of Tanzania (URT). (2010). *National strategy for growth and reduction of poverty II*. Dar es Salaam: Ministry of Finance and Economic Affairs.

van de Walle, N. (2001). *African economies and the politics of permanent crisis, 1979–1999*. Cambridge: Cambridge University Press.

Visram, N. (1997, February). Mkapa's corruption hot potato. *African Business*. Retrieved from http://findarticles.com/p/articles/mi_qa5327/is_n218/ai_n28685303/

World Bank. (2010). *Worldwide governance indicators*. Retrieved from http://info.worldbank.org/governance/wgi/index.asp

The World Bank Group/Multilateral Investment Guarantee Agency (MIGA). (2002). *Tourism in Tanzania: Investment for growth and diversification*. Washington, DC: MIGA and United Republic of Tanzania.

Tourism revenue sharing policy at Bwindi Impenetrable National Park, Uganda: a policy arrangements approach

Wilber Manyisa Ahebwa[a], Rene van der Duim[b] and Chris Sandbrook[c]

[a]Department of Forestry, Biodiversity and Tourism, Makerere University, Kampala, Uganda;
[b]Department of Environmental Sciences, Wageningen University, Netherlands; [c]United Nations Environment Programme World Conservation Monitoring Centre, Cambridge, UK

Debates on how to deliver conservation benefits to communities living close to protected high-biodiversity areas have preoccupied conservationists for over 20 years. Tourism revenue sharing (TRS) has become a widespread policy intervention in Africa and elsewhere where charismatic populations of wildlife remain. This paper analyzes TRS policy at Bwindi Impenetrable National Park (BINP), Uganda, from a policy arrangements perspective. It is based on data collected at BINP and three surrounding parishes, using qualitative methods. It concludes that the governance capacity of the TRS policy arrangement at BINP is low due to the structural incongruence of the dimensions of the policy arrangement (analyzed in terms of actors, resources, rules of the game and discourses). Despite the participatory rhetoric of policy reforms, the Uganda Wildlife Authority remains the most powerful actor: it has control over resources and consequently determines the rules of the game. Local communities do not feel adequately compensated for conservation costs. This issue is exacerbated by weak communications with local people, problems of fair distribution locally and nationally, corruption claims and powerful local elites. To maximize TRS' ability to contribute to conservation through development, inequities in the design of the TRS and dispersion of benefits need to be addressed.

Introduction

Debates on how to deliver the benefits of conservation to local people living close to high-biodiversity areas have preoccupied conservationists for more than two decades, premised on the assumption that conservation goals will be more easily achieved with the support of local people. According to this logic, it is argued that benefits from wildlife should contribute to meeting livelihood needs of communities adjacent to protected areas and to compensate for the costs of living next to a protected area (Adams et al., 2004). One of the most commonly pursued strategies used by international, regional and local conservation entities has been the sharing of revenues from wildlife-based tourism (tourism revenue sharing – TRS). It is argued that TRS can justify conservation campaigns amidst conditions of poverty and limited livelihood opportunities in developing countries (Fisher et al., 2008). TRS has become a widespread policy intervention in Africa and other regions where

97

large populations of wildlife remain, with revenues usually shared on a percentage basis (Hulme & Murphree, 2001; Schroeder, 2008). Conservationists argue that TRS helps to offset conservation costs and improve local attitudes toward conservation (Archabald & Naughton-Treves, 2001).

Revenue sharing programs can take three different forms. First, there are protected area outreach arrangements, where a percentage of park entrance fees is channelled to communities (Archabald & Naughton-Treves, 2001). Second, there are initiatives that involve private companies conducting commercial activities, such as hunting, on community land and then sharing proceeds with the community (Baker, 1997; Becker, 2009; Lindsey, Roulet, & Romanach, 2007; NACSO, 2009; Ochieng, 2011; Saarinen, Becker, Wilson, & Manwa, 2009). Third, there are partnership arrangements, which can involve private and public entities as well as communities in operating tourism "joint ventures". The accruing revenues are thereafter shared based on written agreements guiding such arrangements (Elliot & Sumba, 2010; Spenceley, 2003, 2010; Sumba, Warinwa, Lenaiyasa, & Muruthi, 2007; van der Duim, 2011).

A number of studies that have attempted to evaluate the outcomes of revenue sharing and other incentive-based conservation arrangements in developing countries have revealed mixed outcomes (Ahebwa, van der Duim, & Nyakaana, 2008; Ahebwa, van der Duim, & Sandbrook, in press; Archabald & Naughton-Treves, 2001; Peters, 1998; Schroeder, 2008; Southgate, 2006). Evaluations of incentive-based conservation programs indicate that the approach in practice often falls short of the rhetoric (Spiteri & Nepal, 2006). One feature that has been found to contribute to such failures is the structure and implementation of TRS policies (Archabald & Naughton-Treves, 2001; Schroeder, 2008). This necessitates further research to understand the process by which such policies are arranged and how this reflects the interests of different stakeholders. This paper provides a response to this research need based on the TRS policy intervention at Bwindi Impenetrable National Park (BINP), Uganda, which falls into the "protected area outreach" category as described above. Guided by the Policy Arrangements Approach (PAA), this paper analyzes the introduction and implementation of TRS at Bwindi as a policy arrangement, examines its governance capacity and highlights key critical issues affecting its outcomes.

The policy arrangements approach

In this study, the PAA (Arts & Leroy, 2006; Buizer, 2008; Van der Zouwen, 2006; Van Gossum, Arts, De Wulf, & Verheyen, 2011) guided the analysis of TRS. In this paper, TRS is seen as a policy arrangement, which is defined as a temporary stabilization of the organization (in terms of actors and resources) and substance (in terms of discourses and rules) of a policy domain at a specific level of policy-making (Arts & Leroy, 2006). The institutionalization of a policy domain like TRS is an ongoing process of construction and reconstruction (Liefferink, 2006) and at one point in time, the substantial and organizational aspects of a policy domain "interact" to shape its functioning and outcomes (Van der Zouwen, 2006). Under the policy arrangements framework, the substantial and organizational aspects of a policy domain can be analyzed on the basis of four key dimensions: (1) the actors, (2) resources, (3) the operative rules of the game, and (4) discourses (Arts & Leroy, 2006; Buizer, 2008; Liefferink, 2006; Van Tatenhove, Arts, & Leroy, 2000).

The "actors" dimension entails an analysis of people and organizations involved and excluded in the formation and implementation of a policy intervention as well as those who benefit from it (Buizer, 2008). "Resources" refer to the available assets, which are utilized and deployed by actors to make the policy intervention function. These can be financial, knowledge, contacts or authoritative (Buizer, 2008). Possession or the ability to mobilize and decide the distribution of financial resources, for example, helps to explain the power relations among the actors. "Resources" is the medium through which power is exercised and inequalities explained (Meyer, 2001).

The "rules" dimension of a policy arrangement relates to the formal procedures of decision-making, informal rules and routines of interaction (Van Tatenhove et al., 2000). Rules shape the boundaries within which policy interventions are implemented. For example, they specify how financial resources are allocated, how issues are raised, how evaluation is done and who does what in the process of policy implementation (Ahebwa, 2012). Discourses relate to ideas, storylines or narratives about the concrete policy problem at stake, its causes and possible solutions. It is through the ensemble of these perceptions, or ideas, which are produced and reproduced in certain practices that meaning is attained in the real world (Arts & Leroy, 2006). In this study, discourses were analyzed based on particular narratives or storylines possessed by actors in relation to the implementation of TRS.

The four dimensions of a PAA do not just sum up to define a policy arrangement. They are inextricably interwoven, meaning that a change in one dimension can trigger a change in all other dimensions. For example, the entry of new actors can cause injection of new financial resources, which in turn can necessitate new guiding rules. And in the process, this can cause a shift in the prevailing discourses. This interrelationship is useful in analyzing a policy arrangement at a given period of time (Arts & Leroy, 2006) as it generates deeper understanding of the whole process.

The PAA has proved useful in analyzing developments and changes in policies for periods ranging from three years to over 20 years (Arnouts, 2010; Van der Zouwen, 2006). It has been applied to a broad range of policy arenas including nature (Arnouts, 2010; Van Gossum et al., 2011), water (Wiering & Immink, 2006), agriculture (Liefferink, 2006) and environment (Arts & Leroy, 2006). Moreover, the PAA can be used to investigate the (potential) governance capacity of an arrangement like TRS (Arts & Goverde, 2006). This capacity reflects the extent to which new forms of governance are potentially able to successfully mitigate or solve societal and administrative problems that are legitimately recognized by stakeholders. A high governance capacity means that the institutional preconditions of the policy arrangement contribute to the effective realization of the desired policy impact (van Gossum et al., 2011). The importance of governance within sustainable tourism management is now increasingly recognized (Bramwell & Lane, 2011). To examine this capacity, we borrowed the concept of "congruence" from Arts and Goverde (2006) and Van Gossum et al. (2011). This can be divided into the policy views of the different actors (strategic congruence) and the internal structural congruence of the four dimensions of this policy arrangement. The external congruence with other tourism-related policy interventions is the subject of another research project (see Ahebwa, 2012).

Methodology

This research adopted an interpretive policy analysis approach (Buizer, 2008) focusing on the meanings and perceptions of the actors involved. A researcher informed by the interpretive research paradigm gathers data from the empirical world using qualitative methodologies (Jennings, 2001). In the current study, the interest was rooted in gaining an in-depth understanding of the context, processes and implementation dynamics of TRS: qualitative methods of data collection were therefore more appropriate.

 To collect these meanings and perceptions, interviews were carried out in three parishes surrounding BINP (Bwindi hereafter), namely Nteko and Rubuguri in Kisoro District and Mukono in Kanungu District. The three parishes include several villages. Each village has a village leader answerable to the parish leader (also known as the parish chairperson). Open-ended interviews were conducted with all the village leaders in the three parishes and with the three parish chairpersons. Also, the BWINDI community conservation warden, chairpersons of Community Protected Area Institutions (CPIs; see under the Policy Arrangements analysis) in the three districts surrounding the park, district leaders and coordinator of the International Gorilla Conservation Programme (IGCP; a coalition of Africa Wildlife Foundation, Fauna and Flora International and World Wildlife Fund) in the region were interviewed. The total number of interviews was 25, which corresponds with the required sample size as stated in the literature (Bertaux, 1981; Creswell, 1998; Van Gossum et al., 2011). In addition, 10 focus group discussions were held with residents in each of the three parishes. These focus groups consisted of approximately 15–25 people each, and a deliberate effort was made to involve people of different socioeconomic backgrounds. It was in these discussions that community views about the revenue sharing arrangements were captured. All in-depth interviews and focus group discussions involved questions on TRS discourse, on rules (knowledge of and acceptance of TRS rules and interaction with other rules), on actors (the existence and appreciation of relations with an actor, trust in an actor and why they trust that actor) and on power and resources. Informal discussions were also held in the evenings with members of the community to fill information gaps. Data from interviews and focus group discussions were transcribed, coded and integrated with data from documents. Integrated data were arranged and coded into themes based on the described theoretical framework. This study was conducted between June and September 2009.

 Data collection also entailed a thorough review of relevant documents, including policy documents (TRS, CPI and Community Conservation policies), revenue sharing implementation and review reports, financial disbursement records and minutes of meetings involving Uganda Wildlife Authority (UWA), CPIs, local governments and community associations. Documentary reviews provided baseline data for understanding the history of conservation campaigns and hence the origins of revenue sharing arrangements.

Bwindi Impenetrable National Park

BINP lies in one of Uganda's most densely populated regions, with more than 300 persons per km^2 in some areas and an annual population growth rate of 3.5% (Uganda Bureau of Statistics – UBOS, 2008). The majority of local people are Bantu agriculturalists (Bakiga and Bafumbira) and the minority (0.5%) are Batwa, a Central African forest people. The total population in the three study parishes is approximately 21,000 people with an average household size of 4.6 (UBOS, 2010).

 Historically, the area that is currently gazetted as a park served the community as a source of income (from sales of timber, firewood, alluvial gold and game meat), medicine (medicinal plants) and extra food (wild mushrooms, game meat and honey; Korbee, 2007). Namara and Nsabagasani (2003) further note that the agricultural land around Bwindi has become less productive due to over-cultivation and soil erosion and the park is often seen as a potential fertile area for expansion of subsistence agriculture. Upgrading Bwindi from a forest reserve to a national park in 1991 was intended to protect the "tiny 330-square-kilometre island of biodiversity" (Nowak, 1995) that was threatened by large-scale logging, poaching and other activities by the local people (IGCP, 2008). As a national park, access was forbidden for communities in search of park resources (Hecker, 2005; Namara & Nsabagasani, 2003).

The closure of resource access was not an effective conservation solution. Instead, it ignited resentment among the communities as they were denied income from forest resources and wild foods (Nowak, 1995). This led to conflicts between communities and park staff, manifested in 16 fires started in and around the park by communities in 1992 and other confrontational occurrences (AWF, 2009). Resource deprivation and crop raiding (by baboons, monkeys, gorillas and forest elephants) led to negative community attitudes toward the park (Hamilton, Cunningham, Byarugaba, & Kayanja, 2000; Nowak, 1995). As a result, conservation actors became concerned that local hostility to the park undermined its protection.

To mitigate conflict, various Integrated Conservation and Development (ICD) Interventions were initiated by international conservation and development organizations working at Bwindi. These included the establishment of Multiple Use Zones, a major agricultural development program, and support for farmers to grow substitutes for forest products, such as timber in woodlots (Blomley et al., 2010). A crucial component of the ICD program was the establishment of mountain-gorilla-tracking tourism. At the time of this study, six gorilla groups were open for visitation by up to eight tourists per group per day. A gorilla-tracking permit was US$500 for foreign visitors.

It was a common belief among conservationists internationally that tourism would generate revenue for both conservation and local development, generating jobs and other benefits for local people and, thus, justifying the existence of the park to the communities (Nowak, 1995). According to the logic of ICD, for tourism to earn the support of communities for conservation, there must be meaningful benefits, which accrue to a large number of people. However, tourism around Bwindi is largely dominated by private sector businesses and direct benefits tend to accrue to local elites (Sandbrook, 2006, 2008). In an attempt to ensure greater access to tourism benefits, UWA and other institutions have applied several policy interventions in villages around the park, like the foundation of a community-based tourism project in Buhoma–Mukono (Ahebwa, 2012), the Clouds Mountain Lodge (Ahebwa et al., in press) and the TRS program. The latter is the subject of this paper. We first describe the history of benefit sharing in Uganda and at Bwindi, and then proceed to analyze the current situation using the PAA.

Benefit sharing arrangements in Uganda

Benefit sharing arrangements in Uganda's conservation history can be traced back to the 1950s when colonial officials implemented the approach informally after realizing that forceful approaches to conservation could not yield positive results (Archabald & Naughton-Treves, 2001). However, it is important to note that such arrangements were not enshrined in a policy, did not have an institutional home and were not linked to local compliance with conservation (Archabald & Naughton-Treves, 2001). Rather, residents were given game meat on an informal basis when the Game Department shot wildlife found raiding crops (Naughton-Treves, 1999). These arrangements continued until 1971 when the country plunged into a political crisis that led to a breakdown in the rule of law and loss of control of conservation areas (Hamilton, 1984). Uganda regained peace in 1986 with the coming of the National Resistance Movement (NRM) government that later endorsed and re-ignited biodiversity conservation efforts by rebuilding the National Park system that had collapsed in the period of turmoil (Sebukeera, 1996). The new government's emphasis on grassroots governance and a growing interest in community-based approaches among international donors led to the development of a national tourism revenue sharing policy for all national parks in 1994 (Archabald & Naughton-Treves, 2001).

Bwindi and Mgahinga Gorilla National Park were the first to benefit from the TRS arrangement. These two were prioritized as the surrounding communities had shown stiff resistance to conservation (UWA Official, Research Interview, 2009). The target beneficiaries were "those people living adjoining to the parks who are affected by, and affect the park" (Archabald & Naughton-Treves, 2001, p. 137). This definition of beneficiaries had serious consequences as communities far away from the park also claimed equal benefits as those in the park's vicinity:

> the 1994 mandate for sharing park revenue caused more problems than it solved ... Whereas the intention of the arrangement was to benefit people in frontline parishes, the vague definition of target communities made the issue more complicated to resolve. (UWA Official, Research Interview, 2009)

In 1996, the conservation body (Uganda National Parks, UNPs) which was implementing TRS merged with the Game Department to form the UWA. UWA was charged with making conservation reforms in Uganda, among which was reviewing and improving the 1994 revenue sharing policy. In the review process, UWA realized that apart from the vague definition of target communities, the 1994 revenue sharing arrangement also lacked an institutional home and a legal framework (UWA Official, Research Interview, 2009). UWA, working with support organizations, started working out procedures to improve the performance of the policy. This culminated in the Uganda Wildlife Statute of 1996 (UWA, 2000a).

The new revenue sharing policy differed from that of 1994 in several ways (Adams & Infield, 2003; Archabald & Naughton-Treves, 2001). The 1996 policy provided a legal framework because it had been passed as an Act of Parliament. The target community was defined as those in the neighboring "frontline" parishes, a definition that emphasizes proximity to the park (UWA, 2000b). The 1996 TRS arrangement stipulated a change in revenue sharing from the 1994 policy of 12% of all park income, including income out of user fees, fines, concessions and direct operation of commercial activities, to 20% of gate entrance fees only (UWA, 1996).

Park entrance fees contributed about 80%–85% of park revenues in Uganda by 1996 (UWA, 2000b) as visitor numbers to Ugandan national parks had greatly increased and park laws were increasingly being respected, so there was less revenue generated through fines and all other sources of park revenue remained unchanged (UWA, 2000b). It was assumed at the time that channeling 20% of total gate collections would therefore mean transferring a bigger share of conservation funds to communities. Communities surrounding National Parks with no visitor limitations (like Queen Elizabeth and Murchison Falls) benefited considerably from this percentage change as they had more visitors and hence more funds to develop and expand their livelihood projects. On the other hand, communities surrounding National Parks where visitor numbers were restricted due to ecological reasons (e.g. Bwindi and Mgahinga) got less funds (Table 1).

Table 1 highlights a critical issue of distributive injustice in the wildlife sector which was also found to frustrate revenue sharing arrangements in Tanzania (Schroeder, 2008). Despite the fact that Bwindi tops tourism revenue generation for UWA, it trailed other parks in distribution of TRS funds. In 2009, for example, total revenues out of entrance and gorilla fees were more than 7 billion Uganda Shillings (UGX), comfortably more than

Table 1.   Total and shared tourism revenues generated in the three most visited National Parks in Uganda.

| National park | | Years and amount in UGX shillings | | |
		2005	2007	2009
Bwindi	Total	3,349,712,128	5,121,800,940	7,297,180,333
	Shared	149,491,900	107,713,006	100,004,000
Murchison Falls	Total	1,357,168,768	1,447,768,743	2,031,828,839
	Shared	189,400,531	454,155,365	150,000,000
Queen Elizabeth	Total	1,104,093,653	1,554,425,517	1,809,687,869
	Shared	177,757,600	153,850,000	200,000,000

Source: UWA Accounts Department, 2010.

the other two parks. However, as gorilla-tracking permits, which contribute more than 85% of tourism revenue at Bwindi, are excluded in TRS calculations, TRS funds' allocation to Bwindi was lower than in other parks.

Between 1996 and 2009, a total of 680,349,200 UGX (US$263,000; exchange rate July 2011) was disbursed, representing only 9.3% of the tourism revenues that Bwindi generated in the year 2009 alone (Table 2). Of this, UGX 23,248,000 was spent on projects in Nteko, 61,920,000 in Mukono and 19,398,000 in Rubuguri. The balance was allocated to other parishes bordering the park.

Table 2.   Portion of tourism revenue sharing funds distributed in Mukono, Nteko and Rubuguri Parishes (1996–2009).

| Year | Total TRS funds released in UGX shillings | Portion for the three study parishes | | |
		Nteko	Mukono	Rubuguri
1996	76,000,000	4,000,000	4,000,000	4,000,000
2000	43,819,600	3,400,000	3,717,000	0
2002	89,815,000	3,500,000	3,755,000	3,500,000
2005	149,491,900	0	0	0
2006	114,218,700	5,000,000	5,100,000	4,550,000
2007	107,000,000	3,000,000	41,000,000	3,000,000
2009	100,004,000	4,348,000	4,348,000	4,348,000
Total	680,349,200	23,248,000	61,920,000	19,398,000

Source: UWA Tourism Revenue Sharing Project Report, 2009.

The three study parishes received almost equal shares except in 2007 when a bigger portion was allocated to Mukono specifically to meet the high costs involved in upgrading a road, which is an important access route to the park. The development projects that have been funded for the period 1996–2009 in Mukono, Nteko and Rubuguri parishes are summarized in Table 3. In 2000, Rubuguri parish and in 2005 all the three parishes were unsuccessful in getting project proposals submitted or approved.

Table 3.   Community livelihood projects funded from TRS for the three parishes 1996–2009.

Year	Community livelihood projects funded		
	Mukono	Nteko	Rubuguri
1996	Feeder road	Health unit	Health unit
2000	Health unit	Community campground	–
2002	Health unit	Maternity ward of a health unit	Feeder road
2005	–	–	–
2006	Goat rearing project	Community center	Primary school
2007	Main road rehabilitation Goat rearing project	Goat rearing project	Sheep rearing project
2009	Goat rearing project	Goat rearing project	Sheep rearing project

Source: UWA Revenue Sharing Projects Report, 2009.

The US$5 gorilla levy fee

Gorilla tourism is the key tourist activity and the main revenue generating activity at Bwindi. However, the exclusion of gorilla permit revenues from the TRS scheme results in less funding being available for TRS than at the Savannah National Parks of Uganda. Realizing this limitation, communities around Bwindi and Mgahinga National Parks advocated, through the local government administration, that a levy be deducted from the gorilla permit revenue to boost the share they get from tourism (UWA, 2009). The conservation nongovernmental organizations (NGOs) Mgahinga Bwindi Impenetrable Forest Conservation Trust (MBIFCT) and IGCP operating in the region supported this cause and boosted the communities' bargaining power. They participated in negotiations that involved UWA and the representatives from the three districts (Kisoro, Kanungu and Kabale) surrounding the two parks. This formed the basis for the August 2005 approval of a US$5 levy on every gorilla permit sold, for utilization by communities around Bwindi-Mgahinga Conservation Area (BMCA).

UWA started collecting gorilla levy funds in July 2006. In order to have a significantly bigger fund for effective utilization, the funds are supposed to be disbursed after every two years. Between July 2006 and June 2008, a total of UGX 289,559,783 was collected and disbursed in August 2009 during the celebrations for the 2009 UNEP Year of the Gorilla (Table 4).

Table 4.   Distribution of 2006–2008 Gorilla levy funds.

District	Amount in UGX Shillings
Kanungu	174,506,204
Kabale	74,788,386
Kisoro	40,265,193
Total	289,559,783

Source: UWA Accounts Department, 2010.

Policy arrangements analysis

Actors

At the park level, TRS arrangements over time have been executed by different actor coalitions. Administratively, the revenue sharing funds were initially managed by Park

Management Advisory Committees (PMAC; Archabald & Naughton-Treves, 2001). The PMAC was constituted of district technical staff members selected by park management. However, certain challenges emerged. It was established to cater for park interests in regard to community participation in park management and community interests were not catered for. PMAC members were not elected by the community and did not have the mandate and obligations to represent their interests. PMAC was accountable to the park management and considered themselves as park employees but did not have an institutional framework. In most cases, PMAC was not fully functional and where it functioned there were no community–park interactions. The communities only held meetings when called by the park management. The committee mainly played an advisory role to park management, which meant that issues of community interest in protected area management were not adequately addressed (UWA, 2000b; UWA Official, Research Interview, 2009).

Uganda National Parks (UNPs) attempted to address these issues by trying to adequately provide community representation on PMAC through the formation of Parish Park Committees with the chairperson representing communities on PMAC (UWA, 2000a). Where these committees were formed, most of them were not functional due to conflict and duplication of activities (UWA Official, Research Interview, 2009). Improving community–park relations necessitated a strong institutional link that could effectively and adequately represent the interests and concerns of park management as well as those of communities (UWA CPI Policy, 2000). The absence of effective institutional linkages between park management, communities and other government institutions was characterized by poor communication and information flow, conflicts which often resulted in direct confrontation, marginalization of community participation in protected area management, community deprivation of benefits, resource degradation and general negative attitudes of local communities toward the protected areas (UWA, 2000b). This seriously frustrated conservation efforts (UWA Official, Research Interview, 2009).

Toward the end of 1996, a process to form a new and more appropriate institution that fitted within the framework of legislated community institutions started with collection of the views, ideas and concerns of key stakeholders (UWA, 2000b). The lessons learned from PMAC also guided the process:

> We had a lot to learn from the shortcomings of PMAC and this time, we were determined to form a sustainable, effective and strong institution from the existing government institutions. (Chief Warden BMCA, Research Interview, 2009)

A CPI was formed and the Local Governments system provided the framework for CPI development and the majority of CPI members. "Secretaries for Production", local government officials charged with natural resource management and development at parish, subcounty and district levels are automatically members of the CPIs. Community groups such as resource user groups, youth groups, women's groups and other specialized interest groups that directly or indirectly affect conservation of the park resources are also represented on the CPI. The members of the CPI elect an executive committee to manage the institution's activities, including reviewing proposals and making decisions about TRS funding. They are supported by ex-officio committee members representing UWA and the district environmental office. The ex-officio members are meant to give technical advice and guidance on matters relating to policy, legislation and management objectives of the park (UWA, 2000a).

It is important to note that the majority of members are individuals elected to political positions in the local government. This emerged as a very contentious issue in almost all focus group discussions as CPI members were all branded "politicians" who are driven by the need for votes instead of objective decision-making. In Nteko, for example, it was pointed out that political leaders favor their home villages when it comes to allocation of funds for livelihood projects. To address this problem, the Chief Administrative Officers in each district benefiting from the arrangement, though not included on CPI, have been made the accounting officers:

> They receive the money on behalf of communities and disburse it with guidance from CPI and in turn ask for accountability of the funds released. This was done to minimize corruption and embezzlement of funds that had become rampant in the early stages of its implementation. (Chief Warden Bwindi, Research Interview, 2009)

In view of all the above, it is clear that the TRS policy at Bwindi is implemented by a cross-section of actors. Despite this cross-sectional representation on CPI, it was revealed through informal discussions with communities and from the focus group discussions that the institution of CPI is still unpopular among the communities who are supposed to be the target beneficiaries of this arrangement. One resident in Nkwenda village, Mukono parish, commented:

> Yes, the CPI is there, and I hear that we are represented, but honestly . . . the status quo has not changed . . . The institution has many challenges that UWA should resolve. (Local Resident, Research Interview, 2009)

Resources

Despite the role of several actors in rule setting and implementation, UWA emerges as the most powerful overall actor as it collects and disburses the resources generated by revenue sharing. This gives it the central role in TRS and a position of great influence over the rules of the game, as explained in the following section. UWA is also responsible for establishing a rapport with the people who live around protected areas since creating and increasing goodwill between the park and the community is a key objective of TRS. However, in this sense, UWA lacks the resources needed to fulfill its role, as communication with communities and explanation of the rules of the game is the responsibility of just one UWA employee (the Community Conservation Warden) and he admitted that he is overwhelmed by what he has to do:

> Going around Bwindi is not easy . . . Moreover there is no adequate facilitation for this . . . I try my best, but there is still a lot to be desired in addressing community issues. (Community Conservation Warden Bwindi, Research Interview, 2009)

Because of human and financial limitations, UWA relies on working mainly through the CPIs. Much as community members admit that some projects are being funded by TRS funds, they expressed ignorance about the process of selecting these projects. This suggests that it remains a top-down approach with local elites who are able to gain access to the CPI process deciding for the majority of the community members. CPI members admit that they are supposed to work with local community members and other stakeholders to initiate project proposals where necessary. They confess that at times they do not do so, but argue that, as they are community members themselves, they know community needs and that the costs of consulting all community members in terms of time and money must be taken into consideration.

The implementation of the gorilla levy has also shown the influence of resource distribution among actors in determining policy arrangements. Initially, MBIFCT, being the chief campaigner for the levy, had proposed that the funds be disbursed through its accounts to further the livelihood activities they had initiated. However, this decision was challenged by the Local Governments of Kisoro, Kabale and Kanungu, which argued that the disbursement of the fund through MBIFCT was not provided for in the law, and opted for a direct disbursement of the fund to the District Local Governments. From informal discussions with district officials and councilors, it emerged that the opposition to MBIFCT playing this role in the arrangement was supported by IGCP, which facilitated and coordinated district local governments in attempting to object to the arrangement. It is clear that behind the scenes, there exists rivalry and political wrestling between the two conservation and development organizations (IGCP and MBIFCT):

> These organizations support similar projects and actually do almost similar work ... it seems they are fighting for donors ... if their interest is communities and conservation, they should merge and work together. (Chairman of the Rubuguri Pressure group)

The distribution of TRS resources at Bwindi is based on the number of parishes touching the park. Kanungu happens to have more and Kisoro has the least. However, this criterion is not supported by the people of Kisoro.

> You know Kanungu is a new district created in 2000 ..., they intentionally subdivided their villages and came up with many parishes. This helps them get more funds as opposed to ourselves .... it is unacceptable ... other criteria ... like the population in those parishes should be considered. (Community member of Nteko parish, Research Interview, 2009)

But UWA and IGCP insisted that revenue sharing policy has been well debated and very prudent rules have been put in place to ensure fairness, justice and more importantly to cause an impact on the communities directly affected by the existence of the park.

Rules of the game

Several rules guide the implementation of TRS policy. The rules fall into two categories: disbursement rules which specify the process and the channel of releasing TRS funds, and project selection rules which specify the process and criteria for selecting projects to be funded under TRS arrangements. As described above, UWA is the most powerful actor in TRS and is able to shape rules in favor of conservation objectives. UWA also monitors these funds to ensure that the set rules and conditions are fulfilled. All focus group discussions and informal interactions with the communities revealed that only a few community elites are aware of these rules. The majority of community members know nothing about them. This is also well illustrated by the fact that the majority of members in the communities do not know about the new gorilla levy. However, some elite community members who are informed of the arrangement questioned the levy being set at US$5, or just 1% of the cost of a gorilla permit. According to UWA and ICGP, this was what had been agreed on in the meetings since the bigger percentage of this money goes to finance conservation efforts elsewhere in the country where resources are limited (Adams & Infield, 2003). They argue that Bwindi is a national resource and money cannot only be spent at Bwindi and that, if the communities feel unhappy about it, they should request more discussions for its revision.

The lack of knowledge on rules can be attributed to low levels of education in this region, as legal technicalities cannot easily be understood by the majority who have other priorities:

> We want to see more of our projects funded, and not much attention on technical issues ... We cannot understand them. (An elder in Rubuguri Parish, Research Interview, 2009)

UWA argues that the rules are made in consultation with community leaders who are supposed to communicate them to their respective communities, but this did not happen. At the same time, the majority of the local elites support the rules describing them as more focused to the plight of the local people and to conservation needs.

Overall, TRS-funded projects must be identified within the district and subcounty development plans. The proposals from the communities requesting for TRS funds are prioritized and vetted. Those that fulfill the conditions are selected; these conditions form TRS project selection rules. However, whereas setting and adhering to these rules is important for effective financial management, focus group discussions revealed that the majority of the beneficiary communities find it troublesome to fulfill the set conditions. These include writing proposals, drafting constitutions, opening bank accounts, forming community-based organizations or NGOs and tailoring the proposal to the outlined conditions, all of which prove difficult for local people with a generally low level of education. The repercussion of this has been an emergence of a few local elites who know what to do and are taking advantage of the majority:

> Accessing TRS funds is not easy, we are told to write proposals . . . We don't know that . . . But young people who know this are given the money. (Elderly Respondent in Mukono Parish)

Discourses

Despite the TRS livelihood projects summarized in Table 3, most people in Mukono, Nteko and Rubuguri parishes have no kind words for revenue sharing management by the CPI. In other words, the official discourse is challenged by a local discourse. The official discourse is associated with the underlying motives and ideals of conservation organizations such as UWA and IGCP, reflected in the TRS policy. It reflects UWA's mission to conserve biodiversity and is enshrined in the overall goal for TRS:

> to ensure that local communities living adjacent to PAs obtain benefits from existence of these areas, improve their welfare and ultimately strengthen partnership between UWA, local communities, and local governments, for sustainable management of resources in and around the PAs. (UWA's TRS Policy, UWA, 2000c, p. 9)

The purpose and objectives for implementing TRS are thus tailored to contribute to this goal. Specifically, the TRS policy sets out to achieve three objectives that clearly reflect the international community-based conservation discourse, which especially dominated the conservation debates in the 1980s and 1990s that, if conservation benefits are shared with communities, their attitudes toward conservation will improve and this will help in the campaign to conserve threatened biodiversity. These policy objectives are as follows (UWA's TRS Policy, UWA, 2000):

(1) To provide an enabling environment for establishing good relations between protected areas and their neighboring communities;
(2) To demonstrate the economic value of protected areas and conservation in general to communities neighboring protected areas; and
(3) To solicit support and acceptance of protected areas and conservation from the local communities living adjacent to these areas.

UWA is very optimistic that the TRS arrangement is to a large extent successful. On the other hand, the local governments and communities view TRS differently. Local governments feel that the funds should be handed over to the districts and utilized equally by all parishes in the surrounding districts. They base their argument on the view that the park is their natural resource and should spread benefits to all. They would prefer a different strategy to the current focus on frontline communities. They believe that TRS should be an additional source of revenue for district programs. In fact, one district councilor presented a radical idea, suggesting that Uganda should also decentralize the management of national parks so that the district administration could manage and oversee the national park directly. From the community perspective, they argue that it is their right to share these benefits because the park is "their resource". They even view UWA as an "intruder" having stopped them from accessing park resources. More particularly, they highlighted their problems with CPI in terms of corruption, poor information flow and limited funds. Community members argued that CPI inflates the costs of projects funded. Some of these projects include livelihood projects (goat and sheep rearing), construction of schools, bridges and roads and health units. For example, whereas they admit that goats were purchased for community members, they argued that they were of poor quality (poor breeds), at inflated prices and the distribution procedure by village chairmen favored some community members:

> Yes, a few goats were supplied to community members, but we are aware that a goat was bought at 120,000 UGX, yet the normal price of a good goat in this area is between 60,000-80,000 ... this is dishonesty on their part. (Community member in Mukono Parish, Research Interview, 2009)

Another member of the community in Nteko also expressed discontent with the goat and sheep arrangement:

> the rationale behind a TRS arrangement is to develop communities shouldering the burden of wildlife ... some of community members have these goats, sheep and pigs etc, we would supply CPI at cheaper prices ... but CPI awards contracts to its members, inflate prices, and spoils the whole arrangement.

In protest, most people who received goats slaughtered and ate them. No goat from this arrangement could be seen on a cross-sectional tour of the community and TRS-funded projects and CPI has not followed it up.

A further challenge to the official discourse is that community members argue that they are never consulted on which projects should be funded and never given feedback on what transpires in CPI meetings. An interview with all village committee chairmen, however, revealed that local people are reluctant to attend meetings when invited to get updates on what transpires in CPI. This leads to limited awareness of what is happening. On the other hand, some community members say invitations are given discriminately (only the supporters are invited and others left out) while others argue that turning down meetings is a protest move to demonstrate their dissatisfaction with the arrangement. This puts CPI in the same position as its predecessor's structure (PMAC) because the two institutions almost face the same challenges. The communities further argue that because of visitor limitations at Bwindi, funds for TRS are very limited and therefore cannot make a big impact on the entire population. But UWA argues that it is this dilemma (the limitation of visitor numbers at Bwindi) that led to discussions that gave rise to a US$5 "gorilla levy" to increase TRS funds.

Discussion and conclusion

This paper analyzed the introduction, development and implementation of the TRS program at BINP from a PAA. The paper showed that the governance capacity (Arts & Goverde, 2006; Van Gossum et al., 2011) of this arrangement, that is the extent to which the TRS policy arrangement has been able to successfully mitigate or solve societal problems at Bwindi, is low. The dimensions of the policy arrangement are structurally incongruent: there is no broad acceptance of TRS as a solution, there are two discourse coalitions which are dissimilar in perspective, the regulative instruments that have been established are poorly known, understood and accepted, and the relationships between actors are disturbed and not built on mutual trust. Finally, the TRS is not linked to and integrated in other tourism and nontourism-related arrangements that are in place at Bwindi, like the Buhoma Rest Camp or the Clouds Mountain Lodge (see Ahebwa, 2012; Ahebwa et al., in press).

The internal incongruence of the four dimensions of the TRS policy arrangement is also well illustrated by the fact that although the transfer of management from the PMAC in 1994 to the CPIs in 1996 included the entrance of new community-based actors in the TRS arrangement, at the same time, UWA is still perceived to be the most powerful actor as it has control over resources and consequently determines the rules of the game. Moreover, in this process, local elites were forced into the arms of CPI and UWA in order to get access to and share control over the funds. Therefore, the distributional effects of TRS were and are still subject to discussions in Bwindi, as well as the new rules for disbursing funds and project selection, which are still debated and considered as too "technical to handle" by many. Although the critique to the low funding from TRS has been addressed by the introduction of new resources in the form of the gorilla levy, this has been subject to a dispute between two conservation organizations (IGCP and MBIFCT) and criticized for only being US$5.

All these disputes are reflected in two discourses, an "official" one voiced by UWA and IGCP, reflecting storylines of international and national conservation focusing on linking conservation and development (Newmark & Hough, 2000), and a competing discourse advocated by local communities which challenges the way TRS is implemented. The oppositional discourse calls for more community involvement, more direct individual benefits, distributive justice, more funds to TRS and fewer conditions on TRS funds set by UWA. Similar concerns have been voiced in other developing countries (Schroeder, 2008; Spiteri & Nepal, 2006). TRS is still a statist policy arrangement in which UWA and supporting organizations dominate the arrangement and control crucial resources. Therefore, this research also echoes the findings of Nelson and Agrawal (2008), who argue that there is a reduced likelihood of state institutions (in this case UWA) relinquishing control over resources when they are highly valuable. Whereas CPI and local governments are involved at all levels of TRS implementation, their powers are limited to resource distribution within the framework of UWA's conditional guidelines. The communities on the other hand are the most disadvantaged with neither financial nor knowledge resources. Despite being the central victims of conservation costs, their powers are minimal.

Similar challenges facing revenue sharing schemes of the "protected area outreach" variety have been identified elsewhere (Ahebwa et al., 2008; Archabald & Naughton-Treves, 2001; Schroeder, 2008). The results of this study suggest that this may be due to the inherent imbalance of power in such cases, where the protected area authority will always be able to decide the level of benefit sharing and set basic rules of the game (Barrow & Murphree, 2001). TRS based on commercial activities on community land or formal joint ventures may help to address this imbalance and deliver better outcomes for local people, but even under these arrangements, the imbalances of resources (such as financial and knowledge resources) can result in arrangements that are more rhetorically than practically participatory (Ahebwa et al., in press).

Despite the prevalent performative shortfalls of the TRS scheme at Bwindi, we do not suggest discarding the approach and returning to strict protectionism. Approaches to conservation like TRS are not perfect, but within the constraints facing policymakers, they may offer the best hope for generating local support for conservation. Therefore, to maximize TRS' ability to contribute to conservation through development, we argue that the inequities in the design and dispersion of benefits need to be addressed. In terms of participation, this could include changes in the TRS policy arrangement to more meaningfully include "targeted" local people in decisions about TRS that intimately affect their way of life. In terms of resources allocation, one possible route would be to make an explicit link between benefits from TRS and costs of conservation carried by local people, such as a compensation fund for crop-raiding. Another would be to increase the proportion of gorilla permit revenue shared with local communities to a level sufficient to have a greater impact than the US$5 levy can achieve.

Implementing such policy changes might increase local support for the TRS scheme and ultimately for the existence of the national park. However, it would make the TRS scheme substantially more complex to operate, particularly in the case of compensation, which would entail high transaction costs. Even more problematic though is the fact that reframing the TRS scheme to give greater revenue and decision-making power to local stakeholders would by definition reduce the returns of tourism to UWA and its power to determine the policy arrangement. This would likely be resisted (Nelson & Agrawal, 2008). Furthermore, as this paper has shown, the creation of multi-scale and multi-stakeholder partnerships for conservation built on revenue sharing is a daunting institutional challenge: "neither policy-makers in Uganda nor international conservation organizations that promote the philosophy that wildlife should pay its way to the satisfaction of all parties have yet faced up to the political economic complexity of their 'participatory' objectives" (Adams & Infield, 2003, p. 187). The sharing of tourism revenue with local communities is part of an intuitively convincing narrative of community conservation. However, experiences with implementation suggest a more complex reality, with relatively limited benefits and considerable conflict over resource allocation. An interesting discussion of the complex realities and challenges of the political decentralization of power over natural resources can be found in Mbaiwa and Stronza (2010) writing about Botswana's Okavango Delta. Such challenges must be recognized and responded to wherever TRS is contemplated as a policy for achieving conservation and development.

References

Adams, M.W., Aveiling, R., Brockington, D., Dickson, B., Elliot, J., Hutton, J., et al. (2004). *Biodiversity conservation and the eradication of poverty*. Washington, DC: American Association for the Advancement of Science.

Adams, M.W., & Infield, M. (2003). Who is on the gorilla's payroll? Claims on tourist revenue from a Ugandan National Park. *World Development, 31*(1), 177–190.

Ahebwa, M.W. (2012). *Tourism, livelihoods and biodiversity conservation. An assessment of tourism related policy interventions at Bwindi Impenetrable National Park (BINP), Uganda* (Doctoral thesis). Wageningen University, The Netherlands.

Ahebwa, M.W., van der Duim, R., & Nyakaana, J.B. (2008). Tourism, communities and conservation: An analysis of tourism revenue sharing programme at Lake Mburo National Park, Uganda. In R. van der Duim & M.E. Kloek (Eds.), *Tourism, nature conservation and wealth creation. Thematic proceedings of Atlas Africa conferences volume 4* (pp. 15–26). Arnhem: Atlas.

Ahebwa, M.W., van der Duim, V.R., & Sandbrook, C.G. (in press). Private - community partnerships: Investigating a new approach to conservation and development in Uganda. *Conservation & Society*.

Archabald, K., & Naughton-Treves, N.L. (2001). Tourism revenue-sharing around national parks in western Uganda: Early efforts to identify and reward local communities. *Environmental Conservation, 28*(2), 135–149.

Arnouts, R. (2010). *Regional nature governance in the Netherlands: Four decades of governance modes and shifts in the Utrechtse Heuvelrug and Midden-Brabant* (Doctoral thesis). Wageningen University, The Netherlands.

Arts, B., & Goverde, H. (2006). The governance capacity of (new) policy arrangements: A reflexive approach. In B. Arts & P. Leroy (Eds.), *Institutional dynamics in environmental governance* (pp. 69–92). Dordrecht: Springer.

Arts, B., & Leroy, P. (2006). Institutional processes in environmental governance: Lots of dynamics, not much change? In B. Arts & P. Leroy (Eds.), *Institutional dynamics in environmental governance*. Dordrecht: Springer.

AWF. (2009). *Gorilla conservation*. Retrieved January 28, 2009, from http://www.awf.org/section/wildlife/gorillas

Baker, J.E. (1997). Trophy hunting as a sustainable use of wildlife resources in southern and eastern Africa. *Journal of Sustainable Tourism, 5*(4), 306–321.

Barrow, E., & Murphree, M. (2001). Community conservation: From concept to practice. In D. Hulme & M. Murphree (Eds.), *African wildlife and livelihoods: The promise and performance of community conservation* (pp. 24–37). Oxford: James Currey.

Becker, F. (2009). Tourism, conservation areas, and local development in Namibia; spatial perspectives of private and public sector reform. In J. Saarinen, F. Becker, D. Wilson, & H. Manwa (Eds.), *Sustainable tourism in Southern Africa: Local communities, and natural resources in transition* (pp. 93–115). Bristol: Channel View Publications.

Bertaux, D. (1981). From the life-history approach to the transformation of sociological practice. In D. Bertaux (Ed.), *Biography and society: The life history approach in the social science* (pp. 29–45). London: Sage.

Blomley, T., Namara, A., McNeilage, A., Franks, P., Rainer, H., Donaldson, A., et al. (2010). *Assessing the effectiveness of fifteen years of integrated conservation and development around two gorilla reserves in southwestern Uganda* (Natural Resource Series, Unpublished report). London: International Institute for Environment and Development.

Bramwell, B., & Lane, B. (2011). Critical research on the governance of tourism and sustainability. *Journal of Sustainable Tourism, 19*(4–5), 411–422.

Buizer, M. (2008). *Worlds apart: Interactions between local initiatives and established policy* (Doctoral thesis). Wageningen University, The Netherlands.

Creswell, J.W. (1998). *Qualitative inquiry and research design: Choosing among five traditions*. London: Sage.

Elliot, J., & Sumba, D. (2010). *Conservation enterprise – What works, where and for whom? A Poverty and Conservation Learning Group (PCLP)* (AWF Discussion Paper). Nairobi: African Wildlife Foundation.

Fisher, R., Maginnis, S., Jackson, W., Barrow, E., Jeanrenaud, S., Ingles, A., et al. (2008). *Linking conservation and poverty reduction: Landscapes, people and power*. London: IUCN.

Hamilton, A.C. (1984). *Deforestation in Uganda*. Nairobi: Oxford University Press.

Hamilton, A., Cunningham, A., Byarugaba, D., & Kayanja, F. (2000). Conservation in a region of political instability: Bwindi impenetrable forest, Uganda. *Conservation Biology, 14*, 1722–1725.

Hecker, J.H. (2005). *Promoting environmental security and poverty alleviation in Virunga-Bwindi, Great Lakes Africa* (Part 1: Case study). The Hague: Institute for Environmental Security (IES).

Hulme, D., & Murphree, M. (2001). *African wildlife and livelihoods: The promise and performance of community conservation*. Oxford: James Currey.

IGCP. (2008). *Economics of gorilla tourism in Uganda, ape tourism and human disease: How close should we get?* (Virunga Volcanoes Range Mountain Gorilla Census, 2003. Socio-economic survey [IGCP/CARE/WCS]. Bwindi gorilla census 2006. Summary report. Regional tourism plan summary report). Retrieved October 30, 2008, from http://igcp.org/our_work/our_work.asp

Jennings, G. (2001). *Tourism research*. Singapore: John Wiley Australia.

Korbee, D. (2007). *Environmental security in Bwindi: A focus on farmers* (Research document). The Hague: Institute for Environmental Security (IES).

Liefferink, D. (2006). The dynamics of policy arrangements: Turning round the tetrahedron. In B. Arts & P. Leroy (Eds.), *Institutional dynamics in environmental governance* (pp. 35–68). Dordrecht: Springer.

Lindsey, P.A., Roulet, P.A., & Romanach, S.S. (2007). Economic and conservation significance of the trophy hunting industry in South Africa. *Biological Conservation, 134*(4), 455–469.

Mbaiwa, J.E. & Stronza, A.L. (2010). The effects of tourism development on rural livelihoods in the Okavango Delta, Botswana. *Journal of Sustainable Tourism, 18*(5), 635–656.

Meyer, D.M. (2001). *Communities, contests and power structures. A comparative study of tourism development on Rugen (Germany) and the Isle of Wight (UK) in light of community participation theories* (Doctoral thesis). University of North London, Islington, UK.

NACSO. (2009). *Namibia's communal conservancies: A review of progress 2008*. Windhoek: Author.

Namara, A., & Nsabagasani, X. (2003). *Decentralisation and wildlife management: Devolving rights or shedding responsibility?* (Bwindi Impenetrable National Park, Uganda, Working paper series). Washington, DC: World Resources Institute.

Naughton-Treves, L. (1999). Whose animals? A history of property rights to wildlife in Toro, western Uganda. *Land degradation and Development, 10*, 311–328.

Nelson, F., & Agrawal, A. (2008). Patronage or participation? Community-based natural resource management reform in sub-Saharan Africa. *Development and Change, 39*(4), 557–585.

Newmark, W., & Hough, J. (2000). Conserving wildlife in Africa: Integrated conservation and development projects and beyond. *Bio Science, 50*, 585–592.

Nowak, R. (1995). Endangered species: Uganda enlists locals in the battle to save gorillas. *Science, 267*, 1761.

Ochieng, A. (2011). *Linking tourism, conservation and livelihoods outside protected areas: An analysis of sport hunting intervention around Lake Mburo National Park, Uganda* (Master's thesis). Department of Environmental Science, Wageningen University, The Netherlands.

Peters, J. (1998). Sharing national park entrance fees: Forging new partnerships in Madagascar. *Society and Natural Resources, 11*, 517–530.

Saarinen, J., Becker, F., Wilson, D., & Manwa, H. (2009). *Sustainable tourism in southern Africa: Local communities, and natural resources in transition*. Bristol: Channel View Publications.

Sandbrook, Ch. G. (2006). *Tourism, conservation and livelihoods: The impacts of gorilla tracking at Bwindi Impenetrable National Park, Uganda* (Doctoral thesis). University of London, UK.

Sandbrook, Ch. G. (2008). Putting leakage in its place: The significance of retained tourism revenue in the local context in rural Uganda. *Journal of International Development, 22*(1), 124–136.

Schroeder, R.A. (2008). Environmental justice and the market: The politics of sharing wildlife revenues in Tanzania. *Society and Natural Resources, 21*, 583–596.

Sebukeera, C. (1996). *State of the environment report for Uganda* (Unpublished report). Kampala: National Environmental Authority (NEMA).

Southgate, C. (2006). Ecotourism in Kenya: The vulnerability of communities. *Journal of Ecotourism, 5*(1–2), 80–96.

Spenceley, A. (2003). *Tourism, local livelihoods and the private sector in South Africa: Case studies on the growing role of the private sector in natural resources management* (Sustainable Livelihoods in Southern Africa Research Paper 8). Brighton: Institute of Development Studies.

Spenceley, A. (2010). *Tourism product development. Interventions and best practices in sub-Saharan Africa: Part 1: Synthesis* (Report to the World Bank). Washington: World Bank.

Spiteri, A., & Nepal, K.N. (2006). Incentive-based conservation programs in developing countries: A review of some key issues and suggestions for improvements. *Environmental Management, 37*(1), 1–14.

Sumba, D., Warinwa, F., Lenaiyasa, P., & Muruthi, P. (2007). *The Koija starbeds ecolodge: A case study of a conservation enterprise in Kenya* (African Wildlife Foundation Working Papers). Nairobi: African Wildlife Foundation.

UBOS (Uganda Bureau of Statistics). (2010). *Population and livelihoods report 2010.* Kampala: Author.

UWA. (1996). *Position paper on tourism revenue sharing* (Unpublished report). Kampala: Author.

UWA. (2000a). *Community-protected area institution policy* (Unpublished document). Kampala: Author.

UWA. (2000b). *Community conservation policy* (Unpublished document). Kampala: Author.

UWA. (2000c). *Tourism revenue sharing policy* (Unpublished document). Kampala: Author.

UWA. (2009). *Gorilla levy position paper.* Kampala: Author.

UWA. (2009). *Revenue sharing projects report 2009* (Unpublished document). Kampala: Author.

UWA. (2010). *Extractions from tourism revenue statistical records.* Kampala: Author.

van der Duim, V.R. (2011). *Safari. A journey through tourism, conservation and development* (Inaugural lecture). Wageningen: Wageningen University.

Van Gossum, P., Arts, B., De Wulf, R., & Verheyen, K. (2011). An institutional evaluation of sustainable forest management in Flanders. *Land Use Policy, 28*(2011), 110–123.

Van Tatenhove, J.P.M., Arts, B., & Leroy, P. (2000). *Political modernisation and the environment: The renewal of environmental policy arrangements.* Dordrecht: Kluwer Academic.

Van der Zouwen, M. (2006). Dynamics in nature policy practices across the European Union. In B. Arts & P. Leroy, (Eds.), *Institutional dynamics in environmental governance* (pp. 139–160). Dordrecht: Springer.

Wiering, M., & Immink, I. (2006). When water management meets spatial planning: A policy-arrangements perspective. *Environment and Planning C: Government and Policy, 24*, 423–438.

Community-based cultural tourism: issues, threats and opportunities

Noel B. Salazar

Cultural Mobilities Research (CuMoRe), Faculty of Social Sciences, University of Leuven, Belgium

Using examples from long-term anthropological fieldwork in Tanzania, this paper critically analyzes how well generally accepted community-based tourism discourses resonate with the reality on the ground. It focuses on how local guides handle their role as ambassadors of communal cultural heritage and how community members react to their narratives and practices. It pays special attention to the time-limited, project-based development method, the need for an effective exit strategy, for quality control, tour guide training and long-term tour guide retention. The study is based on a program funded by the Netherlands-based development agency, Stichting Nederlandse Vrijwilligers (SNV), from 1995 to 2001, and on post-program experiences. Findings reveal multiple complex issues of power and resistance that illustrate many community-based tourism conflicts. The encounter with the "Other" is shown to be central and that the role of professional intermediaries in facilitating this experience of cultural contact is crucial. Tour guides are often the only "locals" with whom tourists spend considerable time: they have considerable agency in the image-building process of the peoples and places visited, (re)shaping tourist destination images and indirectly influencing the self-image of those visited too. The paper provides ideas for overcoming the issues and problems described.

Introduction

While social scientists have long taken a critical stance toward the concept of *community*, it remains widely popular in the tourism planning and development discourse. Although not often acknowledged, one of the reasons why community-based tourism (CBT) programs are hindered in their success is because those organizing it ignore the problematic assumptions embedded within the community concept itself (Tosun, 2000). Not surprisingly, the fuzziness of the notion is cleverly exploited in tourism marketing. While CBT is intended to empower people, the representations deployed in constituting the targeted "communities", be they imagined or real, remain largely unexamined. Because of the communicative power of tourism, representations of destinations have direct and potentially significant influences on the people who are being presented, represented and misrepresented, as well as on those (sub)groups who are absent from such representations. It is still common for ethnic minority groups to be depicted as the "exotic Other" in exhibitions, postcards or tourist literature (Smith, 2003).[1] When the tourismified definition of a community identity prevails, the group is frozen in an image of itself or museumized (MacCannell, 1984).

Which images and ideas of community are being (re)produced in CBT projects and policies? Drawing on long-term ethnographic fieldwork in Tanzania, this paper tries to answer this question by analyzing the key role of local tour guides in the representational process. However, it is first essential to delineate the broader scholarly field within which this study engages by briefly reviewing some key ideas on community and its application in CBT. This is followed by an explanation of the research methodology used in this paper and a description of the Cultural Tourism Programme (CTP) in Tanzania as a typical example of CBT, first from a general perspective and then focusing on the role of local tour guides. A critical analysis is made of how well generally accepted CBT policy discourses resonate with the reality on the ground. The concluding section reflects on how the complex challenges revealed by the CTP case studies could be turned into opportunities for sustainable CBT projects in Tanzania and beyond.

Community and community-based tourism

Community is a very elusive and vague term. It is used to refer to not only a locality (e.g. a village community) but also a network of relationships (e.g. cyberspace communities). Most descriptions rely on Eurocentric conceptions that go back to the theorizing of scholars like Tönnies, Marx, Durkheim and Weber (see Amit & Rapport, 2002). According to *The Community Tourism Guide*, for example, a community can be described as "a mutually supportive, geographically specific, social unit such as a village or tribe where people identify themselves as community members and where there is usually some form of communal decision-making" (Mann, 2000, p. 18). Such a notion of community evokes a group of people who have something in common and who are actively engaged with one another in a benign fashion, and such sentiments may be used rhetorically to generate some kind of shared identity where it was only latent (Anderson, 1991). Interestingly, community, "unlike all other terms of social organization (state, nation, society, etc.) ... seems never to be used unfavourably" (Williams, 1976, p. 76). Received ideas about community have distorted and limited empirical research and theory, especially when alluding to out-dated notions of collectivities as fixed in time and space or when invoking community as a unity, as an undifferentiated thing with intrinsic powers that speaks with a single voice. Amit and Rapport (2002) critically examined community as a methodological, theoretical, phenomenological, political and legal construct. They discussed the "slipperiness" of the concept, which they believe is "too vague, too variable in its applications and definitions to be of much utility as an analytical tool" (2002, p. 13). Their analysis reveals that community can equally be a site of violence, political struggle or multiple hierarchies.

In the context of sustainable tourism development, the importance of CBT has clearly been recognized over the past two decades. Nobody will dispute the fact that destination communities must benefit if tourism is to be viable and sustainable in the long term. CBT aims to create a more sustainable tourism industry (at least discursively), focusing on the receiving communities in terms of planning and maintaining tourism development. This idea came to the fore in the 1990s, with Pearce (1992) suggesting that CBT presents a way to provide an equitable flow of benefits to all affected by tourism through consensus-based decision-making and local control of development. While mass or mainstream tourism attracted trenchant criticism as a shallow and degrading experience for developing countries, so-called "alternative" forms of tourism have been viewed much more benevolently and few critiques have emerged (Ryan, 2002).[2] As a particular alternative form of tourism, CBT suggests a symbolic or mutual relationship where the tourist is not given central priority but becomes an equal part of the system (Wearing & McDonald, 2002).

The anticipated benefits of CBT are three (Rozemeijer, 2001, p. 13):

(1) CBT generates income and employment and, as such, contributes to rural development – a benefit that especially applies in remote areas;
(2) the benefits derived from the use of natural resources for tourism will prompt the community to use these valuable resources in a sustainable way; and
(3) CBT adds value to the national tourism product through diversification of tourism, increasing volume and economies of scale.

Four dimensions are considered equally important for sustainable development (Rozemeijer, 2001, p. 15):

(1) CBT should be economically viable: the revenue should exceed the costs;
(2) CBT should be ecologically sustainable: the environment should not decrease in value;
(3) there should be an equitable distribution of costs and benefits among all participants in the activity; and
(4) institutional consolidation should be ensured: a transparent organisation, recognised by all stakeholders, should be established to represent the interests of all community members and to reflect true ownership.

While the above indicates that CBT projects have often been created in the context of ecotourism (e.g. Kontogeorgopoulos, 2005; Snyder & Sulle, 2011), probably the most promising niche to develop CBT programs is cultural tourism, identified by the United Nations World Tourism Organization (UNWTO, 2001) as one of the major growth markets in global tourism. The main strength of CBT, especially in cultural tourism, lies in its potential to empower rural communities and to make a substantial contribution to development and the eradication of poverty (Manyara & Jones, 2007). CBT activities that are designed and implemented through community consensus other than centrally planned (top–down) CTP may cause less negative effects and disruption of rural cultures.

These tourism programs may also enhance the opportunity for spontaneous, rather than contrived, encounters between destination communities and tourists. For these reasons, intergovernmental agencies like the UNWTO and UNESCO have singled out cultural and heritage tourism as the most suitable form of community-based development for developing countries. For many people, (sustainable) cultural tourism development is actually synonymous with CBT involving local people (Lamers, 2001). While the notion of CBT stresses that many of these projects and products are indeed focused on a local community (and its natural and cultural heritage), in practice, they are seldom controlled and managed by that community – "community-centered tourism" would actually be a more accurate term.

Although Murphy (1985) argued a long time ago that communities should play an integral role in the development of tourism and proposed an approach that emphasized the need for community control, the debate still continues as to how an appropriate and sustainable form of community planning should be implemented. Consensus and control are key issues (World Wildlife Fund, 2001), and the political nature of the planning process continues to be a major difficulty (Smith, 2003). A pluralistic approach to community-oriented tourism planning assumes that all parties have an equal opportunity to participate in the political process. Jamal and Getz (1995) provided a critical analysis of collaboration and cooperation, stating that power imbalances often act as a significant barrier to successful collaboration. Reed (1997) suggested that power relations are indeed an integral element in understanding CBT planning and the relative success of collaborative efforts. It is clear that few communities have equal access to political and economic resources, especially indigenous minorities who are often politically, economically and socially disadvantaged (Snyder & Sulle, 2011). CBT can offer such communities the chance to move toward greater political self-determination, but *only* if local control is maximized.

There have been numerous criticisms of CBT. According to Blackstock (2005), the literature on CBT, as presented since the 1990s, has three major failings from a community development perspective. First, it tends to take a functional approach to community involvement (not having the transformative intent of community development and not focusing on community empowerment). Second, it tends to treat the host community as a homogeneous bloc (for whom "consensus" is rare). Thirdly, it neglects the (external power-based) structural constraints on local control of the tourism industry.[3] This has resulted in misunderstandings that are reflected in unsuccessful development or dissatisfied community groups who resent changes, particularly in relation to tourism and tourists.

Attention to multiple interests and identities within communities and their relationships to external actors, political institutions and national policies are critical to understanding the multiple challenges facing CBT (Belsky, 1999). Honey described how many CBT programs are "relational" rather than participatory; "they seek to improve relationships between the community and either the state or the private enterprise through trade-offs rather than to devolve ownership and management of the protected area or tourism project to the local community" (1999, p. 392). Power is people's ability to control the resources required for tourism development – labor, capital, culture and natural resources – and to secure personal returns from having tourism in their community (Brennan & Allen, 2001). Hence, power influences people's willingness and ability to engage in tourism.

Taylor and Davis (1997) conducted a review of the literature concerning the involvement of community members in sustainable tourism development. They argued that to suggest that disparate opinions between groups and individuals can be aligned toward some communal vision fails to recognize that tourism development is fundamentally different from other types of economic development. The economic benefits of tourism may be unevenly distributed but the costs, the intrusion, congestion and rising prices will affect both those who support and those who hate tourism. The main issue centers around the conflict that arises over the planning of the growth and development of tourism where local participation is encouraged by public agencies, but a vociferous minority, in favor or against, influences decisions, the silent majority remaining unheard, suggesting a passive but tacit acceptance.

Even if communities have control over their development, "local control is not necessarily the 'good thing' that many writers imply, particularly where that control is in the hands of development-driven politicians" (Pearce, 1992, p. 26). The control of tourism by players within the community and the pressure to increase visitor numbers could seek to widen community differences as well as creating another destination stereotype. Moreover, the interests of one local community will not necessarily coincide with those of others, nor is it likely that the interests of the local community will be the same for all within the community (Hall, 1994). According to Reed (1997), power relations may seriously alter the outcome of collaborative efforts or even preclude mutual action on the local level. Local power relationships within the community can be factional, as can those of players on the broader stage such as national governments, NGOs and supranational institutions. Empowerment issues, such as who participates, come to the fore: often the disadvantaged (those who need it most) are left out of the process and women are restricted to low-paying service roles (as cooks or cleaners). The emergence of local elites is as likely to produce inequalities within the community, just as these other players produce disparities of benefits at a different level. The word "local" – and, likewise, the word "community" – distracts one from the "intense complexity of micro-politics that all sides are inevitably imbricated within and shaped by" (Meethan, 2001, p. 61).

As Sofield (2003) noted, however, many of the benefits of CBT planning lie in the process, not simply the outcome. By taking the journey down the community engagement and empowerment path, problematic areas, power imbalances, lack of social capacity and capital can be highlighted, which can then work in people's favor (Beeton, 2006). To have a say in the management arena is only one of many ways to ensure that local people benefit from tourism. Rather, the modes of participation are related to the institutional arrangements and the different stages of tourism development present in a community (Li, 2006). To distribute benefits to a community, the tourism initiative need not always involve the community in any rights, tenure or control of the project (Simpson, 2008).

Research methods

This is a qualitative study, guided by the grounded theory approach (Bryant & Charmaz, 2007), whereby descriptive research leads to the development of more meaningful theory and measures. It critically analyzes how well the generally accepted CBT principles, as outlined above, resonate with the reality on the ground. The findings presented here are part of a long-term anthropological study on tourism in Tanzania (Salazar, 2006, 2007, 2009a, 2009b, 2010). Ethnographic fieldwork was carried out over a period of 14 months (June–August 2004, January–August 2007 and February–March 2009), focusing on the northern Arusha Region, together with shorter periods of work in Manyara, Kilimanjaro, Tanga, Dodoma, Dar es Salaam and Zanzibar. The methodology used, distinctively (though not uniquely) anthropological, involved mixed methods. A major part of the fieldwork consisted of extensive observation. As a participant, the author joined tourists on 24 tours, lasting from a minimum of one hour to one week (including overnight stays in some of the communities under study). As an observer, countless hours were spent socializing with local tour guides and informally talking to them (and this in the communities as well as at training institutes). Hundreds of pages of field notes were recorded. The second-most important source of data was interviews. In-depth interviews were conducted and recorded with 30 guides, along with semi-structured interviews with five people involved in guide training; 15 local tour operators; and 13 tourism authorities at local, national and regional levels.

Almost all the interviewed guides agreed to fill in a questionnaire that collected basic demographic information and data on their education, guiding, tour preparation and information resources, travel experience, hobbies and the use of new information and communication technologies. A local assistant carried out 23 additional short, structured interviews with local people. In addition to observations and interviews, various types of secondary data were collected: newspaper and magazine articles; online publications; official documents (e.g. tourism laws and regulations); tour guiding syllabi; and all kinds of tourism-related brochures, pamphlets and other promotional materials. Supplementary data were gathered from tourists by informally chatting with them during safaris. In all instances of data collection, the author was identified as a foreign researcher and, if appro-priate, the official accreditation provided by the Tanzanian Commission for Science and Technology (COSTECH) was shown. All primary data (field notes, interview transcripts) were interpreted with the help of ATLAS.ti, a software package for qualitative data analysis based on the principles of grounded theory (Muhr, 2004).

Extensive background literature research was carried out at various libraries: the Univer-sity of Pennsylvania and the University of California at Berkeley in the US; the University of Dar es Salaam, the Economic and Social Research Foundation, Research on Poverty Alleviation and the Professional Tour Guide School in Tanzania; and the University of Leuven in Belgium. In addition, the African collections of the Africa Museum in Belgium were used. Tapping into various literatures – on anthropology and ethnography, tourism and travel and Tanzania – might have been time consuming, but it allowed the making of theoretical and conceptual connections that would otherwise never have been made. This research is kept up to date through the assistant and by local contacts in Tanzania by using e-mail and short text messages (SMS).

CTP as exemplary CBT?

Although often praised by the tourism sector, NGOs or authorities, promising CBT initiatives are few in number and hard to sustain (Akunaay, Nelson, & Singleton, 2003). The most well-known Tanzanian example is the award-winning Cultural Tourism Programme (CTP). This project was launched in 1995 by the Dutch aid agency Stichting Nederlandse Vrijwilligers (SNV). According to the organization's politically correct sustainable development discourse, in 1994, it received a request for help from a group of young Maasai who wanted to develop tourism in their village – a textbook example of the bottom-up, participatory approach.[4] In reality, tourism is one of SNV's areas of expertise and the agency has extensive experience with CBT in countries such as Bolivia, Botswana, Cameroon, Laos, Nepal and Vietnam (Caalders & Cottrell, 2001). In SNV's development framework, CBT projects are defined as follows:

> Tourism initiatives that are *owned* by one or more defined communities, or run as joint venture partnerships with the private sector with *equitable* community participation, as a means of using the natural resources in a *sustainable* manner to improve their standard of living in an economically *viable* way. (Rozemeijer, 2001, p. 14)

SNV was planning to expand its tourism activities to Tanzania and, unsurprisingly, quickly found local communities interested in jumping on the CBT bandwagon.

CTP was set up as a loose network of local communities, mainly Maasai in northern Tanzania, operating independently from each other and offering individually developed tour packages. These include campsites, home-stays, traditional food and beverage, trained guides and local tours involving natural heritage (forests, waterfalls and caves) and cultural attractions (historical sites and visits to healers, storytellers, artisans and cooking mamas). The main activities on offer are hiking, mountain climbing, cycling, canoeing, fishing and dhow trips. SNV financed the various CTP modules, controlled their expenditures and organized some minimal training for tour guides. The Tanzania Tourist Board (TTB), on the other hand, was responsible for promoting CTP to both local and international travel agencies and tour operators (De Jong, 1999).

Helped by the fact that experiential "meet the people" tourism was becoming in vogue, CTP grew rapidly in its first years of existence. The number of tourists in the 18 initial modules increased from 2600 in 1998 to over 7000 in 2001. For comparison, around the millennium, Tanzania as a whole registered approximately 500,000 international tourist arrivals (UNWTO, 2003). Revenues, very modest when compared to more lucrative safari or hunting business, were distributed partly to local executors and partly to community funds. Because SNV published widely the success of its CTP, the project was awarded the TO DO!99 Award for Socially Responsible Tourism (Adler, 2000). In 2002, the International Year of Ecotourism, CTP was heralded as Tanzania's good practice example of sustainable development by the UNWTO (2002, pp. 237–240). The modules were also widely praised in western guidebooks such as the *Lonely Planet* and the *Rough Guide*.

Due to its perceived economic and institutional sustainability (and because from the start it had been conceived as a 5-year project), SNV withdrew from the program in 2001, although their own philosophy prescribes that a successful CBT venture needs "involvement of an organisation as a partner in project development and commitment to provide continued support" (Rozemeijer, 2001, p. 61). As soon as SNV pulled out, there was a declining cooperation between the different communities involved (van der Duim, Peters, & Wearing, 2005). The intended Tanzania Cultural Tourism Organization, created with the aim of coordinating the various modules, broke down before it even started. Each village dealt only with its own activities, and not everybody in the participating communities was happy with the presence of curious tourists. In some places, the revenues were not distributed properly and there were escalating conflicts over land and natural resources (Nelson, 2003, 2004).

At the time of writing, CTP now has 27 participating communities and many others are waiting to join. However, the various modules offer very similar packages and accessibility is a major factor determining success – villages nearby Arusha (Tanzania's "safari capital") or on the access roads to protected areas are far more popular than more remote ones. Because CTP as a whole badly needed professional management, the TTB assigned a full-time CTP coordinator to develop guidelines and quality standards and to address many marketing problems that arose. In 2005, SNV became involved again, this time by providing two tourism consultants. They identified the following issues as most problematic: standards of accommodation, hygiene for toilets and food preparation, an imbalance of nature-based activities over ones that engage with local culture (although the name of the program suggests otherwise) and the weak interpretation skills of guides (Ashley, 2006). That latter issue is considered next.

CTP tour guiding

> My guide for the [CTP] Osotwa program, Olais Mokolo, resigned from his position as a village executive officer (a local government position) to become a tour guide in order to increase his income. This fact highlights that individuals are benefiting from these programs and do have an incentive to become involved in tourism. (Ofosu-Amaah, 2007, p. 59)

The quote above hints at the importance of "local" tour guides in CTP in particular and CBT in general.[5] They are often the only people with whom tourists spend more time than the average short interaction with other community members. Guiding therefore constitutes a strategic factor in the representation of a community, next to influencing the quality of the tourist experience, the length of stay and the resulting economic benefits for the community (Salazar, 2010). Although emphasized in much of the literature on guiding, the individual goal of guides is not necessarily to become a cultural broker, defined as someone who flattens cultural differences.[6] It is more useful to think of them as small entrepreneurs who, not always successfully, sell their services to a varied group of tourists (Bras, 2000). Guides are not altruistic mediators by vocation, nor can they be expected to submit blindly to CBT rules and regulations. Instead, they sell images, knowledge, contacts, souvenirs, access, authenticity, ideology and sometimes even themselves.

Guides are indispensable to convey to tourists the richness of local natural and cultural heritage. Face-to-face interpretation lies "at the heart and soul" of what guides can and should be doing (Weiler & Ham, 2001, p. 549). In her book on the dynamics of guiding,

Pond (1993) stresses the importance of the skills of delivery over actual knowledge. In addition, they need to understand the currency of their services in a global market that is highly unstable and influenced by continuous changes in consumer preferences (Ap & Wong, 2001). This requires them to endlessly vary, reinvent and customize their services. What guides should and should not do is ideally controlled through mechanisms such as codes of conduct (a form of soft law), professional associations, awards of excellence, formal training, professional certification (or accreditation) and licensing (Black & Weiler, 2005).

Ideally, CTP tour guides are villagers with wide knowledge about the local heritage. They also need to learn (through professional training) how to handle tourists and how to reduce potential negative impacts caused by tourism (cf. Christie & Mason, 2003; Weiler & Ham, 2002). Almost all guides for the initial 18 CTP modules received a brief training from a professional tour guide school in Arusha. Even if these schools mainly focus on wildlife tourism or mountaineering, and with virtually nothing taught on cultural tourism or culture in general, they at least learned some more generic "tricks of the trade" (Salazar, 2010). From the moment SNV withdrew from the project, there was no more financial support for such training. Many of those who were trained have quit their guiding jobs for other (more beneficial) activities outside their villages. Some communities, understanding the importance of guiding for the development of their tourism packages, invested by sending promising villagers to tour guide schools in Arusha. However, these youngsters soon realized that they could earn more money by becoming safari driver-guides and often did not return to the communities that had sponsored their education. While the TTB and SNV recognize that guiding skills are a major problem in many of the CTP modules, there is little happening to change the current situation. SNV, now having "capacity-building" as its organizational priority, claims not to find anyone able to train the local tour guides (even though there are plenty of tour guide schools in Arusha). The brief ethnographic examples below are not meant to criticize the selected modules as such but to illustrate that the current situation can have dramatic consequences for the representation of (often marginal) people, the quality of the services delivered to tourists and the further development of CBT in the area.

In the summer of 2007, the author accompanied a group of American tourists on a typical three-day visit to the Maasai CTP of Mkuru. On their first day, they had a walking safari through the savannah. Their tour guide was not a Maasai but a Meru from a neighboring village (he never identified himself as such though).[7] One of the tourists was a general medical practitioner and very interested in knowing more about how the Maasai use local plants for medicinal purposes. The guide told her that the plants "they" (the Maasai) use have no real healing values but are just used because of tradition. When visiting a Maasai *boma* (livestock enclosure), he was unable to explain how the settlement is structurally organized. After a very brief introduction, he invited the group to "walk around and take pictures". The next day, the group went on a camel safari. At the start, the Meru tour guide introduced all the camels by name. The accompanying Maasai men (one per camel), on the contrary, were never mentioned, let alone properly introduced.

During a CTP tour in Tengeru village, the local Meru guide explained to a group of European tourists that only the Maasai wear blankets, while the Meru wear clothes. He further claimed that the Meru are more developed compared with other "tribes" because they have adapted quicker to modernity, and that the Maasai are certainly more primitive. One of the highlights of the nearby CTP of Il'kidinga, a settlement of Arusha people, is a hike to a hamlet on the top of a hill, with amazing views over the surrounding areas.[8] Upon approaching the hamlet, tourists perceived red blankets on the bushes around the houses.

They all assumed that these were Maasai garments that the women had just washed and were drying in the sun. Little did they know that neither the women who had washed the blankets nor the men who occasionally wear them in this village are actually Maasai. Once inside, the Arusha guide took them to a man (whom the tourists also mistook for a Maasai) who was sharpening a machete. The guide explained that under colonial rule villagers used to buy knives imported from the United Kingdom. Nowadays they purchase cheap knives coming from China. The blades of the imported Asian knives are sharpened and made smaller so that they fit locally crafted protective sheaths. The guide went on to tell that used machetes are sold to visitors because "tourists always like something historic".

Where to go from here?

> Any group or community in today's world should be able to undertake self-criticism and to change in any way it wants to go until it begins to restrict the similar rights of others. The touristic requirement that a group internalize an "authentic" ethnic identity, even if the resulting image is widely held to be a positive one, is no less a constraint than the earlier form of negative ethnic stereotyping. Conforming to the requirements of being a living tourist attraction becomes a total problem affecting every detail of life. (MacCannell, 1984, p. 389)

Tourism is much more than a mere economic activity; it is a complex and dynamic phenomenon, present in virtually every corner of the world and affecting people in multiple ways. The sociocultural effects of tourism, especially in developing countries, are probably the most worrying aspect of a global(ized) sector that offers cut-price packages to remote and exotic destinations. Tourism affects the way cultural practices and landscapes are shaped, and cultural change reflects the influence of tourism as one of the agents in place transformation. Success stories in tourism might not be so hard to find. However, in light of sustainable development, success should never be conceived of as a static result. The fact that external as well as internal factors can disrupt even the strongest and most successful tourism projects should make us cautious (cf. Matarrita-Cascante, Brennan, & Luloff, 2010).

The above examples of the much-acclaimed CTP in Tanzania serve as a sobering example of how widely CBT rhetoric and practice can diverge. The principles of CBT certainly remain laudable. Unfortunately, the implementation of quality standards is often lacking. In the case of Mkuru, the visit to a Maasai community resembled a human zoo: Maasai and tourists staring at one another, with a guide unable to facilitate communication and exchange between the two parties. Because the tourists did not understand Swahili, they never noticed that their "local" guide was not a Maasai but a Meru. Of course, they also did not know that there are growing tensions between Meru and Maasai people in the area because the land they share around Mt. Meru is becoming overcrowded and overstocked. This background information would have led to a very different tour dynamic (and probably a much smaller tip for the guide). The Maasai community visited had no clue about how they were being represented by the Meru guide because they do not speak English.

The current lack of cooperation and consultation between the various CTP modules has a baleful influence on the way different ethnic groups represent one another. In Tengeru, the Meru guide found it necessary to clearly distinguish his ethnic group from the Maasai by denigrating the latter and depicting them as backwards. His comments partly have their origins in the guide's frustration that many foreigners think all Tanzanians are Maasai (Salazar, 2009a; Snyder & Sulle, 2011). The sight of a virile Maasai warrior, dressed in colorful red blankets and beaded jewellery, evokes the romantic image of a modern noble savage – a priceless tourism attraction. This has led to a true Maasai-mania that is profoundly affecting the daily life and culture of Maasai and other communities. Interestingly, the people organizing the CTP tour in Tengeru all wore blue, although this color is not particularly associated with the Meru. They did this to indexically distinguish their ethnic group from the "red" Maasai. In Tengeru, the guides use the opposite strategy; they capitalize on the perceived similarities with the Maasai to attract more tourists. At the same time, by telling tales such as the Maasai machete story, Arusha guides take away some of the magic surrounding the (imagined) Maasai culture, without actual Maasai having any say in whether they like this or not.

The most flagrant case of deceit encountered in the research period was when accompanying a group of international volunteers on their visit to the CTP of Babati and Hanang. The entrepreneur organizing the program was not local, but a Haya from north-western Tanzania. His alleged CBT tours, widely advertised in travel guidebooks and on the Responsible Travel website, bring visitors to the Barabaig, a poor herding people living in the volcanic highlands near Mt. Hanang. The "local" guide, a Chagga from the remote Mt. Kilimanjaro region, has become used to playing the Barabaig. Only, on this particular tour the trick did not work because the volunteers had been in Tanzania for a while and spoke Swahili fluently. They quickly noticed from the interactions the guide had with Barabaig people that he did not speak the local language. They insisted on obtaining information directly from the Barabaig and discovered that many of the things the guide had told them were purely invented. The volunteers were so upset about this that they filed a formal complaint with the TTB. Neither the TTB or SNV nor the CTP coordinator claimed to know about this fraud (which would not be very surprising because they only visit the various modules with announced official delegations).

Conclusion

The only way to overcome this type of situations is to be realistic when planning CBT, taking into account the operational, structural and cultural limits to community participation (Tosun, 2000). Local-level participation is essential for achieving the global goal of sustainable development. However, such involvement often involves a shift of power from local authorities to local actors. Moreover, real consensus and true local control is not always possible, practical or even desired by some of the communities that develop CBT. Planners need insight in this complex web of shifting power relations as well as in the ways different stakeholders imagine CBT. There is clearly a need for fundamental education and training in target communities to accompany tourism development. Local communities must develop strategies for receiving and interacting with tourists as well as displaying themselves and their visible culture (Reid, 2002). This involves finding the right balance between economic gain and cultural integrity.

This paper seeks to stress the key importance of local tour guides in CBT, especially when cultural tourism products are being developed. Because of the communicative power of tourism, representations of cultural heritage have direct and potentially significant influences on the peoples and communities who are being presented, represented and misrepresented. Any CBT program wishing to achieve sustainable success needs tour guides who are well trained and, if possible, local. If guides belong to the community in which the tourism activities are taking place, their insider positionality at least gives them the advantage of knowing what the cultural sensibilities are. This helps to avoid some of the problems discussed above. Professional training is needed, not only to improve guiding and hospitality skills, but also to make guides aware of complex ethical dilemmas, such as disjunctures between local conceptions of community and the ways in which those communities are imagined by visiting tourists. Anthropologists specializing in tourism can play a pivotal role in these programs (Salazar, 2010). Training as such may not be enough to tackle all problems, but it certainly helps tour guides to take better-informed principled decisions about guiding tourists.

The challenge remains to develop forms of tourism that are acceptable to the various interest groups within communities and that are at the same time economically viable and environmentally sustainable. Professionally trained local guides, provided they receive enough incentives for their work (so that they remain motivated to stay), are one of the key elements to achieve sustainable CBT. Apart from providing tourists an unforgettable experience, they can be instrumental in helping communities to have more realistic expectations about tourism development. In the same way that tourism fantasies have a tendency to essentialize "the Other", people in developing countries like Tanzania have a tendency to essentialize tourists and the mythical developed world they come from. The presence of affluent visitors prompts yearnings for change based on an illusionary image of the "good life" abroad, but this also produces tensions between local projects (e.g. modernization vs. cultural conservation). Liminally positioned local guides and sociocultural anthropologists alike are best placed to turn the many challenges facing CBT into worthwhile opportunities and to do this in culturally sensitive ways.

Finally, this paper indirectly asks important questions about the long-term value of short-term projects developed by external agencies and stresses the need for effective exit/handover strategies to be created before the end of such programs.

Acknowledgements

Permission to conduct the research in Tanzania was granted by the Tanzanian Commission for Science and Technology (research permit no. 2007-16-NA-2006-171) and kindly sponsored by the University of Dar es Salaam. The fieldwork was funded by the National Science Foundation (grant no. BCS-0514129) and a grant from the European Commission Directorate General Research (grant no. PIRG03-GA-2008-230892) made it possible to write up the results. An earlier version of this paper was presented at the International Conference on Sustainable Tourism in Developing Countries (ICST-DC) in Dar es Salaam (Tanzania), 10–11 August 2010, where it received the Best Overall Paper Award. I truly thank my Tanzanian research assistant, Joseph Ole Sanguyan, for all his help. All omissions and errors are mine alone.

Notes

1. The continuous process of "othering" peoples in cultural tourism has been extensively discussed in the scholarly literature (e.g. Aitchison, 2001; Bruner, 2005; Dann, 2004; Salazar, 2004, 2010; Van den Berghe, 1994).
2. Broadly defined, "alternative" forms of tourism refer to "those forms of tourism that are consistent with natural, social and *community values* and which allow both hosts and guests to enjoy positive and worthwhile interaction and shared experiences" (Smith & Eadington, 1992, p. 3; emphasis added).
3. Manyara and Jones (2007) even argue that, through foreign resource control and heavy reliance on donor funding, CBT in developing countries promotes neo-colonialism and reinforces dependency.
4. The Maasai, speakers of the Eastern Nilotic Maa tonal language, are a widely dispersed group of seminomadic pastoralists and small-scale subsistence agriculturists who occupy semiarid/arid rangelands in southern Kenya and northern Tanzania – collectively known as Maasailand. In Tanzania, they are said to have lived in the Serengeti plains and Ngorongoro highlands for some two centuries. Alongside the wildlife, the Maasai are the flag bearers of Tanzanian tourism (Salazar, 2009a; Snyder & Sulle, 2011).
5. As the ethnographic examples of this paper illustrate, the qualifier "local" does not necessarily imply that guides are natives of the place where they operate (although they are habitually perceived as such by foreign tourists).

6. The notion of culture broker implies a model of discrete cultures, an assumption contemporary anthropology questions (e.g. Gupta & Ferguson, 1992). Despite criticism (Aramberri, 2001; Sherlock, 2001), the concept is still widely used within tourism studies, where tour guides and other tourism service providers are conceived as intermediaries – be it cultural (Scherle & Nonnenmann, 2008) or social (Jensen, 2010) – between dichotomized host and guest cultures.
7. The Meru people, who have traditionally been farmers, are settled around the base of Mt. Meru.
8. The Arusha people are originally from the foothills of Mt. Meru. Influenced by Maasai ancestry, they still use the Maasai age system and other elements of Maasai social organization. However, they have different clans and abandoned livestock herding in favour of settled cultivation.

References

Adler, C. (2000). *TO DO!99 contest socially responsible tourism: Rationale for the Award.* Ammerland: Studienkreis für Tourismus und Entwicklung.

Aitchison, C. (2001). Theorizing other discourses of tourism, gender and culture: Can the subaltern speak (in tourism)? *Tourist Studies, 1*(2), 133–147.

Akunaay, M., Nelson, F., & Singleton, E. (2003, December, 7–12). *Community based tourism in Tanzania: Potential and perils in practice.* Paper presented at the Second IIPT African Conference on Peace through Tourism: Community Tourism – Gateway to Poverty Reduction, Dar es Salaam.

Amit, V., & Rapport, N. (2002). *The trouble with community: Anthropological reflections on movement, identity and collectivity.* London: Pluto.

Anderson, B.R. (1991). *Imagined communities: Reflections on the origin and spread of nationalism* (2nd ed.). New York: Verso.

Ap, J., & Wong, K.K.F. (2001). Case study on tour guiding: Professionalism, issues and problems. *Tourism Management, 22*(5), 551–563.

Aramberri, J. (2001). The host should get lost: Paradigms in the tourism theory. *Annals of Tourism Research, 28*(3), 738–761.

Ashley, C. (2006). *How can governments boost the local economic impacts of tourism? Options and tools.* London: Overseas Development Institute.

Beeton, S. (2006). *Community development through tourism.* Collingwood: Landlinks Press.

Belsky, J.M. (1999). Misrepresenting communities: The politics of community-based rural ecotourism in Gales Point Manatee, Belize. *Rural Sociology, 64*(4), 641–666.

Black, R., & Weiler, B. (2005). Quality assurance and regulatory mechanisms in the tour guiding industry: A systematic review. *The Journal of Tourism Studies, 16*(1), 24–37.

Blackstock, K. (2005). A critical look at community based tourism. *Community Development Journal, 40*(1), 39–49.

Bras, K. (2000). *Image-building and guiding on Lombok: The social construction of a tourist destination.* Amsterdam: ATLAS Publications.

Brennan, F., & Allen, G. (2001). Community-based ecotourism, social exclusion and the changing political economy of KwaZulu-Natal, South Africa. In D. Harrison (Ed.), *Tourism and the less developed world: Issues and case studies* (pp. 203–221). Wallingford: CAB International.

Bruner, E.M. (2005). *Culture on tour: Ethnographies of travel.* Chicago: University of Chicago Press.

Bryant, A., & Charmaz, K. (Eds.). (2007). *The Sage handbook of grounded theory.* London: Sage.

Caalders, J., & Cottrell, S. (2001). *SNV and sustainable tourism: A background paper.* The Hague: Stichting Nederlandse Vrijwilligers.

Christie, M.F., & Mason, P.A. (2003). Transformative tour guiding: Training tour guides to be critically reflective practitioners. *Journal of Ecotourism, 2*(1), 1–16.

Dann, G.M.S. (2004). (Mis)Representing the "Other" in the language of tourism. *Journal of Eastern Caribbean Studies, 29*(2), 76–94.

De Jong, A. (1999). *Cultural tourism in Tanzania: Experiences of a tourism development project.* The Hague: Stichting Nederlandse Vrijwilligers.

Gupta, A., & Ferguson, J. (1992). Beyond "culture": Space, identity, and the politics of difference. *Cultural Anthropology, 7*(1), 6–23.

Hall, C.M. (1994). *Tourism and politics: Policy, power, and place.* Chichester: Wiley.

Honey, M. (1999). *Ecotourism and sustainable development: Who owns paradise?* Washington, DC: Island Press.

Jamal, T.B., & Getz, D. (1995). Collaboration theory and community tourism planning. *Annals of Tourism Research, 22*(1), 186–204.

Jensen, Ø. (2010). Social mediation in remote developing world tourism locations: The significance of social ties between local guides and host communities in sustainable tourism development. *Journal of Sustainable Tourism, 18*(5), 615–633.

Kontogeorgopoulos, N. (2005). Community-based ecotourism in Phuket and Ao Phangnga, Thailand: Partial victories and bittersweet remedies. *Journal of Sustainable Tourism, 13*(1), 4–23.

Lamers, M. (2001). *Between protection and progress: An actor oriented approach to cultural tourism development in Kenya* (Doctoral dissertation). Maastricht University, Maastricht.

Li, W. (2006). Community decisionmaking: Participation in development. *Annals of Tourism Research, 33*(1), 132–143.

MacCannell, D. (1984). Reconstructed ethnicity: Tourism and cultural identity in Third World communities. *Annals of Tourism Research, 11*(3), 375–391.

Mann, M. (2000). *The community tourism guide: Exciting holidays for responsible travellers.* London: Earthscan.

Manyara, G., & Jones, E. (2007). Community-based tourism enterprises development in Kenya: An exploration of their potential as avenues of poverty reduction. *Journal of Sustainable Tourism, 15*(6), 628–644.

Matarrita-Cascante, D., Brennan, M.A., & Luloff, A.E. (2010). Community agency and sustainable tourism development: The case of La Fortuna, Costa Rica. *Journal of Sustainable Tourism, 18*(6), 735–756.

Meethan, K. (2001). *Tourism in global society: Place, culture, consumption.* New York: Palgrave.

Muhr, T. (2004). *User's manual for ATLAS.ti 5.0* (2nd ed.). Berlin: Scientific Software Development.

Murphy, P.E. (1985). *Tourism: A community approach.* New York: Methuen.

Nelson, F. (2003, February, 20–22). *Community-based tourism in Northern Tanzania: Increasing opportunities, escalating conflicts and an uncertain future.* Paper presented at the Community Tourism: Options for the Future Conference, Arusha, Tanzania.

Nelson, F. (2004). *The evolution and impacts of community-based ecotourism in northern Tanzania.* London: International Institute for Environment and Development.

Ofosu-Amaah, N.G. (2007). *Conservation for sustainable development? Ecotourism in Tanzania* (BA thesis). Harvard College, Cambridge.

Pearce, D.G. (1992). Alternative tourism: Concepts, classifications, and questions. In V.L. Smith & W.R. Eadington (Eds.), *Tourism alternatives: Potentials and problems in the development of tourism* (pp. 15–30). Philadelphia, PA: University of Pennsylvania Press.

Pond, K.L. (1993). *The professional guide: Dynamics of tour guiding.* New York: Van Nostrand Reinhold.

Reed, M.G. (1997). Power relations and community-based tourism planning. *Annals of Tourism Research, 24*(3), 566–591.

Reid, D.G. (2002). Development of cultural tourism in Africa: A community based approach. In J.S. Akama & P. Sterry (Eds.), *Cultural tourism in Africa: Strategies for the new millennium* (pp. 25–34). Arnhem: Association for Tourism and Leisure Education.

Rozemeijer, N. (2001). *Community-based tourism in Botswana: The SNV experience in three community-tourism projects.* Gaborone: SNV Botswana.

Ryan, C. (2002). Equity, management, power sharing and sustainability: Issues of the "new tourism". *Tourism Management, 23*(1), 17–26.

Salazar, N.B. (2004). Developmental tourists vs. development tourism: A case study. In A. Raj (Ed.), *Tourist behaviour: A psychological perspective* (pp. 85–107). New Delhi: Kanishka.

Salazar, N.B. (2006). Touristifying Tanzania: Global discourse, local guides. *Annals of Tourism Research, 33*(3), 833–852.

Salazar, N.B. (2007). Towards a global culture of heritage interpretation? Evidence from Indonesia and Tanzania. *Tourism Recreation Research, 32*(3), 23–30.

Salazar, N.B. (2009a). Imaged or imagined? Cultural representations and the "tourismification" of peoples and places. *Cahiers d'Études Africaines, 49*(193–194), 49–71.

Salazar, N.B. (2009b). A troubled past, a challenging present, and a promising future? Tanzania's tourism development in perspective. *Tourism Review International, 12*(3–4), 259–273.

Salazar, N.B. (2010). *Envisioning Eden: Mobilizing imaginaries in tourism and beyond.* Oxford: Berghahn.

Scherle, N., & Nonnenmann, A. (2008). Swimming in cultural flows: Conceptualising tour guides as intercultural mediators and cosmopolitans. *Journal of Tourism and Cultural Change, 6*(2), 120–137.

Sherlock, K. (2001). Revisiting the concept of hosts and guests. *Tourist Studies, 1*(3), 271–295.

Simpson, M.C. (2008). Community benefit tourism initiatives: A conceptual oxymoron. *Tourism Management, 29*(1), 1–18.

Smith, M.K. (2003). *Issues in cultural tourism studies.* London: Routledge.

Smith, V.L., & Eadington, W.R. (Eds.). (1992). *Tourism alternatives: Potentials and problems in the development of tourism.* Philadelphia: University of Pennsylvania Press.

Snyder, K.A., & Sulle, E.B. (2011). Tourism in Maasai communities: A chance to improve livelihoods. *Journal of Sustainable Tourism, 19*(8), 935–951.

Sofield, T.H.B. (2003). *Empowerment for sustainable tourism development.* Amsterdam: Pergamon.

Taylor, G., & Davis, D. (1997). The community show: A mythology of resident responsive tourism. In M. Stabler (Ed.), *Tourism and sustainability: Principles to practice* (pp. 323–334). Wallingford: CAB International.

Tosun, C. (2000). Limits to community participation in the tourism development process in developing countries. *Tourism Management, 21*(6), 613–633.

United Nations World Tourism Organization. (2001). *Tourism 2020 vision.* Madrid: World Tourism Organization.

United Nations World Tourism Organization. (2002). *Sustainable development of ecotourism: A compilation of good practices.* Madrid: World Tourism Organization.

United Nations World Tourism Organization. (2003). *Tourism Highlights. Edition 2003.* Madrid: World Tourism Organization.

Van den Berghe, P.L. (1994). *The quest for the other: Ethnic tourism in San Cristóbal, Mexico.* Seattle: University of Washington Press.

van der Duim, R., Peters, K., & Wearing, S. (2005). Planning host and guest interactions: Moving beyond the empty meeting ground in African encounters. *Current Issues in Tourism, 8*(4), 286–305.

Wearing, S., & McDonald, M. (2002). The development of community-based tourism: Re-thinking the relationship between tour operators and development agents as intermediaries in rural and isolated area communities. *Journal of Sustainable Tourism, 10*(3), 191–206.

Weiler, B., & Ham, S. (2001). Tour guides and interpretation. In D. Weaver (Ed.), *The encyclopedia of ecotourism* (pp. 549–563). Wallingford: CABI.

Weiler, B., & Ham, S.H. (2002). Tour guide training: A model for sustainable capacity building in developing countries. *Journal of Sustainable Tourism, 10*(1), 52–69.

Williams, R. (1976). *Keywords: A vocabulary of culture and society.* New York: Oxford University Press.

World Wildlife Fund. (2001). *Guidelines for community-based ecotourism development.* Gland: WWF International.

The role of tourism employment in poverty reduction and community perceptions of conservation and tourism in southern Africa

Susan Lynne Snyman

Environmental Policy Research Unit, University of Cape Town & Wilderness Safaris, Johannesburg, South Africa

High-end ecotourism operations in African protected areas often claim to share the benefits of ecotourism with surrounding rural communities through employment as well as "trickle down" effects of revenues that result from such operations. The receipt of benefits from ecotourism is also claimed to promote an appreciation of biological diversity and conservation in surrounding communities. In practice, these claimed benefits can be challenging to measure and no multi-country study has attempted to assess the efficacy of these claims across a variety of circumstances. This study assessed various impacts of ecotourism employment at study sites in Botswana, Malawi and Namibia. Analysis of household income, social welfare impacts and the number of people indirectly affected by ecotourism employment indicates that rural communities are moving towards an engagement with the market economy as a result of ecotourism operations. Monthly income from ecotourism employment was shown to enable households to invest in assets, education and "luxury" goods, which improved financial security and social welfare in remote, rural areas. A thorough analysis of the various factors impacting attitudes towards conservation and tourism showed that ecotourism employment positively affects attitudes, though level of education showed the largest impact.

Introduction

Many rural communities in Africa are characterized by their remoteness, high levels of poverty and unemployment, low level of skills and education, and a high dependency on natural resources for survival (Ellis, 1999). The majority of high-end ecotourism camps are situated in such remote areas, with little development and very few other employment opportunities for local communities. New threats to traditional rural livelihoods posed by climate change mean that, now more than ever, there is an urgent need for alternative – and sustainable – income-generating opportunities, and the panacea is sometimes thought to reside in high-end ecotourism[1] (Ellis, 1999; Nelson et al., 2009).

High-end ecotourism operations in protected areas often claim to share the benefits of ecotourism with surrounding local communities and to ensure a "trickle down" effect of the revenues that result from such operations through community engagement models (Mitchell & Ashley, 2010; Spenceley, 2008). These ecotourism businesses claim to offer efficient, effective and sustainable alternatives that generate meaningful revenue and help to make conservation economically viable through the economic engine of tourism (Mitchell &

Ashley, 2010). The benefits to local rural communities are said to include employment, other income-generating opportunities (both direct and indirect), training, skills development and improved social welfare (Jamieson, Goodwin, & Edmunds, 2004; Mitchell & Ashley, 2010; Spenceley, 2008). At the same time, these economic models are also claimed to promote an appreciation of biological diversity and the conservation of natural resources in rural communities (Bookbinder, Dinerstein, Rijal, Cauley, & Rajouria, 1998; Kiss, 2004; Shibia, 2010; Sifuna, 2010). In practice, these benefits can be challenging to implement, and to date, no multi-country study has attempted to assess the efficacy of these claims across a variety of circumstances.

In the past, communities were able to survive through subsistence farming and, in some cases, government rations and grants (Ellis, 1999). As population growth has escalated, people are finding it harder to survive in this manner and there is a greater need for permanent employment and a steady income (Alexander, 2000; Barrow & Fabricius, 2002). The increasing role of climate change and its effect on subsistence lifestyles is also resulting in a growing dependence on the market economy and a declining ability of traditional subsistence lifestyles to sustain rural populations and satisfy their development aspirations (Ellis, 1999). There are studies indicating that climate change is having a real impact on rural Africa, in terms of changes in climate variability, seasonal shifts and precipitation patterns, and that this situation will deteriorate further (Morton, 2007; Nelson et al., 2009). The biggest vulnerability is that the weather affects the developing countries' main economic activities: farming, fishing and tourism. It is therefore critical that land use choices are made with these factors in mind, and that there is a diversification of rural livelihoods to assist in lowering the risk faced by rural households (Ellis, 1999, 2000; Ellis & Freeman, 2004).

Ecotourism's promised employment and income impacts (Mitchell & Ashley, 2010), as well as the social welfare impacts and limited impacts on the environment, mean that it has the potential to offer a viable and sustainable land use alternative in these remote rural areas. An essential element is to ensure that communities in these areas do in fact receive tangible benefits from ecotourism, and that, therefore, they have a vested interest in conservation of the land and a reduced incentive to engage in alternative land uses, e.g. agriculture, mining and/or livestock farming (Mbaiwa, 2005; Tapela & Omara-Ojungu, 1999). Langholz (1999, in Stronza & Gordillo, 2008) argues that the income earned from ecotourism can minimize or eliminate dependence on activities that exploit natural resources, such as commercial agriculture and cattle farming. It can also lower the risk associated with these weather- and market-dependent income sources.

In 2009, sub-Saharan Africa's travel and tourism was expected to generate US$66 billion of economic activity (US$22 billion directly, or 2.2% of total GDP), and 1.7% of total direct employment (World Travel and Tourism Council [WTTC], 2010). Beyond direct job creation, the infrastructure requirements of tourism (buildings, roads, parks, hotels and airports) mean that there is a direct capital injection and a resultant job creation in tourism that extends beyond the service and hospitality sectors (Ashley & Roe, 2002; Mitchell & Ashley, 2010; Spenceley, 2008). The reinvestment of ecotourism funds into other economic activities by rural villages is an important aspect of community development, and through this, ecotourism can be described as one of the tools promoting local economic development in rural areas (Mbaiwa, 2008). High-end ecotourism, however, is also vulnerable to a number of factors, such as changing exchange rates, political instability, crime rates, impact of air travel on climate change and the costs associated with this, as well as the needs and constantly changing desires of tourists (Ashley & Roe, 2002; Zhao & Brent Ritchie, 2007).

Loss of access to land can impose a number of direct and indirect costs on local communities (Ashley & Roe, 2002; Barrow & Murphree, 2001; Mbaiwa, 2005; Steenkamp & Uhr, 2000). Poor people use natural resources in a number of ways that help them to diversify their livelihoods: trading (e.g. wood, wild fruits), supplying inputs (e.g. for craft making), and for formal or informal employment (e.g. in tourism) (Roe & Elliott, 2006). There are also opportunity costs of foregone opportunities due to a lack of access to natural resources within a protected area, including the protection against shocks – both economic and natural shocks – that could affect the survival of marginal households (Roe & Elliott, 2006). Diversification of livelihoods through, for example, employment in ecotourism can help community members lower this risk (Ellis, 1999; Ellis & Freeman, 2004).

It is frequently argued that employment in ecotourism operations increases people's awareness of the importance of conservation (Shibia, 2010; Walpole & Goodwin, 2001). Stem, Lassoie, Lee, Deshler, and Schelhas (2003), however, found that employment in tourism had minimal influence on conservation perspectives. Tessema, Ahsenafi, Lilieholm, and Leader-Williams (2007) found that local residents generally held positive attitudes towards wildlife and nearby protected areas in their study around four protected areas in Ethiopia. The same finding was established by Mehta and Heinen (2001) for communities around two parks in Nepal. The main reasons given for the importance of wildlife in the Ethiopian study included its attraction to tourists, the hunting opportunities during drought, the enjoyment derived from wildlife viewing and its value for future generations (Tessema et al., 2007). There are, however, studies that do not find a correlation between tourism/economic benefits and more positive attitudes towards conservation (Walpole & Goodwin, 2001), or that suggest that economic benefits alone are not sufficient to encourage conservation (Stem et al., 2003; Stronza & Pêgas, 2008). Stem et al. (2003) found a positive association between tourism employment and conservation practices, while the associations were less clear for conservation perspectives. They also found that participation in indirect tourism benefits showed stronger associations with pro-conservation perspectives than did participation in direct tourism benefits (Stem et al., 2003). Stronza and Gordillo (2008, p. 450) also found that non-economic benefits, such as new skills, broader experiences in managing people and projects, strengthened abilities to negotiate with outsiders, and expanded circles of contacts and support for community efforts, can also influence the chances for conservation.

This study looks at the various factors that impacted on attitudes to tourism and conservation in three southern African countries. An understanding of what factors influence community members' attitudes to tourism and conservation can assist in managing expectations, and it can also be used in education and awareness-raising programmes to improve attitudes and to garner support from communities living in and around conservation areas (Allendorf et al., 2006; Sifuna, 2010; Simelane, Kerley, & Knight, 2006). This understanding is also important because, as pointed out by Emerton (1999), benefit distribution is a necessary, but in itself not necessarily sufficient, condition for communities to engage in wildlife conservation.

De Boer and Baquete (1998) also found that the attitude of local people was influenced predominantly by the degree of crop damage (i.e. the level of human–animal conflict). Efforts to mitigate the human–wildlife conflict would go a long way in assisting with reducing the negative impacts of living alongside wildlife and in the promotion of conservation and ecotourism as viable land uses in rural areas. Numerous other studies (Baral & Heinen, 2007; Hill, 2004; Newmark, Manyanza, Gamassa, & Sariko, 1994; Shibia, 2010) have looked at the effect of human–wildlife conflict on attitudes towards conservation and tourism. In general, these studies focused on one study area and did not compare community attitudes between different countries and conservation areas. The present study compares such attitudes in three southern African countries: Malawi, Botswana and Namibia.

In the majority of rural areas in southern Africa, there are few income-generating and employment opportunities (Ashley & Roe, 2002; Bourdreaux & Nelson, 2011; Scherl et al., 2004; Spenceley & Goodwin, 2007). Many people live a subsistence lifestyle, resulting in those people who are employed being heavily relied upon for support by a large number of people (Ashley & Roe, 2002; Tao & Wall, 2009). Together with this, the impact of HIV/AIDS and the resulting number of orphans has further increased dependency levels in rural areas, with anyone who can find employment supporting a number of other people, not only children and spouses (Drimie, 2002; Snyman, forthcoming). As will be elaborated on in the Results section, the economic impact of job creation and employment in marginal societies is particularly important due to the size of households supported by each wage earner (Salole, 2003).

This study contributes to a greater understanding of the role of high-end ecotourism employment in poverty reduction and its role in the understanding and appreciation of conservation and tourism. This is done through an analysis of extensive primary data collected from 812 socio-economic surveys conducted in the three southern African countries of Malawi, Botswana and Namibia. According to Goodwin and Santilli (2009, p. 9), there has been limited research into the effectiveness of using tourism to deliver economic development and conservation objectives (Bookbinder et al., 1998; Lepp, 2007; Shibia, 2010; Walpole & Goodwin, 2001).

The tourism sites in this study fall into the high-end category by virtue of the accommodation rate charged to guests (in the range of US$220 to US$1484 per person sharing per night) and the low density of beds and vehicles relative to the traversing area. Training and skills development is aimed at offering excellent service standards, due to the high accommodation rate charged and the concomitant high expectations of visitors at these camps. Exclusivity, privacy and attention to detail are characteristics of high-end ecotourism products. This means that the tourism industry is employment-intensive and offers permanent employment, as opposed to other industries in these areas that frequently offer only seasonal employment (Mitchell & Ashley, 2010).

Area of study and methodology

In this study, extensive socio-economic surveys were conducted in camps run by Wilderness Safaris[2] in Malawi, Namibia and Botswana. A total of 194 staff surveys were conducted in six high-end ecotourism camps, constituting a majority of the staff in these camps (ranging from 58% to 74%). A further 618 community surveys were conducted in 25 rural communities, covering 13 different ethnic groups and an average of 28% of households (ranging from 10% to 49%). Wilderness Safaris was chosen for the study as it offers a consistent set of objectives over a broad area in southern Africa. This allows for a comparison of the interactions under changing circumstances, such as due to the varying population density of the area surrounding the conservation area, tenure arrangements and employment in high-end ecotourism. Table 1 summarizes the camps, and communities and ethnic groups surveyed in each country.

The surveys were conducted by both male and female interviewers, and local translators were used in circumstances where the respondent could not speak or understand English. The surveys contained questions relating to demographics, social welfare and

Table 1. The camps, communities and ethnic groups surveyed in each country.[a]

Country	List of camps surveyed	Land ownership	List of communities surveyed	Ethnic groups surveyed
Malawi	Mvuu Camp, Mvuu Wilderness Lodge	National Parks owns the land (*Government*)	Balaka District, bordering Liwonde National Park	Lomwe, Yao, Nyanja, Tumbuka, Tonga
Botswana	Duba Plains, Vumbura Plains, Little Vumbura	Kwedi Concession where camps situated is owned by the Okavango Community Trust (*Community concession*)	Okavango Community Trust (OCT) villages – Seronga, Gunotsoga, Beetsha, Eretsha, Gudigwa	Bayei, Hambukushu, Basarwa, Bakgalagadi
Namibia	Skeleton Coast Camp	Ministry of Environment and Tourism runs Skeleton Coast National Park (*Government*). *Voluntary community levies are paid to the four adjacent conservancies.*	Okondjombo Conservancy; Purros Conservancy; Sanitatas Conservancy; Orupembe Conservancy	Herero, Himba, Damara, Riemvasmaker

[a]For more information on the camps surveyed, see www.wilderness-safaris.com.

living standards, education, employment patterns, income and expenses, health and safety, and attitudes towards tourism and conservation. Each survey was conducted verbally, with the interviewer completing the questionnaire survey during the interview. Each survey took approximately 20–30 minutes when conducted in English, and approximately 25–45 minutes when translated, depending on the respondent's educational level.

All staff who were on duty and available for interview were surveyed, while community households were selected at random, with one member of each household being surveyed. A household is defined here as a group of people living together and sharing income and expenses (Mohr & Fourie, 2003 in Simelane et al., 2006). The surveys consisted of a structured set of questions, with the majority being close-ended questions, with some questions having the option for further explanation. Interviewers introduced themselves to respondents and explained the purpose of the research: a study on the socio-economic impact of conservation and tourism on surrounding communities. The interviewers would have been associated with Wilderness Safaris because of the use of their vehicles in some areas and through the introduction process and explanation relating to the conduct of the surveys, and this may have biased responses. It is impossible to predict the direction of the bias, however, as some respondents may have been negative in order to ensure changes or positive in order to win favour with the private-sector operator in the area (Allendorf et al., 2006).

Respondents were told that the surveys were confidential and their participation in answering all questions in the survey was voluntary. This resulted in some questions not being answered. Non-response to questions did not cluster on particular questions, however, as no particular question had a greater non-response rate than any other question.

Two types of community member are identified in this study: those employed in a high-end ecotourism operation and those living adjacent to a conservation area where the high-end ecotourism operation is situated. This allowed for a comparison of the average community member's household income and that of someone employed in high-end ecotourism, in order to ascertain the influence of this employment.

The IUCN (International Union for Conservation of Nature) defines six categories of protected areas worldwide, depending on the level of protection and use. The categories range from areas under strict protection with limited public access, to areas where recreation is encouraged but there is no resource development and to multiple-use areas that allow resource utilization, recreation and nature conservation (Dudley, 2008). This study includes areas specifically set aside for conservation, which in some cases has resulted in the relocation of local people who were living in the area and who, historically, used the natural resources in the area. It also includes the Namibian conservancy approach, where people live inside the protected area and have access to the natural resources.

Varying opportunity costs of conservation existed in the three countries surveyed. These costs included the income lost due to using the land for conservation or ecotourism as opposed to another use, as well as the costs arising from the human–wildlife conflict that results from conservation (Baral & Heinen, 2007; Hill, 2004; Scherl et al., 2004). Namibia, for example, has a very low opportunity cost of conservation due to the arid nature of most of the country, resulting in few alternative land use options. The population density in the northwest of Namibia in Kunene region, where the research was conducted, was 0.6 persons per square kilometre (Namibia Population and Housing Census, 2001). The study area of Balaka district in Malawi had a population density of 144 persons per square kilometre (Malawi Population and Housing Census, 2008), and it had a high opportunity cost of land set aside for conservation due to the high rainfall and fertile soils, which allows for a number of different land uses. This made it more important that ecotourism operations provided tangible, sustainable benefits to surrounding communities. The population density in the study area of west Ngamiland in Botswana was 2 persons per square kilometre (Botswana Census, 2001).

A drawback of questionnaires can be that people are unwilling to express negative opinions or attitudes to a third party, and they may be reluctant to confess to illegal exploitation practices, such as snaring or collecting plants in a restricted area. However, questionnaires are often a cost-effective method of research (De Boer & Baquete, 1998). This needs to be kept in mind when analyzing the data collected on opinions and attitudes to tourism and conservation in this study. There were negative attitudes expressed by respondents that would indicate that in fact some respondents did not mind expressing negative opinions, and this suggests that the opinions expressed largely were honest.

All data collected were analyzed using SPSS, version 12, and a combination of descriptive statistics and t-tests was used in the analysis.

Socio-economic survey results

Demography

For the three countries, the mean age in years of the respondents was 32.97 in Botswana (min. 17, max. 101), 38.21 in Malawi (min. 15, max. 98) and 33.75 in Namibia (min. 15, max. 93). On average, the community respondents (M = 35.7 years) were slightly older than the staff respondents (M = 33.63 years). The gender of respondents is shown in Table 2.

In Botswana, the majority of the respondents were single (67%), while in Malawi and Namibia, most were married (81% and 42%, respectively), with the figures including traditional and civil marriages. For those employed in high-end ecotourism, the majority were single (51%), whereas most of the community respondents were married (45%).

The 21–30 year age group had the highest average number of years in education (6.82 years), as opposed to older age groups, such as 41–50 year group, who had an average of only 2.57 years in education. For all age groups above the 21–30 year group, the mean number of years in education was lower than 6.82, with the 15–20 year group having a mean of 6.25 years in education. The 21–30 year group also had the lowest percentage (17%) of uneducated respondents (0 years of education) as opposed to the 31–40 year group with 38% uneducated, the 41–50 year group with 52% uneducated, the 51–60 year group with 58% uneducated and the 61–70 year group with 75% uneducated. These results are relevant to the later assessment of the impacts of education and age on attitudes to tourism and conservation, and to the associated recommendations for garnering community support for biodiversity conservation and ecotourism as a viable land use.

Number of dependents

In the surveys conducted for this study, there was an average of 5.81 dependents per community respondent in the three countries studied. For respondents employed in a

Table 2. Gender of the respondents in each country.

Country	Male	Female
Botswana	44%	56%
Malawi	50%	50%
Namibia	63%	37%

Table 3.   Average number of dependents among respondents in each country.

Country	Staff ($n = 193$)	Community ($n = 593$)	Average ($n = 786$)
Malawi	7.95 (min. 1, max. 18)	4.24 (min. 0, max. 17)	5.37 (min. 0, max. 18)
Namibia	6.47 (min.1, max. 10)	7.26 (min. 0, max. 30)	7.15 (min. 0, max. 30)
Botswana	7.84 (min. 0, max. 22)	5.08 (min. 0, max. 36)	5.90 (min 0, max. 36)
Average	**7.42**	**5.81**	**6.01**

high-end ecotourism operation, the average number of dependents for the three countries was higher, at 7.42. This difference was statistically significant ($t(348) = 8.760, p < 0.05$). An outlier number of dependents ($n =100$) for one respondent in the Namibian community study tended to skew the data, with this respondent insisting that this was the number of people that he/she supported. If this value is removed, however, then the average number of dependents for the Namibian community was 7.26 (min. 0; max. 30), which is more realistic, and this was used in the comparisons. It was still higher than the average number of dependents for the staff in Namibia (M = 6.47, min. 1; max 10). Table 3 shows the average number of dependents among respondents in each country, and it illustrates that people employed in ecotourism were supporting a large number of people in these remote rural areas.

In terms of the number of people indirectly affected by the high-end ecotourism operations, Table 4 shows the number of people employed in the surveyed camps and also the average number of their dependents used in the calculations. The table also includes an average amount paid by staff directly to their dependents and does not include other amounts paid on behalf of dependents for food, education, clothing and other expenses.

The total of over 2300 people indirectly impacted by employment in the six camps was significant. This figure excludes the multiplier effects of staff spending in their communities (this is beyond the scope of this paper), and it indicates that the social welfare of a large number of people was impacted by high-end ecotourism operations in these remote rural areas. It is important to note here that employment of any kind results in a positive impact on rural communities, but in the study areas discussed here, there were few other viable, sustainable land use options other than ecotourism, highlighting the very important impact of employment in these tourism camps. Tourism is one of the few businesses able to generate income in impoverished rural areas with high unemployment levels and marginal opportunities for agriculture (Ashley & Roe, 2002; Boudreaux & Nelson, 2011; Scherl et al., 2004; Spenceley & Goodwin, 2007).

With respect to the number of children per respondent, it is interesting to note that the mean number of children for those employed in high-end ecotourism was lower (M = 2.51 children; min. 0; max.10) than for community respondents (M = 3.3 children; min. 0; max. 23). Despite all groups having a similar mean age, Malawi as a whole had the highest mean number of children per respondent (3.99 children; min. 0; max. 23), followed by Namibia (3.34 children; min. 0; max. 16) and Botswana (2.23 children; min. 0; max 10).

Household income impacts

Respondents who were employed in high-end ecotourism operations ($n = 189$)[3] on average had a higher total household income (in US dollars[4]) than average community respondents. The mean staff household income was US$ 233.13 (SE = 20.65) and the mean community ($n = 601$) household income was US$ 100.07 (SE = 8.97). This difference was significant ($t(262.7) = -5.910, p < 0.05$, with a medium-sized effect, $r = 0.34$). Six percent of

Table 4. Number of people indirectly affected by ecotourism employment.[a]

Country	Total no. of staff in the surveyed camps	Average monthly wage per staff member (US$)[b]	Average no. of dependents per staff respondent[c]	Total no. of people indirectly impacted by camp employment[d]	Average monthly amount given to dependents per staff respondent (in US$)	Total payments to dependents per month (in US$)[e]	Total number of people lifted above the poverty line ($1.25 per day[f]): staff and dependents[g]
Namibia (1 camp surveyed – 12 beds)	23	271.51	6.47	149	$95.5	$2196.50	172
Botswana (3 camps surveyed – 58 beds)	173	219.18	7.84	1356	$36.54	$6321.42	1529
Malawi (2 camps surveyed – 42 beds)	108	85.59	7.95	858	$5.64	$609.12	966
Average/Total (6 camps – 112 beds)	**304**	**195.53**	**7.42**	**2363**	**$45.89**	**$13, 950.56**	**2667**

[a]All figures relating to the number of people indirectly impacted, as well as those lifted out of poverty, have been rounded up.

[b]Over and above wages, employees receive gratuities (not included in this analysis) as well as other non-monetary benefits of employment, such as accommodation, food, uniform, and a company HIV awareness/testing and education programme. These figures are based preliminary data from socio-economic surveys conducted by Snyman (forthcoming) and are not official wage figures.

[c]This result is calculated by multiplying the number of people employed in the surveyed camps by the calculated average number of staff dependents.

[d]These figures were obtained from the expenses section of the surveys conducted in the countries. All figures were converted to US$ for comparison purposes using www.xe.com exchange rates on 2 December 2010.

[e]These figures were calculated by multiplying the total number of staff by the average monthly payment to dependents.

[f]World Bank (2011) poverty line figure.

[g]The number of people lifted out of poverty figure is greater than the number of people indirectly impacted, because that figure includes the staff themselves (who have also been lifted out of poverty), whereas the dependents figure does not.

community respondents said that they had no household income, and 59% had a monthly household income of less than $50. In total, 89% of the community respondents had a monthly household income of less than $200.

The population densities of the three study areas varied: in Namibia, it was 0.6 persons per square kilometre; in Botswana, it was 2 persons per square kilometre; and in Malawi, it was 144 persons per square kilometre. A t-test was used to compare the total household income (in US$) in the most densely populated area (Malawi: $n = 246$) with the least densely populated area (Namibia: $n = 104$). This showed that the highly populated area had a lower mean household income (M = US$44.11, SE = 5.058) than the less densely populated area (M = US$263.47, SE = 39.826). This result was significant ($t(106.3) = 5.464$, $p < 0.05$; a medium-to-large effect size was calculated, $r = 0.46$). Despite the fact that this result is significant, there are a number of other important factors, aside from population density, that need to be considered here. For instance, the GDP per capita in Namibia is much higher than that in Malawi. Comparing the impact of population density in Namibia ($n = 104$; density = 0.9 persons per km^2; M = US$263.47, SE = 39.826) with that of Botswana[5] ($n = 251$, density = 3 persons per km^2; M = US$87.2; SE = 10.482) also produced a significant difference ($t(117.531) = 4.28$, $p < 0.05$), but the effect size was small, $r = 0.12$, indicating that on its own, population density did not significantly impact on household income. Other factors, such as GDP per capita, governance and local economic development, need to be taken into consideration (but are beyond the scope of this paper).

A total of 33% of the staff respondents had had a permanent job before. For 77% of the staff respondents, their current job in high-end ecotourism was therefore their first permanent job. For the community respondents, only 22% had ever had a permanent job in their lives, and only 12% were currently employed. This figure, however, excludes those community members who were not at home because they were in full-time employment.

For 77% of the staff respondents, the salary that they earned in high-end ecotourism was the sole source of income in the household. For 95% of the staff respondents too, their salary was the main source of income in the household. The mean number of household income sources for staff respondents ($n = 194$) was 1.24 (min. 1; max. 3), and for community respondents ($n = 617$), it was 1.33 (min. 0; max. 4). The main sources of household income for community respondents were casual labour, family/spouse, pension (in Namibia) and using/selling natural resources for farming, weaving, thatching, etc. The majority of community respondents relied on subsistence farming for the provision of food for the household, and in Malawi, many respondents relied on cash crops, such as cotton and tobacco.

Social welfare impacts

Cattle are generally regarded as a sign of wealth in most African communities (Low, Kemp, & Doran, 1980). In Botswana and Malawi, staff had more cattle per household on average than did the community members. This was not the case in Namibia, however, where community respondents had on average more cattle per household (M = 57.36) than did staff members (M = 41.41). This is most likely due to the fact that the community respondents in the Skeleton Coast concession area were predominantly Himba (semi-nomadic people who rely on livestock for their survival). In rural areas of Africa, cattle often represent a "pension" system for households, as they are a form of wealth and can be sold to provide very important household income (Low et al., 1980). Staff members' ability to afford cattle assists in ensuring future financial security as well as in increasing

Table 5. Percentage of respondents who owned or had access to a mobile phone.

Country	Staff (n = 194)	Community (n = 618)
Malawi	72%	27%
Namibia	94%	15%
Botswana	94%	46%
Average	**87%**	**29%**

social status. Further, 87% of staff members had access to, or owned, a mobile phone in their household, compared with only 29% of community respondents (see Table 5).

Only 4% of the community respondents owned, or had access to, a motor car in their household, whereas 21% of the staff respondents did. Table 6 shows the top categories of monthly expenditures as a percentage of the total monthly household expenditures. Average expenditure patterns of staff and community members show that staff members spent a smaller percentage of their salaries on food, and more income on "luxury goods", as opposed to community members who spent more on "necessities" (e.g. paraffin, transport). It is argued (Namibian Central Bureau of Statistics, 2006), therefore, that the greater the percentage of household income spent on food, the "poorer" the household as they have less available income for "luxury goods".

Attitudes to tourism and conservation

Comparison of data collected from staff employed in ecotourism operations and random community members supports the argument that employment in tourism increases people's awareness of the importance of conservation, although a significant difference was not found ($t = 2.388$, df $= 772$, $p > 0.05$). The majority of community members did think that it was important to conserve natural resources (average 84%), though the average was

Table 6. Top categories of monthly household expenses as a percentage of total expenditure.

Expenditure	Percentage of total	Expenditure	Percentage of total
Botswana *community*	(n = 261)	Botswana *staff*	(n = 101)
Food	28	Food	25
Casual labour	11	Savings	12
Toiletries	8	Education/school fees	11
Gas/paraffin/candles	8	Money to dependents	8
Fuel expenses	7	Mobile phone airtime	8
Malawi *community*	(n = 251)	Malawi *staff*	(n = 76)
Food	46	Food	39
Loans	20	Education	12
Cleaning materials	6	Money to dependents	7
Clothes	6	Accommodation/rent	7
Paraffin	4	Mobile phone airtime	6
Namibia *community*	(n = 106)	Namibia *staff*	(n = 17)
Food	35	Food	18
Transport	12	Money to dependents	16
Cleaning materials	9	Accommodation/rent	8
Savings	8	Savings	6
Alcohol	8	Accounts	6
Toiletries	8	Toiletries	6

Table 7.   Percentage of respondents who felt that conservation was important.

Country	Staff (n = 194)	Community (n = 618)
Malawi	99%	80%
Namibia	100%	91%
Botswana	98%	82%
Average	**99%**	**84%**

not as high as for those employed in ecotourism (99%). The main reasons given by staff respondents for the importance of conservation were for tourism and for future generations. Only 13% of the community members surveyed (n = 618) said that they did not think that conservation was important. Only two (1%) of the staff surveyed (n = 194) said that they did not think that conservation was important. For community members, the most positive responses were in Namibia (91%), with Botswana (82%) and Malawi (80%) also having a majority of community respondents feeling that conservation was important (Table 7).

Respondents were asked whether or not they considered that Wilderness Safaris and the tourism camps in the conservation areas where they lived had created jobs for local people. Eighty-eight percent of the staff respondents said that they felt that the camps did create jobs for local people, whereas only 62% of the community respondents agreed with that. Respondents were asked which land use they felt created the most jobs for local people in the area. Forty-seven percent of community respondents said that agriculture created the most jobs, followed by tourism (24%). For staff respondents, the majority said tourism (66%), followed by agriculture (22%). For the land use that benefited local people the most, the community respondents said that this was agriculture (61%), followed by tourism (14%). Half (50%) of the staff respondents said that tourism benefited local people the most, followed by agriculture (33%). These results are not unexpected, as it makes intuitive sense that those employed in tourism will see a greater, more tangible benefit from it than those who do not receive direct benefits. It also supports the view that employment in high-end ecotourism increases people's positive perceptions of conservation and tourism as a land use. The importance of subsistence agriculture for the survival of the majority of households in rural areas explains the importance placed on agriculture as a land use.

Table 8 shows that 81% of the staff surveyed felt that tourism helped to reduce poverty in the area. Fifty percent of the community respondents felt that tourism reduced poverty, with Botswana having the highest percentage (70%) of community respondents responding positively to this.

Impact of human–animal conflict on attitudes to tourism and conservation

Analysis was undertaken of the impact of problems with wild animals on attitudes to tourism and conservation. Ninety-seven percent of the respondents who said that they did

Table 8.   Percentage of respondents who feel that tourism reduces poverty in the area.

Country	Staff (n = 194)	Community (n = 618)
Malawi	55%	37%
Namibia	100%	42%
Botswana	87%	70%
Average	**81%**	**50%**

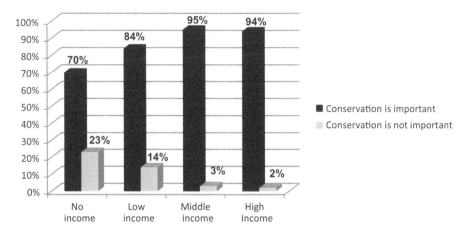

Figure 1.   Importance of conservation to different income groups.

not have problems with wild animals felt that conservation was important, as opposed to only 85% of those who said that they did have problems with wild animals. Problems with wild animals also seemed to have influenced attitudes towards tourism. Eighty-two percent of those with no problems felt that tourism created jobs for local people, as opposed to 65% of those who did have problems. Sixty-nine percent of those who had no problems with wild animals felt that tourism camps reduced poverty in the area, and this compared with 55% among those who did have these problems.

Impact of level of household income on attitudes to tourism and conservation

Respondents' total household income (in US$) was divided into the following categories: no income ($0, $n = 30$), low income ($1–100, $n = 467$), middle income ($101–350, $n = 228$) and high income ($351 and above, $n = 65$). Twenty-two respondents did not answer the section on household income, so did not fall into any of these categories. The importance of conservation to the four categories was then assessed. As anticipated, the middle- and high-income groups had more respondents who thought that conservation was important (95% and 94%, respectively). The group with no income had the lowest percentage (70%) who felt that conservation was important, with 84% in the low-income group feeling that conservation was important. In the four categories from no income up to high income, the percentage of respondents who felt that conservation was *not important* was as follows: 23%, 14%, 3% and 2% (Figure 1).

Education and employment impacts on perceptions of conservation and tourism

The results indicate that staff ($n = 193$) on average had a higher number of years of education (M $= 8.8$ years, SD $= 3.48$) than the average community member ($n = 617$) (M $= 4.82$ years, SD $= 4.38$). This result was found to be significant ($t(399) = -12.983$, $p < 0.05$), with a large effect ($r = 0.54$). This highlights the importance of education in securing permanent employment. Consideration was given to the impact of education on perceptions of the importance of conservation. In the survey, it was found that those who felt that conservation was important ($n = 704$) had a mean of 6.26 years of education, while those who did not think that conservation was important ($n = 83$) had a mean of 2.42 years of education. To ascertain the impact of employment and education on perceptions of conservation, a separate assessment was made only of staff members.[6] Among this group, it was found that those who felt that conservation was important ($n = 191$) had a mean of 9.31 years of education, as opposed to those who did not feel that conservation was important or who were not sure ($n = 3$), who had a mean of 6.33 years of education. In general, it appears that education per se does play an important role in positive perceptions of conservation.

When the sample was divided into those who were employed (in any job, not exclusively high-end ecotourism) and those who were unemployed, 96% of the employed respondents felt that conservation was important, in contrast to 83% of the unemployed respondents. Interestingly, of the unemployed respondents, 14% felt that conservation was not important, and only 2% of the employed respondents felt that it was not important, with the remainder not answering, not knowing or being undecided. This result suggests that permanent employment (and the security of monthly income) has a positive relationship with positive perceptions.

Impact of age on attitudes to conservation

In this study, it was also found that respondents who were younger ($M = 34.83$ years, $SE = 0.510$) were more positive about conservation and tourism than those who were older ($M = 38.21$ years; $SE = 1.903$). This difference, however, was not significant.

Discussion

Although the analysis focused on the staff of one high-end ecotourism operator, the camps and areas surveyed represented a wide cross-section of ecotourism operations under varying tenure arrangements, with varying ethnic groups, differing population densities and differential rates charged to visitors. There is applicability, therefore, to a wide spectrum of high-end ecotourism operators in southern Africa as well as to other operators engaging with communities (e.g. in Canada and Australia).

While conducting the surveys, it was clearly evident that permanent employment (irrespective of the form) and a monthly salary were important in terms of social welfare, financial security, development and empowerment (Mitchell & Ashley, 2010). The security of a steady income allowed households to invest in non-essential goods, such as higher education, infrastructure, mobile phones, and other "luxury" goods, all of which were seen to improve social welfare and status in the community. These "luxury" goods could be said to improve social welfare, often through improvements in communication and transport. When conducting the surveys, the author often had community respondents saying that the high-end ecotourism staff had "nice houses" and could afford to "buy nice things". A number of staff members could afford "luxury goods", such as generators in areas with no electricity, better education for family members, mobile phones, televisions and motor cars. Staff members usually used local builders to construct their homes: this created a multiplier effect in the rural communities that went beyond the direct payment of wages and salaries to staff members (Mitchell & Ashley, 2010), but this is beyond the scope of this paper. The perception in the communities that was noted by the author was that employment in high-end ecotourism afforded one the opportunity to have a better general standard of living than the average community member. Other, often "unmentioned" benefits associated with tourism employment included the provision of staff accommodation and food, flexible work schedules and part-time employment (Meyer, 2008, p. 567; Mitchell & Ashley, 2010; Spenceley, 2008). The high percentage of staff respondents who had never had a permanent job before indicates the importance of the training and skills development obtained from jobs in high-end ecotourism in these remote areas.

In Botswana and Malawi, the average number of dependents for respondents employed in high-end ecotourism was much higher than that for community members, indicating the importance of salaries earned in high-end ecotourism in terms of supporting a large number of people in these areas. Support was mostly given through buying food and paying for education for dependents. In Namibia, the situation was different, largely due to the fact that the Himba people living in the Skeleton Coast concession area lived in large extended family groups, with many people living together and sharing income and expenses (the mean for the community (including the outlier figure) was 8.1 dependents and excluding the outlier of 100, it was 7.26, min. 0 and max. 100).

To a certain degree, the link between employment and gender was determined by local cultural traditions, where women stay at home to look after the children and homes, and men seek employment. This would also explain the greater percentage of females in the community surveys (also evidenced by Odindi & Ayirebi, 2010). It also illustrates the important need to focus on engaging specifically with women with respect to conservation and natural resource use and to the impact of households on biodiversity conservation, as they are more frequently the ones collecting and using natural resources in the rural areas (Allendorf et al., 2006; Odindi & Ayirebi, 2010).

As was expected, respondents employed in high-end ecotourism operations generally had more positive attitudes towards conservation and tourism, as they were directly receiving tangible benefits from it (Stem et al., 2003; Walpole & Goodwin, 2001). What was surprising was the high percentage of community respondents who felt that conservation was important, despite incurring significant costs in terms of loss of livestock and crops from wild animals, as well as a loss of, or reduced access to, natural resources (also evidenced by De Boer & Baquete, 1998; Driscoll, Hunt, Honey, & Durham, 2011; Mehta & Heinen, 2001; Sekhar, 2003). Education appears to be one of the key factors in garnering community support for, and understanding of, the importance of conservation and tourism as an alternative land use (Gadd, 2005; Larson, 2010; Shibia, 2010; Stem et al., 2003; Teye, Sönmez, & Sirakaya, 2002). In line with this study, Allendorf et al. (2006) also found a positive correlation between number of years of education and positive attitudes towards protected areas in Upper Myanmar. Mehta and Heinen (2001) also found in their Nepal study that high school graduates were in a better position to understand the importance of conservation areas, and this resulted in positive attitudes. In this study, larger households tended to be more positive about conservation than smaller households, but this difference was not found to be significant. Tessema et al. (2007) also found that larger families valued protected areas more.

Younger respondents were more positive about conservation and tourism than older respondents, though the difference was not significant and is possibly due to the higher education levels of younger respondents, rather than the actual age. Shibia (2010) found a significant difference in the relationship between the age of the respondents and their attitudes to conservation around the Marsabit National Park in Kenya. As was found in this study, he found that young respondents were more positive towards conservation (Shibia, 2010). Tessema et al. (2007) found the opposite: they found that older residents valued protected areas more. De Boer and Baquete (1998) found no significant influence of household size, ethnic group, religion, gender or educational level on attitudes to the protected area in their Mozambique study.

De Boer and Baquete (1998) stated that an awareness of benefits from the conservation area, together with education programmes encouraging the sustainable use of natural resources, could result in an acceptance of restrictions on use. While conducting the surveys for this study, it was evident that unless community members were themselves employed in high-end ecotourism or had a family member employed in ecotourism or conservation, there was limited awareness of the direct, tangible benefits of ecotourism and conservation. Education in this area is critical to the long-term success of conservation as a sustainable land use (a similar result was also found by Tessema et al., 2007). A willingness and eagerness to learn more about conservation and ecotourism was felt in all the communities surveyed. It would appear from the study results that problems with wild animals led to less positive perceptions and attitudes to tourism and conservation (Baral & Heinen, 2007; De Boer & Baquete, 1998; Shibia, 2010), highlighting a role for effective human–animal conflict mitigation measures in improving attitudes (Worah, 2002).

Allendorf et al. (2006) found that socio-economic status significantly affected attitudes towards protected areas, but that perceptions of these protected areas, particularly positive perceptions, were better predictors of attitudes and had a much larger effect on attitudes than socio-economic variables. De Boer and Baquete (1998) found that the income of employed people decreased their dependence on natural resources in the Maputo Elephant Reserve in Mozambique. This possibly also could explain the increased positive attitudes for higher-income groups in this study, as they were not as affected by the negative impacts of conservation areas, such as restrictions on resource use and crop or livestock damage by wild animals, as they had alternative income sources to buy necessities and the associated security of livelihood diversification (Ellis, 1999; Ellis & Freeman, 2004). The results clearly illustrate that households with lower total income tended to feel that conservation was less important than those with a higher total household income.

The direct benefits that ecotourism employees received through their salaries and wages and skills training offered tangible, measurable impacts that could be directly related to conservation. Largely due to the nature of community living, other members of the community were able to see these benefits in the lives of other community members and to relate this to conservation and tourism. Over and above this, a number of community members in this study felt that conservation was important for their children and for future generations. This was a far-sighted approach in traditionally poor, rural communities that are often thought to live in terms of daily survival (this positive attitude was also found by De Boer & Baquete, 1998; Mehta & Heinen, 2001; Sekhar, 2003).

Conclusions

Stronza and Gordillo's respondents remarked that "ecotourism is not a solution to our economic concerns, and it is not a panacea" (2008, p. 459). This is a profound statement that reflects the need to manage community expectations and to ensure that the community does in fact receive tangible benefits from ecotourism. The importance of empowerment and development of rural communities is essential in ensuring the sustainability of ecotourism in rural areas (Alexander, 2000; Grossman & Holden, 2009). Wise investment of community income from ecotourism into sustainable projects is also critical to the long-term success of ecotourism as a land use (Ashley, De Brine, Lehr, & Wilde, 2007). Providing ecotourism employment opportunities for educated youth in rural areas can assist in lessening the move of young people to urban areas in search of employment, and thereby it can assist in keeping rural families closer together. There is, however, the potential negative impact of accelerated population growth around protected areas, which Wittemeyr et al. (2008)

found could lead to increased pressure on natural resources and the availability of land. But their results have since been challenged by Joppa, Loarie, and Pimm (2009), who argue that population growth that does occur near protected areas is likely to result from a general expansion of nearby population centres.[7]

In order to encourage community support for conservation and the consequent protection of natural resources, a direct connection needs to be ascertained between conservation and ecotourism and the benefits that accrue to the community from it, whether collective or individual. The timing of benefit distribution is also important and should be as quick as possible in order to establish a link between income and conservation (Mulonga & Murphy, 2003). Creating awareness of intangible benefits will also assist in establishing links with conservation and ecotourism, e.g. skills training and infrastructure upgrades. While undertaking the surveys for this study, many respondents commented on the improved roads since ecotourism operations had been established, as well as improvements to schools and clinics, and in terms of scholarships, feeding schemes and water provision (Ashley & Roe, 2002).

Reducing poverty in rural areas can help to reduce pressure on biodiversity by reducing the need for unsustainable use, providing opportunities for alternative livelihoods, and by placing people in a position where they can choose to conserve (Walpole & Wilder, 2008), rather than be forced to. Diversification of rural livelihoods will also reduce dependencies, as well as pressure on natural resources (Ellis, 1999; Okello, Buthman, Mapinu, & Kahi, 2011).

The private sector, in the form of high-end ecotourism, has much to offer in the realm of community conservation and high-end ecotourism (Ashley, 2005; Spenceley, 2003). The necessary start-up funding, skills, expertise and marketing capabilities ensure that the business then has a higher likelihood of succeeding (Spenceley, 2003). Essential to this process is the empowerment of local people so that ultimately they can take over the management, operation, as well as potentially, the ownership of the business (Lepp, 2007; Teye et al., 2002). If this does not happen, then ecotourism can serve to entrench rather than alleviate poverty in rural communities, through the restrictions on land use and the damage caused by wild animals on crops and domestic livestock. Mitigation measures to reduce the human–wildlife conflict will improve attitudes to tourism and conservation, and consequently, support for them as viable land uses (Worah, 2002). The private sector has an important role to play in this area in terms of education, training and skills transfer. It is also critical that the private sector partners with a community structure that is efficient, representative and legitimate and that will distribute the benefits equitably (Ashley et al., 2007).

The results in this study show that attitudes of communities around conservation areas differ depending on household income levels, education, population density and age groups. These results are important in terms of managing relations between conservation areas and adjacent communities. Community projects and the establishment of ecotourism operations in rural areas need to be aligned with the expectations of the communities, and be based on the varying income levels, education and general social welfare in the area, and be designed accordingly (Simelane et al., 2006).

Communities are heterogenous in their composition, in the natural resources available to them and in the economic conditions that they face (Barrow & Fabricius, 2002). There is thus no one solution that will work for all communities. There is a need for basic guidelines that cover all community-based natural resource management (CBNRM) areas, and then specific guidelines for countries and within countries, and for specific communities and cultural groups, based on the economic conditions of the area and the alternative income-generating opportunities in the area (Snyman, forthcoming). According to Emerton (1999), community incentives to conserve wildlife, and the various conditions that this depends on, vary at different times for different people. Prevailing economic conditions play an important role in social welfare, and from there, in the economic and financial situation of households. This in turn plays a role in determining households' attitudes to conservation and tourism, which may also vary over time.

If conservation is to remain as a primary land use in a number of rural areas in Africa, then it is important that communities living in and around these areas have an appreciation and understanding of conservation (Alexander, 2000). The introduction, implementation and sustainability of community engagement projects relies heavily on an understanding of the cultural, economic, as well as non-economic characteristics of the communities concerned. It is essential that the differences in communities are understood and taken into consideration in community engagement projects (Simelane et al., 2006).

The results of this study have highlighted the critical importance of tourism employment in remote, rural areas in terms of reducing poverty, improving the social welfare of local communities and promoting biodiversity conservation. The key is to find ways that can increase the impacts of tourism employment, which are limited by the size of the tourism operation (Spenceley & Snyman, forthcoming). Over and above increasing tourism employment, the study's results indicate that financial management training and advice should be given to tourism staff and community members to encourage them to save, reduce debt and invest wisely.

Further research conducted in 2010 in Zambia, Zimbabwe and South Africa will extend this study further and provide a comparative analysis across the region (Snyman, forthcoming).

Acknowledgements

The author gratefully acknowledges financial support from SIDA (Swedish International Development Cooperation Agency) through University of Göteborg in Sweden and the Environmental Policy Research Unit in the School of Economics at the University of Cape Town. Special thanks are due to Wilderness Safaris for the funding, accommodation and transport to conduct the surveys for this research. Thanks to Chris Roche and Derek de la Harpe, and to four anonymous referees for valuable comments, input and guidance.
Thanks to all the interviewers, translators, staff and community members who helped with and/or participated in the surveys for this research.

Notes

1. The term "ecotourism" was coined by Cebellos-Lascurain in 1980 and redefined by him (in Scheyvens, 1999, p. 245) 16 years later as "environmentally responsible, enlightening travel and visitation to relatively undisturbed natural areas in order to enjoy and appreciate nature (and any accompanying cultural features both past and present) that promotes conservation, has low visitor impact, and provides beneficially active socio-economic involvement of local populations" (Salole, 2003).
2. Wilderness Safaris is a private ecotourism company operating over 70 camps in six southern African countries; for more information, see www.wilderness-safaris.com.
3. Seventeen community respondents did not complete the income section, with five staff respondents not giving household income information.
4. All incomes were converted to US dollars for comparison purposes.
5. These two countries have a GDP per capita that is more similar: Namibia $6658, Botswana $10,866.

6. This analysis was done to determine whether or not it was the effect of employment in ecotourism and education from the employer that affected attitudes to conservation, or general education.
7. Other criticisms of Wittemeyr et al.'s (2008) paper can be found in *Conservation and Society* (Vol. 9, Issue 1, 2011).

References

Alexander, S.E. (2000). Resident attitudes toward conservation and black howler monkeys in Belize: The Community Baboon Sanctuary. *Environmental Conservation, 27(4)*, 341–350.

Allendorf, T., Swe, K.K., Oo, T., Htut, Y., Aung, M., Aung, M., et al. (2006). Community attitudes toward three protected areas in Upper Myanmar (Burma). *Environmental Conservation, 33(4)*, 344–352.

Ashley, C. (2005). *Facilitating pro-poor tourism with the private sector: Lessons learned from "pro-poor tourism pilots in southern Africa"* (Working Paper No. 257). London: Overseas Development Institute.

Ashley, C., De Brine, P., Lehr, A., & Wilde, H. (2007). *The role of the tourism sector in expanding economic opportunity* (Corporate Social Responsibility Initiative Report No. 23). Cambridge, MA: Kennedy School of Government, Harvard University.

Ashley, C., & Roe, E. (2002). Making tourism work for the poor: Strategies and challenges in southern Africa. *Development Southern Africa, 19(1)*, 61–82.

Baral, N., & Heinen, J.T. (2007). Resources use, conservation attitudes, management intervention and park-people relations in the Western Terai landscape of Nepal. *Environmental Conservation, 34(1)*, 1–9.

Barrow, E., & Fabricius, C. (2002). Do rural people really benefit from protected areas – rhetoric or reality? *Parks, 12(2)*, 67–79.

Barrow, E., & Murphree, M. (2001). Community conservation: From concept to practice. In D. Hulme & M. Murphree (Eds.), *African wildlife and livelihoods: The promise and performance of community conservation* (pp. 24–37). Oxford: James Currey.

Bookbinder, M.P., Dinerstein, E., Rijal, A., Cauley, H., & Rajouria, A. (1998). Ecotourism's support for biodiversity conservation. *Conservation Biology, 12(6)*, 1399–1404.

Botswana Census. (2001). Retrieved May 11, 2009, www.cso.gov.bw. Botswana: Central Statistics Office.

Boudreaux, K., & Nelson, F. (2011). Community conservation in Namibia: Empowering the poor with property rights. *Economic Affairs, 31(2)*, 17–24.

De Boer, W.F., & Baquete, D.S. (1998). Natural resource use, crop damage and attitudes of rural people in the vicinity of the Maputo Elephant Reserve, Mozambique. *Environmental Conservation, 25(3)*, 208–218.

Drimie, S. (2002). *The impact of HIV/AIDS on rural households and land issues in southern and eastern Africa.* A background paper prepared for the Food and Agricultural Organisation, Sub-Regional Office for Southern and Eastern Africa. Pretoria: Integrated Rural and Regional Development, Human Sciences Research Council. Retrieved June 6, 2011, http://www.oxfam.org.uk/resources/learning/landrights/downloads/hivbackg.pdf

Driscoll, L., Hunt, C., Honey, M., & Durham, W. (2011). *The importance of ecotourism as a development and conservation tool in the Osa Peninsula, Costa Rica.* Report for the Centre of Responsible Tourism (CREST). Retrieved April 5, 2011, http://www.responsibletravel.org/resources/documents/reports/Tinker_Final_Report_MASTER.pdf

Dudley, N. (Ed.). 2008. *Guidelines for applying protected area management categories.* Gland: IUCN.

Ellis, F. (1999). *Rural livelihood diversity in developing countries: Evidence and policy implications* (ODI Natural Resource Perspectives, No. 40). London: Overseas Development Institute. Retrieved May 21, 2010, http://www.odi.org.uk/nrp/40.html

Ellis, F. (2000). The determinants of rural livelihood diversification in developing countries. *Journal of Agricultural Economics, 51*(2), 289–302.

Ellis, F., & Freeman, H.A. (2004). Rural livelihoods and poverty reduction strategies in four African countries. *Journal of Development Studies, 40*(4), 1–30.

Emerton, L. (1999). *The nature of benefits and the benefits of nature: Why wildlife conservation has not economically benefitted communities in Africa. Community conservation research in Africa: Principles and comparative practice* (Paper No. 9). Manchester: Institute for Development Policy and Management, University of Manchester.

Gadd, M. (2005). Conservation outside of parks: Attitudes of local people in Laikipia, Kenya. *Environmental Conservation, 32*(1), 50–63.

Grossman, C., & Holden, P. (2009). Towards transformation: Contractual national parks in South Africa. In H. Suich & B. Child (Eds.), *Evolution and innovation in wildlife conservation: Parks and game ranches to transfrontier conservation areas* (pp. 357–372). London: Earthscan.

Goodwin, H., & Santilli, R. (2009). *Community-based tourism: A success?* (ICRT Occasional Paper No. 11). Leeds: ICRT and GTZ.

Hill, C.M. (2004). Farmers' perspectives of conflict at the wildlife-agriculture boundary: Some lessons learned from African subsistence farmers. *Human Dimensions of Wildlife, 9*(4), 279–286.

Jamieson, W., Goodwin, H., & Edmunds, C. (2004). *Contribution of tourism to poverty alleviation: Pro-poor tourism and the challenge of measuring impacts.* For Transport Policy and Tourism Section, Transport and Tourism Division, UN ESCAP, Bangkok. Retrieved November 11, 2009 http://www.haroldgoodwin.info/resources/povertyallleviation.pdf

Joppa, L.N., Loarie, S.L., & Pimm, S.L. (2009). On population growth near protected areas. *PLoS One, 4*(1), e4279.

Kiss, A. (2004). Is community-based ecotourism a good use of biodiversity funds? *Trends in Ecology and Evolution, 19*(5), 232–237.

Larson, K. (2010). *Attitudes concerning conservation in two different wildlife areas in Kenya* (Student Report No. 320). Uppsala: Department of Animal Environment and Health, Ethology and Animal Welfare Programme, Swedish University of Agricultural Sciences.

Lepp, A. (2007). Resident's attitudes toward tourism in Bigodi village, Uganda. *Tourism Management, 28*, 876–885.

Low, A.R.C., Kemp, R.L., & Doran, M.H. (1980). Cattle wealth and cash needs in Swaziland: Price response and rural development implications. *Journal of Agricultural Economics, 31*(2), 225–236.

Malawi Population and Housing Census. (2008). *Preliminary report.* Zomba: National Statistical Office.

Mbaiwa, J. (2005). Wildlife resource utilization at Moremi Game Reserve and Khwai community area in the Okavango Delta, Botswana. *Journal of Environmental Management, 77*(2), 144–156.

Mbaiwa, J. (2008). The realities of ecotourism in Botswana. In A. Spenceley (Ed.), *Responsible tourism: Critical issues for conservation and development* (pp. 205–224). London: Earthscan.

Mehta, J.N., & Heinen, J.T. (2001). Does community-based conservation shape favourable attitudes among locals? An empirical study from Nepal. *Environmental Management, 28*(2), 165–177.

Meyer, D. (2008). Pro-poor tourism: From leakages to linkages. A conceptual framework for creating linkages between the accommodation sector and "poor" neighbouring communities. *Current Issues in Tourism, 10*, 558–583.

Mitchell, J., & Ashley, C. (2010). *Tourism and poverty reduction: Pathways to prosperity.* London: Earthscan.

Morton, J.F. (2007). The impact of climate change on smallholder and subsistence agriculture. *PNAS, 104*(50), 19680–19685.

Mulonga, S., & Murphy, C. (2003). *Spending the money: The experience of conservancy benefit distribution in Namibia up to mid-2003* (DEA Research Discussion Paper No. 63). Windhoek: DEA.

Namibian Central Bureau of Statistics. (2006). *Namibia household income and expenditure survey (NHIES 2003/2004).* Windhoek: National Planning Commission.

Namibia Population and Housing Census. (2001). Kunene Region, Census Indicators. Retrieved August 2, 2011, http://www.npc.gov.na/census/index.htm

Nelson, G.C., Rosegrant, M.W., Koo, J., Robertson, R., Sulser, T., Zhu, T., et al. (2009). *Climate change: Impact on agriculture and costs of adaptation* (Food Policy Report). Washington, DC: International Food Policy Research Institute.

Newmark, W.D., Manyanza, D.N., Gamassa, D-G.M., & Sariko, H.I. (1994). The conflict between wildlife and local people living adjacent to the protected areas in Tanzania: Human density as a predictor. *Conservation Biology, 8*(1), 249–255.

Odindi, J.O., & Ayirebi, G.K. (2010). Communities and conservation: In search for a win-win situation in the Great Fish River Reserve. *Journal of Sustainable Development in Africa, 12*(1), 13–26.

Okello, M.M., Buthman, E., Mapinu, B., & Kahi, H.C. (2011). Community opinions on wildlife, resource use and livelihood competition in Kimana Group Ranch near Amboseli, Kenya. *The Open Conservation Biology Journal, 5*, 1–12.

Roe, D., & Elliott, J. (2006). Livelihoods and conservation – arguments shaping the debate: Pro-poor conservation: The elusive win-win for conservation and poverty reduction? *Policy Matters, 14*, 53–63.

Salole, M. (2003). *Torra conservancy and tourism development merging two disparate worlds in rural Namibia* (Unpublished master's thesis). School of Management Studies for the Service Sector, University of Surrey, UK.

Scherl, L.M., Wilson, A., Wild, R., Blockhus, J., Franks, P., McNeely, J.A., et al. (2004). *Can protected areas contribute to poverty reduction? Opportunities and limitations*. Gland: IUCN.

Sekhar, N.U. (2003). Local people's attitudes towards conservation and wildlife tourism around Sariska Tiger Reserve, India. *Journal of Environmental Management, 69*, 339–347.

Shibia, M.G. (2010). Determinants of attitudes and perceptions on resource use and management of Marsabit National Reserve, Kenya. *Journal of Human Ecology, 30*(1), 55–62.

Sifuna, N. (2010). Wildlife damage and its impact on public attitudes toward conservation: A comparative study of Kenya and Botswana, with particular reference to Kenya's Laikipia region and Botswana's Okavango Delta region. *Journal of Asian and African Studies, 45*, 274–296.

Simelane, T.S., Kerley, G.I.H., & Knight, M.H. (2006). Reflections on the relationships between communities and conservation areas of South Africa: The case of five South African National Parks. *Koedoe, 49*(2), 85–102.

Snyman, S. (forthcoming). *The economics of ecotourism: The socio-economic impact of ecotourism on rural communities in 6 southern African countries*. PhD dissertation (in progress). School of Economics, University of Cape Town, South Africa.

Spenceley, A., & Goodwin, H. (2007). Nature-based tourism and poverty alleviation: Impacts of private sector and parastatal enterprises in and around Kruger National Park, South Africa. *Current Issues in Tourism, 10*(2–3), 255–277.

Spenceley, A., & Snyman, S. (forthcoming). Poverty reduction and sustainable tourism in Africa. In K. Bricker, R. Black & S. Cottrell (Eds.), *Ecotourism and sustainable tourism: Transitioning into the new millenium*. Burlington, MA: Jones & Bartlett.

Spenceley, A. (2003). *Tourism, local livelihoods and the private sector in South Africa: Case studies on the growing role of the private sector in natural resource management, sustainable livelihoods in southern Africa* (Research Paper No. 8). Brighton: Institute of Development Studies.

Spenceley, A. (Ed.). (2008). *Responsible Tourism: Critical issues for conservation and development*. London: Earthscan.

Steenkamp, C., & Uhr, J. (2000). *The Makuleke land claim: Power relations and community-based natural resource management* (Evaluating Eden Series: Discussion Paper No. 18). London: IIED.

Stem, C.J., Lassoie, J.P., Lee, D.R., Deshler, D.D., & Schelhas, J.W. (2003). Community participation in ecotourism benefits: The link to conservation practices and perspectives. *Society and Natural Resources, 16*, 387–413.

Stronza, A., & Gordillo, J. (2008). Community views of ecotourism. *Annals of Tourism Research, 35*(2), 448–468.

Stronza, A., & Pêgas, F. (2008). Ecotourism and conservation: Two cases from Brazil and Peru. *Human Dimensions of Wildlife, 13*, 263–279.

Tao, T.C.H., & Wall, G. (2009). Tourism as a sustainable livelihood strategy. *Tourism Management, 30*, 90–98.

Tapela, B.N., & Omara-Ojungu, P.H. (1999). *Towards bridging the gap between wildlife conservation and rural development in post-apartheid South Africa: The case of the Makuleke community and the Kruger National Park.* Retrieved September 19, 2007, http://www.egs.uct.ac.za/sagj/omara.htm

Tessema, M.E., Ahsenafi, Z.T., Lilieholm, R.J., & Leader-Williams, N. (2007). Community attitudes to wildlife conservation in Ethiopia. In S. Weber and D. Harmon (Eds.), *Proceedings of the 2007 George Wright Society Conference "Protected areas in a changing world"* (pp. 287–292). Hancock, MI: The George Wright Society.

Teye, V., Sönmez, S.F., & Sirakaya, E. (2002). Resident attitudes towards tourism development. *Annals of Tourism Research, 29*(3), 668–688.

Walpole, M.J., & Goodwin, H.J. (2001). Local attitudes towards conservation and tourism around Komodo National Park, Indonesia. *Environmental Conservation, 28*(2), 160–166.

Walpole, M.J., & Wilder, L. (2008). Disentangling the links between conservation and poverty reduction in practice. *Oryx, 42*(4), 539–547.

Wittemeyr, G., Elsen, P., Bean, W.T., Coleman, A., Burton, O., & Brashares, J.S. (2008). Accelerated human population growth at protected area edges. *Science, 321*, 123–126.

Worah, S. (2002). The challenges of community-based protected area management. *Parks, 12*(2), 80–90.

World Bank. (2011). Extreme poverty rates continue to fall. Retrieved June 13, 2011, http://data.worldbank.org/news/extreme-poverty-rates-continue-to-fall

World Travel and Tourism Council (WTTC). (2010). Travel and tourism economic impact: Sub-Saharan Africa. Retrieved September 26, 2011, http://www.wttc.org/site_media/uploads/downloads/sub-saharan_africa2.pdf

Zhao, W., & Brent Ritchie, J.R. (2007). Tourism and poverty alleviation: An integrative research framework. *Current Issues in Tourism, 10*(2–3), 119–143.

Tourism and poverty alleviation in Fiji: comparing the impacts of small- and large-scale tourism enterprises

Regina Scheyvens and Matt Russell

School of People, Environment and Planning, Massey University, Palmerston North, New Zealand

This paper explores the pro-poor tourism literature's proposition that businesses "at all levels and scales of operation" can contribute to poverty alleviation, and questions the view that small-scale "alternative" forms of tourism development are preferable in delivering wide-ranging benefits to the poor. Based on research in Fiji, it uses the multidimensional view of poverty modelled on Zhao and Ritchie's integrative research framework for "anti-poverty tourism" that identifies three determinants: "opportunity", "empowerment" and "security". The paper reveals that both small- and large-scale tourism make positive contributions to revenue generation, job creation and community development, but there is considerable potential for local procurement and labour conditions to improve. Poverty has increased in Fiji, despite rising tourism arrivals, but this problem is complex and is linked to agricultural decline. An underlying concern is that tourism policy in Fiji encourages development of large, foreign-owned resorts, while indigenous businesses often do not receive the support they require to be successful in the long term. Thus, indigenous Fijian participation in the tourism sector is predominantly as employees or as recipients of lease monies, and rarely as those directly involved in tourism planning and development, therefore limiting the pro-poor potential of the sector in Fiji.

Introduction

In the last decade, the notion that tourism growth can contribute considerably to poverty alleviation has been pushed strongly in development circles. This is in stark contrast to the 1970s and 1980s, when social scientists rigorously critiqued the nature and impacts of tourism in the "developing world" (Britton, 1982; Bryden, 1973; Hills & Lundgren, 1974). These studies, focused particularly on small-island economies in the Caribbean and Pacific, employed dependency theory to show how western ownership of the tourism industry – from hotels to operators to airlines – perpetuated and reinforced relations of domination and control between "First" and "Third" world nations. At that time, Fiji was said to provide a textbook example of the "structurally dependent economy" (Britton, 1982, p. 24), which – due to inequalities inherent in the world economic system – could only assume a subordinate and largely passive role in tourism development.

Pro-poor tourism (PPT) is built, at least in part, upon the critical response to such characterisations of tourism development. While narratives heavily informed by discourses of dependency rightly emphasised structural inequalities and the political economy of global tourism, they also produced their own set of conceptual limitations that hampered a more nuanced understanding of tourism growth in developing countries. Targeted towards mainstream or mass tourism, they tended to lose some of their explanatory power when faced with small-scale and alternative models of tourism development, which often exhibited a greater degree of indigenous ownership and control (Brohman, 1996; Hampton, 1998). In addition, exposés of the ways in which unequal market relations are reproduced and reinforced through tourism development are certainly important and necessary, but many commentators *only* identified the development constraints facing island states, while failing to identify their strengths. Such approaches tend to neglect the significant agency exercised by governments and local communities in managing their tourism assets (Scheyvens & Momsen, 2008, p. 495).

A central, and perhaps contentious, proposition of the PPT literature is that businesses "at all levels and scales of operation" have the potential to contribute to poverty alleviation (Pro-Poor Tourism Partnership, 2005, p. 1). This marks it out as distinctive from views that look in the main towards "alternative" forms of tourism development – including ecotourism, cultural tourism and voluntourism – to broaden the socio-economic benefits of tourism growth. Certainly, small-scale and alternative forms of tourism enterprise have significant and proven developmental benefits (Scheyvens, 2008; Wanhill, 1999; Wilson, 1997); however, a one-sided focus on alternative tourism alone means overlooking the developmental potential of the mass or mainstream tourism market, when mainstream tourism actually accounts for the bulk of tourism flows (Jafari, 2001). Mass tourism is sometimes viewed by communities as more profitable, less risky and more beneficial than alternative tourism (Butler, 1990; Weaver & Oppermann 2000). Thomlinson and Getz (1996), for example, show how mainstream enterprises can generate more material benefits and are more likely to remain viable in a deregulated and competitive economic environment. Thus, for example, ". . . [while] small is beautiful in the context of ecotourism . . . small is also vulnerable" (Thomlinson & Getz, 1996, p. 197). As Burns explains, larger-scale forms of tourism can be far more desirable than small-scale options on a number of levels:

> Exhortations to "leave only footprints" . . . carry an ironic and unintentional truth because footprints with no dollars attached do little to develop the industry to a level of critical mass that can supply large-scale employment and a reliable stream of tax revenues to be used to implement beneficial government policies including health, education, and welfare (2004, p. 25).

Thus, while the number of small-scale alternative tourism operators on the market have greatly escalated since the late 1980s, the changes they are implementing will mean little overall if the mainstream tourism industry, dominated by transnational companies, fails to reassess and reorganise its operations (Sobania, 1999, p. 81). The PPT approach addresses this issue because it is more *problem*-driven than theory-driven: thus, rather than ignoring the systemic inequalities associated with international tourism, PPT advocates searching for ways to encourage all forms of tourism, including mass and large-scale ventures, to be more pro-poor.

In the period since the groundbreaking early research of the PPT partnership, interest in the relationship between tourism in developing countries and poverty reduction has increased dramatically. However, despite a growing consensus around the *potential* for poverty reduction through tourism, the actual relationship between the two "largely remains *terra incognita* for tourism academics" (Zhao & Ritchie, 2007, p. 10). This paper contributes to such discussions by directly examining the impacts of businesses at different scales in the most popular tourism destination in the South Pacific: Fiji. This involves looking across the spectrum of tourism development: from small-scale, locally owned backpacker establishments to larger-scale, foreign-owned resorts. Our discussion is divided into three main parts. It begins with a brief overview of issues associated with rising poverty in Fiji in the context of the Government's current tourism plans and policy. Then, it compares and discusses the poverty alleviation impacts across case studies at different tourism development levels. The final section analyses the core research findings.

Tourism development and poverty in Fiji

Significance of tourism to Fiji's economy

Fiji has the largest tourism industry of any South Pacific country, employing approximately 14.5% of the total workforce and driving overall economic development in the country (Milne, 2005, p. 12; Narayan, 2005, p. 1157). Like many Pacific states, the country's reliance on tourism has increased greatly as traditional export sectors such as sugar have declined. While sugar is still Fiji's most important crop, the loss of preferential European markets through the termination of the Lomé Convention, combined with the mass expiry of mainly Indo-Fjian held land leases in 2006, means that its contribution to GDP has shrunk from 13.5% in 2000 to just under 6% in 2008 (Mahadevan, 2009, p. 3; Narayan, 2005). Other export sectors such as fisheries and garment manufacturing have also suffered dramatic short-term erosion (Mahadevan, 2009; Narayan & Prasad, 2003).

In contrast, tourism export earnings were US$364 million in 2005, 12.5% of GDP (Ministry of Tourism, 2007, p. 4). More recent estimates including both direct and indirect contributions (the latter, e.g., involving purchases by hotels from suppliers and government tourism sector spending) put the GDP contribution of tourism at 27.8% for 2011 (World Trade and Travel Council [WTTC], 2011, p. 3). Despite the damage wrought on the industry by endemic political instability (since 1987, the country has undergone four coups and 16 changes of government), overall, Fiji has exhibited steady growth in visitor arrivals. Between 1999 and 2009, the average annual growth in visitors was 4.2%, comfortably exceeding the Pacific regional average of 3.2% (Scheyvens & Russell, 2009, p. 6). It should be noted, however, that this is less than the World Tourism Organization's projected 5% yearly increase in the world tourist market towards 2020 (Ashe, 2005) and well below the 9% annual increase projected for the Asia Pacific region (Ministry of Tourism, 2007, p. 2).

Poverty in Fiji

Growth in tourism has not, unfortunately, translated into equitable or broadly based development. In 1977, approximately 15% of households lived below the poverty line. This figure rose to 25.5% in 1990–1991, and to 34.4% in 2002–2003, the date of the most recent household expenditure survey (Mahadevan, 2009, p. 14). A study by Narsey (2007) shows that poverty is worst among rural people with 39% of rural indigenous Fijians and 47% of rural Indo-Fijians living below the poverty line.[1] The cost of closing the poverty gap was estimated to have risen from 1.9% of GDP in 1977 to 5.2% in 2002–2003: the cost of eradicating poverty is now a staggering US$90 million annually (Mahadevan, 2009, p. 16). Fiji is ranked 108th on the United Nations Development Programme (UNDP)'s Human

Development Index, compared with 42nd in 2002 (United Nations Development Programme [UNDP], 2009, p. 1).

Factors influencing rising poverty in Fiji poverty are multiple and complex; however, an overriding factor is the declining contribution of the sugar sector. In 1990–1991, two-thirds of Fiji's households received income from agriculture (Ahlburg, 1996, p. 3); however, the declining sugar industry and the expiry of land leases have dramatically increased the number of people living below or near the poverty line (Narsey, 2007; Walsh, 2002). Statistically, rural Indo-Fijians are more likely to fall into poverty than rural indigenous Fijians, and as Sriskandarajah (2003, p. 315) emphasises, rural Indo-Fijian's vulnerability is greatly exacerbated by their lack of access to communally held land and concomitant resources available within broad social networks.

More broadly, Walsh (2002, p. 336) pointed to the structural adjustment policies initiated after the 2000 coup, with cutbacks in government employment, the weakening of wage bargaining power and labour unions, and the introduction of value-added tax (VAT) on all expenditure, including basic necessities. Under pressure from the World Trade Organization, successive governments in Fiji have reduced tariffs on numerous items, with government revenue from tariffs declining from 33% of total tax revenue in the mid-1980s to 18% by 2002 (Chand, 2004, p. 8). Following VAT's introduction in 2002, taxes on consumption accounted for 45% of all tax revenue. Taxes on income, however, declined from 52% of all tax revenue before VAT to 30% in 2003, placing the taxation burden most heavily on the poorest in society (Chand, 2004, p. 7).

Tourism development plans and policy

Given these pressures, government tourism policy has stressed the desire to maximise both social and economic benefits of industry growth. The government's *Tourism Development Plan 2007–2016* puts special emphasis on achieving a "balance between [the] four planks of prosperity: social, cultural, environmental and economic" as the "key to sustainable tourism development" (Ministry of Tourism, 2007, p. 4). But while successive tourism development plans emphasise equitable development, the main policy thrust continues to focus on industry growth through increased foreign investment (Scheyvens & Russell, 2009, pp. 9–12). The vast majority of resources go towards achieving the overriding ambition of the *Tourism Development Plan 2007–2016*, which is "achieving 1.1 million visitor arrivals and tourism infrastructure exceeding 16,000 rooms" (Ministry of Tourism, 2007, p. 2) – a doubling of tourist numbers over the 2009 levels. To achieve this, the government offers generous incentives for the development of five-star hotels, including a 100% write-off on all capital expenditure in any one year during a period of eight years; carry forward of losses of up to six years; duty-free import of most capital equipment, machinery and plant; and a waiver on corporate tax on profits for 20 years (Narayan, 2000, p. 17).[2] There are no restrictions on repatriation of profits, resulting in leakage. Berno estimates that current levels of foreign exchange leakage from tourism are 60% (cited in Veit, 2007, p. 2).[3]

Given this orientation towards large-scale growth, the Fijian government has been widely criticised for failing to take steps to ameliorate the most negative impacts of high levels of foreign ownership. These include unequal spatial and geographic development (Rao, 2006), significant long-term leakage and repatriation of profits (Berno, 2006; Narayan & Prasad, 2008), and perhaps most significantly, failing to develop linkages between tourism facilities and local economies (Berno, 2006; Mahadevan, 2009; Narayan & Prasad, 2003; Rao, 2006; Veit, 2007).

The Native Lands Trust Board and tourism development

Fiji's tourism industry is unique in being both the largest in the region and having the most comprehensive legislative and policy framework for situating tourism development within the institution of customary tenure[4]. Today, 89% of land in Fiji is still under customary tenure and governed by traditional leadership structures. The primary means of increasing participation in the tourism industry has thus been through lease deals between *mataqali* (landowning clans) and developers, enacted through the agency of the Native Land Trust Board (NLTB).

A core function of the NLTB is negotiating on behalf of landowners the leasing of customary land to tourism developers for up to 99 years. Thus, the Board has been involved in all major tourism projects in Fiji and is often the driving force behind many proposals for new tourism infrastructure (Harrison & Brandt, 2003, p. 145). The NLTB is required to secure a fair lease payment, provide regulation and protection of the interests of both parties during the lease period, and "increase Fijian socio-economic equity [and] participation in all aspects of the tourism industry" (Native Land Trust Board [NLTB], 2006, p. 7). To achieve this, the Tourism Policy of NLTB requires that, provided they meet "normal employment requirements", first preference be given to members of the landowning community for all staff posts, small-service operations such as taxi stands or entertainment services, as well as for the supply of all food, providing they meet a "standard satisfactory to the lessee" (NLTB, 2006, p. 11, 18).

Larger-scale resorts are also expected to grant landowners at least one seat on the Board of Directors of the company, and a minimum of 10% free shares (NLTB, 2006, p. 11). While a village may have several different *mataqali*, it is the *mataqali* owning the land on which the resort is situated that is the formal recipient of these benefits. The government has recently sought to widen the advantages derived from lease deals by requiring the lessee to assist the village in the improvement of their water supply, health provision, village hall infrastructure and village electrification (NLTB official, December 2009).

It is significant that the NLTB does not actively encourage joint ventures, as potential conflict between landowners and developers is viewed as an impediment to investment (NLTB official, December 2009). Thus, while small-scale, family-owned enterprises do co-exist with large foreign-owned businesses, the core focus of tourism policy is on increasing local partnership with foreign developers, rather than local ownership and management of tourism infrastructure.[5] Of 132 tourism projects implemented between 1988 and 2000, 94% were foreign-owned, including joint ventures, with just 6% in local ownership (Narayan & Prasad, 2003). As Douglas notes, "Tourism development plans call for indigenous par-ticipation and control of tourism, yet the principal area of participation continues to be as landholders" (1997, p. 91). For local ownership of community-based ventures to increase in future, Farrelly (2011) argues that there may need to be reform of Fiji's local traditional decision-making systems.

Small- and large-scale tourism – a comparison

Methodology

Research reported in this paper was undertaken as part of a NZAID (New Zealand Agency for International Development)-funded research project *Sharing the Riches of Tourism: Exploring How Tourism Can Contribute More Effectively to Poverty Alleviation in the Pacific*. The Fijian component of this research involved an extensive literature review, fol-lowed by three periods of fieldwork in Fiji between June 2009 and March 2010, involving

Regina Scheyvens, Adi Vale Bakewa and Azmat Gani. The first research phase involved semi-structured interviews with economics and development studies academics, government personnel (from the Ministry of National Planning, Reserve Bank of Fiji and Ministry of Tourism), NGO officials (from ECREA and Fiji Council of Social Services), a tourism industry representative and four resort managers. This collected background data on the state of tourism in Fiji and how well it was contributing to poverty alleviation. Between December 2009 and March 2010, more comprehensive case studies were conducted in three different areas to assess the poverty alleviation impacts at different scales of tourism development: this involved one large resort, one medium-sized resort and four small-scale and/or backpacker resorts. Adi did follow-up interviews with members of the landowning community and others living nearby two of the case study resorts, and she delved further into the workings of two indigenous businesses established with assistance from nearby resorts.

The challenges involved in rigorously tracking and quantifying benefit flows from businesses to communities are well documented by PPT researchers (e.g. Goodwin, 2006; Harrison, 2008). Harrison (2008, pp. 861–862) notes how it is often impossible to calculate the benefits tourism brings to communities, given the resources required for systematic and comparative monitoring and analysis, as well as the difficulties inherent in gauging more intangible long-term benefits not directly related to wealth distribution or employment. This study faced the additional challenge of a sensitive political climate, which for example, made it difficult to openly discuss land tenure issues with NLTB officials. As such, interviews were targeted at drawing out experiences of individuals or small groups of related people (e.g. *mataqali* members or resort staff) and their perceptions of tourism development. We aimed to canvass a diversity of viewpoints in the case study areas, from business owners, senior management, local and expatriate staff members, community representatives, and also both local residents involved and not involved directly in tourism. Most respondents are quoted anonymously and the names of the tourism resorts and backpacker ventures are likewise not revealed in accordance with ethical guidelines for research confidentiality.

We employ a multidimensional view of poverty modelled on Zhao and Ritchie's (2007, pp. 12–14) integrative research framework for "anti-poverty tourism": this identifies three determinants, "opportunity", "empowerment" and "security", as the key conditions for successful poverty alleviation. We explain these determinants next, and in some cases have added to Zhao and Ritchie's ideas by drawing from Scheyvens (2011, p. 25) on the desired results of tourism regarding poverty reduction. Zhao and Ritchie use "opportunity" to refer to the access of poor people to economic opportunities (2007, p. 13). This could include the chance to engage in paid employment or to earn income from sale of goods or services to the tourism sector, as opposed to the traditional charity-based approach to poverty reduction. Ideally, these economic opportunities should increase people's long-term self-reliance (Scheyvens, 2011, p. 25). "Empowerment" aims to enhance and strengthen the poor's participation in political processes and local decision-making, as well as removing the barriers that work against them building their assets (Zhao & Ritchie, 2007, pp. 13–14). The goal here should be that all people can develop their capabilities, have a sense of control over their wellbeing and lead dignified lives (Scheyvens, 2011, p. 25). The third determinant, "security" is targeted at consolidating "opportunity" and "empowerment" via a reduction in the poor's vulnerability to factors such as environmental disasters, economic downturn or ill-health. Zhao and Ritchie (2007, p. 14) suggest that a social security system should support the poor during hard times. To Scheyvens (2011, p. 25), "security" would also include enabling poor people to secure their rights via, for example, effective legislation protecting customary land rights, or an employment contract which provides a resort worker with fair working conditions and job security. As Zhao and Ritchie stress: "To achieve the most desired effect in poverty alleviation, all of the three components should be concurrently strengthened" (2007, p. 13). A comparison of the small- and large-scale ventures based on Zhao and Ritchie's ideas is provided in Table 1.

Small-scale tourism: Yasawa Island Backpacker resorts

The Yasawa Islands of Fiji provide a perceived backpackers' haven, with approximately 15–20 small enterprises catering to budget- to mid-range tourists. A few resorts are on privately owned land; the rest are on communal land and are locally owned and operated by family groups. Tourists using this accommodation travel approximately 3 hours to the Yasawa Islands from the mainland of Viti Levu, on the Yasawa Flyer, a catamaran operated by tour company Awesome Adventures. A "hop on - hop off" ticket enables stops at different islands and resorts along the way. Further background to the Yasawas can be found in Kerstetter and Bricker (2009).

Community members in the Yasawas can benefit both formally and informally from their association with backpacker tourism. Paid employment from backpacker resorts is an important formal benefit for some local residents, particularly since there are so few economic opportunities in the Yasawas. This also extends to entertainment activities contracted by tourist resorts, usually performed by locals from the landowning village. Community members may benefit from the receipt of lease monies paid to the *mataqali*. In one case, the chief used some of this money to establish a piped water supply in the village, to improve the quality of life of all residents. Informal benefits come from donations from school and village visits, sale of handicrafts, and setting up of a tour or village enterprise for tourists – for example, one family had set up a tea shop on the beach near to backpacker resorts (Backpacker Owner Operator, Yasawas, December 2009).

Small-scale, family-owned operations possess a number of unique strengths, one being their resilience to the vicissitudes of international tourist markets (see Biggs, Hall, & Stoeckl, in press). This is particularly so when there are good land-based or marine resources from which they can derive a livelihood. The 2009 global recession impacted Fiji's tourism dramatically, with arrivals falling by 7.8% (*Fiji Times*, December 2, 2009). However, most people normally employed in tourism in the Yasawas could still meet their livelihood needs due to access to land, *qoliqoli* areas (traditional fishing grounds), as well as falling back on the income of family members. As one villager explained to us, when the tourists do not come, ". . . I go back to option B – *qoliqoli* to catch crabs and sell in the market" (Villager, Yasawas, March 2010). Given the high level of temporary and casual labour throughout the tourism industry, the communal land tenure system and *qoliqoli* rights, combined with an ability to draw on alternative income sources, are critical for reducing community-level vulnerability to economic shocks.

Where small-scale tourism businesses are located on customary land, the procurement of local goods is usually quite high, if available. Overall, small operators prefer to source food locally rather than from the mainland, but in some parts of the Yasawas, the poor soils, dry climate and lack of irrigation technology limit agricultural production (Backpacker Owner Operator, Yasawas: December 2009). Most operators will source a very high proportion of their fish locally. One backpacker resort that takes up to 60 guests purchases around US$200 of locally caught fish per week, providing an income for several fishing people (Owner Operator, Yasawas, December 2009).

However, small-scale, family-owned businesses can also be somewhat vulnerable in a market dominated by large-scale enterprises. As Leah-Burns has noted in the context of

Table 1. Comparison of the poverty reduction impacts between small- and large-scale resorts in Fiji.

	Small-scale, indigenous Fijian-owned resorts	Large-scale, foreign-owned resorts on land leased from indigenous Fijian owners
Opportunity		
Wages	Usually paid the minimum wage, but sometimes less. Many staff work 60–70-hour weeks but are only paid for a 40-hour week. Beneficially, most live nearby and can return home daily.	Those without qualifications/experience usually begin on the minimum wage. Some establishments pay overtime, others expect employees to work extra hours without pay. Opportunity cost: many staff, especially those on offshore islands, migrate to work and spend long periods away from home and family; villages suffer loss of productive workers.
Opportunities for progression	Individuals usually employed without needing any formal qualifications, but there are limited opportunities for progression.	Employees require at least 6th form education, and some resorts offer good opportunities for progression, building this in to planning for all employees. Senior positions often dominated by expatriates.
Lease money	Families usually gain access to *mataqali* land informally, so do not directly compensate the *mataqali* for the land.	Lease monies are paid to the *mataqali* via NLTB twice yearly. In some cases, this is shared between all adult members, while at other times, it is used for community projects, e.g., upgrading the water supply system. At still other times, chiefs co-opt funds. Opportunity cost: the land that is tied up in a 99-year lease sometimes could have been used for other productive purposes, e.g., agriculture, housing.
Economic linkages	Most fish, fruit and vegetables sourced locally. Menus partly dictated by what is available locally. Some building materials and furnishings, e.g., woven mats, sourced from within Fiji. Encourage visits to nearby villages, where handicrafts are sold and donations are made to schools and churches.	Most purchase fresh produce and fish from large suppliers who import a lot of produce. Hotel chain may limit options by dictating food safety standards and auditing suppliers. Building materials and furnishings often sourced from outside Fiji. Most buy handicrafts for the resort store locally or allow a local handicraft stall on site.
Empowerment		
Training for employees	Usually not provided, apart from some on-the-job training specific to employee's role.	On-the-job training provided as well as subsidies for courses offered by external providers. May provide "cross training" to expose employees to jobs in other areas of the resort.
Respect for community culture and traditions	Help to rejuvenate interest in traditional dance and song through employing local *meke* groups and choirs and taking tourists on tours of their village.	Help to rejuvenate interest in traditional dance and song through employing local *meke* groups and choirs.

(Continued on next page)

	Small-scale, indigenous Fijian-owned resorts	Large-scale, foreign-owned resorts on land leased from indigenous Fijian owners
Support for indigenous business ownership and development	Backpacker ventures that are indigenous-owned and as such offer a source of pride to families and clans. They in turn might support other small local enterprises, such as tours, or offer their own activities. Many indigenous businesses struggle to succeed as businesses, however, due to lack of access to credit and training or mentoring, plus community demands on the business.	Entertainment services typically contracted from landowning village. Will often utilise larger locally owned businesses, such as laundry or security services. In a minority of cases, resorts will support the establishment of landowner business enterprises, which are a source of pride in their communities.
Participation in decision-making	Some indigenous business owners gain roles on tourism bodies, where they can assert their interests.	Most resorts employ a community liaison officer to facilitate communication with landowners, but this does not necessarily give landowners any decision-making power. One landowner representative might be given a seat on the board of directors of a resort.
Security		
Job security	Low. Many employees are members of the extended family and have no contracts. Employees brought in from outside the area are likely to be on monthly contracts. Likely to have their hours cut if there is a downturn in the sector.	Low. Staff have contracts but most are on temporary monthly contracts (i.e. one year or more). Likely to have their hours cut if there is a downturn in the sector.
Medical benefits	None – but employer likely to help with specific requests (e.g. if a close family member is sick).	In some cases, subsidised benefits are available for all staff – most typically only for senior supervisors and managers.
Environmental resilience	Will abide by rules of local chiefs regarding Marine Protected Areas where no fishing is allowed. Do not always have adequate sanitation systems in place (e.g. septic tanks located close to protected lagoons).	Likely to donate to environmental causes which reflect their business interests, e.g. Marine Protected Areas. May include an automatic donation to such causes on guest bills. Will promote careful use of resources (e.g. energy and fresh water) as this saves the businesses money.
Economic resilience of communities	Access to customarily held land provides a subsistence "fall back option" and reduces vulnerability to economic shocks.	NLTB has a legal duty to ensure landowners retain enough land for their own subsistence needs. Employees who migrate from other areas are most vulnerable if their hours are cut or their contract is not renewed.
Contributions to community groups	Varies: some give occasional donations to schools, sports groups and churches; others continuously expected by chief or other leaders to give to such groups in cash or kind – while this provides a source of social security, it may jeopardise business viability.	Give in response to specific requests from schools, sports groups and churches, but not keen to support ad-hoc requests for assistance from individuals. May also encourage donations from their guests for community development or environmental projects.
Land rights	Usually based on *mataqali* land as is their right.	Resorts on native lands are all under lease agreements arranged and managed via the NLTB. However, some resort owners feel they have purchased the land and that landowners no longer have any formal rights regarding that land.

Source: Structure based on Zhao and Ritchie (2007).

Fiji, "large foreign companies often thrive in an environment where small local ventures fail" (2003, p. 90). She cites seven local tourism enterprises on the island of Beqa that struggled to remain financially viable, largely due to their inability to raise sufficient capital for advertising compared with the larger, foreign-owned competition (2003, p. 90). In our research, we found direct examples of larger players exerting their power in ways which disadvantage smaller businesses. For example, the monopoly enjoyed by Awesome Adventures, mentioned previously as the only provider of fast sea transport to the Yasawas, has served to severely disadvantage some small-scale operators. While appreciating that without this transportation service, only small numbers of intrepid travelers would venture to the Yasawa islands, only backpacker resorts that are prepared to pay a 30% commission are actively promoted by Awesome Adventures. This made a significant difference to custom – we saw establishments connected to Awesome Adventures with around 30 guests, while nearby properties were empty or had only one or two guests. Although a 30% commission was regarded as standard by a number of people in the tourism industry, this is beyond the means of many small, locally owned enterprises operating with small margins.

Smaller-scale operations also face an additional challenge not faced by larger, foreign-owned enterprises: their responsibility to fulfill the social and cultural expectations of the wider community. The backpacker businesses studied all made significant contributions to their communities over the long term. For example, they would be asked to print tests or certificates for the local school on their photocopier, or to provide fuel for a boat to take boarding school pupils home in the holidays or to donate food and drink for a church fundraising event. While this assistance was highly valued by nearby communities, some backpacker owner-operators found that balancing the desires and expectations of the wider community with the imperatives of running a business was often challenging; it could sometimes threaten business viability. While these kinds of issues are certainly not exclusive to small-scale indigenous enterprises, locally owned businesses operate on small margins and are much more deeply embedded within traditional cultural hierarchies, making demands from the local school, church or chief for "free" goods and services very difficult to navigate.

Working conditions and training in the small-scale backpacker resorts compared un-favorably with large-scale ventures. Most employees we spoke to received the minimum wage (US$1.30/hr for a licensed business), did not receive a contract and were expected to work long hours. While employment legislation in Fiji states that a normal working week is 48 hours over a maximum of six days, with overtime paid for additional hours worked, this rarely occurs in practice among small-scale tourist businesses. A number of workers interviewed said they were routinely expected to work a 12-hour day (while being paid for eight hours), and they received irregular holidays, if at all. Some worked seven days a week, only taking a break if they fell ill (Backpacker staff, Yasawas, December 2009), and it is common practice for permanent staff members to have their pay reduced in low seasons (Backpacker Owner Operator and Backpacker staff, Yasawas, December 2009). It is also uncommon for individual staff to receive any substantive form of training which could enhance their skills, job satisfaction and employment opportunities elsewhere.

Large-scale tourism resorts

The practices of large-scale resorts are often very different from those of small-scale backpacker ventures, and this has implications for their ability to contribute to poverty alleviation. The discussion to follow is based largely on one Coral Coast resort, referred to here as Resort A, which has much in common with other resorts in this popular tourist area on Fiji's main island, but also draws on interviews conducted at three other resorts in the first phase of this research. Resort A has over 100 rooms and a 4.5-star rating, and is located on lease-hold land. An upmarket establishment, it caters primarily to the family and general holiday-maker markets from New Zealand and Australia. It is owned by a foreign family, and one of the managers expressed pride in the quality of the resort's relationship with the landowning community, indicating that in contrast to larger chain resorts, the family-run nature of this resort allowed management to be more responsive to community needs (Resort A's Manager, December 2009).

In conforming with NLTB requirements, the *Turaga ni Mataqali* (chief of the *mataqali*) sits on the company's Board of Directors, and the company employs a landowner representative to act as an intermediary between the landowning *mataqali* and Resort A. The manager estimates that 15–20% of the resort's total workforce is from the landowning *mataqali*, with 35–40% from the wider community where the *mataqali* is based. More local people are employed during special events, such as weddings and other large functions. While the manager claimed that there are good chances for advancement within the company, he expressed frustration because he still has to rely primarily on expatriate staff to fill supervisory and managerial roles. He said that although hiring more expensive expatriate staff is not the preferred option, "local manpower is horrendously short at the moment. We're finding it incredibly difficult to get good qualified personnel beyond an elementary supervisory level" (Resort A's Manger, December 2009).[6]

As noted in the PPT literature, larger companies will typically offer superior wages, are more likely to abide by labour laws and, importantly, will invest considerably more in training and capacity-building than locally owned operations (Meyer, 2008, p. 577). These points were certainly supported in this study. Many employees at Resort A were receiving rates of pay in excess of the minimum wage, and a number of those interviewed had received a pay increase in the past year. All received training of some sort, and if they chose to undertake training outside the resort at their own cost, this significantly improved their opportunities for promotion. Some employees had opportunities to broaden their skills base by cross-training across departments. This involves pairing an employee with someone proficient in the area they wish to train in over a set period of time; so, for example, a chef may receive training in reception or a member of the housekeeping staff may get training in bar service (Resort A's Food and Beverage Manager, December 2009).

Other large-scale resorts investigated as part of this study provided additional benefits to staff, including progression planning for every staff member, including gardeners, housekeeping and maintenance staff, and access to online training resources provided by their parent company (in hotels run by international chains) and externally run training courses. Larger resorts also have resources to offer employment benefits simply not attainable in smaller-scale operations, including health insurance and retirement schemes. At one internationally branded resort, employees could access health insurance for themselves and their family for US$1.30 per week, with the resort paying the other US$3.90 per week.

While there are real benefits for employees at larger resorts, their job security is still not guaranteed. Following international trends, there is a high level of casualisation throughout the hospitality sector in Fiji, whereby having the majority of employees on temporary contracts is considered normal. At Resort A, only one-third of around 250 employees were permanent (on one year or longer contracts), and over half were on temporary (monthly) contracts. The remaining staff were casuals who were employed for specific tasks (such as painting) for just a few days or weeks (HR Manager, Sonaisali, December 2009). Additionally, there appears to be minimal forewarning about available work. A staff member on a temporary contract said to us: "You just look at the monthly roster. If your name doesn't appear you know you just stay home" (Resort A's Receptionist, December 2009).

Procurement of local goods is an important way in which tourism can contribute to poverty reduction. At Resort A, a reasonable amount of goods are procured locally. For example, in-house landscaping staff provide some of the resort's flowers for decorative purposes, and tailors employed full time by the resort produce all staff uniforms as well as bedding, towels, and furniture covers for guest rooms. Approximately 50% of food is sourced locally via intermediaries, that is, suppliers which deliver straight to resorts. While the Head Chef says that there is a high demand for locally produced food (particularly fish, fruit and vegetables), he argues that due to their requirements in terms of quantity, quality and consistency, they are forced to rely primarily on wholesalers, who in turn import a significant proportion of their product. While there is certainly potential for greater local food purchasing at this resort, they compare favourably with an internationally branded resort located not far away: the manager here estimated that they imported 80% of the food they required, and he noted that "head office" offshore set a number of standards for them to meet which could inhibit procurement of local produce.

The lack of local purchasing of fish in many large resorts seems a major anomaly, considering the richness of the resource all around them. As explained by Resort A's Head Chef, however, the amounts of seafood required – which requires significant standardisation, processing and packaging – is not conducive to buying local. They purchase 120 kg of frozen mahimahi and 30 kg of tuna a week, along with 80 kg of lobster. Ironically, this fish is rarely fresh: "Tourists expect fresh fish . . . [But] most of the fish processed through any company here gets frozen and delivered to you" (Resort A's Head Chef, December 2009).

While the PPT literature suggests that there are many ways in which large resorts can support locally owned businesses, it is rare to find resorts in Fiji which are willing to go beyond paternalism and actively assist with the establishment or mentoring of such businesses. Resort A was, however, an exception. The Manager assisted the *mataqali* to establish their own taxi company, which is based at the resort's taxi base, drawing up specific performance requirements, assisting with the formation of pricing structures and with negotiating the vehicle lease deal (Resort A's Manager, December 2009; and Taxi Company's Manager, February 2010). The taxi company grew to employ 10 people (six drivers and four other staff members), and depending on occupancy rates at the resort, generates between US$1000 and US$2000 weekly. Two drivers and the manager were interviewed, and all talked with pride of the achievements of the enterprise. They spoke of the benefits of gaining new experience and the knowledge and confidence to operate a business, and the increased morale and self-esteem which has resulted for the landowning *mataqali*. One *mataqali* member said that the success of the business had shown ". . . that Fijians can excel in business, like our Indian counterparts" (Landowner, Feburary 2010).

Comparing pro-poor potential in Fiji at different scales of tourism development

It is clear that businesses at both ends of the scale can contribute significantly to strengthening the "three determinants of poverty alleviation", outlined in Zhao and Ritchie (2007): opportunity, empowerment and security. Table 1 summarises some of the different ways in which small- and larger-scale tourism enterprises in Fiji contribute to poverty reduction according to Zhao and Ritchie's three criteria; the discussion below elaborates on these issues.

In terms of the determinant of "opportunity", which focuses on access of poor people to economic opportunities, both small- and large-scale resorts in Fiji make a significant contribution. Local Fijians involved in tourism – whether members of the landowning *mataqali* receiving lease monies, those directly employed in tourism businesses or those living in areas close to resorts – can clearly gain significant livelihood benefits from tourism (Interviews, December 2009 and February 2010). Those employed in large resorts, overall, had greater opportunities for progression and received better wages and working conditions than many people working in small resorts. However, in small resorts, most employees had the benefit of working close to home rather than having to migrate to work in a place far removed from their family and land. Working conditions in smaller resorts suffer as businesses operating on small margins face often vigorous competition. As Wanhill comments, the high degree of market fragmentation and competition characteristic of the tourism sector means "market mechanisms do not create socially optimal solutions" for small business development (1999, p. 144).

Far more in terms of lease monies can be gained from larger-scale resorts, with a 500-bed resort paying in the order of US$100,000 annually for their lease, compared with US$2500 per annum for smaller backpackers, and US$45,000 per annum for medium-sized resorts (NLTB, 2006, appendix 2). Similarly, larger resorts bring greater volumes of tourists and are much more likely to provide opportunities for a community to independently exploit the benefits of tourism by setting up their own small enterprises. However, bigger lease deals also carry an opportunity cost, with large tracts of community land, which could have potentially been used for agriculture, housing or similar, being tied up in 99-year leases. Some respondents further voiced concern that landowners can become overly dependent on lease payouts and neglect other opportunities, for example, to earn a living or to engage in fishing or farming. Distribution of lease monies is another issue. While in some *mataqali*, all adult members receive regular lease payments; in others, the monies are held collectively for community projects such as upgrading village infrastructure. In other cases, chiefs have managed to co-opt a significant proportion of the funds (Interviews, December 2009 and February 2010).

While almost all respondents acknowledged that tourism had increased economic op-portunities within their communities, it was evident that there was a level of dissatisfaction amongst some non-landowning *mataqali* about uneven distribution of employment op-portunities and money earned from tourism. Significantly, such complaints were largely voiced within communities associated with small-scale enterprises, perhaps because these businesses had a lower turnover of revenue and therefore less capacity to generate devel-opmental benefits over an entire community. In these situations, tourism was likely to be viewed by non-landowning *mataqali* as undermining village unity. In contrast, a respondent from a non-landowning *mataqali* in an area dominated by larger resorts said that tourism had served to incorporate the village under a common direction:

> [Tourism has] improved unity. All issues on tourism that concern the village – the elders sit together and decide. The village development committee is a channel of communication from the hotel to [a local business] to the village headman and then to the village development committee. So there is transparency and trust (Villager, February 2010).

While economic opportunities in terms of lease monies and employment are good in the case of large resorts, there are lost opportunities in terms of procurement of local goods, such as fruit and vegetables. Given the sugar industry's downturn and the dramatic rise in rural poverty, there is no doubt that enormous development opportunities for poor farmers and fishing people are being missed through inadequate linkages with tourism enterprises. Berno (2006) has estimated that US$15 million annually is spent by the tourism sector on importing food products that could be grown or produced in Fiji. The staggering volume of imported produce consumed by the tourism industry in Fiji becomes apparent when one compares the revenue generated by one of the smaller tourism wholesalers with a larger one which took part in our research. The large company, which supplies directly to a number of major hotels, imports an estimated 99% of their product, with turnover between US$400,000 and US$750,000 weekly (Large-scale food supplier, March 2010). In contrast, two smaller companies, which source between 80% and 90% of their food locally and supply a mixture of small-, medium- and large-scale establishments, generate between US$350 and US$600 weekly (Small-scale suppliers, March 2010). Overall, large resorts are less adaptable to the local environment and more poorly connected with local suppliers. While small- to medium-scale resorts are generally better integrated into their local economies, lack of coordination and access to technology among producers prevents them from supplying larger resorts with the products they require.

The Fijian Government has stated its desire to increase the productivity of domestic agriculture towards import substitution, and recognises the importance of linkages with tourism operations to reduce poverty and stimulate domestic consumption (Veit, 2007). However, the Ministry of Agriculture is heavily under-resourced in terms of skilled labour and funds, and past agricultural development initiatives have not developed to fruition (Mahadevan, 2009, p. 6). While there is much to be done on a government level to expand and sustain tourism–agriculture linkages, there is significant scope for resorts to further develop procurement policies which prioritise purchasing of local goods and services. From the perspective of the owner of a large, Suva-based importer, the primary problem is not the quality or consistency of Fijian produce, but rather that most chefs at upscale resorts are expatriates, and are overly "fussy", expecting all produce to meet "European standards" (Large-scale food supplier, March 10). The Ministry of Tourism notes the increased demand for locally produced food among tourists, but says the industry has failed to make Fijian cuisine sourced from local ingredients an "integral part of the Fijian experience" (2004, 8).

Shifting now to look at the determinant of "empowerment", Zhao and Ritchie stress that the aim is to enhance the poor people's participation in political processes and local decision-making, as well as removing the barriers that work against them building their assets (2007, pp. 13–14). While NLTB has been effective in securing enhanced economic opportunities as well as a level of subsistence security via its protection of customary tenure systems in Fiji, it has not created an environment conducive to increased levels of indigenous ownership of the tourism product, nor has it facilitated landowners having a greater say in the nature and direction of tourism development in Fiji. Government policy, including the tax holidays and incentives described previously, allows for the subsidisation of the largest resorts over long periods of operation, while small business development is relatively neglected.

It is unfortunate that there have not been more efforts to develop businesses owned and run by indigenous Fijians because comments indicating that genuine empowerment had been felt at the community level were most evident where people ran their own small-scale enterprises, whether supplying fresh fish to a resort or the landowners' taxi business associated with Resort A (Interviews, December 2009 and February 2010). Undoubtedly, businesses owned by indigenous Fijians are a source of genuine pride to communities and they tend to be run by people who have a long-term interest in the environmental and social sustainability of their ventures, rather than being only moti-vated by profits. A concern, however, is that indigenous businesses regularly fail at least partly due to lack of ongoing support in terms of capacity-building, access to credit or mentoring.

Small resorts provided few opportunities for their employees to receive training and to progress within the business. Often these employees do not have job descriptions nor a clear idea of any performance criteria which they should meet and which could then be rewarded. While, on the other hand, large-scale resorts provide superior wages and training opportunities, this did not necessarily translate into "ladders" to middle and senior management.

Moving on to Zhao and Ritchie's third component, security, this is taken to mean a re-duction in the vulnerability of the poor to factors such as environmental disasters, economic downturn or ill-health, and provision of social security to support the poor during hard times (2007, p. 14). Many respondents emphasised the advantages of employment in large resorts or receiving lease monies, which enabled them to improve their resilience through access to better health and education services, and build homes using more permanent construction materials which might withstand future cyclones. However, job security in resorts is not guaranteed, with the majority on temporary contracts.

While involvement in small-scale resorts is unlikely to yield such good economic returns as they do not offer the same employment benefits or wages as larger businesses, these resorts provide a source of social security for relatives and friends who come to the owners when needing a loan or other financial contribution to help with an unexpected expense, such as a medical bill. Large resorts will plan to donate to certain community development causes, such as schools and sports teams, but tend to discourage ad-hoc requests for assistance from nearby residents. Small resorts often respond positively to such requests because of their close relationships with those in the community. While providing communities with a form of assistance and security, paradoxically, this may undermine the economic viability of some small resorts.

In terms of land rights and economic resilience, the NLTB guarantees that the interests of landowners cannot be legally excluded from the operations of tourism businesses.[7] As Sofield put it, the NLTB's Policy for Native Land ensures that communities are "incorporated into the habitus of the resort" (2003, p. 325), and provides a legislative framework that allows communities to balance traditional obligations and values with participation in the commercial economy. And, in rural areas particularly, access to communal resources is what Firth (2000, p. 191) has referred to as "an informal system of social security", serving to blunt the sharpest edges of industry shocks. This was clear in the Yasawas, where people turned to their marine and land resources to meet their livelihood needs when there was a downturn in tourism in 2009. Some managers of large resorts were very respectful of the relationship they had with landowning groups, with one stating: "Our relationship with the community remains at the heart of everything we do" (Manager of a large resort, June 2009). Others, however, felt that leased land had been "sold" to them and that the indigenous owners no longer had any rights over it: "The LOC [landowning community] did own this place, but they gave it away, yet they still believe they own it and try to impose their regime on hotels here" (Manager of a large resort, June 2009).

Conclusion

The PPT literature asserts that tourism can benefit poor people and business interests, whether large or small. This paper has shown that there are certainly many instances where tourism enterprises in Fiji at various scales are bringing direct and indirect benefits to the poor – primarily centred on lease money, jobs and contributions to community development – which largely hinge on the legislative and policy framework of the NLTB. There is also a good deal of untapped potential to increase these benefits, particularly to expand the downstream benefits of the large resorts. This study has, however, identified a number of issues impeding the poverty alleviation potential of tourism in Fiji. In particular, there are still underdeveloped linkages between tourism and the wider economy and a heavy reliance on imported products, particularly among large-scale operators. There are also poor employment conditions in a number of the small-scale resorts, and inadequate job security for most employees in large-scale enterprises, and there is a lack of sustained governmental support for small enterprise development. Overall, indigenous Fijian participation in the tourism sector continues to be predominantly as employees or as recipients of lease monies, and rarely as those directly involved in tourism planning and development.

While in the past there was a tendency to see tourism as predominantly a private sector activity where market forces rule, today there is growing attention to the comprehensive role states must assume if tourism development is to meet the goals of sustainability and poverty reduction (Harrison, 2008; Schilcher, 2007; Sofield, 2003). As Harrison has argued, meaningful poverty reduction effectively relies on the state: ". . . the impacts of any pro poor tourism project, even if on a large scale, are likely to be limited unless a state's entire tourism strategy is constructed around poverty alleviation. In effect, [pro poor tourism] requires a *developmental* state" (2008, p. 863 – emphasis original). And, as Schilcher notes, such policies require strong institutions capable of proactively intervening in market forces and redistributing financial resources (2007, p. 71).

Thus, the potential for tourism to work in a more pro-poor manner in Fiji in future is underpinned by the government's overall approach to development. Currently, there are significant tensions between the government's goals, which purport to seek to develop tourism in a sustainable, equitable manner while simultaneously promoting rapid growth of the sector, including a doubling of tourist arrivals by 2016. It is critical that the Fijian government is fully aware of the negative implications of a one-sided focus on large-scale growth funded by external sources, rather than simply focusing on positives such as job creation, lease money and tax revenue (whatever is left after various exemptions apply). This focus on growth leads to an emphasis on encouraging investment in large-scale initiatives by external developers. For example, the NLTB has a duty to secure the kind of participation that benefits communities, yet it is also under pressure to provide an environment that is as attractive as possible to foreign investors. Due to this, NLTB officials do not promote joint ventures, as they are viewed as being unnecessarily risky and an impediment to foreign investment (NLTB Official, Suva, December 2009). If the Fiji government is serious about tourism contributing to more equitable development, it should broaden the distribution of economic opportunities from tourism and move communities beyond dependence on lease arrangements. An important issue raised by Farrelly (2011) is the need to better understand, and perhaps reform, how Fiji's local traditional decision-making systems work if community-based tourism enterprises are to be effectively supported. Furthermore, one of the best ways to strengthen local enterprise is to encourage partnerships between communities and larger tourism investors. Options include providing investment advice, mentoring schemes, access to credit, and support for cooperative organisations or marketing networks which brand local enterprises within a destination. Greater support to small- and medium-scale tourism enterprises could stimulate regional entrepreneurship and job creation, and help to meet the NLTB's stated goal of increasing indigenous ownership in tourism.

Governments in the developing world that want tourism to contribute to poverty alleviation must be willing to balance the desire for foreign investment and growth with other priorities, which may include widespread sharing of the benefits of development and local control over the nature of development. This is likely to require difficult trade-offs. As

Chok, Macbeth, and Warren suggest: "Tourism development that generates net benefits for the poor and protects the environment ... will place restrictions on human activity and challenge our current rapid expansion development model" (2007, p. 51). Such trade-offs in Fiji might include weighing up the value of investing more resources in agriculture and formulating viable and innovative strategies for increasing linkages between large-scale resorts and local producers in a context whereby other government ministries are chronically understaffed and underfunded.

Pro-poor outcomes do not automatically arise from rapid growth of the tourism sector: the success of such initiatives is heavily dependent on a government's willingness to provide a facilitating policy environment specifically targeting the poor and establishing policy frameworks and institutions that ensure ongoing support. This can occur where both large-scale and small-scale tourism ventures exist; however, where governments favour large-scale development funded by foreign investors and fail to engage the local population in ownership of tourism businesses or provide a voice for them in tourism planning and management, the pro-poor potential of tourism is significantly impeded.

Acknowledgements

Vinaka vakalevu (thank you very much) Associate Professor Azmat Gani and Adi Vale Bakewa, who assisted with data collection in Fiji for this research. Sincere appreciation also goes to our research participants, who gave their valuable time to share their thoughts and experiences with us.

Notes

1. Nearly half of the Fiji Islands' population is non-indigenous, mostly Indo-Fijians, whose ancestors arrived as indentured labourers in the late nineteenth century. Most Indo-Fijians do not own land, and large numbers lease land from indigenous Fijian landowners for agriculture. While poverty among indigenous Fijians is increasing, Indo-Fijians are more likely to experience extreme forms of deprivation (Walsh, 2002).
2. Thus, some of the largest resorts in Fiji pay very minimal tax throughout long periods of operation. In 2005, a high-growth year, tourism exports accounted for F\$729 million in export earnings, but only an estimated (best case) F\$139 million tax revenue for the Fijian government (Ministry of Tourism, 2007, p. 4).
3. Note however that some researchers now suggest that the term "leakage" has been misused and misinterpreted in an overly negative manner by tourism scholars (Mitchell & Ashley, 2010, p. 82).
4. Customary land in Fiji is land owned and governed by the values and customs of the *mataqali*, a clan-like unit primarily composed of groups of families linked through kinship ties, which has come to represent the basic social unit of indigenous Fijian society (Sofield, 2003, p. 286). Although kinship networks are often grouped together to form larger territorial and political units, the *yavusa* and *vanua*, respectively, it is the *mataqali* category of land ownership that is reified and protected by Fijian law.
5. An NLTB official interviewed for this study could name only two operative joint venture arrangements.
6. This perceived shortage of skilled labour could be legitimately questioned by several important providers of education and training to the tourism and hospitality sector in Fiji.
7. See Scheyvens and Russell (in press) for a full analysis of the role of the NLTB in tourism development.

References

Ahlburg, D.A. (1996). *Summary of a report on income distribution and poverty in Fiji*. Suva: University of the South Pacific Press.

Ashe, J.W. (2005). *Tourism investment as a tool for development and poverty reduction: The experience in Small Island Developing States (SIDS)*. Paper presented at the Commonwealth Finance Ministers Meeting, 18–20 September, Bridgetown, Barbados.

Berno, T. (2006). Bridging sustainable agriculture and sustainable tourism to enhance sustainability. In G. Mudacumura, D. Mebratu, & M.S. Haque (Eds.), *Sustainable development policy and administration* (pp. 207–231). New York: Taylor & Francis.

Biggs, D., Hall, C.M., & Stoeckl, N. (in press). The resilience of formal and informal tourism enterprises to disasters – reef tourism in Phuket. *Thailand Journal of Sustainable Tourism, 20*(5).

Britton, S. (1982). Tourism dependency and development: A mode of analysis. In S. Williams (Ed.), *Tourism: Critical concepts in the social sciences* (pp. 23–45). New York: Routledge.

Brohman, J. (1996). New directions for tourism in the Third World. *Annals of Tourism Research, 23*(1), 48–70.

Bryden, J. (1973). *Tourism and development: A case study of the Commonwealth Caribbean*. Cambridge: Cambridge University Press.

Burns, P.M. (2004). Tourism planning: A third way? *Annals of Tourism Research, 31*(1), 24–43.

Butler, R. (1990). Alternative tourism: Pious hope or Trojan horse? *Journal of Travel Research, 28*(3), 40–45.

Chand, G. (2004). Overview of current economic conditions in Fiji. Retrieved 1 August 2010, from http://student.fnu.ac.fj:82/Lautoka%20Campus/2011/Trimester%203/SCHOOL%20OF%20COMMERCE/Economics/Ecn502/Readings/Overview%20of%20current%20economic%20conditions%20in%20Fiji].pdf.

Chok, S., Macbeth, J., & Warren, C. (2007). Tourism as a tool for poverty alleviation: A critical analysis of "pro-poor tourism" and implications for sustainability. In C.M. Hall (Ed.), *Pro-poor tourism: Who benefits?* (pp. 34–55). Clevedon: Channel View Publications.

Douglas, N. (1997). Applying the life-cycle model to Melanesia. *Annals of Tourism Research, 24*(1), 1–22.

Farrelly, T.A. (2011). Indigenous and democratic decision-making: Issues from community-based ecotourism in the Boumā National Heritage Park, Fiji. *Journal of Sustainable Tourism, 19*(7), 817–835.

Fiji Times. (2009, December 2). Tourism earnings to fall $50m. Retrieved 30 August 2009, from http://www.fijitimes.com/story.aspx?id=134711

Firth, S. (2000). The Pacific Islands and the globalisation agenda. *The Contemporary Pacific, 12*(1), 178–192.

Goodwin, H. (2006). Measuring and reporting the impact of tourism on poverty. Retrieved 30 August 2009, from http://www.haroldgoodwin.info/resources/measuring.pdf

Hampton, M.P. (1998). Backpacker tourism and economic development. *Annals of Tourism Research, 25*(2), 639–660.

Harrison, D. (2008). Pro-poor tourism: A critique. *Third World Quarterly, 29*(5), 851–868.

Harrison, D., & Brandt, J. (2003). Ecotourism in Fiji. In D. Harrison (Ed.), *Pacific Island tourism* (pp. 139–151). London: Cognizant Publications.

Hills, L., & Lundgren, J. (1974). *The impact of tourism: A methodological study with examples from the Caribbean and possible lessons for the South Pacific*. Montreal: Department of Geography, McGill University [Mimeographed].

Jafari, J. (2001). The scientification of tourism. In V.L. Smith & M. Brent (Eds.), *Hosts and guests revisited: Tourism issues of the 21st century* (pp. 28–41). New York: Cognizant Communication.

Kerstetter, D., & Bricker, K. (2009). Exploring Fijian's sense of place after exposure to tourism development. *Journal of Sustainable Tourism, 17*(6), 691–708.

Leah-Burns, G.L. (2003). Indigenous responses to tourism in Fiji: What is happening? In D. Harrison (Ed.), *Pacific Island tourism* (pp. 82–93). New York: Cognizant Communication.

Mahadevan, R. (2009). The rough global tide and political storm in Fiji call for swimming hard and fast but with a different stroke. *Pacific Economic Bulletin, 24*(2), 1–23.

Meyer, D. (2008). Pro-poor tourism: From leakages to linkages. A conceptual framework for creating linkages between the accommodation sector and "poor" neighbouring communities. *Current Issues in Tourism, 10*(6), 558–583.

Milne, S. (2005). *The economic impact of tourism in SPTO member countries*. Suva: South Pacific Tourism Organisation (SPTO).

Ministry of Tourism. (2004). *Report on the food policy for the travel and hospitality conference, Naviti resort, November 17th 2004*. Suva: Planning and Research Section, Ministry of Tourism.

Ministry of Tourism. (2007). *Fiji's tourism development plan 2007–2016*. Suva: Department of Tourism, Ministry of Tourism.

Mitchell, J., & Ashley, C. (2010). *Tourism and poverty reduction: Pathways to prosperity*. London: Earthscan.

Narayan, P.K. (2000). Fiji's tourism industry: A SWOT analysis. *The Journal of Tourism Studies, 11*(2), 15–24.

Narayan, P.K. (2005). The structure of tourist expenditure in Fiji: Evidence from unit root structural break tests. *Applied Economics, 37*, 1157–1161.

Narayan, P.K., & Prasad, B.C. (2003). Fiji's sugar, tourism and garment industries: A survey of performance, problems, and potentials. *Fijian Studies, 1*(1), 3–28.

Narayan, P.K., & Prasad, B.C. (2008). Reviving growth in Fiji: Are we swimming or sinking? *Pacific Economic Bulletin, 23*(2), 5–26.

Narsey, W. (2007, June 10). Truth behind our poverty. *Fiji Times*. Retrieved 29 August 2009, from http://www.fijitimes.com/story.aspx?id=64272.

Native Land Trust Board (NLTB). (2006). *A tourism policy for Native Land 2006–2010*. Suva: Author.

Pro-Poor Tourism Partnership. (2005). *Key principles and strategies of pro-poor tourism*. London: Author.

Rao, M. (2006). *Challenges and Issues in pro-poor tourism in South Pacific Island countries: The case of Fiji islands*. Working Paper, Employment and Labour Market Studies, School of Economics, University of the South Pacific, Suva, Fiji.

Scheyvens, R. (2008). On the beach: Small-scale tourism in Samoa. In J. Connell & B. Rugendyke (Eds.), *Tourism at the grassroots: Visitors and villagers in the Asia-Pacific* (pp. 131–147). London: Routledge.

Scheyvens, R. (2011). *Tourism and poverty*. New York: Routledge.

Scheyvens, R., & Momsen, J.H. (2008). Tourism in small island states: From vulnerability to strengths. *Journal of Sustainable Tourism, 16*(5), 491–510.

Scheyvens, R., & Russell, M. (2009). *Sharing the riches of tourism: Exploring how tourism can contribute more effectively to poverty alleviation in the Pacific, a report funded by NZAID*. Palmerston North: Massey University.

Scheyvens, R., & Russell, M. (in press). Tourism, land tenure, and poverty alleviation in Fiji. *Tourism Geographies, 13*(4).

Schilcher, D. (2007). Growth versus equity: The continuum of pro-poor tourism and neoliberal governance. In C. Michael Hall (Ed.), *Pro-poor tourism: Who benefits?* (pp. 56–83). Clevedon: Channel View Publications.

Sobania, I. (1999). *Turning green?: A case study of tourism discourses in Germany in relation to New Zealand* (Doctoral dissertation). Retrieved 1 June 2010, from http://worldcat.org/oclc/154607694

Sofield, T. (2003). *Empowerment for sustainable tourism development*. London: Pergamon.

Sriskandarajah, D. (2003). Inequality and conflict in Fiji: From purgatory to hell? *Asia Pacific Viewpoint, 44*(3), 305–324.

Thomlinson, E., & Getz, D. (1996). The question of scale in ecotourism: Case study of two small ecotour operations in the Mundo Maya region of Central America. *Journal of Sustainable Tourism, 4*(4), 183–200.

United Nations Development Programme. (2009). Human development report 2009: Fiji. Retrieved 1 Aug 2010, from http://www.undp.org.fj/index.php?option=com_publications&Itemid=44

Veit, R. (2007). Tourism, food imports and the potential of import-substitution policies in Fiji. Paper prepared for Fiji AgTrade, Ministry of Agriculture, Fisheries and Forests, Suva, Fiji.

Walsh, C. (2002). Poverty in Fiji and the Pacific Islands: Defining an agenda for poverty reduction. In *Proceedings of the First Asia and Pacific Forum on Poverty* (Vol. 1) (pp. 230–346). Manila: Asian Development Bank.

Wanhill, S. (1999). Small and medium tourism enterprises. *Annals of Tourism Research, 27*(1), 132–147.

Weaver, D.B., & Oppermann, M. (2000). *Tourism management*. Brisbane: John Wiley & Sons.

Wilson, D. (1997). Paradoxes of tourism in Goa. *Annals of Tourism Research, 24*(1), 52–75.

World Travel and Tourism Council. (2011). *Travel and tourism economic impact 2011: Fiji*. Retrieved 3 May 2011, from http://www.wttc.org/bin/pdf/original_pdf_file/fiji.pdf

Zhao, W., & Ritchie, B. (2007). Tourism and poverty alleviation: An integrative research framework. In C. Michael Hall (Ed.), *Pro-poor tourism: Who benefits?* (pp. 9–29). Clevedon: Channel View Publications.

A critical analysis of tourism, gender and poverty reduction

Hazel Tucker and Brenda Boonabaana

Department of Tourism, University of Otago, Dunedin, New Zealand

Research on gender and poverty reduction through tourism has largely focused on the notion of women's "economic empowerment". Yet, there is still insufficient understanding about what is involved in enabling women to participate in tourism in development contexts and in ensuring they benefit economically. The paper explores the complexity of the changes that necessarily are involved in the relationships between tourism development, gender and poverty reduction, and it does this through two case studies of non-western tourism development settings, one a rural township and World Heritage Site in central Turkey, and the other a parish in south-western Uganda. The analysis identifies a variety of socio-cultural factors that constrained and enabled women and men to engage in tourism development and to benefit from it. It also explores the ways in which individuals negotiated the gendered discourses by resisting and also participating in particular cultural practices. It is concluded that the relationships between tourism, gender and poverty reduction must be approached through a nuanced understanding of the significant changes that are implicated in these relationships, as well as through a consideration of the fluid and contradictory ways in which women and men are positioned, and position themselves, in relation to those changes.

Introduction

Some scholars have pointed to the importance of gaining an understanding of how gender relations shape, and are shaped by, tourism processes over time, and how gender relations inform issues of inequality and control in tourism (Aitchison, 2001; Kinnaird & Hall, 1996; M. Swain, 1995; Tucker, 2007). Despite the importance of gaining this understanding, the relationships between gender, tourism development and poverty reduction remain little understood. Numerous studies have found that the relative benefits of tourism development reflect already existing inequalities, so elite groups usually dominate tourism development efforts and monopolize the benefits, and these groups usually comprise men (Hitchcock & Brandenburgh, 1990; Scheyvens, 2000; Stonich, Sorensen, & Hundt, 1995). Moreover, it is broadly understood that in many contexts, women miss out on the employment opportunities and related benefits of tourism development due to the culturally defined, normative notions of gender identity, roles and relations (Scheyvens, 2000; Tucker, 2007). Some pro-poor tourism development projects, therefore, have deliberately targeted women's "economic empowerment" by encouraging and supporting women's involvement in small and micro-enterprises (Ferguson, 2010a). The intention of such "empowerment" is to establish a process "by which those who have been denied the ability to make choices acquire such ability" (Kabeer, 2005, p. 13). Undoubtedly, such "empowerment" is far from straightforward, however, as it is a process that demands significant change.

Poverty reduction and gender equality comprise Goals 1 and 3, respectively, of the Millennium Development Goals (Kabeer, 2005), but the relationships between gender development and poverty reduction continue to be highly contested. For instance, gender, and development policies and projects which espouse women's "economic empowerment" as a means to achieve broader poverty reduction have been criticized for their "instrumentalist" approach to the relationships between gender equality and development (Chant, 2006; Ferguson, 2010a), as well as for their tendency to be dominated by western liberal and/or radical feminist theories (Ferguson, 2009). It is argued that these theories are Eurocentric and tend to be essentializing in their approach to gender and women's empowerment (Kabeer, 1999; Oyewumi, 2002; Syed, 2010). It is important, therefore, to move beyond simplistic and fixed ideas of women's "economic empowerment", particularly in non-western contexts, and to consider more fully the cultural complexity and the shifting dynamics of how gender norms, roles and inequalities affect, and are affected by, development and poverty reduction outcomes.

This paper explores the complexity of the changes necessarily involved in the relationships between tourism development, gender and poverty reduction. It does this by considering how women are discursively positioned in these relationships in two different non-western settings, one a small township and World Heritage Site in central Turkey, and one a parish in south-western Uganda. The assessment has two aims. The first aim is to highlight the importance of the culturally specific character of how gender relations interact with tourism development when looking at the relationships between gender and poverty reduction through tourism. This links to the second aim, which is to emphasize the importance of examining both how gender relations affect poverty reduction in tourism development contexts and how poverty reduction through tourism development in turn affects gender relations. The intention is to look beyond instrumentalist approaches to women's "economic empowerment" in order to consider the broader complexities of gender relations and how, over time, they interact with tourism development.

Feminism, development and tourism

Although a detailed account of the "gender and development paradigm" (Moser, 1989; Singh, 2007) is beyond the scope of this paper, it is useful to outline some of the key phases of development and approaches within this paradigm. There was a growing awareness during the 1970s that poverty throughout the world was more prevalent among women than among men, and this "feminization of poverty" led to calls for the integration of gender awareness into all poverty reduction and development interventions (Chant, 2007; Chen et al., 2005; Singh, 2007; Whitehead, 2003; Zuckerman, 2001). This awareness prompted the emergence of what was called Women in Development (WID), a phase of the gender and development paradigm which was informed by liberal feminism and was based on the idea that women are a vulnerable group in need of help in accessing employment and income-generating projects. The way in which gender and development thinking has progressed since then has paralleled the evolution of feminist thinking. Thus, the next phase, called Women and Development (WAD), was informed by Marxist feminism, and later what were designated as Gender and Development (GAD) policies emerged in the 1980s as a response to the radical and socialist critiques of the earlier WID approach (Singh, 2007). The GAD approach prompted the view that *gender equality* rather than solely women must be the focus, and it also advocated the need to take into consideration the socio-cultural construction of gender. With this broadening of focus came analyses and critiques of the concept of "empowerment", prompting a rejection of the idea of universal "standard" criteria which can be applied in all cultural contexts (Chant, 2006). Further, feminist post-structuralism was argued to be particularly appropriate for the study of gender and development in cross-cultural settings. This approach rejects the essentialization of gender and views the subjectivity of both women and men to be fluid and also culturally and historically constructed (Singh, 2007).

It has been argued, however, that in the majority of contemporary gender and de-velopment policies, "gender" continues to be "primarily used as a synonym for women, conforming to Women in Development (WID) . . . notions about the participation of women in economic development" (Ferguson 2010a, p. 5). Ferguson's (2010a) concern is prompted in particular by micro-enterprise funding being targeted at women under the "gender" banner with the idea of promoting women's "economic empowerment". Ferguson (2010a) points out that this is one of the key foundations of contemporary gender and development policy more generally because it is the World Bank's approach and it is also implicated in the World Bank's tourism development policy. According to Ferguson, the World Bank's ap-proach constructs women's economic empowerment through the tourism micro-enterprise "as a 'fix' for the 'gender problem'" (2010a, p. 5), which in turn also becomes a "fix" for the "poverty problem". Advocates of the GAD approach have also questioned the value of focusing development efforts on women rather than on "gender equality" (Awumbila, 2006; Chant, 2007; Ferguson 2010a). As Awumbila argues, "Focusing on women in isolation from their social relationships does little to address the power imbalances rooted in these social relations that lead to women's greater vulnerability to poverty" (2006, p. 159).

Ferguson also argues that "in recent World Bank publications on gender and the MDGs [Millennium Development Goals], it is clear that gender inequality is viewed not so much as a problem in itself, but rather as a barrier to economic development and poverty reduction" (2009, p. 15). According to Ferguson, even where "gender equality" is the stated aim, "women's economic empowerment" is "constructed not as a goal in its own right, but as a means for achieving other development outcomes" (2010a, p. 6). This instrumentalist approach is prompted by research showing that in the hands of women, productive resources are often more beneficial to the wider household and community than they are when in the hands of men (Chen et al., 2005; Okin, 2003; Silberschmidt, 2001). Furthermore, poverty reduction is not the only development outcome that might be contributed to through women's active involvement in tourism. For example, Scheyvens (2000) argues that because women's roles tend to place them in close connection with the natural environment, they develop specialist knowledge of that environment, as well as an interest in protecting it. Therefore, "any agency interested in promoting effective ecotourism should encourage the active involvement of women, even if their primary concern is not gender equity" (Scheyvens, 2000, p. 235). Indeed, Chant notes that there is a problem because gender and development projects tend to lead to "women working for development", more than development "working for women" (2006, p. 102).

In addition to the problem of "instrumentalist" approaches, Ferguson argues that in reality "feminist research on micro-enterprise projects suggests that 'economic empower-ment' from such projects is limited" (2010a, p. 7). Ferguson (2010a) cites a number of micro-enterprise initiatives targeted at women in a variety of development contexts, and she concludes that control over loans and benefits tends to be maintained by men, that any benefits accrued by women tend to be made by women who are already better off and that gender inequalities continue to constrain women's entrepreneurship and their chances of active involvement. Even where micro-enterprise projects do seem to empower women, the *longer-term implications* of these projects for women, men and the broader community are questionable. They are especially questionable when projects are initiated by outsider groups who are not fully cognizant of the cultural nuances of gender relations in that society. This applies for an ecotourism project run by a Dutch NGO that both van der Cammen (1997) and Scheyvens (2000) argue has successfully worked to economically empower Maasai women in Tanzania. According to Scheyvens (2000), the NGO staff managed to persuade the men that they should allow women to be actively involved in tourism by convincing the men that this would help them to attract both development funding and culturally responsible ecotourists. The NGO staff worked with groups of women to help them to build up their confidence and skills and to assist them to set up such tourism products as walking safaris and beadwork shops. Scheyvens (2000) and van der Cammen (1997) conclude that empowerment had been achieved because the Maasai women largely were able to retain the income they earned, such as through selling beadwork.

However, Chant (2006) further cautions against situations where the definitions of women's empowerment are based on the values of outsiders, and where there is a lack of regard for the *implications* of such empowerment. Similarly, Kabeer states:

> To attempt to predict at the outset of an intervention precisely how it will change women's lives, without some knowledge of "being and doing" which are realizable and valued by women in that context, runs into the danger of prescribing the process of empowerment, and thereby violating its essence, which is to enhance women's capacity for self-determination. (1999, p. 462)

According to Kabeer (1999), the very notion of women's empowerment is based on western ideas of how gender relations ought to be, rather than on how they actually are. And he argues that such a normative standpoint is not sufficiently informed about women's own perceptions of their possibilities and constraints. As Singh also argues, "A primary goal of Western feminism is equality between men and women. In developing countries, however, these goals become unrealistic . . . For many women, adopting the goals of Western feminism would mean losing their families, the primary source of support for the fulfilment of their social, psychological and economic needs" (2007, p. 104). From this perspective, externally organized pro-poor tourism projects aimed at women's economic empowerment might be problematic if the longer-term implications of the resulting changes are not considered.

Thus, the discussion that follows, rather than dwelling on women's "economic empowerment" per se, draws on critiques of the gender and development paradigm and takes the view that the relationships between tourism, gender and poverty reduction must be approached through a nuanced understanding of the significant changes implicated in these relationships, and through consideration of the fluid and contradictory ways in which women and men are positioned, and position themselves, in relation to these changes. Post-structural feminism is taken as a useful approach which attempts to understand "how individuals negotiate gendered discourses contingent on specific historical contexts by resisting or participating in those cultural practices" (Azzarito, Solmon, & Harrison, 2006, p. 224). In this view, women are recognized as active participants who make choices and participate in structuring and negotiating their identities, rather than being seen as "victims" or "problems" (Azzarito et al., 2006; Weedon, 1997). Singh (2007) argues that a feminist post-structuralist approach does not assume a stationary, simplistic and standardized definition of women, and thus it is particularly appropriate for studies of gender and development in cross-cultural settings.

In the gender and tourism literature, the relative benefits of tourism development for women and men are widely understood to reflect local socio-cultural norms regarding gender relations and the division of labour based on gender (Apostolopoulos & Sönmez, 2001; Ferguson, 2009; Gibson, 2001; Harvey, Hunt, & Harris, 1995; Kinnaird, Kothari, & Hall, 1994; Long & Kindon, 1997; Scott, 1997; Wilkinson & Pratiwi, 1995). Feminist research has highlighted how in cases where women are heavily involved in tourism production, there is a clear segmentation of men's and women's work, with women's employment being concentrated in such low-paid, part-time and seasonal areas as hospitality, cleaning and retail work (Ferguson, 2009; Sinclair, 1997a, 1997b). This clear segmentation is most obvious in larger-scale tourism enterprises, and thus small and micro-enterprises, and especially family-run businesses have often been found to be relatively beneficial for women because of the economic opportunities they offer them as well as the chances they offer them to improve their status within and outside of the household (Gibson, 2001). Based on her study of a wide range of contexts, Scheyvens (2000) also notes that small-scale, community-focused tourism initiatives offer the highest potential for enhancing the lives of economically marginalized groups, including rural women. Similarly, Gentry (2007) argues that alternative forms of tourism based on small-scale businesses are likely to be more beneficial for local women, as compared with mass tourism, which often attracts transnational corporate tourism businesses and external labour. The issue of tourism's scale is why many pro-poor tourism projects that target women tend to be based on encouraging tourism micro-enterprises as part of small-scale community or eco-tourism projects, such as the one in Mukono parish, which is examined in this paper. The World Bank's gender and poverty reduction tourism projects in Central America are also based predominantly on small-scale and "alternative" forms of tourism development (Ferguson, 2010a).

In many cultural contexts, however, even small and micro-scale businesses may not allow women's involvement. One reason for this is that women may be prevented from doing particular types of work if such work is culturally inappropriate. Wilkinson and Pratiwi (1995) report that this applies in the case of rural Java, where guiding work has prostitution connotations. The emphasis in many cultural contexts on women's household and reproductive responsibilities can also severely limit women's ability to work outside the home and in tourism (Ferguson, 2010b). Where social norms restrict women to domestic space, women might miss out all together on formal employment opportunities, and this may be particularly prominent in certain socially conservative Muslim societies (Sönmez, 2001; Tucker, 2007). In contrast, it has been noted that tourism can offer possibilities for gender roles and relationships to be *re*negotiated (Gibson, 2001; Long & Wall, 1995; Meethan, 2001; Scheyvens, 2000; Sinclair, 1997a, 1997b; Swain & Wallentin, 2008; Tucker, 2007). When considering the relationships between tourism, gender and poverty reduction, it is crucial to understand how this renegotiation can take place, and also what its implications may be.

The study contributes to understanding in this field by examining what can be involved in promoting women's economic participation in tourism in development contexts and in helping them to benefit from it. This is explored through two case study settings where "traditional" gender norms and roles have until recently prevented women from engaging in tourism in substantive ways, or indeed, in any other formal employment or work outside of the household. The two settings illustrate some of the socio-cultural factors that constrain and enable women and men to engage in tourism work and to benefit from it. These examples also illustrate the very complex and necessarily gradual nature of the processes of socio-cultural change involved in the relationships between gender, tourism and poverty reduction. The two case study tourism development settings are introduced next.

Gender and tourism development: the two settings

Tuyezere (2007) points to religious beliefs as having a strong role in the ways in which gender relations are reinforced and "naturalized" in a society. Consequently, Syed (2010) argues that research on gender and development needs to take account of both the socio-cultural and the religious contexts that affect the complex nature of gender relations. There is insufficient space here to explore in great depth the effects of religion per se on gender relations and tourism development. Yet the two case studies involve communities following two of the world's main religions, and as such, they complement each other to provide a broad understanding of the processes of socio-cultural change implicated in the relationships between gender, tourism development and poverty reduction. The first setting is the small township of Göreme in central Turkey, and the second is Mukono parish in south-western Uganda. Both are rural contexts which traditionally have depended on subsistence farming, and both represent conservative patriarchal societies. A key criterion for examining these two case studies is that both are societies where traditionally women had limited access to income and formal work outside of the home. In addition, they are both cases where "community-based tourism" has developed and is thought to have significantly reduced poverty in their communities. In both cases, tourism entrepreneurship and employment is now a major source of income for the local community, and women have begun to find employment and to establish micro-enterprise activity.

While these two settings have several similarities, they also differ in many respects beyond their different religious contexts. Mukono parish has experienced external intervention through NGO-funded projects, whereas Göreme's tourism development has predominantly been established from within the community and has not involved any targeted donor or NGO-funded "tourism development" interventions. Mukono parish more overtly represents a "developing country" context, with poverty still seen as a widespread and extreme problem; while in Göreme, there has been significant economic and social development over the last three decades, largely due to the successful growth of tourism in the region but also because of political, economic and social reform at the national level. Nonetheless, many households in Göreme are still considered to be at the margins of poverty, and a recent increase in women's involvement in tourism is helping to lift some households further out of poverty. The two settings are not included here to make direct comparisons between them. Rather, these two settings are used to illustrate that the processes of discursive construction are common to both despite their dissimilarities. These cases demonstrate the importance of considering the particular local socio-cultural influences on gender relations and tourism development, and also how women are discursively positioned in relation to tourism and poverty reduction.

The methodology used in both settings is based on an interpretative approach, with the fieldwork guided by the anthropological methods of participant observation and semi-structured, in-depth interviews. The Göreme case is part of a long-term ethnographic study, conducted by Tucker, and which began in 1995 by looking at the socio-cultural changes initially brought about by tourism in the village, and it has since developed into a longitudinal study researching the continuing tourism development and its ongoing implications for society and culture in the area (see, in particular, Tucker 2003, 2007, 2010). A primary focus of the study has been the ongoing dynamics of the relationships between tourism development and gender relations in this socially conservative society. During Tucker's most recent periods of fieldwork in Göreme, in 2009 and 2010, her interviewing focused particularly on women who had recently begun to work in tourism for the first time.

The Mukono setting presented here is part of a larger research project looking at the relationships between community-based tourism, and gender roles and relations in Mukono parish. This research was conducted by Boonabaana, who is herself from a neighbouring parish and so shares a cultural background and language similar to the community studied. The fieldwork material here was collected through in-depth interviews with Mukono women and men, those involved and those not involved in tourism (a total of 44 in-depth interviews were conducted). Use was also made of participant observation, such as attending tourism activities, meetings and local interactions, and document review methods. Fieldwork was conducted for 12 months between 2009 and 2010.

The analysis next outlines the relationships between gender, tourism and poverty reduction in Göreme.

Göreme, gender relations and tourism work

Since the mid-1980s, Göreme and the wider Cappadocia area have become a major focus for Turkey's cultural tourism development. The primary tourist attraction in the region remains the Göreme Open-Air Museum, designated a World Heritage Site in 1985. Göreme township is within the Göreme National Park area, which surrounds the Open-Air Museum, and consequently, it did not see the same large-scale tourism-related investment and construction that was seen in some other towns in Cappadocia. Göreme's tourism thus developed through small or micro-businesses that were mostly locally owned and operated (Tucker, 2003). Prior to the development of tourism, the Göreme community largely relied on subsistence farming, although some men found employment in nearby towns and some went further afield to become truck drivers. At that time, too, some Göreme people were driven by economic hardship to take advantage of migration programmes to northern Europe.

Today, the majority of Göreme households are engaged in tourism-related work or entrepreneurial activity, even though most have also retained their land in order to continue their subsistence farming alongside their tourism business activities (as Bryceson points out, retaining land as a fallback is a way of "safeguarding peasant survival in the face of adversity" [2000, p. 312]). There is a population of approximately 2000 people in the township, and also around 80 small guest houses (*pansiyons*) and "boutique" hotels, 25 tour and activity operators, 30 restaurants, 10 bars, 15 carpet shops, several general stores and numerous other souvenir shops and stands.

During the development of tourism in Göreme in the 1980s and 1990s, men became the tourism entrepreneurs and gained tourism employment, while women largely remained occupied with garden and farming work for household consumption and with other domestic work. This is because, in accordance with Islamic codes and practice, in Göreme society, there is strict segregation of the sexes, with a well-defined distribution of economic and social activity according to gender that is upheld by the principles of shame and honour (*namus*) (Tucker, 2003). Despite significant social and economic change in Turkey over recent decades, Göreme and the wider Cappadocia region has remained a pocket of rural conservatism. In Göreme, a major way in which gender segregation is manifested is in relation to movement outside of the home. While men may move around freely in public space, it is improper for women to do so. Rather, women stay within the strict boundaries of domestic space unless specific permission to do otherwise is granted by a close male relative.

Involvement in tourism is highly gendered, therefore, through the ideological, social and spatial gender separation in Göreme. As tourism has developed there, tourism work has been considered a man's activity as it is regarded as inappropriate for women to work in the "public" sphere. Generally, women have been excluded from participating in tourism work, and they have only been able to access the tourism economy indirectly through the earnings of their husband or other male household members. Women's legitimacy to be in, and to work in, such "public" spaces as the central streets is limited by the principles of shame and honour, and an associated culture of gossip. As one woman reported, "I can't even go to the shops or the market, because of tourism." Another Göreme woman explained, "My husband won't allow me to enter public places, so I couldn't be a waitress. He wouldn't allow it. Also, I don't have the confidence."

In more recent years, however, there has been an increase in women's paid employment in local tourism small businesses as well as in women's micro-scale entrepreneurial activity associated with tourism. These activities represent a significant shift in the ways in which moral and spatial boundaries relating to gender are now manifested in Göreme. Tucker (2007) looked in depth at what had enabled this shift to take place, arguing that a variety of social, political and economic realms have converged to create an environment in which the boundaries of *namus* (shame and honour) associated with Göreme women's work have slowly shifted. Some of these factors are aspects of broader social changes, in particular national-level improvements in education for women and girls. Other factors are directly related to tourism, such as foreign female incomers (tourists who have become resident in Göreme) who have demonstrated new forms of cultural possibility, especially regarding gender relations and roles.

In addition, the moral and spatial boundaries surrounding women's activities are slowly being pushed out, and very gradually, women are becoming more confident and comfortable in public/tourism space, as well as less susceptible to gossip, than they were previously. The main area of employment for women is in the *pansiyons* (guest houses) and boutique hotels. During the first two decades of Göreme's tourism development, most guest houses were small and informally run. During the past decade, however, many of these establishments have grown to become larger, more formal and compartmentalized "boutique hotels". This compartmentalization has created a "back stage" space where women have started to be employed. As one woman who works in a *pansiyon* said, "*Pansiyon* work is okay because a *pansiyon* is like a house. There aren't any men, for example, in the laundry or kitchen." It is necessary for a *pansiyon* to be formalized in this way, and for it to be considered a respectable establishment, for a woman's husband to grant her permission to work there *and* for a woman to feel comfortable working there. A few younger, unmarried women have also, after gradual exposure to tourists and tourism, mastered enough language and service skills, as well as enough confidence, to graduate through to the more public areas, such as into hotel reception or restaurant work. While these young women have sometimes been the subject of gossip, the fact that they have by and large persisted in their employment, often supported and encouraged by foreign resident friends, means that the spatial boundaries and boundaries of shame relating to gender and tourism work are gradually shifting and being stretched out (Tucker, 2007).

This shifting of moral and spatial boundaries, which has allowed women to begin entering tourism employment and tourism/public space, has become especially important in recent years in relation to poverty reduction. In general, the Göreme women who are engaging in tourism work are either the head of their household (divorced or widowed), and they struggle to provide for themselves and their children, or the wives or daughters of households which are struggling to make a living, even though the men of the household may be involved in tourism. Wages are low in Göreme and so men who do not have their own business may earn only a meagre income. Some struggle even when they do have their own business. Tucker (2010) reports that unlike the relatively level playing field that characterized the early years of Göreme's small-business development, inequalities are now emerging, with an increased difference between success and non-success. Some businesses are maturing and thriving, while others have stagnated and struggled to survive. The owner-operators of the struggling businesses can only make a meager living at best. One woman who works in her husband's small shop on the main street, selling snacks, drinks and tobacco products to a largely tourist market, explained that she had wanted to do the day-time shift in the place of the young man who her husband had previously employed (most tourism businesses in the town are open from early morning until late evening). She said that previously there was very little money left after they had paid the wage of the worker, but now that she splits the long working day with her husband, all of the shop's small profit comes into the household. Initially, the husband had resisted his wife's suggestion of her working in the shop, but because that same year a few other women had started to work in the central businesses (mostly mothers helping in their son's cafes, again because income was not enough to pay wages), a precedent had been set, and so he decided that they would give it a try. The woman said that she was uncomfortable at first being in the shop in the main street, and that both her and her husband had feared there would be gossip. However, she had gradually got used to being there, and was also comforted by the fact she was not the only woman helping in their family businesses on the main street.

The shifting of moral and spatial boundaries has clearly allowed some households, when there is an economic necessity, to involve women in tourism work. Change in gender norms, however, is a slow process. There still remain strict limitations on women's abilities to work, both at the ideological and at the practical levels. Childcare is a particular issue that inhibits women's ability to work, especially if the children are young. The busiest time for tourism, and when there is most likelihood of work being available, is during the summer months, but this is when the long school holidays occur. Consequently, women with younger school-age children would only be able to work in a *pansiyon* or other tourism business if they had female relatives who were available and willing to look after their children.

Some women who lacked childcare and thus were unable to go out to work have attempted to earn a little money from their home by selling handicrafts to passing tourists. These women live in the township's older neighbourhoods and have capitalized on their "traditional" cave-dwelling lifestyle by inviting tourists in to view their "cave-house" with the aim of then selling handicrafts to them. Despite there being much gossip about this activity, some women have continued out of economic necessity, particularly those who are divorced or widowed and who do not have the social links and standing to gain regular employment in a *pansiyon*. The married women who engage in this type of entrepreneurial activity acknowledged that they would not be able to work in tourism other than doing this sort of activity because they could not obtain permission from their husband. Having their cave-house as an attraction and selling handicrafts from home therefore provides these women with an opportunity to engage with the tourism economy and to earn some money of their own that they would otherwise not have.

Despite these positive changes in Göreme, the women's earnings are still contributing only in a minimal way to poverty reduction. As already mentioned, wages are in any case low, and within the work places they are entering, women tend to gain only the least remunerative jobs. On a very practical level, the employment of women in tourism significantly adds to the women's workloads because their household-centred reproductive and food production duties continue even if tourism-related work is taken up. However, particularly for divorcees and widows and for households struggling on a small tourism income, the ability for women to contribute to the household economy is significant, whether it is through saving the family business from having to pay a wage to a non-family member or through their earning a small wage from another business. What is also clear in Göreme is that a significant shift has occurred in the society's normative notions of gender identities and roles, and that this has been necessary in order for women to be able to start working in the "public" spaces of tourism.

The analysis next examines the discursive processes of gender, tourism and poverty reduction in the very different cultural context of Mukono parish in Uganda.

Mukono parish, community tourism initiatives and gender

Mukono parish is located in Kayonza subcounty, Kanungu District in south-western Uganda. It has a population of just over 5000, and their ethnicity is predominantly Bakiga. There are 11 villages in the parish, six of which are in the "tourism zone". Considerable socio-economic progress has been realized in recent years through tourism development because of its close proximity to the Bwindi Impenetrable National Park, a UNESCO World Heritage Site popular for gorilla ecotourism. However, there is still significant deprivation, and the local community is still thought to be largely gripped by poverty. This community was formerly faced with an extreme scarcity of livelihood opportunities, being dependent on subsistence farming, but during the past decade and a half, tourism has emerged as an alternative and relatively lucrative livelihood opportunity. Due to the funding gained from tourism, schools, clean water and health centres have now been established for the first time in the area. Also, the women and young people have begun to earn an income of their own for the first time.

This research focused specifically on the major small-scale community tourism businesses in the area, which were: the Buhoma Community Rest Camp initiative, a community walk initiative, the Bwindi Advanced Market Gardener's Association vegetable initiative, and cultural performances and handcraft businesses run by women's groups. These are community-run tourism initiatives and they exclusively employ Mukono locals, both men and women, but initially they were funded by external (international and national Ugandan) NGOs. Profits from these initiatives pay employees' wages, sustain the businesses and are reinvested in other communal projects, such as schools, water infrastructure and roads. The rest camp caters for the accommodation, food and beverage needs of tourists, while the community walk initiative provides a "local cultural experience" through 10 designated stopping sites, including a women's craft shop, juice and local beer production households, a traditional medicine healer, and a Kalehe/pygmy ("Batwa") group cultural performance and craft market. The Bwindi Advanced Market Gardener's Association vegetable initiative works as a linkage between local farmers and tourism businesses, helping in the production and marketing of produce for tourist lodgings and providing cooking classes for tourists. Various women's groups present cultural performances and run handicraft businesses. Some women who do not belong to any of these groups may weave baskets to sell privately, while a few other women are employed as sales staff in craft businesses.

Among these NGO-initiated projects, the only initiative targeted specifically at women is the cultural performances and handicraft businesses run by women's groups. Thus, this is the one sector that has only women involved, although one initiative targeted at a Batwa (pygmy) group involves a mixed group of men and women. In all, there are approximately 10 women's groups involved in this sector. The other initiatives and sectors have a "community-wide" focus, and between them, they directly employ approximately 40 men and 15 women. In this non-cultural performance/handicraft sector, men tend to be in the better rewarded management positions, while women generally occupy the low-ranking, low-paying and insecure jobs, notably housekeeping, gardening and guiding. The community walk initiative is staffed by five female and four male guides, and the vegetable initiative's "individual" membership comprises approximately 100 men and 140 women.

Over time, Mukono men have been relinquishing many of their "household breadwinner" responsibilities to women. This trend originated and became accepted when men previously had left their families for work in colonial plantations, mines and factories situated far from Mukono parish, leaving women with all the household responsibilities. Very few men leave the parish to gain employment today, however, largely due to tourism development. While some men now have tourism-related jobs, many have developed alcohol-drinking and "womanizing" habits, which according to the participants were influenced by legacies from pre-colonial and pre-Christian polygamous marriages. Many women have embraced the tourism opportunities available largely because many men are developing alcoholism and leaving women to fend for themselves and for their children. Indeed, one woman dubbed tourism development "a saviour". Through their small-scale tourism businesses, they are earning an income and thereby offsetting some of their pressing economic difficulties. Women's economic involvement in tourism, therefore, presents a fundamental change for these women.

However, specific cultural and religious beliefs continue to strongly influence the gender dynamics and gendered behaviours of the Mukono community. Firstly, beliefs in witchcraft mean that a man who is seen to help out in the household is accused of being subject to witchcraft propagated by his own wife. Christian beliefs also have a considerable influence in reinforcing particular gender relations. As one woman pointed out, "When you are religious, you see the way things are supposed to be. The Bible even says that women should be submissive to their husbands." Another woman described the current male drinking and womanizing behaviour as "just a gene from God". Simultaneously, women themselves place significant value on persisting with their marriage and keeping the family together, and doing so, as one woman said, "through thick and thin". Such persistence earns them community respect.

Secondly, for women to work in tourism and directly to benefit from it, they constantly had to negotiate and renegotiate gender norms within the context of local gossip as well as threats to their personal comfort and safety. Some of the women interviewed complained about being unable to get involved in tourism work because they lacked the presentable clothes which they considered were necessary for women to wear for work and during women's group meetings. Other women who worked in such positions as tour guides were accused of being "rebels" by some community members, and especially older relatives. (Ferguson (2010b) similarly notes that in Central American tourism development projects, guiding was not considered suitable work for women). Further, some women reported being subjected to sexual harassment from outsider men who come into the area for tourism work, such as tour-bus drivers, national park employees and soldiers stationed there to provide tourist security.

Lastly, one of the major barriers for married women is the necessity to gain their husbands' permission to work. In the context of Mukono, men's role in permission-giving is influenced by their cultural roles as *banyineka* (household owners) and as decision-makers who must direct and control the lives of their wives and children. A woman who works as a housekeeper commented on this, "A man is the head of the family and the woman has to listen to her husband. We know that is the rule and we go by that." A local man whose wife makes and sells handicrafts privately to tourists also said, "My wife makes baskets, but I don't want her to do dancing. I want her to perform her other wife duties at home, but not to come home late . . . those clubs that demand her to stay there till 8 or 9 pm, no way. Would she really want me to cook?" As well as wanting his wife to be at home to perform her household "wife duties", he went on to say how his wife's employment in a tourist lodge or performance group would automatically create "doubt", because "a lot of things take place there . . . a woman can't refuse sex when offered money". Thus, for married women, gaining their husband's permission is central to their entry into paid tourism work, and women must constantly negotiate this in order to retain good marital relations.

In turn, because local men are beginning to appreciate women's development efforts, some men and parents are beginning to relax their negative attitudes towards their wives and daughters working in tourism. Women are being seen to significantly improve not only their own personal situation but also that of their household, and even that of their neighbours through the provision and sharing of basic household items, such as salt, soap and sugar. One woman commented, "Most families here are surviving on the power of women. Actually, that's why we thank tourism so much." Similarly, a man said in his interview, "When my wife sells her baskets, she tells me what she wants to buy and if she buys a dress, I feel happy and relieved because I would have been the one to buy it." Undoubtedly, there is a growing appreciation of women who work and earn, despite the barriers.

In addition, because some tourism work, such as craft-making, is home based, women are able to combine it with their household responsibilities. Guiding work is also part time and thus it allows for flexibility around household duties. Thus, the nature of much of the tourism work in Mukono, being part-time, home based and flexible, has facilitated women's entry into tourism. These factors have also helped women to retain their husbands' approval, since they are able to keep some time to perform household duties. Time management is another strategy that women are employing, such as by trying to schedule their meetings and cultural performances at times which do not clash with their household responsibilities. However, this usually means that these women must work very long days to make sure everything gets done and to avoid their husband's reprimands.

Overall, women's workload is significantly increased if they work in tourism because that work is always combined with managing their household duties. Some women, particularly if they have full-time and less flexible work, manage to gain paid or unpaid/family help, especially for childcare. For example, one woman, who is a manager of a private craft business, hires a maid for childcare and also gets a supporting hand from relatives. She said, "I pay the maid who takes care of my daughter, and my brother's wife takes care of my elderly mum on my behalf. I send her money and she takes care of the farming for my mum, takes care of the animals at home, and makes food available." Many women enlist the help of a family member while they are working, such as a sister or sister-in-law. Even where such domestic helpers are not paid directly in cash, they would be given small gift items which they otherwise lack, such as salt or sugar. Women working in tourism also frequently employ gardening labour because keeping productive gardens is a crucial part of the identity of "hardworking *Bakiga*" women, an identity which is culturally highly valued.

The opportunities for small-scale tourism income in Mukono are thus perceived as slowly bringing the community out of abject poverty, including women and their households. Women spend their income on pressing family needs, including their children's education, clothing, food and household items. They also help relatives and neighbours, thus creating a positive "trickle-down effect" with their small earnings. Moreover, the women's ability to interact and network with fellow women and other workmates, and to share "development" ideas, is having further positive outcomes. For example, some women's cultural groups have become informal lending and borrowing institutions for their members, with members pooling resources for self-help. Some women have also invested in property (land and rental houses), the ownership of which used to be solely in the hands of men. In turn, this safeguards their economic future, even in the event of divorce or separation, since women's groups' collective investments restrict their husbands from claiming their property for sale or personal use. Overall, the fact that women have become breadwinners for the first time has enabled them to "bring something to the table" and to "buy salt", as they put it, and it has also allowed them to form networks, to help others and to have increased levels of confidence and self-esteem.

Tourism, gender practices and poverty reduction: Mukono and Göreme settings

> You know there are men who would proudly say that my wife is actually the best cook. How is he going to say that you are a good cook when you are even not cooking for him? By the time you reach home, you are very tired and you can't show him that love that he expects you to give to him. It is that time when you are not at work and not in the office that you need to welcome your husband and be there for him, serve him and show him love, and if you don't do that, you are actually not like a wife. Money is not all. You may work, make money, but if you are not happy in your family, it has no meaning. For me I would love to balance my roles as a woman and also my work here. My family matters so much, and so making my children and husband happy makes me happy. (Mukono woman who works in a craft business)

The settings and processes examined so far illustrate many of the socio-cultural factors that constrain and enable women to begin to engage in tourism work and to benefit from it, and also how women discursively position themselves, and are positioned by others, in relation to tourism and poverty reduction. In both contexts, women seek their husband's permission to work in the tourism realm. In Göreme, this is related to tourism operating predominantly in the "public" realm, with the Turkish word for permission (*izin*) encompassing the notion of protection as much as that of control (see Tucker 2003). In Mukono, permission is sought from husbands more because tourism work is seen as distracting a woman from her household duties, but it is also linked to men's fears about the relationship between tourism work and women's promiscuity. (Such fears have also been identified elsewhere, such as in Botswana [Mbaiwa, 2005]). While permission for women to work in tourism has gradually been negotiated in both Göreme and Mukono, this was done in ways which would not cut too severely, or too quickly, against the socio-cultural norms and expectations. Women's own negotiation of the norms and expectations, therefore, was necessarily a gradual process, with women devising ways to fit tourism work in and around their usual roles and practices. It is precisely because their decisions and actions appear often to be compliant and resistant to change that these two illustrative settings provide important insights into the multiple and contradictory ways in which women and men negotiate and constantly reposition themselves within gender discourses.

Both settings illustrated that "a husband's permission", or in other words, men's position of power and control, is far from being the only factor, or even the main factor, in determining a woman's ability to take up formal employment in the tourism sphere. In both cultural contexts, the women themselves desired to heed the cultural expectations by fulfilling their household and marriage duties. As also suggested by Singh (2007), because the family and the household are the main source of social, economic and emotional support for most women, the goals of western feminism might be both unrealistic and irrelevant. Informed by post-structuralist feminism ideas, this is where it appears clear that individuals negotiate the gendered discourses by both resisting *and* participating in particular cultural practices. Furthermore, the study settings here support the argument within post-structuralist feminism that "a woman's identity is a temporal duality of positions, meaning that women carry within them the positions of power and powerlessness at the same time, rather than the either/or position suggested by most discourses" (Singh, 2007, p. 106).

As well as the fine line between women's *wanting* and *needing* to maintain good marital relations, this position of simultaneous power and powerlessness and of simultaneous resistance and participation is seen in both Göreme and Mukono in the fine line between women's wanting and needing respect within their community. In the Muslim society of Göreme, that respect is associated with *namus*, or honor and shame, which in turn is closely connected with the duality of public and private/domestic space. In Mukono, community respect is connected with a woman persisting with her marriage and also her fulfillment of household and gardening duties. In both Göreme and Mukono, women actively participate in these gender discourses and are reluctant to step outside of their usual role and their usual (domestic) space. As we saw in both settings, there are also specific tourism jobs deemed inappropriate for women, such as "front stage" work (hotel reception work and restaurant waiting) in Göreme and guiding and working at lodgings in Mukono. As already mentioned, this is also seen in other contexts. For instance, Ferguson explains that guiding is seen as inappropriate for women in some Central American tourism settings and also notes that women, as much as men, "expressed the opinion that guiding and diving were 'not for women'" (2010b, p. 869). The same situation occurs in Göreme and Mukono, where in relation to their work in tourism being deemed inappropriate, both women and men fear community gossip, while being perpetrators of such gossip.

Gossip has long been argued to confirm and reinforce norms and to control individual moral conduct (Gluckman, 1963). More recent discussions of the practice and meaning of gossip have looked at how people use gossip to argue about moral standing (Pietila, 2007; Stewart & Strathern, 2004). Such arguments are more likely to take place at times of significant change, because this is when the parameters of moral conduct and standing are under threat. At such times, gossip is a method used by a community for "fixing social boundaries and moral codes" (Zinovieff, 1991, p. 132). The important point here is that by both fearing and perpetuating gossip, women's positioning in relation to gender norms and tourism development is contradictory and discursive. Again, rather than being a situation where patriarchy is operating in a repressive and unitary way, women's active participation in the social practice of gossip reflects a complex environment of gender relations in which power and resistance are both multi-directional and contested.

Women's subjectivity is also discursively constructed in relation to their social re-production roles in Göreme and Mukono. Part-time and flexible tourism work to some extent enables women to work around childcare and other household responsibilities. Some women also negotiate the help of relatives, friends or paid helpers for childcare and other household and gardening duties. There is clearly a tension for women, however, in trying to juggle tourism work outside of the home with social reproduction duties, particularly childcare. It is also clear that women who work in tourism carry a double burden, and that their overall workload is increased. Globally, the majority of social reproduction work – domestic tasks, parenting and other types of social care – is carried out as unpaid labour in the home and is undertaken by women (Ferguson, 2010b; Waylen, 2000). Again, in Göreme and Mukono, women actively participate in these gender practices, as was shown in the interview extract at the start of this section, thus reproducing the discourse that social reproduction is ultimately women's responsibility.

In both settings, private "home-based" production and selling of handicrafts has been taken up by women who are unable to work outside of the domestic realm. In relation to women in India, Kantor (2003) argues that development interventions should support women's home-based micro-economic enterprises, and indeed, many tourism development projects purposefully promote this kind of enterprise because it is seen as encouraging "the retention of the nuclear family and 'traditional' ways of living" (Ferguson, 2010b, p. 880).

In this context, Ferguson (2010b) discusses a rural tourism project in Costa Rica which is hailed throughout Central America as a "model" for tourism development and which aims to provide families with an income through offering accommodation and food in their own home to tourists. As Ferguson (2010b) points out, however, such policy does nothing to challenge the notion that social reproduction is "women's work". Moreover, women's involvement in a "family business" is likely to add to their unpaid workload. This appears also to be the case for the women in Göreme who help out at the family shop or cafe. While their unpaid labour is perceived as helping to keep their own household out of poverty, effectively, it is still unpaid labour which is added to the social reproduction labour within the household that these women already do.

In relation to household earnings and poverty reduction, women's tourism work in Göreme does not appear to have replaced men's tourism productive work at all. Men in Göreme are still the main income earners and women's work and earnings are supplementary, unless in a woman-headed household. In contrast, in Mukono, women's work is considered to be a major contributor to household poverty alleviation, since many men appear to be replacing their "household breadwinner" responsibilities with drinking, gaming and womanizing habits. Depictions of men in situations of poverty as "violent, lazy, drunken problems" are common in many gender and development policies (Cleaver, 2002), and this is an interesting area for further critical attention (Bedford, 2007, p. 304). However, for the purposes of the present discussion, the important point is that because women's work in tourism in Mukono has in many households replaced the dependence on men's earnings, the cultural norms regarding gender roles and relations seem to become more easily relaxed. As men and other family and community members increasingly appreciate women's development efforts, it is becoming easier for women to negotiate their husband's permission and local gossip is decreasing. In other words, because women's role in poverty reduction is becoming highly valued within the whole Mukono community, it appears to be having significant implications for gender roles and relations in this society. In Göreme, on the other hand, men are still the predominant income earners for the majority of households and cultural norms regarding gender roles and relations still retain a strong grip on the acceptance of women's tourism work.

Nonetheless, while tourism enterprise has facilitated a greater level of financial independence for more women in Mukono than in Göreme, many Göreme women now have a greater *possibility* of participating in tourism, and of earning an income from it, than they did previously. It is too early yet to say how this increased actual or potential financial independence might affect women's choices regarding marriage, divorce and other related life choices. Yet there seems no doubt that the previous certainty of women's financial dependence on men has now shifted, and that consequently, poverty reduction through tourism in both Mukono and Göreme will have significant implications for future changes in gender relations. At the same time, though, the benefits that women have received from participation in tourism have *necessitated* substantial changes in gender relations, and such changes have been shown here to require gradual, multiple and often seemingly contradictory processes of negotiation.

Conclusion

To date, the research on gender and poverty reduction initiatives, including initiatives with a focus on tourism, have usually concentrated on the notion of women's "economic empowerment". It has been explained how this approach has been criticized for taking an "instrumentalist" approach to "the poverty problem", and also for its tendency to be based on Eurocentric ideals about how gender relations ought to be, rather than based on how they actually are in each particular socio-cultural context. This was illustrated in the example discussed earlier of an "ecotourism" project in Tanzania, wherein men were persuaded by external NGO workers to allow women to engage in tourism micro-enterprise activities. However, in line with feminist critiques of the gender and development paradigm, the in-depth examination in this paper of two tourism development settings has shown that there is a need to treat with caution claims by tourism and poverty reduction projects to "have achieved", or even to be aiming for, women's "economic empowerment".

First, the idea influenced by earlier radical and liberal feminist theories that women are oppressed by a unitary notion of patriarchal power has been shown to be problematic. The analysis here has contested the idea that all that is required is for *men* to be persuaded to allow *women* to participate in tourism work, doing this by showing that gender power is multiple, contested and fluid, rather than being possessed by men to be used in relations of control over women. This is why pro-poor tourism projects which espouse quick-fix notions of "empowerment" in relation to women, tourism and poverty reduction might be considered naive. Moreover, such projects might also remain limited in their ability to meet their aims unless, firstly, they take into account the full complexities of the socio-cultural norms surrounding gender roles and relations in the locale in question, and secondly, they recognize women's agency in negotiating power relations. In both the Göreme and Mukono cultural contexts, women themselves simultaneously resist and participate in the cultural practices and expectations regarding their spatial and social reproduction roles.

Second, as Swain and Wallentin argue, the process of women's empowerment in relation to tourism development can only take place "when women challenge the existing norms and cultures of a society to effectively improve their well being" (2008, p. 24). Tourism development in both Göreme and Mukono shifted the boundaries of norms and expectations in relation to gender discourse and practices, but this was also shown to be necessarily gradual and enacted "from within" in line with local ways of "being and doing" (Kabeer 1999, p. 462). The women's income-generating projects which do not pay attention to women's and men's own perceptions of their constraints and possibilities in relation to tourism, or to the possible *implications* of such significant and complex changes, are unlikely to be successful in their poverty reduction efforts and may also be detrimental to women. As Chant (2006) points out, albeit in relation to non-tourism-focused gender and development efforts, a perceived "threat" posed by improvements in women's economic status can result in men taking over projects, controlling the income that is derived or even *increasing* their overall authority and control within the home. The complexity and pervasiveness of gender norms and relations means that there can be no "quick fix" to gender and poverty issues.

Finally, regarding the instrumentalist tendencies of the "tourism for women's economic empowerment" approach, the present analysis has indicated how a situation can result where women are working for development rather than development working for women. This was seen in the fact that tourism created a "double burden" of work for the women of both Mukono and Göreme. In line with Ferguson's (2010b) study of the relationships between tourism development and social reproduction in Central America, the two case studies show that there must always be full consideration of women's social reproduction roles in gender-focused poverty reduction. Furthermore, while the Mukono case does reflect the idea that productive resources in the hands of women might be more beneficial to the household and the wider community than when they are in the hands of men, the Göreme case does not. What both settings show, therefore, is that it is crucial to consider the cultural specifics of gender relations in each particular tourism development context when exploring the relationships between gender, tourism and poverty reduction. It also is evident that because the implications for the gender relations involved in poverty reduction initiatives through tourism development are complex and often seemingly contradictory, it is necessary to view the relationship between gender, tourism development and poverty reduction as a discursive and ongoing process.

References

Aitchison, C.C. (2001). Theorising other discourses of tourism, gender and culture: Can the subaltern speak (in tourism)? *Tourist Studies, 1*(2), 133–147.

Apostolopoulos, Y., & Sönmez, S. (2001). Working producers, leisured consumers: Women's experiences in developing regions. In Y. Apostolopoulos, S. Sönmez, & D. Timothy (Eds.), *Women as producers and consumers of tourism in developing regions* (pp. 3–18). Westport, CT: Praeger.

Awumbila, M. (2006). Gender equality and poverty in Ghana: Implications for poverty reduction strategies. *GeoJournal, 67*, 149–161.

Azzarito, L., Solmon, M.A., & Harrison, L. (2006). "...If I had a choice, I would": A feminist poststructuralist perspective on girls in physical education. *Research Quarterly for Exercise and Sport, 77*(2), 222–239.

Bedford, K. (2007). The imperative of male inclusion: How institutional context influences world bank gender policy. *International Feminist Journal of Politics, 9*(3), 289–311.

Bryceson, D. (2000). Disappearing peasantries? Rural labour redundancy in the neo-liberal era and beyond. In D. Bryceson, C. Kay, & J. Moooij (Eds.), *Disappearing peasantries?: Rural labour in Africa, Asia and Latin America* (pp. 299–326). London: ITDG Publishing.

Chant, S. (2006). Contribution of a gender perspective to the analysis of poverty. In J.S. Jaquette & G. Summerfield (Eds.), *Women and gender equity in development theory and practice: Institutions, resources and mobilisation* (pp. 87–106). Durham, NC: Duke University Press.

Chant, S. (2007). *Gender, generation and poverty.* Cheltenham: Edward Elgar.

Chen, M., Vanek, J., Lund, F., Heintz, J., Jhabvala, R., & Bonner, C. (2005). *Progress of the world's women: Women, work & poverty.* New York: United Nations Development Fund for Women (UNIFEM).

Cleaver, F. (Ed.). (2002). *Men and masculinities: New directions in gender and development.* New York: Zed Books.

Ferguson, L. (2009). *Analysing the gender dimensions of tourism as a development strategy* (Working Paper No. pp03/09). Madrid: ICEI, Universidad Complutense de Madrid.

Ferguson, L. (2010a). Interrogating gender in development policy and practice: The World Bank, tourism and microentreprise in Honduras. *International Feminist Journal of Politics, 12*(1), 3–24.

Ferguson, L. (2010b). Tourism development and the restructuring of social reproduction in Central America. *Review of International Political Economy, 17*(5), 860–888.

Gentry, K.M. (2007). Belizean women and tourism work: Opportunity or impediment? *Annals of Tourism Research, 34*(2), 477–496.

Gibson, H. (2001). Gender in tourism: Theoretical perspectives. In Y. Apostolopoulos, S. Sönmez, & D. Timothy (Eds.), *Women as producers and consumers of tourism in developing regions* (pp. 19–43). Westport, CT: Praeger.

Gluckman, M. (1963). Gossip and scandal. *Current Anthropology, 4*(3), 307–316.

Harvey, J.M., Hunt, J., & Harris C.C. Jr (1995). Gender and community tourism dependence level. *Annals of Tourism Research, 22*(2), 349–366.

Hitchcock, R.K., & Brandenburgh, R.L. (1990). Tourism, conservation and culture in the Kalahari desert, Botswana. *Cultural Survival Quartery, 14*(2), 20–24.

Kabeer, N. (1999). Resources, agency, achievements: Reflections on the measurement of women's empowerment. *Development and Change, 30*, 435–464.

Kabeer, N. (2005). Gender equality and women's empowerment: A critical analysis of the third millennium development goal. *Gender and Development, 13*(1), 13–24.

Kantor, P. (2003). Women's empowerment through home-based work: Evidence from India. *Development and Change, 34*(3), 425–445.

Kinnaird, V., & Hall, D. (1996). Understanding tourism processes: A gender aware framework. *Tourism Management, 17*(2), 95–102.

Kinnaird, V., Kothari, U., & Hall, D. (1994). Tourism: Gender perspectives. In V. Kinnaird & D. Hall (Eds.), *Tourism: A gender analysis* (pp. 1–28). Chichester: John Wiley.

Long, V., & Wall, G. (1995). Small scale tourism development in Bali. In M. Conlin & T. Baum (Eds.), *Island tourism: Management, principles and practice.* Chichester: John Wiley.

Long, V.H., & Kindon, S.L. (1997). Gender and tourism development in Balinese villages. In M.T. Sinclair (Ed.), *Gender, work and tourism* (pp. 91–119). London: Routledge.

Mbaiwa, J.E. (2005). The socio-cultural impacts of tourism development in the Okavango delta, Botswana. *Journal of Tourism and Cultural Change, 2*(3), 163–185.

Meethan, K. (2001). *Tourism in global society: Place, culture, consumption.* Basingstoke: Palgrave.

Moser, C.O.N. (1989). Gender planning in the third world: Meeting practical and strategic needs. *World Development, 17*, 1799–1825.

Okin, M.S. (2003). Poverty, well-being, and gender: What counts, who's heard? *Philosophy & Public Affairs, 31*(3), 280–316.

Oyewumi, O. (2002). Conceptualising gender: The Eurocentric foundations of feminist concepts and the challenge of African epistemologies. *Jenda: A Journal of Cultural and African Women Studies, 2*(1), 1–9.

Pietila, T. (2007). *Gossip, markets, and gender: How dialogue constructs moral value in post-socialist Kilimanjaro.* Madison, WI: University of Wisconsin Press.

Scheyvens, R. (2000). Promoting women's empowerment through involvement in ecotourism: Experiences from the Third World. *Journal of Sustainable Tourism, 8*(3), 232–249.

Scott, J. (1997). Chances and choices: Women and tourism in Northern Cyprus. In T. Sinclair (Ed.), *Gender, work and tourism.* London: Routledge.

Silberschmidt, M. (2001). Disempowerment of men in rural and urban East Africa: Implications for male identity and sexual behaviour. *World Development, 29*(4), 657–671.

Sinclair, T. (1997a). Issues and theories of gender and work in tourism. In T. Sinclair (Ed.), *Gender, work and tourism* (pp. 1–15). London: Routledge.

Sinclair, T. (1997b). Gendered work in tourism: Comparative perspectives. In T. Sinclair (Ed.), *Gender, work and tourism* (pp. 220–234). London: Routledge.

Singh, S. (2007). Deconstructing "gender and development" for "identities of women". *International Journal of Social Welfare, 16*, 100–109.

Sönmez, S. (2001). Tourism behind the veil of Islam: Women and development in the middle east. In Y. Apostolopoulos, S. Sönmez, & D.J. Timothy (Eds.), *Women as producers and consumers of tourism in developing countries* (pp. 113–142). Westport, CT: Praeger.

Stewart, P.J., & Strathern, A. (2004). *Witchcraft, sorcery, rumours and gossip.* Cambridge: Cambridge University Press.

Stonich, S.C., Sorensen, J.H., & Hundt, A. (1995). Ethnicity, class and gender in tourism development: The case of the Bay Islands, Honduras. *Journal of Sustainable Tourism, 3*(1), 1–28.

Swain, M. (1995). Gender in tourism. *Annals of Tourism Research, 22*(2), 247–266.

Swain, R.B., & Wallentin, F.Y. (2008). *Economic or non-economic factors – what empowers women?* Unpublished working paper, Department of Economics, Uppsala University.

Syed, J. (2010). Reconstructing gender empowerment. *Women's Studies International Forum, 33,* 283–294.

Tucker, H. (2003). *Living with tourism: Negotiating identities in a Turkish village.* London: Routledge.

Tucker, H. (2007). Undoing shame: Tourism and women's work in Turkey. *Journal of Tourism and Cultural change, 5*(2), 87–105.

Tucker, H. (2010). Peasant-entrepreneurs: A longitudinal ethnography, *Annals of Tourism Research, 37*(4), 927–946.

Tuyezere, A.P. (2007). *Gender and development: The role of religion and culture*. Kampala: Fountain Publishers.

van der Cammen, S. (1997). Involving Maasai women. In L. France (Ed.), *The earthscan reader in sustainable tourism* (pp. 162–163). London: Earthscan.

Waylen, G. (2000). Gendered political economy and feminist analysis. In J. Cook, J. Roberts, & G. Waylen (Eds.), *Towards a gendered political economy* (pp. 14–38). Basingstoke: Macmillan.

Weedon, C. (1997). *Feminist practice and poststructuralist theory*. Malden, MA: Blackwell.

Whitehead, A. (2003). *Failing women, sustaining poverty: Gender in poverty reduction strategy papers*: Report for the UK Gender and Development Network. Oxford: Oxfam GB.

Wilkinson, P., & Pratiwi, W. (1995). Gender and tourism in an Indonesian village. *Annals of Tourism Research, 22*(2), 283–299.

Zinovieff, S. (1991). Inside out and outside in: Gossip, hospitality and the Greek character. *Journal of Mediterranean Studies, 1*(1), 120–134.

Zuckerman, E. (2001). *Engendering Poverty Reduction Strategy Papers (PRSPs): Why it reduces poverty and the Rwanda case*. Paper presented at the WIDER Development Conference on Debt Relief, Helsinki, Finland.

Can ecotourism deliver real economic, social, and environmental benefits? A study of the Osa Peninsula, Costa Rica

Carter A. Hunt[a], William H. Durham[b], Laura Driscoll[c] and Martha Honey[d]

[a]Department of Recreation, Park and Tourism Management, Pennsylvania State University, University Park, Pennsylvania, PA, USA; [b]Department of Anthropology, Stanford University, Stanford, CA, USA; [c]Department of Environmental Science, Policy, and Management, Berkeley, University of California, Berkeley, CA, USA; [d]Center for Responsible Travel, Washington, DC, USA

Doubt persists about ecotourism's ability to make tangible contributions to conservation and deliver benefits for host communities. This work in Costa Rica's Osa Peninsula tests the hypothesis that ecotourism in this region is more effective at improving well-being for local residents, at enhancing their access to key resources and information, and at supporting biodiversity conservation than other locally available economic sectors. Data from 128 semi-structured interviews with local workers, both in ecotourism and in other occupations, together with associated research, indicate that ecotourism offers the best currently available employment opportunities, double the earnings of other livelihoods, and other linked benefits. Locally, ecotourism is viewed as the activity contributing most to improvements in residents' quality of life in the Osa Peninsula and to increased levels of financial and attitudinal support for parks and environmental conservation. Ecolodge ownership by local people is substantial, and many local ecotourism workers plan to launch their own businesses. The data offer a convincing rebuttal to arguments that ecotourism does little to address poverty or disparities in access to resources and equally rebuts claims that ecotourism is simply a part of the "neoliberal conservation toolkit" that cannot help but exacerbate the very inequalities it purports to address.

Introduction

Debate persists about the impact of tourism on local environments and local livelihoods near protected areas (Bookbinder, Dinerstein, Rijal, Cauley, & Rajouria, 1998; Higham, 2007; Higham & Luck, 2007; Kiss, 2004). Key issues are tourism's contributions to local livelihoods, income creation, and protected areas (see Mayer, 2014; Whitelaw, King, & Tolkach, 2014). This paper looks at those issues and the rapid growth of ecotourism as a specific form of leisure travel to natural areas (Boo, 1989; Ceballos-Lascurain, 1996; Honey, 2008; Ziffer, 1989). There has been considerable scholarship on this topic (reviewed by Agrawal & Redford, 2006; Fennell & Weaver, 2005; Stronza, 2001; Weaver & Lawton, 2007), and Costa Rica has emerged as arguably the world's most iconic eco-tourism destination (Honey, 2008). Ecotourism in Costa Rica began to take off in 1987 when the Central American Peace Plan officially ended the region's various civil wars and its architect, Costa Rican President Oscar Arias, won the Nobel Peace Prize. By the early 1990s, ecotourism had propelled foreign visits to become the country's leading export and Costa Rica remains today a major ecotourism destination (Honey, 2008).

While elsewhere in Costa Rica, other models of tourism (such as all-inclusive resorts and vacation homes) compete with ecotourism (Almeyda, Broadbent, & Durham, 2010a, 2010b; Broadbent et al., 2012; Honey, Vargas, & Durham, 2010; van Noorloos, 2011), in Costa Rica's Osa Peninsula, the local economy is driven by small-scale nature-based tourism, much of it embodying the definition of ecotourism espoused by the International Ecotourism Society as "responsible travel to natural areas that conserves the environment and improves the welfare of local people" (The International Ecotourism Society [TIES], https://www.ecotourism.org/what-is-ecotourism). The promotional materials of the Costa Rican Institute for Tourism (ICT) prominently promote the Osa Peninsula as a place where "ecotourism features as the main product" (http://www.visitcostarica.com).

The Osa Peninsula region, therefore, offers an excellent context in which to ground test the economic, social, and environmental impacts of ecotourism. In addition, university researchers, NGO personnel, and concerned citizens are alarmed that new, governmental expansion plans have been made without a solid understanding of the Osa Peninsula's ecotourism-based economy or the likely impacts of large-scale conventional tourism developments (such as those to the north in Guanacaste & Manuel Antonio along Costa Rica's Pacific Coast) on both local livelihoods and biodiversity conservation on the Peninsula (Arroyo Mora et al., 2012). The present study of the key impacts of ecotourism in the Osa region is designed to fill a critical gap in knowledge and to help to stimulate an informed debate about the proposed development of a large-scale hydroelectric dam (Umaña, 2013), a new international airport (Murillo, 2012), and the resultant tourism trajectories for the Osa region.

More specifically, this paper assesses ecotourism in the Osa Peninsula by asking: How well does small-scale ecotourism provide income and employment opportunities for area residents? Does it lead to increased support for protected areas among local residents in comparison with other local livelihoods? Does it offer a higher quality of life than existing livelihood alternatives? In short, how beneficial is ecotourism in the region – economically, socially, and environmentally?

To explore these questions, the authors trained and led a team of field researchers to work in Osa in August 2010. The overarching hypothesis we test here, using data from that fieldwork, is that ecotourism in the region represents a different and better livelihood for those employed in the sector than the opportunities offered to those local residents employed in the existing local livelihood alternatives (e.g. construction, transportation, artisanal gold mining, retail, small-scale and plantation agriculture including African oil palm and cattle). Our analysis focuses on data gathered through semi-structured interviews from 70 ecotourism employees and 58 local residents working in other sectors, and is supported with corroborative qualitative and secondary data from other sources. We now review the ecotourism scholarship that frames this analysis.

Ecotourism, conservation, and development

When Budowski (1976) suggested a symbiotic relationship between tourism and conservation, he helped open discussion of whether tourism will generally contribute to favorable development outcomes or not (deKadt, 1979; Smith, 1977). Spurred on in the 1980s by the Brundtland Report's seminal definition of sustainable development (World Commission on Environment and Development [WCED], 1987) and a growing focus on integrated conservation and development projects (Brandon & Wells, 1992), policy-makers, researchers, conservationists, and community activists became interested in the new concept of ecotourism as a specific, more beneficial form of tourism (Honey, 2008; Smith & Eadington, 1992).

By the time The International Ecotourism Society (TIES) was founded in 1990, there were scores of ecotourism experiments in destinations around the world. TIES' definition (quoted above) distinguishes ecotourism from traditional types of tourism because, for the first time, it describes not only the tourism activity – recreational travel to natural places – but also the intended impact of that travel – that it "conserves the environment and improves the welfare of local people". Thus, with the advent of ecotourism, tourism for the first time embedded ethical values and positive outcomes into its definition. In contrast, nature tourism is defined simply as travel to enjoy and experience nature, with no reference to impact. Ecotourism was the earliest – and in many parts of the world remains the best known – of a new genre of tourism terminology. Recent years have seen the emergence of a range of similar terms describing impacts as well as activities, including pro-poor tourism, geotourism, and responsible tourism. While these terms differ slightly, they share the core proposition that these types of tourism, done well, will bring positive benefits to both conservation initiatives and host communities, and all form part of wider discussions and developments in tourism under the sustainable tourism umbrella.

The rise of ecotourism has also prompted a deeper debate, with critics arguing that ecotourism is simply a permutation within a neoliberal conservation agenda (Fletcher, 2014; Igoe & Brockington, 2007) that leads "biodiversity or nature to become commodities and natives to become labor" (West, Igoe, & Brockington, 2006, p. 257) in a global economic restructuring designed to facilitate the spread of free markets. Skeptics have taken on not only ecotourism specifically (e.g. Horton, 2009; Hunt, 2011; Kiss, 2004), but also more broadly integrated conservation and development projects (as in Terborgh, 1999; West & Carrier, 2004). Fletcher (2012), for instance, in his writing on the Osa Peninsula, argues that ecotourism is simply one more piece of the neoliberal conservation toolkit – what he calls the "Master's Tools" – that cannot help but exacerbate the very inequalities it purports to address.

While these and other scholarly debates continue (for excellent reviews, see Higham, 2007; Higham & Luck, 2007; Weaver & Lawton, 2007), ecotourism has continued to gain traction in the Americas, "arguably the region with the greatest amount and diversity of ecotourism activity in the world" (Stronza, 2008, p. 8). Ecotourism development was strong in Costa Rica in particular (Boo, 1989; Hall, 2000; Ziffer, 1989). By the time former president Jose Maria Figueres Olsen announced in his 1996 essay, "Sustainable Development: A New Challenge for Costa Rica", that the country would be "offering itself to the world as a 'laboratory' for this new [sustainable] development paradigm" (Figueres Olsen, 1996, p. 190), Costa Rica was already a test bed for ecotourism in practice (Ceballos-Lascurain, 1996; Honey, 2008).

Two years later, the Costa Rican Tourism Institute (ICT) launched one of the world's first and most stringent certification programs to measure the environmental, social, and economic impacts of accommodations and to award one to five "green leaves" depending on how a business scored. The voluntary CST program, which was created by a team of government officials, academics, tourism business leaders, and NGOs, has grown by fits and starts but has at last gained real traction, with many hotels lining up to be certified. At present, Costa Rica has 226 certified hotels, including 19 in the Osa Peninsula region. ICT has also launched sustainable certification programs for beaches, rental cars, tour operators, and tourism attractions. These initiatives have helped to put concrete measurable criteria behind ecotourism labels and to differentiate between genuine eco-tourism businesses and those that have simply appropriated the name for marketing purposes.

Today ICT marketing materials continue to state that "ecotourism features as the main product" in the Osa Peninsula. However, ecotourism is not a homogeneous product. Our research found that the 105 accommodation facilities we identified as operating in the region vary considerably in both the activities offered to visitors and the benefits provided to conservation and the local community. For some, performance is reflected in their eco-rating under the CST program; for others, measures of impact are more casual. Yet, individual lodges provide a range of ecotourism offerings, including intense overnight treks through Corcovado National Park for "hard" ecotourists and shorter local rainforest hikes coupled with spa- and wellness-oriented programs catering to "softer" ecotourists (Weaver, 2005). Overall, visitors come to the Osa Peninsula primarily to pursue a range of nature-based ecotourism opportunities, with Corcovado National Park being the main attraction (Hunt & Durham, 2012).

This study builds on anthropological methods our group implemented previously (e.g. Almeyda et al., 2010a) to assess whether ecotourism in the Osa Peninsula is meeting its twin tenets of "conserving the environment" and "improving the welfare of local people". We ask whether Osa residents working in ecotourism have better earnings, more opportunities for advancement, better quality of life, and more positive attitudes towards national parks than their peers working in other jobs, including local shops and businesses, wage labor, small-scale agriculture, African oil palm plantations or other local livelihood options. The overarching hypothesis tested here is that ecotourism in Osa is more effective at improving the well-being of local people, at giving them access to important resources and information, and at supporting biodiversity conservation than are existing alternative livelihoods. To be able to accept this assertion, empirical data must lead us to reject the following null hypotheses:

(1) that the employment opportunities in ecotourism do not offer higher and more stable earnings than employment in other sectors;
(2) that ecotourism does not contribute more to existing parks, protected areas or local environmental ethics than does other employment; and
(3) that ecotourism does not reduce disparities in access to important resources, including education, jobs, job training, and conservation knowledge and information.

In the sections below, we empirically test these null hypotheses against the quantitative and qualitative data collected during fieldwork in the two primary gateway communities for tourism to the Osa Peninsula. Our approach provides a multiple case-control study of individuals working in the ecotourism industry with demographically similar individuals living in the same communities whose livelihoods are not derived directly from the tourism industry. Before proceeding to results, we first provide a description of the study region and our methodology.

Study methods

Study site – the Osa Peninsula

The Osa Peninsula in the southern Pacific coast of Costa Rica is home to one of the country's biodiversity gems – Corcovado National Park. However, the creation of the park in 1978, and its management since then has been rife with conflicts (Cuello, Brandon, & Margoluis, 1998). Much of this conflict involved the 50-year presence and sudden withdrawal of the United Fruit Company (UFC) banana plantations in the early 1980s. Many former UFC workers turned to gold mining in the park and settled in bordering areas of the Golfo Dulce Forest Reserve. Additional multinational subsidiaries – including Ston Forestal (van den Hombergh, 2004) and currently PalmaTica (Beggs & Moore, 2013) – have had similar, if less intense, impact on the region. In recent decades, much external investment in this region has focused on exclusionary conservation efforts (Appendix A in Hunt, Durham, & Menke, 2013), conducted with its "back to the communities". As a result, local residents enjoyed little change in quality of life resulting from strict protection and became embittered towards the national park (Nuñez, Borge, & Herrera, 2007). We document further details about the regional context and other development efforts underway in the Osa and Golfito region elsewhere (Hunt et al., 2013).

The Osa Peninsula's geographic remoteness and seasonal wet weather have acted thus far as barriers to large-scale tourism development. However, these barriers could well change if and when a proposed new international airport in Palmar Norte is built. As the Liberia airport in Costa Rica's northernmost Pacific province of Guanacaste demonstrates (Morales & Pratt, 2010), a commercially viable international airport requires a large number of arrivals, which in turn require large hotels and resorts. The completion of this state-supported project – along with the new bridges, coastal highway, and other roads throughout the region – opens the Osa for large-scale tourism-related development. The prospect of the above model moving into the Osa region is creating consternation among many local residents, researchers, and environmental NGOs (van Noorloos, 2011; Morales & Pratt, 2010).

If such an intensive style of development were to occur in Osa, the region's tropical biodiversity could be quickly decimated as it has been in other Latin American regions (Terborgh, 1999; Vandermeer & Perfecto, 2005). If, as is probably more likely, the Osa falls prey to Manuel Antonio-style desarrollo hormiga ["ant-like development"] – chaotic and intense tourism development involving a mix of small, medium, and larger hotels, large numbers of vacation homes, and a correspondingly intense real estate speculation – the region's biodiversity may be equally in jeopardy (Broadbent et al., 2012; Honey et al., 2010). Such circumstances make it timely to assess ecotourism's impact in the Osa Peninsula and to consider the most appropriate trajectory of future regional development planning.

Research design

To assess the impact of ecotourism on the Osa Peninsula, we gathered ethnographic data from ecotourism lodge owners and managers, ecotourism employees, neighboring local residents not directly involved in tourism, and visitors to the region. In addition to this original data, we also gathered archival data from earlier studies, ICT documentation, NGO reports, and popular press articles. These sources of data are summarized in Table 1. As noted in the table, the focus of our analysis here is on residents of the Osa Peninsula. In particular, we compare ecotourism employees to other local residents who do not work directly in the tourism industry yet who otherwise share many demographic similarities. We gathered data on these two groups from two communities in the Osa Peninsula. The research design can thus be characterized as a multiple case control study with criteria for selection being ecotourism as the primary livelihood.

Table 1. Overview of data collection.

Source	Type	Emphasis	#
Ecolodge operators	Structured interviews	Land acquisition, product acquisition, salaries, social and environmental practices, and certifications	11
Ecolodge employees*	Structured interviews	Demographics, household expenditures, household income, attitudes toward protected areas and conservation, perceived environmental threats, proposed airport, proposed hydroelectric project, and presence of foreigners	70
Local residents not employed in tourism*	Structured interviews		58
Tourists	Structured interviews	Trip characteristics, expenditures, Costa Rican itinerary, parks visited, importance of social and environmental responsibility, certification, carbon offsets, environmental attitudes, and demographics	73
Ecolodge Websites	Text	Content analysis of ownership information	91

*Analysis here focuses on the subset of data from these two sources.

Our research efforts focused on the communities of Puerto Jimenez and Drake's Bay for two reasons. First, these are the primary gateway communities to the Osa Peninsula and to the region's showcase – Corcovado National Park. Ecotourism activities are far denser around these communities than anywhere else on the Osa Peninsula. Furthermore, Puerto Jimenez and Drake's Bay house the Peninsula's two regional airports, both receiving daily domestic flights operated by NatureAir and Sansa Airlines. As gateways to the Osa region, Puerto Jimenez and Drake's Bay are the most logical and efficient locations for an assessment of the impacts of ecotourism in the region.

Two field teams worked in the Osa Peninsula during August 2010; the first author led one research team and third author coordinated the other. The second author provided in-field supervision and the fourth author assisted with office interviews. The research teams also included eight Spanish-speaking research assistants recruited from Stanford University and two additional assistants enlisted from the Golfito branch of the Universidad de Costa Rica (one for each team). During research preparation and while in Costa Rica, all team members were instructed in field research methodology and proper research protocol, including Stanford's Internal Review Board guidelines for human subjects research.

To develop a sampling frame, we began with an exhaustive web-based survey of tourism businesses offering accommodation in the study region. We identified 105 unique lodges operating on the Osa Peninsula. Prior to arrival, we distilled this list to include only ecotourism lodges operating specifically in the two gateway towns. With advice from an NGO that works in the region (*Fundación Corcovado*), we selected a sample of 10 lodges representing a range of sizes and amenities, and these 10 consented to be part of the study. Four of the lodges in our sample provided temporary lodging at reduced rates for the research teams.

Each team conducted structured interviews with lodge owners and managers, lodge employees, tourists, local residents and business owners, NGOs, international and local realty offices, former lodge operators, and government departments. Analysis of the full data-set is beyond the scope of a single manuscript. We focus here on a control case comparison of households where the primary wage earner works in ecotourism with neighboring households where the primary wage earner does not work directly in tourism of any kind. As indicated by an asterisk in Table 1, the bulk of our analysis is derived from the data gathered through structured interviews with 128 local Costa Rican residents sampled from two sub-populations of Osa Peninsula residents: those residents ($N = 70$) whose primary employment is in one of the 10 ecolodges that consented to participate and those residents ($N = 58$) from the same communities not currently employed in tourism, interviewed in their homes and businesses.

For tourism employees, we interviewed all consenting employees of each of the 10 ecolodges, minus those who were away during the study period. For the sake of efficiency during fieldwork, interview data from non-tourism counterparts were collected with a convenience sample of heads of households during door-to-door visits to houses and shops in Drake Bay and Puerto Jimenez, along transects formed by the main commercial street in each town. Although limited by non-random selection, we demonstrate below that these sub-groups were nonetheless matched on many demographic characteristics and thus we believe they provide valid comparisons. In cases where interviewees from either group did not provide a complete response to each question, we indicate any such variation in overall *n*-values in the figures and tables.

An identical interview protocol was followed with both groups of interviewees and was designed to gather both quantitative and qualitative data. The protocol organized interview questions according to key themes including: (1) residents' demographic information; (2) employment, income, and expenditure information for all household members; (3) resident attitudes toward national parks and toward environmental conservation; (4) resident perceptions of the current issues facing the Osa (e.g. knowledge of the proposed international airport, attitudes toward the presence of foreigners, and attitudes toward tourism expansion); and (5) resident evaluations of their own quality of life and the factors most responsible for the current quality of life.

In addition to the focal data from residents working in tourism and counterparts not working in tourism, we also gathered information in separate structured interviews with hotel managers and owners (Table 1). These lengthy interviews yielded data on numerous themes not all of which are directly relevant to our analysis here but did help substantiate their environmental and social practices and therefore their "authenticity" as ecolodges (e.g. lodges' environmental policies, certifications, water management, energy consumption, waste treatment, chemical use, grounds keeping, tourist activities, monthly purchases, philanthropic activities in the community, and challenges to sustainability in the Osa). Here we draw upon select qualitative information from these manager and owner interviews when their comments provide additional insight into the impact of ecotourism in the region.

Finally, the field team gathered data from tourists who had concluded their stays and were waiting in the pre-boarding area of the Drake's Bay and Puerto Jimenez regional airports (Table 1). Those structured interviews assessed trip expenditures, information about other areas visited in Costa Rica, knowledge of ecotourism, and efforts to ensure social and environmental responsibility during the travel. These data do not specifically relate to the current analysis and are not assessed here. Aspects of their analysis have, however, been published elsewhere (Hunt & Durham, 2012).

Quantitative data gathered were analyzed using contingency tables, *t*-tests, Pearson correlation coefficients, and analysis of variance. Qualitative data were entered into an Excel database and coded by thematic content. Our analysis focuses on both quantitative measures of difference and the descriptive inferences derived from qualitative data that differentiate tourism employees and non-tourism employees. Where relevant, we also include corroborating secondary data analyzed in our other research efforts in the region of the Osa Peninsula. The results of these combined quantitative and qualitative analyses are reported below.

Results

Analysis of data from the fieldwork described above produced the following findings related to our hypotheses. First, we found that tourism workers were far more likely to have been born in the Osa region than non-tourism workers – 58% vs. 35% ($p < 0.05$), a 1.7-fold difference. This result means that locals can and do find employment in the local tourism sector and that they see an economic advantage for doing so. We also found local workers in tourism to be on average younger than non-tourism workers (Table 2). The residents in our sample who primarily work in tourism were more often males, whereas those primarily not working in tourism were more likely to be females (a difference compounded by the fact that non-tourism workers were interviewed in their homes and businesses during daytime hours). Employment for those not working directly in tourism came from small-scale agriculture, African oil palm production, small businesses (e.g. general stores or *pulperias*; small eateries or *sodas*), taxi driving, construction, fishing, teaching, cooking, truck driving, hair styling, carpentry, and cashiering. Due in part to an average age difference, non-tourism workers were more likely to be married than tourism workers. Non-tourism household sizes also tended to be slightly larger than tourism workers' households, although the average for both groups was between three and four people per household. Female interviewees had reportedly lived in the area for less time on average than males, and non-tourism workers reported slightly longer average periods of residency in the area than tourism workers.

Tourism and non-tourism livelihoods in Osa Peninsula

Tourism workers' monthly *individual* income is nearly twice as high as those of workers not in tourism – US$709.70 vs. US$357.12 (Table 3), a significant difference even with income's substantial variability across our samples. For ecolodge employees, incomes for the month prior to the survey ranged from a low of US$366.59 for kitchen assistants and housekeeping staff to US$4788.92 for a freelance guide. Among non-tourism

Table 2. Demographics of the sample of local residents (total $N = 123$).

Demographic descriptors	Tourism	Non-tourism	N	p-value
Married [P]	21 of 65	31 of 58	–	0.0178*
Male	44 of 65	25 of 58	–	0.0061**
Average household size[δ]	3.37	3.54	65	0.6164
Average interviewee age[δ]	29.61	35.02	71	0.0511
Female average years residency[δ]	13.93	14.98	39	0.8249
Male average years residency[δ]	19.83	28.08	58	0.0330*
Combined average years residency[δ]	18.3	20.46	97	0.4603

[P]Chi-square test used.
[δ]*t*-test used.
*Result significant at the 0.05 level.
**Result significant at the 0.01 level.

Table 3. Monthly individual and household income in US$, aggregate means ($N = 116$).

Community	Tourism		Non-tourism		p-value[A]	
	Self-only	Household	Self-only	Household	Self	Household
Puerto Jimenez	620.36	638.46	367.30	519.10	0.4027	0.5283
Drake Bay	747.99	840.10	345.54	486.78	0.0285*	0.1562
Full sample	709.70	784.47	357.12	503.27	0.0292*	0.2125
Lowest month	467.16		310.05		0.0299*	

[A]t-test used. Here, p-values were calculated comparing self-only incomes and household incomes separately between tourism and non-tourism.
*Result significant at the 0.05 level.

respondents, one person employed as an artisan reported the lowest non-zero monthly income in the sample (US$96.47). A farmer who had just sold his harvest reported the highest monthly income (US$1929.42), but acknowledged that it was *only* during harvest time that his income would reach this level.

Differences in average *household* income between tourism employees and others were more pronounced in Drake Bay than in Puerto Jimenez, the latter being larger and more economically diverse. Tourism workers in Drake Bay reported household incomes 1.7 times that of their non-tourism counterparts, whereas Puerto Jimenez tourism employees reported household incomes 1.2 times those of their non-tourism neighbors. In contrast to the overall average incomes reported in Table 3, tourism workers reported income lows (that is, earnings of the lowest/worst income month of the year) of on average US$467.16, while non-tourism workers reported income lows at an average level of US$310.05, a 1.5-fold difference that is also statistically significant ($p < 0.05$). Our data demonstrate that, for our sample, ecotourism provides higher income than other local employment opportunities. Qualitative information confirms this to be true during the "worst" months of the year when tourist arrivals are low.

Monthly household expenses are roughly the same for households with and without tourism workers (Table 4). Across categories of food, utilities, personal investments, and

Table 4. Average reported monthly expenses by category.

Expense	Tourism US$ (N)	Non-tourism US$ (N)	p-value[A]
Food	$184 (64)	$204 (51)	0.5112
Housing	$49 (63)	$41 (51)	0.7115
Utilities	$48 (62)	$66 (52)	0.1429
Savings	$54 (59)	$42 (51)	0.7303
Transportation	$18 (62)	$51 (52)	0.1272
Recreation	$30 (63)	$39 (50)	0.6326
Education	$13 (62)	$34 (51)	0.0321*
Investment	$26 (61)	$24 (51)	0.8870
Medical costs	$15 (62)	$28 (51)	0.1265
Other	$49 (57)	$66 (46)	0.4143
Total	$373 (64)	$389 (50)	0.7903

[A]t-test used.
*Result significant at the 0.05 level.

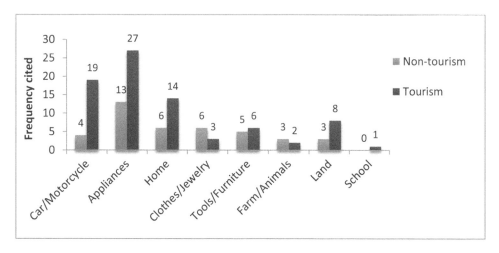

Figure 1. Disposable income allocation: Tourism vs. non-tourism.

recreation, household expenses for the two groups fell into broadly similar distributions. Food was the largest expense for both groups, with housing, utilities, and savings also falling into the top five for both groups. Data on lesser expenses exhibited few differences between tourism workers and non-tourism workers. Tourism workers did, however, report spending significantly less on education than their non-tourism counterparts. This difference may be explained by the age, sex, and family size differences between the groups we have noted above: that tourism workers tended to be younger, male, and have slightly smaller families, while non-tourism workers tended to be older, predominantly female, and have somewhat larger families. Until further work is done on the topic of education, the best we can say is that tourism workers wind up with more disposable income than non-tourism counterparts (US$338 per month vs. US$162). This difference, in turn, is reflected in higher spending on recreation among tourism workers.

Tourism workers were more likely than non-tourism workers to feel that their jobs had allowed them to progress financially. Tourism workers answered "yes" to this question at a rate of almost 2 to 1, with 63% feeling their work had improved their circumstances. By comparison, just under half of non-tourism workers (48%) answered "yes" to the same question. To gain greater insight into consumer behavior, from those who said "yes" we asked what specific things the extra money enabled them to buy. In free-listed responses, interviewees most frequently cited home appliances, home improvements (e.g. purchases of furniture, tools, etc.), and construction of a new house (Figure 1). Tourism workers gave more varied responses than non-tourism workers, including the only respondents who mentioned financing their own further education.

Tourism workers invested much more often in vehicles (24% of tourism responses vs. 10% of non-tourism responses), which is not unexpected as many have a distance to commute between home and their work in ecolodges. Tourism employees were also more in favor of starting their own tourism-related business than their non-tourism counterparts (23% vs. 18% in the 5-year timeframe and 19% vs. 15% in 10 years) or their own non-tourism businesses (27% vs. 18% in 5 years and 33% vs. 29% in 10 years). Overall, tourism workers were more likely to indicate a desire to start their own business, whether in tourism or not (27% vs. 18% in 5 years and 33% vs. 29% in 10 years).

Table 5.   Local attitudes toward protected areas and oil palm.

Topic	Tourism ($N = 65$)				Non-tourism ($N = 58$)				p-value[A]
	Positive	Negative	Mixed	NR	Positive	Negative	Mixed	NR	
Opinion on national parks	85% (55)	2% (1)	12% (8)	2% (1)	74% (43)	3% (2)	16% (9)	7% (4)	0.3513
Opinion on private reserves	37% (24)	11% (7)	5% (3)	48% (31)	31% (18)	5% (3)	7% (4)	57% (33)	0.5180
Opinion on oil palm plantations	31% (20)	20% (13)	18% (12)	31% (20)	47% (27)	21% (12)	10% (6)	22% (13)	0.2700

Note: NR = no response.
[A]Chi-square test used. Significance reported as p-value.

Support for conservation

Two questions assessed attitudes toward national parks and private reserves (Table 5). When asked "How do you feel about the existence of national parks and protected areas?" respondents gave overwhelmingly positive responses (85% positive for tourism workers and 74% for non-tourism workers). Fewer respondents ventured an opinion on the same question regarding *private* reserves, with more than 52% of the sample declining to comment. Given the role of African oil palm as a driver of change in agricultural landscape mosaics in the region (Beggs & Moore, 2013), we gauged attitudes toward oil palm by asking "do you think the expansion of oil palm plantations in the region is good or bad for the community?" Opinions did not differ greatly between the two groups, with roughly equal numbers of individuals giving negative opinions (21% of non-tourism workers and 20% of tourism workers) and a larger number of individuals expressing positive opinions (47% of non-tourism workers and 31% of tourism workers).

Respondents were then asked to identify and evaluate threats to local biodiversity. Individuals from both tourism work and non-tourism work overwhelmingly agree that the worst threat to local species diversity is hunting, followed by deforestation (Table 6). To explore employment-related changes in environmental behavior, respondents were asked to comment on their extraction of forest products during the previous year, under conditions of anonymity. Among non-tourism workers, 37.5% said they had extracted items (such as wood, plants, and seeds) from the forest in the last year, compared to 17.5% − less than half as many − for tourism workers, a finding that just misses statistical significance ($p = 0.051$).

Our interview data from the operators of nearby Danta Lodge and of Aguila de Osa in Drake's Bay suggest that forest cover has largely regenerated since these two projects were initiated on former pasture land. This reinforces our earlier findings around the Lapa Ríos ecolodge (Almeyda et al., 2010a). Based on the reported occupancy rates, the reported rates of participation in hiking in the park, and the current park entrance fees, we conservatively estimate approximately US$25,000 of support to Corcovado National Park from just these three lodges. This estimate does not include entrance fees to nearby Caño Island Reserve, the Terraba-Sierpe National Wetlands, Piedras Blancas National Park or any number of private reserves operating in the region.

Community benefits and engagement

Many of the ecolodges in our sample provide funds to their local communities for conservation and development needs. Several lodges in Drake's Bay, for example, contribute to

Table 6. Comparison of perceived threats to local species diversity ($N = 123$).

| | Tourism | | Non-tourism | | |
Threat	Drake	Jimenez	Drake	Jimenez	Total
Hunting	21 (48%)	7 (19%)	6 (22%)	9 (29%)	43
Deforestation	7 (16%)	5 (24%)	1 (4%)	10 (32%)	23
Human presence	8 (18%)	2 (10%)	5 (19%)	4 (13%)	19
Pollution	7 (16%)	1 (5%)	3 (11%)	2 (6%)	13
Food scarcity	2 (5%)	0	2 (7%)	1 (3%)	5
Construction	0	1 (5%)	0	3 (10%)	4
Tourism	0	0	3 (11%)	0	3
Capture for pets	0	0	2 (7%)	0	2
Mining	0	1 (5%)	0	0	1
Global warming	0	1 (5%)	0	0	1
Airports	0	1 (5%)	0	0	1
No threats	3 (7%)	0	2 (7%)	0	5
No response given	5 (11%)	9 (43%)	9 (33%)	11 (39%)	34

Note: $N = 65$ Tourism, 58 non-tourism. Multiple responses per subject were permitted.

the Fundación Corcovado, which provides annual contributions to local development funds, bolsters environmental education curriculum in local schools, promotes recycling in the community, and supports local sea turtle conservation efforts. One of the Fundación Corcovado's successful initiatives is an environmental education and art program in the local school that led to elementary school students, many of whom had never left the Peninsula, earning the chance to represent their community in San Jose.

On the critical issue of ownership, we took a closer look at the "universe" of ecolodges in the Osa region. Our web-based census of 105 lodges operating in the region revealed that 91 lodge websites (87%) provide information about ownership. Of these 91 lodges, 35 (38.5%) indicate being locally owned and operated by Costa Rican citizens. Although we were unable to secure information on the start date for all of these 91 lodges, given the dominance of foreign owned ecolodges in the early decades of tourism in the Osa (Cuello et al., 1998; Horton, 2009), the owners we spoke with claimed that most of the locally owned business growth has occurred in recent years. The ratio of local to foreign ownership of new projects in coming years is thus likely to increase and be paralleled in other tourism-related sectors including transportation, restaurants, and other services. Access to employment via both foreign and locally owned lodges and access to new business opportunities in tourism continue to be created in the Osa region.

Beyond income, employees of these ecolodges acquire English language skills that are not otherwise available through work in other sectors. Interviewees at several lodges described English classes being offered as a no-cost part of employee training. Additionally, ecolodges generate capacity outside of the tourism sector. One locally owned business outside of Puerto Jimenez – Danta Corcovado Lodge – offers funding and facilities in support of women's groups who meet in the community. This lodge has also sponsored house painting and tree-planting campaigns, plus the building of an educational center, a recycling program, and a health clinic, thus establishing a link between ecotourism, community services, and health care access.

Table 7. Comparison of local attitudes and perceptions.

Topic	Tourism (N = 65)				Non-tourism (N = 58)				p-value[A]
	Positive	Negative	Mixed	NR	Positive	Negative	Mixed	NR	
Aware of new airport	87% (56)	13% (9)	–	–	57% (33)	43% (25)	–	–	0.0002**
Opinion on new airport	34% (22)	25% (16)	28% (17)	15% (10)	47% (27)	5% (3)	17% (10)	31% (18)	0.0043**
Opinion on cruise ships	48% (31)	12% (8)	13 (20%)	20% (13)	45% (26)	19% (11)	12% (7)	24% (14)	0.5104
Opinion on houses of foreigners	23% (15)	37% (24)	22% (14)	18% (12)	38% (22)	17% (10)	12% (7)	33% (19)	0.0138*
Opinion on foreigner presence	30% (19)	14% (9)	15% (10)	42% (27)	29% (17)	12% (7)	16% (9)	43% (25)	0.9764
Opinion on sale of land to foreigners	19% (12)	31% (20)	23% (15)	28% (18)	22% (13)	34% (20)	19% (11)	24% (14)	0.8844

Note: NR = no response.
[A]Chi-square test used. Significance reported as p-value.
*Result significant at the 0.05 level; 95% confidence that observed difference is not the result of chance.
**Result significant at the 0.01 level.

Another component of access – access to strategic information – was assessed quantitatively in our survey. When asked about governmental plans to build a new international airport in Palmar Sur, a majority of both tourism employees and those not working in tourism favored the airport, which they see as bringing development and increased employment opportunities. Those in ecotourism were statistically better informed, with 87% of tourism respondents citing awareness of the plan (Table 7). In contrast, just 57% of the non-tourism workers expressed awareness of the proposed airport. Ecotourism workers were also more likely than non-tourism workers to oppose the airport (25% vs. 5%). Those in favor of the airport gave responses like, "I suppose the airport is good because it will bring more tourists, so the community will develop and there will be more work". Those opposed cited fears of crowding and overdevelopment. In the words of one interviewee, "I hope they do not build it... we'll become Jacó!" referring to a heavily developed resort area farther north along the Pacific coast. While it is not clear how additional knowledge about the airport affects support or opposition to it, the indications are clear that with tourism comes increased access to information, and this information is an important resource for assessing the implications of different development scenarios including those involving this new international airport.

A majority of ecotourism workers and non-tourism workers indicated a desire for more tourists in the Osa (63% for tourism workers and 76% for non-tourism workers), though tourism workers gave a higher percentage of qualified answers (16% vs. only 2% from those not working in tourism). Examples of qualified answers include, "More tourism would be good, but I hope there is balance, and I hope there are real economic benefits for us" and "I hope there are more tourists, but it would depend on the type of tourism they bring". Such responses highlight a desire to reap the benefits of increased economic activity from tourism, while avoiding its negative environmental and social impacts found along the Pacific coast north of the Osa Peninsula. Tourism workers have had more access to information about potential negative consequences of certain forms of tourism development (e.g. such as that seen in the northern province of Guanacaste resulting from the beginning of direct flights from the USA to the Liberia airport) and exhibit a more cautionary attitude toward tourism development as a result of their involvement in tourism.

Discussion

Hypotheses revisited

In the context of the Osa Peninsula, then, the data collected here call into question each of the three null hypotheses proposed earlier. They are:

(1) that the employment opportunities in ecotourism do not offer higher and more stable earnings than employment in other sectors;
(2) that ecotourism does not contribute more to existing parks, protected areas or local environmental ethics than does other employment; and
(3) that ecotourism does not reduce disparities in access to important resources, including education, jobs, job training, and conservation knowledge and information.

Our data show that ecotourism offers local residents higher incomes – nearly double earnings per month – than other employment opportunities. The data also indicate that Osa residents view ecotourism as contributing more than other businesses to both improvements in quality of life and benefits for conservation of the region's rainforest. Our findings offer an important, if localized, confirmation of the value of stay-over ecotourism for livelihoods and conservation – two key tenets of ecotourism – in the Osa Peninsula.

With respect to the second hypothesis, we found that all lodges provide economic benefits directly to Corcovado National Park, through both entrance fees paid by visitors and, in some cases, donations by the lodge owners. For instance, several lodges have contributed directly to both reforestation and natural regeneration of tropical forest adjacent to the national park, and this confirms an earlier dual remotely sensed and ethnographic analysis (Almeyda et al., 2010a). Furthermore, many ecotourism businesses contribute to tree-planting programs in the surrounding communities. The qualitative evidence also indicates an increased level of support for parks and environmental protection among tourists visiting the Osa Peninsula. Again, our data suggest that ecotourism delivers on its promise.

Finally, our data also offer a convincing rebuttal to arguments that ecotourism does little to address poverty or disparities in access to resources. As we found, the lodges of our sample offer higher paying employment opportunities for local residents, proactively promote the conservation of nature, and offer increased access to educational, health, and information-related resources. Compared to alternative development trajectories in the Osa, from bananas to palm oil plantations to cattle ranching and fishing, it is clear that ecotourism is providing greater benefits for biodiversity conservation and community development. Our interviewees noted that the higher incomes and training they have received through their work in ecotourism create access to new ecotourism-related opportunities, including new businesses – more than a third of which are now locally owned. As a result, foreign ownership is now far from universal in Osa. Although surely warranting confirmation in future longitudinal analyses, we found a trend toward increasing local ownership of businesses as a result of ecotourism in the region. In Osa, what Fletcher (2012) calls the "Master's Tools" (instruments of neoliberal capitalism) thus appear to be helping with both poverty and local access to resources.

Ecotourism, conservation, and development revisited

Analysis of the interview data about the impacts of ecotourism in and around the communities of Drake Bay and Puerto Jimenez contributes to several ongoing discussions about ecotourism and its benefits to conservation and the host community. First, our finding of a

1.7-fold overall difference in household incomes between those with members working in tourism and those whose members are employed elsewhere makes it clear that ecotourism offers higher incomes for local residents. This finding stands in contrast to many other tourism destinations, including resorts along Costa Rica's north and central Pacific coast, that typically employ outside labor for construction and then employ non-locals in higher paying office positions (Honey, 2008; Honey et al., 2010; Hunt & Stronza, 2011). Ecotourism provides higher income jobs and opportunities for self-improvement and advancement which can help to slow the outflow of youth from the Osa Peninsula, thereby breaking the vicious cycles of impoverishment, resource degradation, and migration outlined by Durham (1995, 2008) and explored empirically in a nearby tourist destination by Hunt (2011).

However, by the same token, the line between ecotourism and non-tourism sectors was less distinct than we expected: those interviewed stated that virtually everything in the Osa Peninsula is dependent upon ecotourism. The direct and indirect economic activity generated by ecotourism is critical, for instance, for local shop owners, farmers, fishers, and road workers. As one interviewee put it, "without tourism, no one would have money to spend in my store". Ecotourism plays a pivotal or "keystone" role in the economic network of the Peninsula: even those residents who do not derive their primary income from the payroll of a hotel, airline or other tourism-related business still consider themselves to be sustained by the tourism industry. Indeed, those surveyed and interviewed credit ecotourism with overall positive changes in local educational opportunity, job training, and value given to nature, as reflected in the decline in hunting and deforestation in the region. Other ecotourism destinations in Central and South America have shown similar positive results (Hunt & Stronza, 2011; Stronza, 2010; Wunder, 2000).

Our findings also corroborate other writings indicating that local employment influences such things as commitment to community, sense of place, and attitudes towards conservation (Almeyda et al., 2010a; Honey et al., 2010; Horton, 2009; Stronza & Durham, 2008). In addition, it indicates that ecotourism provides the increased income and employment opportunities that are necessary for ensuring favorable conservation-related outcomes of ecotourism (Alexander, 2000; Belsky, 1999; Campbell, 1999; Hunt & Stronza, 2011; Stronza 2010; Vasconcellos Pegas & Stronza, 2009)

Such outcomes are critical given this region's history of conflicts between people and parks. It appears that ecotourism's contributions to local livelihoods and conservation have helped to shift attitudes among Osa residents (as reported also in Almeyda et al., 2010a). Much like Horton (2009) and Cuello et al. (1998) have shown, our findings suggest that ecotourism — with its commitment to benefiting both local livelihoods and the environment — has improved local attitudes toward national parks and conservation. While more research is needed to understand the reasons behind these differences, they are consistent with the findings of others (Buckley, 2010; Hunt & Stronza, 2011; Saarinen, Becker, Manwa, & Wilson, 2009; Stronza & Durham, 2008) who report that ecotourism has sensitized employees to environmental issues and contributes to increased support for protected areas and conservation.

Our data are only a first look at a relatively small sample, and they cover only a short-time horizon. However, they do suggest that, in the Osa region, ecotourism reduces disparities by *increasing* the access of local and poor people to strategic resources. With increased access to information, higher paying jobs, and educational and training possibilities comes increased social capital, which has been identified as a key factor in improved development and livelihood outcomes (Bebbington, 1999; Jones, 2005), including that of the Osa region (Hunt et al., 2013).

Conclusion

The Osa Peninsula is the last remaining section of Costa Rica's Pacific coast where eco-tourism is the dominant type of tourism and a significant sector of the local economy. It, therefore, offers an appropriate setting to ground test some of the indicators of the economic, social, and environmental impacts of ecotourism compared with other employment alternatives. As described here, a field team conducted 128 interviews with local residents of the Osa in and around Drake Bay and Puerto Jimenez, including 70 interviews with ecolodge employees and 58 with residents not working in tourism, in order to test a key hypothesis that ecotourism in the Osa represents a different, and better, form of economic activity than the existing extractive alternatives – such as timber, gold mining, plantation agriculture, cattle, etc.

Overall, the findings from this multiple case control study demonstrate that ecotourism is a high-value economic activity in the Osa Peninsula. It is perceived as providing stable, better paying jobs, and more opportunity for advancement than other economic endeavors. Further, it is credited with helping to shift local attitudes toward positive perceptions of Corcovado National Park and the other protected areas. Although not evenly spread throughout the Peninsula, ecotourism's economic reach is wide, with most other types of businesses tying their well-being directly or indirectly to the health of the tourism sector.

Further research is needed to anticipate the effects of several pending large-scale developments in the Osa region – including, but not limited to, the proposed international airport and the Diquis Hydroelectric project. Both projects have the potential to rapidly increase land speculation and larger scale tourism and vacation home developments, thereby undermining the model of small-scale, nature-based ecotourism that today is dominant in the Osa Peninsula. Concern remains that these proposed infrastructural projects stand to tip the Osa Peninsula in favor of a more mass tourist model characteristic of the north and central Pacific coast, and to undermine the sustainable income, employment, and more equitable access to key resources afforded by ecotourism. In addition to its value to other researchers and other ecotourism areas elsewhere in the world, the research presented here may be of particular value to those shaping future development decisions and policies in the Osa region.

Acknowledgements

This study was made possible through a grant from the Tinker Foundation. We are grateful to Fundacion Corcovado for their assistance throughout the complexities of fieldwork logistics. Our thanks go to the residents and businesses of Puerto Jimenez and Drake Bay who shared with us their invaluable knowledge and experience in countless interviews and conversations with our research teams. We are very grateful for the time they granted us, and for their patience and wisdom in sharing perspectives on their home. We also wish to acknowledge the efforts of our student research assistants: Stanford University students Caroline Adams, Molly Oshun, Joshua (Mac) Parish, and Anne Scalmanini, and Andrea Cordero Retana and Isabel Arias Sure of the Golfito branch of the University of Costa Rica.

References

Agrawal, A., & Redford, K. (2006). *Poverty, development, and biodiversity conservation: Shooting in the dark? (Working Paper No. 26)*. New York: Wildlife Conservation Society.

Alexander, S.E. (2000). Residents attitudes towards conservation and black howler monkeys in Belize: The Community Baboon Sanctuary. *Environmental Conservation, 27*(4), 341–350.

Almeyda, A.M, Broadbent, E.N., & Durham, W.H. (2010a). Social and environmental effects of ecotourism in the Osa Peninsula of Costa Rica: The Lapa Rios case. *Journal of Ecotourism, 9* (1), 62–83.

Almeyda, A.M., Broadbent, E.N., & Durham, W.H. (2010b). Ecotourism impacts in the Nicoya Peninsula, Costa Rica. *International Journal of Tourism Research, 12*(6), 803–819.

Arroyo Mora, D., Cattgens, A.A., Campos Mora, C., Chang Vargas, C., Cortez Muños, G., Madrigal Olivares, A., . . . Monestel Herrera, H. (2012). *Estudio multidisciplinario: Aproximaciones al Megaproyecto Hidroeléctrico El Diquís [Multi-disciplinary study: Approaches to the El Diquís hydro-electric mega-project]*. San Jose, CA: Grupo Independiente de académicos e investigadores de la Universidad de Costa Rica.

Bebbington, A. (1999). Capitals and capabilities: A framework for analyzing peasant viability, rural livelihoods and poverty. *World Development, 27*(12), 2021–2044.

Beggs, E., & Moore, E. (2013). *The social landscape of oil palm production in the Osa-Golfito region*. San Jose, CA: Iniciativa Osa-Golfito (INOGO), Stanford University.

Belsky, J.M. (1999). Misrepresenting communities: The politics of community-based rural ecotourism in Gales Point, Belize. *Rural Sociology, 64*(4), 641–666.

Boo, E. (1989). *Ecotourism: The potentials and pitfalls*. Washington, DC: World Wildlife Fund.

Bookbinder, M.P., Dinerstein, E., Rijal, A., Cauley, H., & Rajouria, A. (1998). Ecotourism's support of biodiversity conservation. *Conservation Biology, 12*(6), 1399–1404.

Brandon, K.E., & Wells, M. (1992). Planning for people and parks: Design dilemmas. *World Development, 20*(4), 557–570.

Broadbent, E.N., Almeyda Zambrano, A.M., Dirzo, R., Durham, W.H., Driscoll, L., Gallagher, P., . . . Randolph, S.G. (2012). The effects of land use change and ecotourism on biodiversity: A case study of Manuel Antonio, Costa Rica, from 1985–2008. *Landscape Ecology, 27*(5), 731–744.

Buckley, R. (2010). *Conservation Tourism*. Wallingford: CAB International.

Budowski, G. (1976). Tourism and environmental conservation: Conflict, coexistence, or symbiosis?. *Environmental Conservation, 3*(1), 27–31.

Campbell, L.M. (1999). Ecotourism in rural developing communities. *Annals of Tourism Research, 26*(3), 534–553.

Ceballos-Lascurain, H. (1996). *Tourism, ecotourism, and protected areas: The state of nature-based tourism around the world and guidelines for its development*. Gland: IUCN.

Cuello, C., Brandon, K., & Margoluis, R. (1998). Cost Rica: Corcovado National Park. In K. Brandon, K. Redford, & S. Sanderson (Eds.), *Parks in peril: People, politics, and protected areas* (pp. 143–192). Washington, DC: Island Press.

deKadt, E. (1979). *Tourism: Passport to development?* Oxford: Oxford University Press.

Durham, W. (2008). The challenge ahead: Reversing vicious cycles through ecotourism. In A. Stronza & W. Durham (Eds.), *Ecotourism and conservation in the Americas* (pp. 265–272). Wallingford: CAB International.

Durham, W.H. (1995). Political ecology and environmental destruction in Latin America. In M. Painter & W. Durham (Eds.), *The social causes of environmental destruction in Latin America* (pp. 249–264). Ann Arbor: University of Michigan Press.

Fennell, D., & Weaver, D. (2005). The ecotourium concept and tourism-conservation symbiosis. *Journal of Sustainable Tourism, 13*(4), 373–390.

Figueres Olsen, J.M. (1996). Sustainable development: A new challenge for Costa Rica. *SAIS Review, 16*(1), 187–202.

Fletcher, R. (2012). Using the master's tools? Neoliberal conservation and the evasion of inequality. *Development and Change, 43*(1), 295–317.

Fletcher, R. (2014). *Romancing the wild: Cultural dimensions of ecotourism.* Durham, NC: Duke University Press.

Hall, C.A.S. (Ed.). (2000). *Quantifying sustainable development: The future of tropical economies.* San Diego, CA: Academic Press.

Higham, J. (2007). Ecotourism: Competing and conflicting schools of thought. In J. Higham (Ed.), *Critical issues in eco-tourism: Understanding a complex tourist phenomenon.* Oxford: Elsevier.

Higham, J., & Luck, M. (2007). Ecotourism: Pondering the paradoxes. In Higham, J. (Ed.), *Critical issues in eco-tourism: Understanding a complex tourist phenomenon.* Oxford: Elsevier.

Honey, M. (2008). *Ecotourism and sustainable development: Who owns paradise?* (2nd ed.). Washington, DC: Island Press.

Honey, M., Vargas, E., & Durham, W. (2010). *Impact of tourism related development on the Pacific Coast of Costa Rica: Summary report.* Stanford, CA: Center for Responsible Travel.

Horton, L.R. (2009). Buying up nature: Economic and social impacts of Costa Rica's eco-tourism boom. *Latin American Perspectives, 36*(3), 93–107.

Hunt, C. (2011). Passport to development? Local perceptions of the outcomes of post-socialist tourism policy and growth in Nicaragua. *Tourism Planning and Development, 8*(3), 265–279.

Hunt, C.A., & Durham, W.H. (2012). Shrouded in a fetishistic mist: Commoditization of sustainability in tourism. *International Journal of Tourism Anthropology, 2*(4), 330–347.

Hunt, C., Durham, W., and Menke, C. (2013). *Sustainable development centered on human well-being in Osa and Golfito, Costa Rica: A social diagnostic analysis.* San Jose, CA: Iniciativa Osa-Golfito (INOGO), Stanford University.

Hunt, C., & Stronza, A. (2011). Missing the forest for the trees? Incongruous local perspectives on ecotourism in Nicaragua converge on ethical issues. *Human Organization, 70*(4), 376–386.

Igoe, J., & Brockington, D. (2007). Neoliberal conservation: A brief introduction. *Conservation and Society, 5*(4), 432–449.

Jones, S. (2005). Community-based ecotourism: The significance of social capital. *Annals of Tourism Research, 32*(2), 303–324.

Kiss, A. (2004). Is community-based ecotourism a good use of biodiversity conservation funds? *TRENDS in Ecology and Evolution, 19*(5), 232–237.

Mayer, M. (2014). Can nature-based tourism benefits compensate for the costs of national parks? A study of the Bavarian Forest National Park, Germany. *Journal of Sustainable Tourism, 22*(4), 561–583.

Morales, L., & Pratt, L. (2010). *Analysis of the Daniel Oduber Quirós International Airport, Liberia, Guanacaste.* Stanford, CA: Center for Responsible Travel (CREST).

Murillo, K. (2012). *El Proyecto de Aeropuerto Internacional para el Sur: Contexto, Percepciones, y Perspectivas* [*The international airport project for the south: Context, perceptions, and perspectives*]. San Jose, CA: Iniciativa Osa-Golfito (INOGO), Stanford University.

Nuñez, M., Borge, C., & Herrera, B. (2007). *Inversiones en la conservación de la biodiversidad en al Área de Conservación Osa, Costa Rica (1995–2005): Implicaciones para su futuro* [*Investments in Biodiversity Conservation in the Osa Conservation Area (ACOSA), Costa Rica, from 1995–2005: Implications for its future*]. San Jose: SINAC-ACOSA.

Saarinen, J., Becker, F., Manwa, H. & Wilson, D. (2009). *Sustainable tourism in southern Africa: Local communities and natural resources in transition.* Bristol: Channel View Publications.

Smith, V. (Ed.). (1977) *Hosts and guests: The anthropology of tourism.* Philadelphia: University of Pennsylvania Press.

Smith, V.L., & Eadington, W.R. (1992). *Tourism alternatives: Potentials and problems in the development of tourism.* Philadelphia: University of Pennsylvania Press.

Stronza, A. (2001). The anthropology of tourism: Forging new ground for ecotourism and other alternatives. *Annual Review of Anthropology, 30*, 261–283.

Stronza, A. (2008) The bold agenda of ecotourism. In A. Stronza & W. Durham (Eds.), *Ecotourism and conservation in the Americas* (pp. 163–176). Wallingford: CAB International.

Stronza, A. (2010). Commons management and ecotourism: Ethnographic evidence from the amazon. *International Journal of the Commons, 4*(1), 56–77.

Stronza, A., & Durham, W. (2008). *Ecotourism and conservation in the Americas*. Wallingford: CAB International.

Terborgh, J. (1999). *Requiem for nature*. Washington, DC: Island Press.

Umaña, Álvaro. (2013). *El Proyecto Hidroeléctrico El Diquís y el Humedal Nacional Térraba-Sierpe: Análisis de impactos potenciales y viabilidad futura* [*The El Diquis Hydroelectric Project and the Terraba-Sierpe National Wetland: Analysis of potential impacts and future viability*]. San Jose, CA: Iniciativa Osa-Golfito (INOGO), Stanford University.

van den Hombergh, H.G.M. (2004). *No stone unturned: Building blocks of environmentalist power versus transnational industrial forestry in Costa Rica* (Doctoral dissertation). Amsterdam: Faculty of Social and Behavioral Sciences, University of Amsterdam.

van Noorloos, F. (2011) Residential tourism causing land privatization and alienation: New pressures on Costa Rica's coasts. *Development, 54*(1), 85–90.

Vandermeer, J., & Perfecto, I. (2005). *Breakfast of biodiversity: The political ecology of rain forest destruction*. Oakland, CA: Food First Books.

Vasconcellos Pegas, F., & Stronza, A. (2009). Ecotourism equations: Do economic benefits equal conservation? In A. Stronza & W. Durham (Eds.), *Ecotourism and Conservation in the Americas* (pp. 163–176). Wallingford: CAB International.

Weaver, D. (2005). Comprehensive and minimalist dimensions of ecotourism. *Annals of Tourism Research, 32*(2), 439–455.

Weaver, D., & Lawton, L.J. (2007). Twenty years on: The state of contemporary ecotourism research. *Tourism Management, 28*(5), 1168–1179.

Wells, M., & Brandon, K. (1992). *People and Parks: Linking Protected Area Management with Local Communities*. Washington, DC: The World Bank.

West, P., & Carrier, J.C. (2004). Ecotourism and authenticity. *Current Anthropology, 45*(4), 483–498.

West, P., Igoe, J., & Brockington, D. (2006). Parks and peoples: The social impact of protected areas. *Annual Review of Anthropology, 35*, 251–277.

Whitelaw, P.A., King, B.E.M., & Denis Tolkach, D. (2014). Protected areas, conservation and tourism – financing the sustainable dream. *Journal of Sustainable Tourism, 22*(4), 584–603.

World Commission on Environment and Development (WCED). (1987). *Our common future: Report of the world commission on environment and development*. New York: United Nations.

Wunder, S. (2000). Ecotourism and economic incentives – an empirical approach. *Ecological Economics, 32*(3), 465–479.

Ziffer, K.A. (1989). *Ecotourism: The uneasy alliance*. Washington, DC: Ernst & Young/Conservation International.

Value chain approaches to assessing the impact of tourism on low-income households in developing countries

Jonathan Mitchell

Overseas Development Institute, London, UK

This paper examines two issues: the emergence of pro-poor tourism as an idea and how the impacts of tourism on local communities around developing world tourist destinations can be measured. Pro-poor tourism was initially conceived in the period 1999–2000 at the conceptual and policy level. More recently, the critical knowledge gap has been found to be that of having reliable evidence to support policy development and action. This paper describes and justifies an action research approach to value chain analysis which allows researchers to "trace the tourism dollar" in developing country tourist destinations. The approach also supports the identification of opportunities to enhance positive tourism impacts on the poor and explains how to develop a shortlist of feasible high impact interventions. Poverty is defined, and a conceptual framework for understanding the linkages between the tourist sector and the local economy is outlined. Value chain analysis is also defined and seven key reasons are given for its use. Field experience with this approach in 12 different developing country destinations is shown to be an empirical basis for suggesting that the methodology is conceptually robust and a practical way of alleviating poverty, allowing researchers and the industry to work together effectively.

Introduction

Whilst the most popular international tourist destinations remain those in already-affluent countries, such as France and Spain, the market share of international tourism arrivals in developing countries is increasing rapidly. In 2008, just over 40% of international tourist trips had a developing country destination (World Bank, 2010). Countries such as China, Turkey, Mexico and Malaysia have a large and increasing share of global tourist flows. Figure 1 provides a visual comparison of the volume of global tourism flows in 2005. It is interesting to compare the significant tourism flows in the emerging southern destinations, with the powerhouses of the world economy, such as the United States, Japan and Germany.

Developing country tourism is not the exclusive preserve of middle-income countries. Although still a small share of global tourism activity (some 1.4% of international tourist arrivals), tourism is the leading export sector and source of foreign exchange for virtually all (non-oil) exporting of the least developed countries[1] – the poorest 49 countries in the world (Honeck, 2008).

Figure 1. A tourist-eye view of the world. Note: The area of each country is proportional to the number of international tourist arrivals. Source: SASI Group and M. Newman (2006) – based upon data from *World Development Indicators*.

This paper examines two issues: the emergence of pro-poor tourism (PPT) as an idea, and how can the impact of tourism on local communities around tourist destinations be measured?

The emergence of pro-poor tourism as an idea

A small group of researchers[2] around the time of the Millennium Development Summit in 1999 coined the term "pro-poor tourism" (or PPT). The intention of this early work for the UK's Department of International Development was simple, to explore how tourism could contribute to poverty reduction (Ashley & Goodwin, 2007). PPT aimed to put "poverty at the heart of the tourism agenda" and the Pro-Poor Tourism Partnership was formed in 1999 to work on this agenda. It seems incongruous to suggest in a special issue on "Tourism and Poverty Reduction" of the *Journal of Sustainable Tourism* in 2012 but, these simple assertions were a revelation a decade ago.

At that time, many tourism researchers had negative perceptions of the ability of the tourist industry to benefit host countries. Although the size of the tourist sector in developing countries was recognised, "tourism pessimists" claimed that the great majority of the potential benefits "leaked" back to the countries of origin through the activities of international tour operators, foreign-owned hotels and the high import propensity of tourism in developing countries (cited in Bolwell & Weinz, 2008; Brohman, 1996; Jules, 2005). In addition, tourism employment was regarded as seasonal, low-paying and exploitative (Clancy, 2001; Slob & Wilde, 2006). Furthermore, poor people were seen as particularly vulnerable to the costs of tourist development – through lost access to, and depletion of, natural resources.

Many in the mainstream commercial tourist sector also tended to see poverty reduction in destinations as the responsibility of others. This viewpoint has coexisted with the assumption that tourism activity is generally benign for destinations. "Tourism-euphoric" commentators pointed to the jobs and economic activity created by the mainstream tourist sector. Tourism-led growth is regarded by some as almost ubiquitous in its benign effects and international organisations, such as the UNWTO (United Nations World Tourism Organization) and World Travel and Tourism Council, have invested significant energy into asserting not only the importance of tourism as an economic sector, but also the benefit which tourism delivers to local communities around tourist destinations. If tourism is inherently good for development, the role of tourism policymakers in developing countries was little more than to deliver as many tourists to destinations as possible.

It was apparent to the early PPT practitioners that many of the rather strident claims – of both the "tourism pessimists" and "tourism-euphoric" commentators – were often based on remarkably weak foundations. There was no agreed method of measuring the impact of tourism activity on host destinations and a striking absence of rigorous analysis (Mitchell & Ashley, 2010). Partly due to this evidence gap, and also because researchers, the development sector and the tourist industry itself lacked the institutional framework to communicate with each other, the opportunity for informed debate between these sharply contrasting positions was largely missed.

Gradually an institutional architecture began to evolve. The Travel Foundation was created as an NGO (non-governmental organisation) to bring the outbound travel industry, government and non-governmental bodies together to focus on environmental and socio-economic impacts at tourist destinations. The International Centre for Responsible Tourism at Leeds Metropolitan University has successfully brought mainstream industry and researchers together. Most mainstream tour operators now have a sustainable development or corporate social responsibility department. The Overseas Development Institute (ODI) has spent a decade stimulating and working with development agencies to develop a more nuanced approach to tourist development. These are important, although early, steps. The institutional architecture in which debates about the destination impacts of tourism can take place is much more conducive in 2010 than it was at the turn of the Millennium.

However, other than isolated case studies of individual supply chains, we found ourselves in 2005 without the research tools to answer the most basic economic question: how does tourism affect the lives of poor people living around tourist destinations?

How can the economic impact of tourism on local communities around tourist destinations be measured?

Attempting to answer this question raises three important issues: definitional, conceptual and research methods. None are straightforward and, after several years of effort, we are not there yet. However, we have been trying to sharpen our performance in these areas and can provide some guidance.

Definitions

One of the most difficult issues facing PPT is how to define poverty. The most straightforward approach is to adopt the "dollar a day" (per person at 1995 purchasing power parity level) measure of extreme poverty, recently amended to $1.25 by the World Bank. This definition of poverty has the advantage that it is universal and facilitates comparisons between destinations in different countries.

However, in many of the contexts in which PPT practitioners work – meaning low-income countries and often examining supply chains that extend deep into rural areas – "dollar a day" poverty lines are of limited relevance because almost the whole population falls below the poverty line. International poverty thresholds obscure the real differences in wellbeing between households existing significantly below the poverty line and much better-off households that are on, or near, the international poverty line – who would often not be regarded as resource "poor". For this reason, nationally defined poverty levels – which reflect how people perceive poverty – are often very much lower than "dollar a day" poverty thresholds.

The trade-off is between a universal definition of poverty, which may not be appropriate in specific contexts, and a more flexible definition of poverty which, whilst always lower than "dollar a day" thresholds, resonates locally. It is difficult to apply the former when research is being funded by local organisations – so the ODI has tended to adopt the more restrictive (i.e. lower) poverty line. As a consequence of this, findings about the pro-poor impact of tourist destinations in different countries have not been strictly comparable.

PPT draws from the concept of pro-poor growth. This emerged as a counter to the belief that the benefits of development would inevitably "trickle down" to poor households. The need to focus on the distributional consequences of growth was prompted by the empirical observation that in some countries – particularly in Latin America and Africa, rather rapid rates of economic growth were demonstrably not improving the livelihoods of low-income households. This mirrored the more general belief that the central focus of development should be to reduce poverty – in line with the Millennium Development Goal 1 (MDG1; see http://www.undp.org/mdg/goal1.shtml).

The broad definition of pro-poor growth (summarised in Ravallion, 2004) labels growth as pro-poor, as long as the poor benefit (i.e. absolute or relative poverty falls, even if inequality increases). Most episodes of growth would, therefore, fall under this so-called World Bank definition of pro-poor growth. Applied to the tourism sector, this would require that net benefits to the poor are positive. In practice, this would be difficult to assess, as positive flows tend to be financial and evident, whilst the negative effects of tourism are more often non-financial impacts on livelihoods (access to resources) or even more intangible assets such as culture. In terms of policy usage, this broad definition may lead a few to recognise the need to assess the negatives, but would probably lead many more to simply reassure themselves that tourism growth in inherently pro-poor.

The narrow definition of pro-poor growth (expounded by Kakwani & Son, 2003) re-quires that the poor benefit proportionately more than others, so that inequality is reduced along with poverty. In other words, tourism is only pro-poor if it reduces inequality as well as directing resources to poor people. Although the authors have found some examples of supply chains into the tourism value chain that may meet this restrictive definition of PPT, they are few and far between. In fact, much developing country government public expen-diture fails to be redistributive in this sense. Tourism is a private-sector-driven activity and needs to generate returns to the owners of businesses in order to be sustainable. There can be few commercial activities that successfully meet this benchmark of pro-poor growth.

The policy implications of defining most tourism (indeed most private sector develop-ment) as anti-poor are questionable. This is a poor rationale for not developing the tourist industry if it can generate substantial net benefits for poor people that exceed their oppor-tunity costs (what they would be doing if there was no tourism) – particularly if these net benefits can be increased via the type of deliberate interventions highlighted in this review. This thought is echoed in criticisms of both the narrow and wide definitions.

Osmani (2005) argues that "pro-poor growth demands a break with the past that makes growth more conducive to poverty reduction . . . from the point of view of the poor; there must be an improvement over business as usual" (p. 9). So, by this definition, "pro-poor" growth is simply growth that benefits the poor more than some previous benchmark. In practical terms, this moves us away from categorising whether a growth experience is or is not pro-poor, and focuses minds on (1) enhancing poverty-reducing impacts and (2) comparing whether a particular set of policies is likely to be more pro-poor than another. This emphasis on boosting net benefits is embraced by the definition of PPT posted by the Pro-Poor Tourism Partnership. This need to shift emphasis from the conceptual to the practical level is also recognised by Ravallion (2004) who argues that "the real issue is not whether growth in pro-poor but how pro-poor it is" (p. 4).

The faddish "development industry" has now largely moved beyond the term pro-poor growth and is using terms such as "inclusive" or "shared" growth. These terms are compatible with Osmani's pragmatic definition of a pattern of growth which creates more opportunities for low-income households than what preceded it.

The definition of tourism itself is not entirely straightforward. Tourism is "the activities of people travelling to and staying in places outside their unusual environment for no more than one year for leisure, business, and other purposes not related to an activity remunerated from the place visited". This definition, from the UNWTO, seems clear but often is not applied by policymakers – who often equate "tourist" with "foreigner" or "leisure traveller". In reality, tourism is much more characterised by domestic and business travellers than many recognise.

In addition, definitions of the "tourist sector" are problematic. According to the 1993 international standard System of National Accounts (SNA), the tourist sector is defined by the economic sub-sectors of hotels, restaurants and part of the transportation sub-sector. However, tourist spending drives demand for goods and services throughout the economy. Careful work on Tourism Satellite Accounts – which is a demand-based definition that examines where in the economy tourist spending takes place, rather than being driven by adding the activity in predetermined economic sub-sectors – leads to interesting results. Estimates vary in different countries, but typically the restrictive definition of tourism driven by SNA results is an estimate of the scale of tourism which is about half the level based upon an examination of tourist demand. This definitional issue is particularly important for PPT practitioners because generally the poorest households which receive income from tourist demand are the farmers, fishers and craft sellers who fall outside the SNA-defined "tourist sector". For this reason, it is important to take the broader definition of tourism in order to avoid simply assuming away much of the pro-poor impact of tourism – as the conceptual framework below highlights.

The range of tourism products themselves has important methodological implications. Applying a global value approach to a standard package tourist product is relatively straight-forward. This is particularly the case when the chain is vertically integrated, where the outbound tour operator controls the retailing of holidays and also the airline used, and often has a long-term relationship with the accommodation and excursion service provider in destination. In destinations characterised by independent travel, it is often much more challenging to obtain meaningful information about tourist spending beyond the destination itself (because tourists would have arrived at destination using a diverse variety of transport modes and routes from a rich variety of sources).

Conceptual framework

Our conceptual framework for understanding the linkages between the tourist sector and the local economy is outlined in Figure 2. The main value of this framework is to appreciate the scope of the several different pathways by which the tourist sector can transfer benefits (and dis-benefits) to local communities in and around tourist destinations. These can be summarised in three pathways: Pathway 1 are direct effects; Pathway 2 captures the indirect

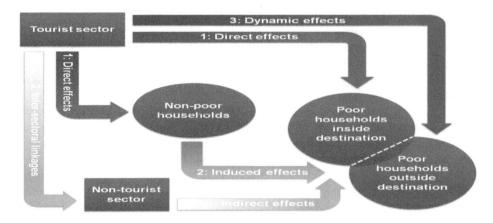

Figure 2. Conceptual framework for understanding linkages between tourism and the local economy – the three pathways. Source: Mitchell and Ashley (2010).

and induced impacts; and Pathway 3 captures the longer-term, dynamic effects of tourist development.

The first pathway includes direct flows from the narrowly defined "tourist sector" to low-income groups in the local economy. These include the wages of workers from poor backgrounds in hotels, restaurants, guides and transport companies and any benefits for communities from Corporate Social Responsibility initiatives and community equity schemes. The first round impacts of direct effects are usually fairly local to the destination (i.e. local people working in the tourist sector or a local orphanage supported). However, direct effects may benefit communities distant from the destination through mechanisms such as the remittances of low-income workers who migrate to the destination for work, but send funds home to relatives.

The second pathway includes indirect flows where tourist expenditure stimulates activity outside the tourist sector – for instance hotel construction wages and supplies, food and beverages. Supply chains for goods and services beyond the tourist sector may be significantly longer than direct linkages. Often the food consumed by tourists is not grown in the local economy, and may benefit low-income groups far from the destination (and sometimes beyond the borders of the host country).

Induced effects are an important impact resulting from the spending of tourist workers' wages in the local economy. Through induced impacts, the wages paid to non-poor workers can benefit low-income communities if they supply the goods and services on which workers spend their wages.

The third pathway includes the dynamic effects (both positive and negative) of tourist activity on the local economy. Direct, indirect and induced effects are all short-term impacts: a hotel is opened and workers are employed; food is purchased and wages are spent. Dynamic effects are the longer-term impact of a hotel on the local economy such as payment of tax to support services to the local population, the upgrading of skills in the local labour market resulting from the training of hotel staff, or the changed access of local communities to natural resources.

An increasingly critical point about this conceptual framework is not what it includes, but what it excludes. Our focus has been on "tracing the tourist dollar" and to a large extent on financial transactions. The inclusion of livelihood effects which do not involve a financial transaction (like access to natural resources) can only be integrated into this framework with difficulty. At least as important, this framework is designed to examine the effects of tourism activity on low-income households. However, increasingly researchers are under pressure to take account of the environmental costs of tourist activity and demonstrate the trade-off with any socio-economic benefits. With recent advances in environmental economics, and specifically the explicit pricing of carbon, it is possible to explore this trade-off of environmental costs and socio-economic benefits using cost-benefit analysis techniques. However, the fact remains that this conceptual framework is focused upon answering questions about the impact of tourism on low-income households, not assessing the environmental impacts of tourism.

We now turn to the research methods which will generate the data required to populate this conceptual framework.

Research methods

In terms of ways of capturing these three pathways, ODI staff members have reviewed the available research methods. A sensible way of categorising this diverse literature is to group it in terms of what the researchers themselves are trying to achieve. The four categories of research methods in Table 1 address four quite distinct questions:

(1) What are the economic effects of tourism on the rest of the economy?
(2) How big is "tourism"?
(3) In what ways does tourism affect poor people?
(4) How can tourism be expanded?

Many researchers are looking at different parts of the conceptual framework in Figure 1 but few are examining all the possible effects of tourist development on the host population. In addition, we found that much of the effort invested by tourism researchers on Tourism Satellite Accounts and Master Plans, is not moving us significantly closer to our goal of understanding tourism destination impacts on low-income households (see Table 2).

In response to this analysis, the ODI narrowed down the choice of research tools which can answer the research question about how to assess the impacts of tourist development on low-income households at the destination to four areas: livelihood analysis, enterprise analysis, local economic mapping and pro-poor value chain analysis. As Table 2 indicates, the drawback of the first three approaches is that they have a clear focus on the rather

Table 1. A categorisation of tourism research tools.

Primary objective of analysis	Different research methods
Assess the economic effects (direct, indirect, static & dynamic) of tourism activities on the (macro) economy	Regression analysis, social accounting matrices, computable generalised equilibrium models
Describe the size of the tourist sector	Tourism Satellite Accounts
Measure impacts of tourism on poor people or local economies at tourist destinations	Livelihoods analysis, enterprise analysis, local economic mapping and pro-poor value chain analyses
Develop and enhance the tourism sector, its growth and competitiveness.	Tourism Master Plans and conventional value chain analysis

Note: Our assessment revealed the volume and quality of existing analysis, but also the partial nature of individual tools. The field is characterised by pockets of excellent, but isolated, scholarship.

Table 2. An overview of the research approaches.

Research methods	Input–output analysis	Tourism satellite accounts	Regression analysis	Computable Generalised Equilibrium Modelling (and SAM)	Micro enterprises/livelihoods analysis	Local economic mapping (pro-poor value-chain analysis)	Master planning	Conventional value chain analysis
Research focus:								
Size of tourism-related economy	√√√	√√√	√	√√		√	√	
Competitiveness of tourism sector			√	√		√	√√√	√√√
Impact of tourism on macro–economy	√√√	√√	√√√	√√√			√	
Impact of tourism on poor people			√	√√√	√√√	√√√	√	
Geographical scale	Regional/national	National	National/international	Regional/national	Local	Destination	National	Tourist product
Policy relevance	√	√	√√	√√√	√√√	√√√	√√√	
Extent of application	Widespread	Growing considerably	Widespread	Limited	Limited	Very limited	Ubiquitous	Very limited
Consideration of								
Non-financial issues	No	No	No	No	√	Some	Few	No
Direct effects	√	√	√	√	Some	√	√	√
Secondary effects	√	√	√	Some	No	Some	Some	√
Dynamic effects	No	No	Some	Some			Few	No
Cost	Modest	High	Modest	Reasonable	Modest	Modest	High	Reasonable
Implemented by	Academics	Public bodies and consultants	Academics	Academics	Researchers/practitioners	Researchers	Consultants	Consultants and academics

Notes: indicates no relevance, √; indicates some relevance, √√; indicates high relevance, √√√.
Source: Mitchell & Ashley, 2010

local and direct and indirect impacts. Most are unable to either take into account dynamic effects or to assess the competitiveness of the tourism product itself. Both of these are important weaknesses because empirical evidence suggests that many of positive socio-economic impacts of tourism are found in the dynamic pathway. Also, it is important to understand the health of the tourist sector itself. Linking low-income households more closely to an ailing economic sector is not developmentally progressive. It is also important to understand that tourism does not exist primarily to benefit poor people. Tourism is a private sector enterprise and, unless researchers understand the economics of tourism itself, they are in a poor position to engage with the tourist sector and propose realistic changes which will have a positive impact on low-income households.

It was for this reason that value chain analysis was selected as the chosen research tool, and that the conventional value chain approach (which, as is discussed below, was originally conceived as a business tool) itself has to be adapted to incorporate a pro-poor dimension.

What are value chains?

Value chains do not exist in the sense of their having a tangible reality: they are simply a framework for trying to understand how the world works. The value chain describes the full range of activities required to bring a product or service from conception, through the different phases of production (involving a combination of physical transformation and the input of various producer services), delivery to final consumers and final disposal after use (Kaplinsky & Morris, 2001).

Value chains are frequently confused with other concepts, such as clusters. Clusters analysis also shares many similarities with value chain analysis. A cluster is a sectoral and geographical concentration of an enterprise within a region or even one specific urban area (for example Bollywood films in Mumbai and tourism in Sharm-El-Sheik). The rationale for focusing on clusters is that cooperation between firms in a cluster can improve the efficiency of participating enterprises above the level that would be possible without cooperation (through improved access to inputs, cost-sharing for research and development (R&D), improved marketing and advocacy, development of economies of scale and scope, etc.). It is especially helpful in explaining the observed reality of clusters in many developing economies, and in understanding why many of these clusters include small firms (Schmitz & Nadvi, 2000).

Value chains, then, are a way of understanding the interaction of people and firms with markets – whether domestic or global. In value chains, primary actors perform a selection of (primary) functions. These typically include input supply, production, processing, storage, wholesale (including export), retail and consumption. Actors who perform similar functions are regarded as occupying the same functional "node", for example the input supply node, production node, retail node and so on. Secondary actors, or ancillary workers, perform (secondary) service roles that support primary functions, such as transportation, brokerage and service processing. As goods in value chains are exchanged and transformed, they "flow downstream", in a series of transactions that add value and costs.

The key point about value chains is that they recognise that the firms linking suppliers to producers to processors and intermediaries to the customer at the end of the chain are the critical determinants of trade, whether these are domestic, regional or global. All stakeholders along a specific value chain need to cooperate and to coordinate their activities to keep the end customer happy. Chain coordination allows "driving" agents to institute measures which reduce costs and risks whilst increasing the speed and reliability of supply, or which increase sales (Gibbon, 2001).

The concept of the value chain has risen to the fore in recent years to reflect major changes in market conditions (Kaplinsky & Morris, 2001). From the demand side, global markets have become increasingly demanding of variety and quality, and the resulting chains of production have become increasingly suffused with standards. Many of these standards require linked processes throughout the chain. For example, in Travelife certification, a "chain of custody", involving environmental and social standards, has to be passed all the way from the outbound tour operator through the supply chain to individual suppliers (i.e. accommodation, excursions, animation, etc.) at the destination (see www.travelife.org).

From the supply side, firms have increasingly concentrated on their core competences and, although they have been reluctant to own their suppliers and customers, they have needed to ensure that these conform to chain standards in order that they can achieve systemic efficiency in global markets. These two factors have meant that chain coordination – referred to as "chain governance" (Gereffi, Sturgeon, & Humphrey, 2005) – is a necessary component of value chain competitiveness. Here, Gereffi has made the widely cited distinction between chain governance executed by key buyers ("buyer-led chains") and that in which the governance role is played by a holder of core technology ("producer-driven chains") (Gereffi, 1994). International tourism is a classic buyer-led chain where international tour operators have the economic power to demand that standards are met throughout the chain.

Where do value chains come from?

Value chains are relatively value free as a framework and therefore have been applied in some very different contexts (see the excellent discussion in Altenburg, 2007):

- The francophone *filière* approach of the 1960s, which was used to delineate the scope of analysis for agricultural commodity exports (cotton, rubber, cocoa and coffee), principally from France's former colonies. This was essentially a technocratic exercise undertaken by agricultural scientists motivated by a desire to improve the efficiency of the value chains.
- The management science approach to supply chain management and outsourcing, to explore "make or buy" decisions based on the distinction between core and non-core competencies of corporations. Offshoring gathered momentum in the clothing industry in the 1970s as Northern companies moved their production functions to developing countries, which offered lower labour costs. Now, the great majority of consumer electronics, footwear, toys, bicycles, computers and clothes are produced outside Organisation for Economic Co-operation and Development (OECD) and middle-income countries. Increasingly, higher-value functions (such as call centres, R&D, etc.) are being outsourced to developing countries.
- Porter's (1985) value chain concept, which is based on the observation that location-specific conditions (rather than the factor cost differentials of neoclassical theory) determine the competitive advantage of locations. Porter's analysis emphasises the importance of local rivalry and specific demand conditions. This approach has had a large influence on local economic development and cluster thinking.
- Gereffi (1994) and several others coined the global value chain concept following empirical studies of globalised production across several sectors of the economy. This approach differed from the earlier filière school because the governance of value chains was identified as a central theme – based on sociological notions of economic

power allowing lead firms to impose the parameters of contracts and subcontracts in their supply chain and collect above average profits (or rents) as a consequence.

The evolution of global value chains, and increased competition amongst firms at different stages of the value chain, has resulted in new opportunities and challenges for new entrants. On the one hand, the global fragmentation of production in theory means that many low-income countries can plug into global value chains and therefore benefit from "catch-up" growth (through resultant technology transfer, learning by doing, etc.). On the other hand, some of the routes used in the past to achieve industrial development may not be as viable. Global value chain analysis focuses on the dynamics of inter-firm linkages within this system, and the way in which firms and countries are integrated globally. But it also goes beyond firm-specific linkages to reveal the dynamic flow of economic, organisational and coercive activities between producers within different sectors on a global scale (Kaplinsky & Morris, 2001).

This raises the question of how producers (firms, regions or countries) participate in the global economy, rather than whether or not they should do so. Its approach is therefore analogous to the new trade theory literature in that the results are ambiguous: trade openness is not always beneficial to an economy; if it is managed in the wrong way, trade may have long-term detrimental effects. As Kaplinsky & Morris (2001) put it, "if they [producers] get it wrong, they are likely to enter a 'race to the bottom', that is a path of immiserating growth in which they are locked into ever-greater competition and reducing incomes" (p. 26).

How can value chains help?

Value chain analysis can make an important contribution to pro-poor economic development for seven key reasons.

Firstly, value chains are particularly well suited to understanding *how poor people can engage*, or engage more beneficially, with domestic, regional or international trade. The contribution of the global value chain thinkers was a recognition of something very important to the resource poor in rural areas – their lack of power compared with the lead firms setting the "rules of the game" in the value chain. Trade is about productivity and factor costs, but also about the use of brute economic power to extract value from the chain.

Secondly, value chain analysis has *economic viability and sustainability* at its core because of its focus on markets and commercial viability (as well as development concerns). This is an important advance on more "traditional" enterprise development projects, which have often focused almost exclusively on producers (or the supply side), to the neglect of sources of demand. Ironically, "traditional" approaches to enterprise development (by both external donors and the state) have often paid insufficient attention to the existing market systems in which their interventions took place. Value chain analysis is therefore compatible with market development approaches to development. Value chain analysis provides a framework for engagement with both business and beneficiary groups. Successful value chain development projects, therefore, aim for win–win outcomes for all participants. This implies that there is nothing "anti-development" about generating incentives for the already rich to get richer, providing it is done in a way that includes, and benefits, groups of poor people.

Thirdly, value chains are a strong qualitative *diagnostic tool*, capable, if employed with skill, of identifying critical issues and blockages for specific target groups and then generating robust and effective policies and development strategies. The key point is that a sound value chain analysis does not simply provide a robust explanation for why the resource poor are poor. It also provides a logical framework to formulate concrete intervention strategies to change the circumstances of the poor. In this sense, value chains are a normative, as well as a diagnostic, tool to understand what reality currently is – and how it can be changed for the better.

Fourthly, and related, value chain analysis identifies the *core rents payable and barriers to entry* that determine who in the chain benefits from production for diverse final markets. This helps to focus minds on how best to facilitate the participation of the poor in these chains. There may be little point in assisting producers to enter chain links characterised by excessive competition (i.e. where there are no barriers to entry). On the other hand, poor producers can also be assisted in creating their own barriers to entry through upgrading strategies, for example brands of estate coffee produced and sold into global markets by Central American coffee farmers. Figure 2 outlines five of the key triggers for value chain upgrading: the need to improve system efficiency, product quality, product differentiation, social and environmental standards, and the business environment.

Fifthly, value chain analysis is *inherently scalable*. This is important because, following the logic of the MDGs (and particularly MDG1), external donors are increasingly concerned with reducing poverty at scale. Developing value chains which, if successful, benefit only a few tens of beneficiaries is – quite rightly – becoming difficult to justify. Even if the initial focus of a value chain development exercise is on a single producer group or firm, there is no reason why the same logic cannot be applied to a cluster of firms or a region or country.

Sixthly, value chain analysis is *relatively evidence-based and action-oriented*. This form of analysis provides tangible recommendations for what specific firms in a specific value chain – and their governments – can do to increase their competitiveness and development impact.

Finally, value chains provide a clear way forward as a *policy and restructuring tool*. International evidence shows that achieving systemic competitiveness requires cooperation along the chain, as well as within links in the chain. After all, a chain is only as strong as its weakest link. So the establishment of a collation of interested parties involved in promoting participation by the poor, or the restructuring of value chains, is often a necessary process to ensure that appropriate global competitiveness is realised. Ideally, this includes both private sector parties concerned with endogenous rents and public sector participants concerned with exogenous rents for there is evidence of both market failure and state failure. Realising global competitiveness involves a joint journey of discovery.

It is for these reasons that value chain analysis has had a profound impact on development studies in recent years and, we believe, has much promise for both measuring and improving the impact of tourism in developing country destinations.

Applying value chain analysis to the tourist sector

The ODI has developed an approach, based upon value chain analysis, which "follows the tourist dollar" through the tourist value chain and associated supply chains. We understand that this approach is partial. It has a focus on economic transfers and on direct, indirect and induced impacts. The treatment of non-economic issues and longer-term dynamic effects is less systematic and, in an ideal world, a pro-poor value chain analysis would be complemented with equilibrium modelling and a livelihoods analysis.

Our methodology has been written up in detail elsewhere (see Ashley, Mitchell, & Spenceley, 2009). In essence, we examine the total expenditure of tourists (spending on the package as well as discretionary spending) and follow this expenditure flow to under-stand who benefits and how. "Pro-poor income" (PPI) – the wages and profits earned by

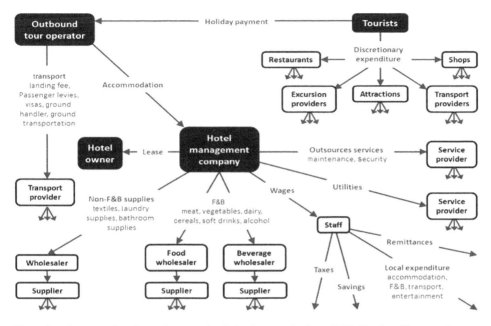

Figure 3. An example of a tourism supply chain. Source: Author. (F&B, Food and beverage)

resource-poor households from tourist spending – can then be compared with total tourism expenditure to assess how pro-poor is tourism at the destination. Tourist destinations differ in terms of their size and complexity. At one end of the spectrum is an all-inclusive hotel with an exclusivity agreement binding it to receiving guests from one overseas tour operator and limited discretionary spending by tourists in-country. At the other end of the spectrum is a large destination with many hotels serving different markets (different source markets, package arrangements, purpose of travel – each with a distinctive local economic footprint) and many independent travellers with large amounts of discretionary expenditure. In the latter example, it is only possible to sample hotels to build up a picture of the destination value chain as a whole.

Figure 3 illustrates a package tourism value chain for a single hotel and demonstrates the scope of analysis required to "trace the tourism dollar" effectively. It is immediately apparent that this kind of analysis requires tourists to work with a wide range of stakeholders within the value chain (tour operators; hotel managers; hotel staff; tourists; suppliers such as shop owners, guides, farmers, food wholesalers; as well as tourists themselves). The nature of supply chains has a significant impact on their economic footprint – is the fish supplied by the wholesaler imported frozen from Europe or caught locally by artisanal fishermen, for instance? It is important to follow these supply chains as far down as possible because this is often where the pro-poor impact either is or is not found.

There are also important decision-makers outside the value chain. These include the local tourist association, government tourist department, small business association, tourist training college and others in the external enabling environment – which often have a significant impact on how the tourist value chain operates. It is useful to locate potential participants in the value chain who are currently excluded, in order to understand the barriers to entry for the chain.

The approach is structured around three different phases. These phases may be undertaken concurrently but in some situations will be more easily done separately allowing some time for reflection in between:

- *Phase 1: Diagnosis of current situation and context*: This phase includes tools to map the tourism value chain (or economy of the destination), and the participation of the poor within it. The purpose here is to understand financial flows and how the tourism sector currently works. This phase also helps to understand the policy and regulatory context and the existing tourism market.
- *Phase 2: Project opportunities, prioritisation and feasibility*: This phase includes a systematic approach to develop a "long list" of project options. It then guides the move towards a "short list" of high priority interventions that should be implemented, by applying specific criteria that include the likely impact of the intervention on poverty.
- *Phase 3: Project planning*: This section is used to package proposed interventions into bankable projects that can be assessed by potential financiers. The section provides a structure for reports, and tools to assist in developing institutional arrangements, targets and indicators for monitoring, and also project budgets.

The basic elements of "what to do" in a pro-poor value chain assessment, and "why", are outlined in Table 3, with a series of component steps.

Institutions vary enormously in the resources they dedicate to the project scoping and planning process. For example, the diagnostics of tourism value chains have been conducted in as little as 20 staff days per destination – although more resources are needed for more robust analysis.

What is notable about this approach is that it is possible, generally with a team of two specialist researchers – normally working with a team of local stakeholders – to complete the data collection for the diagnostic phase (Phase 1) and Steps 6 and 7 of Phase 2 within about two weeks. This is possible because the ODI has developed a series of standard tools to conduct the analysis (i.e. hotel manager surveys, inbound tour operator surveys, tourist surveys, retailer surveys, etc.). This approach is greatly enriched by involving local stakeholders in a participatory analysis and should including formal rounds of feedback to "ground truth" the analysis with a panel of experienced local stakeholders.

It is ideal to have a break in the fieldwork for analysing the data collected, writing up findings and organising further consultation, before moving into Step 8 (shortlisting and selecting) and then the planning of projects (Phase 3). This is because it is important to analyse and understand what the results of – typically about 100 – interviews are before proceeding to defining interventions to enhance the pro-poor impact of the destination. Whilst Phases 2 and 3 are less intensive in terms of data collection, they are nevertheless demanding in terms of both consultation and analysis.

The ODI has undertaken these analyses on destinations in about a dozen countries with funding from multilateral organisations (World Bank, International Trade Centre, United Nations Development Programme; Commonwealth Secretariat and European Commission), non-governmental organisations (SNV), and the private sector.[3]

- Africa: Tanzania (safari and hiking on Kilimanjaro), Rwanda (gorilla viewing), Ethiopia (business tourism in Addis Ababa and historic/cultural tourism on the Northern and Southern circuits), The Gambia (package beach), Ghana (business tourism in Accra), Cape Verde (package beach), Tunisia (package beach), Libya (new tourist development);

Table 3.   The what and why of pro-poor value chain analysis.

Phase	Step	What to do?	Why?
Phase 1: Diagnosis	Step 1	Preparation	To define the destination, target group and the project team and review panel
	Step 2	Map the big picture: enterprises and other actors in the tourism sector, links between them, demand and supply data and the pertinent context	To organise a chaotic reality, understand the overall system
	Step 3	Map where the poor do, and do not, participate	To avoid erroneous assumptions about poor actors, to take account of the less visible suppliers
	Step 4	Conduct fieldwork interviews in each node of the chain with tourists and service providers, including current and potential low-income participants	To provide data and insights for Steps 5–8
	Step 5	Track revenue flows and pro-poor income. Estimate how expenditure flows through the chain and how much accrues to poor people. Consider their returns and factors that enable or inhibit earnings.	To follow the dollar through the chain down to the poor, and how to assess how returns can be increased
Phase 2: Scope and prioritise opportunities	Step 6	Identify *where* in the tourism value chain to seek change. Which node or nodes have the greatest opportunity (or rent) accessible for low-income groups	To select areas ripe for change, draw upon Steps 1–5. To ensure Steps 6–8 are focused on priority areas
	Step 7	Analyse blockages, options, & partners in the nodes selected, to generate a long list of possible interventions	To think laterally and rationally in generating the range of possible interventions
	Step 8	Prioritise projects on the basis of their impact and feasibility	To generate a project shortlist, comprising projects most likely to deliver impact
Phase 3: Planning	Step 9	Intervention feasibility and planning	Package selected interventions for funding and implementation

Note: These steps have to be iterative and cannot be entirely sequential. For example, some initial thinking from Step 6 (where to focus) will probably inform Step 5. Some thinking on partners' activity will inform Step 6, but be more detailed in Step 7.
Source: Mitchell and Ashley (2009)

- Asia: Lao People's Democratic Republic (cultural in Luang Prabang), Vietnam (business tourism in Da Nang and cultural in Hoi An), Cambodia (business tourism in Phnom Penn and cultural in Siem Reap);
- Latin America: Brazil (beach resorts in Salvador area); and
- Europe: Turkey and Greece (all-inclusive resorts).

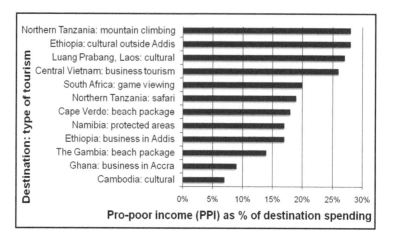

Figure 4. Share of destination tourist spending reaching the poor. Source: Mitchell and Ashley (2010).

A robust empirical basis for understanding the destination economic impacts of tourism is beginning to emerge from this experience over the past five years. It is to these findings that we now turn.

How, and how much, does tourism affect the lives of poor people?

Firstly, in line with the first hypothesis of PPT, international tourism can, sometimes, be an effective way to transfer funds from rich tourists to resource poor people. There are destinations where for every $4 spent by a tourist in-country, $1 reaches the poor people. This is a highly progressive rate of conversion from aggregate trade receipts to pro-poor benefits and compares favourably with many agricultural value chains.

In the "better practice" examples cited in Figure 4, where over 20% of tourists' expenditure at the destination accrues to low-income participants in the value chain, a pro-poor impact is generally the result of strong indirect (like hotel construction or agricultural supply chains to tourists) and dynamic linkages (like the taxation of tourists providing a large share of government redistributive spending). In middle-income countries, direct linkages (such as the wages paid to hotel workers) are often a major source of the benefit flow from tourists to low-income communities.

However, just because tourism can benefit the local community does not mean that this effect is inevitable. Figure 4 provides examples – cultural tourism in Cambodia and business tourism in Ghana – where less than one-tenth of tourist in-country spending reaches the resource-poor. In these instances, the enabling environment for tourism is poor, which allows for significant "elite capture" (both legal and informal) of the benefits from tourism.

The second hypothesis of PPT was that whatever the current level of pro-poor performance of a destination is, there is scope to increase the benefit flow to the poor. An important aspect of our approach is not just to measure and understand how tourism currently affects local communities, but also to make practical suggestions for how to increase this impact. In every destination in which we have worked, across Africa, Asia, Latin America and Europe, the ODI has made recommendations to significantly increase the pro-poor impact of tourism. These recommendations are prioritised in terms of the speed of implementation, resources required and the scale of the pro-poor impact.

Sometimes our recommendations involve changes to the regulatory and enabling environment or the operating practices of individual tour operators and hoteliers. When proposing change for the private sector, our goal is to develop a business case when pro-poor interventions can be implemented that are financially viable. The goal is to find interventions which have higher returns – both commercially and socially.

The third hypothesis of PPT, that any type of tourism can be pro-poor, has particular resonance. It is clear that the old prejudices about the impact of different kinds of tourist products are often not supported by the evidence. Business tourism is strongly pro-poor in Central Vietnam and much less so in Ethiopia. Cultural tourism is positive for local communities in Laos but not in Cambodia. Package tourism does not perform particularly well in The Gambia but performs better in nearby Cape Verde and is integral to the most pro-poor destination we have found anywhere – hiking on Mt. Kilimanjaro in Tanzania. There is as little empirical basis for suggesting mainstream tourism is inherently bad for development as for the view that community-based/ecotourism/cultural tourism is ubiquitously good for development.

Conclusions

We conclude that significant advances are being made towards the goal of assessing the impact of tourism development on low-income households in destination areas:

(1) This form of analysis is fraught with definitional difficulties regarding the fundamental building blocks of any analysis (Who is poor? What is pro-poor? What is tourism?) but these difficulties are inherent to the analysis of any economic sector which seeks to broaden the spread of benefits to low-income households.
(2) The conceptual model is a useful framework to guide the analysis of the impact of tourism on low-income groups. However, it is partial and – to remain relevant – will increasingly have to be applied together with the analysis of non-financial impacts of tourist development.
(3) Value chain analysis does provide a useful research method to assess destination impacts. The ODI's work has shown that it can be adapted to have a specific "pro-poor" focus and is suitable for analysing the tourist sector. In addition, the approach has been refined to allow relatively quick and affordable analyses.

There are indications that this methodological advance is allowing research into the impacts of tourism to rejoin the mainstream of development economics and so become fundable by mainstream development agencies. In addition, the value chain approach aligns closely with how the private sector sees tourism supply chains, and so allows researchers to work directly with the industry whilst speaking the same language.

Notes

1. Least Developed Countries is a United Nations Category for the countries with the lowest indicators of human socio-economic development and is based on meeting low-income, human resource weakness and economic vulnerability criteria.
2. The Overseas Development Institute, based in London; the International Institute for Environment and Development, based in London and Edinburgh; and the International Centre for Responsible Tourism, now based in Leeds, with independent sister organizations in nine other countries.

3. See material in the public domain at http://www.odi.org.uk/resources/search.asp?database= resources&theme=27.

References

Altenburg, T. (2007). *Donor approaches to supporting pro-poor value chains*. Report prepared for the Donor Committee for Enterprise Development Working Group on Linkages and Value Chains, German Development Institute for the Organisation for Economic Co-operation and Development. Retrieved 17 January, 2012, from http://www.fao-ilo.org/fileadmin/user_upload/fao_ilo/pdf/DonorApproachestoPro-PoorValueChains.pdf

Ashley, C., & Goodwin, H. (2007). *'Pro poor tourism': What's gone right and what's gone wrong?* Overseas Development Institute Opinion 80, 31/5/2007. Retrieved 17 January, 2012, from http://www.odi.org.uk/opinion/details.asp?id=3853&title=odi-opinions

Ashley, C., Mitchell, J., & Spenceley, A. (2009). *Opportunity study guidelines the tourism-led poverty reduction programme*. Geneva: International Trade Centre.

Bolwell, D., & Weinz, W. (2008). *Reducing poverty through tourism*. International Labour Organisation Sectoral Activities Programme Working Paper 266, Geneva.

Brohman, J. (1996). New directions in tourism for third world development. *Annals of Tourism Research, 23*(1), 48–70.

Clancy, M. (2001). Mexican tourism: Export growth and structural change since 1970. *Latin American Research Review, 36*(1), 128–150.

Gereffi, G. (1994). The organization of buyer-driven global commodity chains: How U.S. retailers shape overseas production networks. In G. Gereffi & M. Korzeniewicz (Eds.), *Commodity chains and global capitalism*. London: Praeger.

Gereffi, G., Sturgeon, T., & Humphrey, J. (2005). The governance of global value chains. *Review of International Political Economy, 12*(1), 78–104.

Gibbon, P. (2001). Upgrading primary production: A global commodity chain approach. *World Development, 29*(2), 345–363.

Honeck, D. (2008). *Poverty alleviation and the Doha development agenda: Is tourism being neglected?* World Trade Organisation, Economic Research and Statistics Division Staff Working Paper ERSD-2008-13, Geneva, Switzerland.

Jules, S. (2005). *Sustainable tourism in St. Lucia: A sustainability assessment of trade and liberalisation in tourism services*. Winnipeg, Manitoba: International Institute for Sustainable Development.

Kakwani, N., & Son, H. (2003). Pro-poor growth: Concepts and measurement with country case studies. *The Pakistan Development Review, 42*(4), 417–444, Part I (Winter 2003) .

Kaplinsky, R., & Morris, M. (2001). *A handbook for value chain analysis*. Ottawa, ON: International Development Research Centre.

Mitchell, J., & Ashley, C. (2009). *Value chain analysis and poverty reduction at scale*. Overseas Development Institute Briefing Paper 49. Retrieved February 20, 2012, from http://www.odi.org.uk/resources/download/2675.pdf

Mitchell, J., & Ashley, C. (2010). *Tourism and poverty reduction: Pathways to prosperity*. London and Virginia: Earthscan.

Osmani, S. (2005). *Defining pro-poor growth*. UNDP International Poverty Centre for Inclusive Growth, One Pager (#9), Brasilia. Retrieved 17 January, 2012, from http://www.ipc-undp.org/pub/IPCOnePagerBook.pdf

Porter, M. (1985). *Competitive advantage, creating and sustaining superior performance*. New York: The Free Press.

Ravallion, M. (2004). *Defining pro-poor growth: A response to Kakwani*. UNDP International Poverty Centre for Inclusive Growth, One Pager (#4), Brasilia. Retrieved 17 January, 2012, from http://www.ipc-undp.org/pub/IPCOnePagerBook.pdf

Schmitz, H., & Nadvi, K. (2000). Clustering and industrialization: Introduction. *World Development, 27*(9), 1503–1514.

Slob, B., & Wilde, J. (2006). *Tourism and sustainability in Brazil: The tourism value chain in Porto de Galinhas, northeast Brazil*. Amsterdam: Centre for Economic Research on Multinational Corporations (SOMO).

World Bank. (2010). *World development indicators*. Washington, DC: Author.

Tourism–agriculture linkages in rural South Africa: evidence from the accommodation sector

Christian M. Rogerson

School of Tourism & Hospitality, Faculty of Management, University of Johannesburg, Johannesburg, South Africa

This paper explores issues in the development of linkages between tourism and agriculture in developing world situations, a key challenge for pro-poor tourism. It contributes to the limited literature on food sourcing by tourism accommodation establishments by analysing tourism–agriculture linkages in the food supply chains of 80 luxury African safari lodges (ASLs) in rural South Africa. The results disclose important constraints on the establishment and strengthening of local linkages relating to lack of local production quality, consistency and volume required by ASLs. The role of transport, wholesale intermediaries and the rapid turnover of ASL procurement managers is also shown. Price was not a major factor, and contrary to some claims, most ASLs are not foreign owned or staffed by foreign chefs unused to local produce. Positive trends include rising South African food quality and variety, increasing niche market production and increasing tourist interest in fair trade and local foods. For policy intervention, the greatest significance is the failure of many local community initiatives, and the need for training, capacity building and support for local producers to enter the food supply chains. The key need, however, is to overcome poor communication and deep mistrust between food supply decision-makers and local producers.

Introduction

In their recent review paper on progress in the geography of tourism, Hall and Page (2009, p. 11) stress that poverty reduction and pro-poor tourism must be considered as key issues for the future of international tourism management over the next five to 10 years. Pro-poor tourism scholars highlight several reasons why local farmers in developing countries should supply tourism enterprises with food products (Meyer, 2006; Rueegg, 2009; Torres & Momsen, 2004). In many developing countries, tourism projects have been initiated in regions or localities where the livelihoods of the poor are dominated by food production. It is emphasized, therefore, that supplying formal tourism establishments with food products can build upon the existing skills of the poor without changing their livelihood strategies (Torres & Momsen, 2004, p. 302). Moreover, the provision of food products involves utilizing the productive assets of the poor in terms of land and labour. New skills learned in the production of food for tourism establishments potentially might also allow farmers to transfer such skills to other food supply chains. Further, proponents suggest an untapped potential exists for poor people to furnish "authentic" locally produced food for which there is a growing demand (Meyer, 2007). Another compelling argument for strengthening local tourism–agriculture linkages relates to its impacts in terms of reducing the "carbon foodprint" of tourism establishments. New research demonstrates that the advantages of localizing food production extend to reduced greenhouse gas emissions and the making of low carbon destinations, an essential element for sustainable tourism development (Gössling, Garrod, Aall, Hille, & Peeters, 2011).

This study contributes in two significant respects to deepen our limited understanding of tourism–agriculture linkages in the developing world. Firstly, it charts new territory and addresses the geographical gap in scholarship relating to tourism–agriculture linkages in the region of sub-Saharan Africa, which is a growing part of the international tourism economy (Rogerson, 2007; Rogerson & Rogerson, 2011). The findings in this paper represent in part a response to the call made for additional "comparative research" in order to better interpret the links between tourism and agriculture (Telfer & Wall, 2000, p. 443), and more especially, between tourism accommodation or lodging establishments and food producers (Meyer, 2007; Timothy & Teye, 2009). Secondly, the research focus here is not upon the linkages of agriculture with mass tourism or beach resorts, which has been examined in research in the Caribbean, Mexico and Indonesia (Meyer, 2006; Telfer & Wall, 2000; Timms, 2006; Torres & Momsen, 2011). Instead, the analysis is of the food supply chain and local impacts of luxury safari lodges which would be classed broadly as "alternative tourism" products associated with wildlife or ecotourism. Evidence is presented from interviews conducted during 2009 with safari lodges at a range of different localities across South Africa concerning food supply chains in general and specifically of tourism–agriculture linkages (Hunt, 2010). South Africa provides an appropriate setting for such an investigation, for the country has been at the forefront of policy innovation and practice relating both to pro-poor tourism (Ashley & Haysom, 2008; Ashley & Roe, 2002; Rogerson, 2006; Rogerson & Visser, 2011; Spenceley, 2008) and to maximizing the benefits of tourism for local economic development (Rogerson, 2002, 2006; Rogerson & Rogerson, 2010; Visser & Hoogendoorn, 2011).

The nexus of tourism and agriculture

The broad relationship between tourism and agriculture in the developing world is considered as multi-faceted, complex and variable (Torres & Momsen, 2011). It ranges across a spectrum from situations of "conflict where tourism competes with agriculture for land, water and labour to symbiosis where the tourism industry purchases local agricultural products and uses the agricultural landscape for agritourism" (Telfer & Wall, 2000, p. 423). Tourism offers a potential to galvanize local agricultural development through backward linkages that allow local farmers to supply the food needs of tourism establishments (Rueegg, 2009; Torres & Momsen, 2004). Accordingly, strengthening the linkages between agriculture and tourism is central to promoting symbiosis rather than conflict between the two sectors. The benefits of a closer relationship include decreased linkages through imports, improvement in tourism industry food supplies, increased tourist access to local foods and improved sustainability for tourism, not least through alleviation of poverty (Torres & Momsen, 2011).

Across the experience of the developing world, the food supply chain to the tourism sector is therefore acknowledged to be an important potential source of pro-poor impacts (König, 2007; Meyer, 2007; Mitchell & Ashley, 2006, 2009, 2010; Rueegg, 2009; Torres

& Momsen, 2004). As food and beverages are considered to account for approximately one third of tourist expenditure in destinations (Meyer, 2006, p. 20), the promotion of local food production for tourism consumption can "affect significantly the economic and social impact of tourism" (Belisle, 1983, p. 498). According to Torres (2003, p. 562), the failure to stimulate local supplies represents "both a lost opportunity for local agriculture and a hemorrhaging of tourism benefits". In terms of attaining the objectives set by pro-poor tourism, the supply chain to tourism enterprises is especially significant because it can disperse the benefits of tourism spatially well beyond that of the destination, in such a manner farmers "need never meet a tourist to benefit from the sector" (Mitchell, Ashley, & Mann, 2007, p. 3). It is observed, however, that whilst the linkages between tourism and agriculture in developed countries have been interrogated across a range of different contexts (e.g. Brown, Cox, & Fox, 1991; Cox, Fox, & Bowen, 1994; Fleischer & Tchetchik, 2005; Hermans, 1981; Knowd, 2006; Sims, 2009; Skuras, Dimara, & Petrou, 2006; Telfer, 2000), much less attention has been given to this important topic in the environment of the developing world.

Since the early 1980s when Belisle (1983, p. 509) bemoaned "the paucity of research into the relationships between tourism and food production", only a small number of investigations have appeared in the developing world. Of note is that the majority of existing scholarship centres upon detailed case studies, which have been conducted in the Caribbean (Belisle, 1983; Momsen, 1998; Timms, 2006), Mexico (Torres, 2002, 2003; Torres & Momsen, 2004) or Indonesia (Telfer & Wall, 1996, 2000). The largest body of research focuses upon tourism–agriculture linkages in the circumstances of enclavic mass tourism resorts (such as Cancun) or of beach tourism in small island tourism economies (e.g. Lombok or St Lucia). Only recently has the geographical research frontier on tourism–agriculture linkages extended to encompass a wider range of developing world destinations (see König, 2007; Rueegg, 2009; Torres & Momsen, 2011).

Scholarship on tourism–agriculture linkages isolates several critical factors that constrain the involvement of local producers in tourism supply chains. Existing research draws attention to a suite of different influences that impact upon food supply procurement patterns and backward linkage development (Torres & Momsen, 2011). The characteristics and strength of linkages are considered to be associated with several demand-related, supply-related (or production-related) and marketing or intermediary factors (Meyer, 2007; Rueegg, 2009; Torres, 2003). Meyer (2007, p. 569) asserts that in order to both support the procurement of local inputs for accommodation establishments and maintain sustainable linkages between tourism and agriculture, "the demand, supply and marketing and intermediary related factors as well as government policy need to be taken into account". In terms of production-related issues, factors of significance are environmental considerations, the nature of local farming systems, the lack of local production of goods or types and quality of food demanded by tourists and/or the high prices of local products (König, 2007; Lacher & Nepal, 2010; Meyer, 2006, 2011). One critical demand-related factor is the nature of tourism development with foreign-owned or managed enterprises and expatriate chefs reliant upon imports and evolving only weak links to local producers (Meyer, 2006; Torres, 2003). In addition, larger and higher-end hotels exhibit a trend towards using imported foods rather than locally grown produce (Meyer, 2011; Telfer & Wall, 2000). Importantly, the existing research suggests that the opportunities for "creating demand for local foods are greatest among certain nationalities and with more adventurous non-mass tourists" (Torres, 2003, p. 548).

Torres (2003) stresses that significant marketing- or intermediary-related factors can also assume a vital role in defining tourism–agriculture linkages. Among the most influential can be the availability and quality of regional transport and distribution infrastructure, kickbacks paid to local chefs by large food suppliers and the inexperience of local producers in marketing. In addition, Meyer (2006, p. 31) highlights the frequently limited communications between the tourism and agricultural sectors which "means that there is generally limited awareness of what is required by tourists and what can be produced locally to satisfy the demands of the tourism sector". Although the available scholarship paints an uneven picture, it does point to the general conclusion that most tourism establishments in the global South source their food (and other services) from wherever is cheapest, most reliable, most easily accessible and of assured quality (Meyer, Ashley, & Poultney, 2004; Torres, 2003). Most importantly, the predominant pattern is for high-end tourism establishments to source from distant and mainly large suppliers rather than from local small enterprises or poor entrepreneurs (Torres & Momsen, 2004). The implications of sourcing food products from distant large-scale suppliers for local economies and for local economic development are to reduce severely the pro-poor impacts of tourism projects.

Safari lodge tourism in South Africa

Since the 1994 democratic transition, South Africa has emerged as one of the leading tourism destinations in Africa (Rogerson, 2007; Rogerson & Visser, 2004). The largest segment – over 70% – of the country's nine million recorded international tourists (2009) are from sub-Saharan Africa and travel to South Africa primarily for purposes of business, shopping or visiting friends and relatives (Rogerson, 2009; Rogerson & Visser, 2006). The cohort of approximately two million long-haul international visitors – mainly from Western Europe and increasingly from North America – represents the highest income-earning segment of the tourism economy of South Africa. Although this particular group encompasses a growing stream of business tourists, the majority of South Africa's long-haul international tourists are leisure travellers, many of them attracted to the country by its range of "exotic" wildlife attractions (Rogerson, 2009; Rogerson & Visser, 2006).

The African safari lodge (ASL) represents a form of high-value, low-volume accommodation that provides non-consumptive game-viewing experiences in an atmosphere of luxurious hospitality. Although this form of tourism might be considered a niche tourism activity, across much of southern Africa it is viewed as a mainstream tourism product (Ashley & Roe, 2002; Massyn & Koch, 2004; Rogerson & Visser, 2011). The ASL originated in small rustic camps which were set in areas with large amounts of wildlife. Initially, ASLs were built mainly for friends and family, or hunters and adventure travellers who wished to "safari" through the wildlife and wilderness areas of Africa. Historically, the ASL phenomenon began in South Africa at locales such as the Sabi Sands Game Reserve during the 1930s. Especially from the 1960s, growing numbers of Northern tourists began to travel in search of "wild Africa" because of increased disposable incomes, expansion of leisure time as well as technological advancements in aviation. During the 1980s as the demand for this form of tourism further escalated, so did both the levels of luxury and the cost of tourist bed nights. Accompanying the growing profitability of safari lodges, ASLs expanded throughout the region of southern Africa, led mainly by developments taking place in South Africa.

Massyn and Koch (2004, p. 103) contend that what makes an ASL different from other forms of accommodation is that it offers "the preserved remnants of Africa's charismatic mega fauna and biological diversity in a global context, which is experiencing waves of species extinction elsewhere". Additionally, ASLs use the draw card of "romance", marketing their products with a heavy focus on the created "legends" and imagery of "wild

Africa" (Massyn & Koch, 2004). A considerable growth in the number of ASLs has taken place in South Africa during the past 15 years coincident with the ending of apartheid, the dropping of international sanctions on the country and South Africa's image change from global pariah to "rainbow nation". Nevertheless, the nature of the safari lodge has been impacted by wider structural changes in the tourism economy (Massyn & Koch, 2004, p. 106). During the last decade, the conservation industry witnessed a number of important shifts, not least the rise in community-based conservation programmes throughout southern and east Africa, the growth of "green movements" and a stronger emphasis on social consciousness. Taken together, this triggered an increase in the numbers of travellers to Africa, who wish to participate in forms of tourism that "give back" to the communities and environments they visit (Ashley, de Brine, Lehr, & Wilde, 2007).

In response to these changes, a "new generation" of ASLs appeared, which no longer are focused exclusively on marketing a luxurious "wild Africa" image. Instead, the "new wave" of ASLs incorporates into their enterprise marketing the elements of environmental protection and community development (Massyn & Koch, 2004). Many lodges are marketed now as more "authentic" by using responsible tourism best practice as their unique selling point, often linked to their membership of new certification schemes such as Fair Trade in Tourism. A last critical influence upon the changing nature and practice of South African safari lodges has been that of the national government. One consistent tenet of tourism planning in the post-apartheid period is that of fostering "responsible tourism". National government has actively pursued the positioning of tourism as a key driver in the country's economy and as a vehicle to advance the livelihoods of people who were previously disadvantaged under apartheid (Republic of South Africa, 2011; Spenceley, 2008). The 1996 White Paper on the Development and Promotion of Tourism promoted the development of responsible and sustainable tourism approaches (Rogerson & Visser, 2004). This focus has continued to the present day such that the primary vision of South Africa's recently (2009) constituted National Department of Tourism is to forge "the conditions for responsible tourism growth and development by promoting and developing tourism, thereby increasing job and entrepreneurial opportunities and encouraging the meaningful participation of previously disadvantaged individuals" (Republic of South Africa, 2010). The promotion of responsible tourism practices is a central thread in South Africa's National Tourism Sector Strategy released in 2011 (Republic of South Africa, 2011).

The South African government's support for inter-sectoral linkages in the form of local procurement is strong. One emphasis in the country's Responsible Tourism Guidelines is on the need for greater levels of local procurement. The guidelines urge the private sector to, *inter alia*, "buy locally made goods and use locally provided services from locally owned businesses where ever quality, quantity, and consistency permits. Monitor the proportion of goods and services the enterprise sources from businesses within 50 km and set a 20 per cent target for improvement over three years" (Spenceley et al., 2002). Furthermore, the Responsible Tourism Manual for South Africa stresses the need for the tourism industry to forge stronger linkages with local communities through procurement practices:

> Linkages between different tourism enterprises and services in a locality can help to create a strong destination, and provide a network of various attractions. For a tourism enterprise, creating local linkages is about changing the ways in which it spends its money – not about spending more of it! Geographical neighbours make good business partners (once they are equipped to provide consistent products and service). The local "geographic family" linkage ensures a strong ethic of feedback and responsibility (Spenceley et al., 2002, p. 28).

In South Africa, ASLs are spatially situated mostly in remote areas of extreme natural beauty – national parks, reserves and low-populated scenic regions – where local communities suffer from high levels of poverty and low levels of economic development (Massyn & Koch, 2004). Normally, the ASL is the sole or main employer in its immediate surrounding area. Owing to their location and the high-paying customers they attract, arguably ASLs offer a strong potential to initiate pro-poor tourism impacts in rural areas. Recently, considerable attention has attached to the potential of safari lodge tourism as a vehicle for pro-poor local economic development in South Africa (Rogerson, 2006; Rogerson & Rogerson, 2010). Indeed, certain research demonstrates that participation in the supply chain could be more beneficial to the poor than direct involvement in core tourism activities (Ashley & Haysom, 2008; Kirsten & Rogerson, 2002). It is observed that the consumption and preparation of food is acknowledged to be a central facet of the visitor experience at ASLs. Because of their remote locations, there are no alternative options for tourists to purchase food services. The "safari" experience is marketed as an inclusive package, which includes luxury accommodation, spectacular game viewing and gourmet food. Accordingly, in view of the substantial food procurement spend of ASLs, the development of backward linkages between tourism and agriculture is viewed as potentially highly significant for determining the local impacts of tourism.

Food supply linkages in South Africa – method and profile

To ascertain the extent of tourism–agriculture linkages in the safari lodge industry, the first step was the preparation of a database of all ASLs in South Africa. For the purposes of this investigation, "luxury ASLs" were defined as those accommodation establishments that offer non-consumptive game-viewing experiences and charge a daily rate of over US$200 per person per night. The establishment of this database drew upon a number of sources, most importantly of the Indaba tourism attendance listings (Hunt, 2010). In addition, this source was supplemented by an Internet research of safari establishments as well as of lodge marketing associations and provincial tourism organizations. The analysis disclosed a total of 235 luxury safari establishments spread across the country. In addition, there are a substantial number of other ASLs that charge less than US$200 per person per night, which were omitted from the study.

The spatial distribution of the 235 luxury ASLs in South Africa is illustrated in Figure 1. It is evident that the highest concentration of ASLs can be found in north-eastern parts of South Africa within the two provinces of Limpopo and Mpumalanga, which have the largest amount of land set aside for wilderness conservation purposes. At the regional level, the distribution of these lodges exhibits a number of distinct clusters that form around South Africa's major national parks, most importantly the Kruger National Park, the Addo Elephant National Park and the Isimangaliso Wetland Park. Each of these three major parks is surrounded by several private game reserves that offer non-consumptive game-viewing experiences and house a range of different safari lodge operations. Together, these three clusters contain 163 or 69.4% of the categorized luxury ASLs in the country.

Although South African ASLs are situated in rural areas, apart from those in the Kalahari area of the Northern Cape, few would be considered as remote. The average distance from a luxury ASL to the nearest community settlement and nearest urban centre was calculated, respectively, as 23.8 km and 74 km. Considerable variations exist between the different clusters. ASLs in the Madikwe, Addo Elephant and Cape Town clusters are situated less than 20 km from their nearest community settlement, whereas those in the Waterberg and Southern Kruger are on average over 35 km away. In relation to the nearest urban centre, however, the Madikwe and Waterberg ASLs were on average over 100 km distant, whereas ASLs in the Addo Elephant cluster were less than 40 km away. The factor of location to

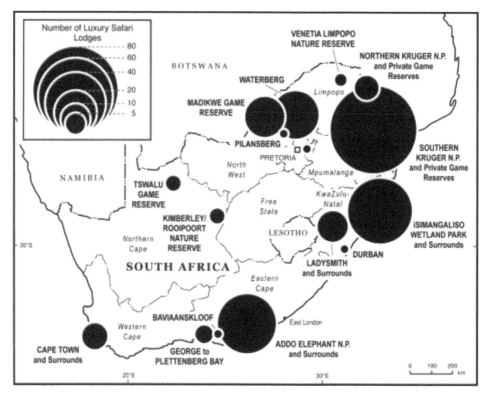

Figure 1. The geographical distribution of South African safari lodges, by local grouping (Source: Author).

the closest community and the nearest urban centre emerges in accounting for variations between clusters in patterns of food sourcing (Hunt, 2010).

It should also be noted that variations occurred in the average daily price of accommodation. The most costly were ASLs situated in the private game reserves of the Southern Kruger and Madikwe clusters where average daily rates were over ZAR4300; the least expensive were lodges in the Waterberg (R2700) and Cape Town and its surroundings (R2872; 7.3 ZAR = US$1, as of August 2011). With the exception of two ASLs in Madikwe which were owned by local communities (but operated by a tripartite management involving also the provincial parks board and the private sector), all remaining lodges were under full private sector ownership. As a whole, 77.5% of the surveyed ASLs were owned by domestic South African companies. The high levels of domestic control recorded in the luxury ASL sector in South Africa contrast with the significant extent of external ownership of ASLs recorded in surrounding countries in the region of southern Africa (Mbaiwa & Darkoh, 2006; Spenceley, 2008).

Patterns of sourcing

In this and the following section, the findings are analysed concerning patterns of food sourcing and barriers to the development of local linkages between tourism and agriculture. The results are drawn from 56 detailed interviews, which were conducted during 2009 with members of ASL management and chefs across South Africa. As many of the

Table 1. Food, menu and supplier decisions: ASLs in South Africa.

Decision	By chef	By chef and management	By management	Total
Foods served and menu decisions	34	25	21	80
Food supplier decisions	8	24	48	80

survey interviewees were responsible for food supply decisions at more than one lodge, the enterprise survey captured information for 80 different ASLs. This data from the enterprise survey were supplemented by additional interviews which were undertaken with key ASL food suppliers as well as a short investigation of the food preferences of the international clientele of ASLs (Hunt, 2010). As far as possible, the enterprise survey was structured to reflect the geographical distribution of ASLs. Of the total 80 ASLs for which data were obtained, 59 or 73% were derived from the three leading ASL cluster locations. A slight under-representation in the survey is recorded from ASLs surrounding the Isimangaliso Wetland Park because of the unwillingness of some operators there to participate in this investigation. The research process allowed the collection of both quantitative and qualitative materials; the former gives evidence of the organization of food sourcing, whereas the latter provides insight into the range of factors that shape ASL food supply chains.

An important initial finding relates to the information on food sourcing decisions which are made at ASLs. It is evident from Table 1 that in the majority of cases, chefs are important in taking decisions regarding the choice of food and menus to be prepared whereas management personnel assume a more significant role in decisions regarding food procurement and sources of supply. In order to meet the required five-star standards of cuisine, the ASLs require high-quality food supplies and ingredients. For the successful production of competitive gourmet cuisine, the survey respondents stressed the imperative for access to a wide variety of quality fresh supplies for which reliable delivery can be assured. In addition, high-quality processed goods such as olive oil, chocolate, puff pastry or spices are also essential supplies. For their clientele, the lodges require a wide variety of goods including, for example, a choice of specialized cheeses, different meat options or several varieties of fresh fruit. As one supplier interviewee explained: "we have very picky clients that require high quality specialised goods".

In order to source the range of specialized food supplies, the majority of ASLs procure their produce through an intermediary supplier. Of the 80 ASLs which supplied information, 73 or 91% used an intermediary supplier; only seven lodges stated that they sourced all their goods by themselves. The choice for an intermediary supplier was on grounds of convenience. As one respondent observed: "it is easier to go through a middleman who does all the bartering, sourcing and delivery for you". For the important group of luxury ASLs in the Sabi Sands private game reserve, a part of the Southern Kruger cluster, one intermediary distributor is the exclusive source of all fresh produce goods. In the ASL food chain, the role of the intermediary supplier is thus crucial in making decisions regarding the choice of supplier as well as in establishing standards that local producers must attain if they wish to enter the supply chain.

As the ASLs utilize a range of specialized food products, information was collected for the source of supply of eight different categories of food: (1) vegetables, (2) fruit, (3) eggs, (4) dairy products, (5) meat products, (6) luxury goods, (7) tinned goods and (8) dried goods. Information was obtained on where lodges sourced their supplies for produce rather than the original source of supplies, an issue that was addressed through the second set of supplier interviews.

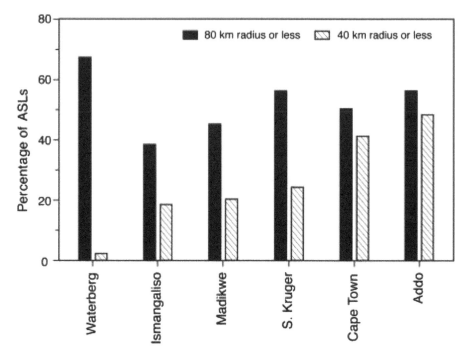

Figure 2. Percentage of ASLs in each area which source the bulk of their goods within a 40 km and an 80 km distance from source establishment to the ASL.

Figure 2 provides a comparison of the six ASL clusters in respect of sourcing goods from within a 40 km and an 80 km radius for each ASL location. It is apparent that considerable spatial variability exists in geographical patterns of food procurement. For example, in the Cape Town and Addo clusters, up to 40% of food goods required by ASLs can be sourced from suppliers within a distance of 40 km or less; this distance is much less than that for ASLs in other parts of South Africa. Behind this relatively high level of local sourcing in these two regions is the proximity of ASLs to well-established local agricultural sectors, good infrastructure and agro-processing capabilities. Important variations exist between different categories of food goods. In terms of the eight different food groups, the research disclosed the distance to suppliers for the bulk of ASL requirements. Not surprisingly, the most specialized goods, such as luxury goods (which would include high-value processed goods such as caviar or specialized chocolates), record a longer average sourcing distance (188 km) than is the position for eggs (73 km), fresh vegetables (80 km) or fruit (80 km).

In terms of local economic development impacts in rural areas of South Africa, what emerges is the potential for local sourcing of supplies of eggs, fresh fruit and, in particular, fresh vegetables. Nationally, for domestic consumption, South Africa is mostly self-sufficient in the production of fresh vegetables; only a relatively small amount of fresh vegetables is imported. Table 2 reveals the patterns of sourcing of vegetables within South Africa for the different ASL clusters. It is apparent that a high proportion of vegetables consumed by ASLs is locally sourced. In total, 35% of the lodges surveyed in South Africa source the bulk of their fresh vegetables from within a 40 km radius of where they are located and 59% from within 80 km. It must be noted, however, that these percentages vary considerably for different areas of the country. On average, it is estimated that each ASL orders 250 kg of vegetables per month that is delivered in batches at least once a week.

Table 2. Distance travelled by the bulk of vegetables and percentage of ASLs that source the bulk of their vegetables within 80 km and 40 km, South Africa.

	Average distance (km) to vegetable source establishment	Vegetables sourced within 80 km radius (%)	Vegetables sourced within 40 km radius (%)
Isimangaliso Wetland Park & surrounds	119	33.33	22.22
Addo Elephant Park & surrounds	52.44	68.75	62.5
Waterberg & surrounds	92.17	66.67	0
Cape Town & surrounds	68.57	57.14	57.14
Madikwe Game Reserve & surrounds	71.25	62.5	37.5
Southern Kruger	79.5	66.67	33.33
Average for South Africa	80.48	59.17	35.45

Some ASLs demand vegetable deliveries on a daily basis in order to ensure the freshness of ingredients. One respondent commented that: "I order regularly in low volumes as it is hard to keep goods fresh and it is also important for pest control as rotting vegetables is a problem" (Eastern Cape). More than half of the ASLs, which are not located within a national park (55%), actually grow a proportion of their own vegetable produce and fresh herbs themselves. Further, "top-up" supplies in particular are sourced from local enterprises or directly from local farmers. In the Addo Elephant Park and surrounding cluster as well as the Cape Town cluster respondents explained that small amounts of vegetables were sourced directly from local farmers, albeit only as a "back up" supply arrangement.

Importantly, it was disclosed that the majority of South African ASLs source the bulk of their fresh produce from established urban-based distributors or suppliers. By far the most significant of these sources is the main wholesale fruit and vegetable market in Johannesburg; for those lodges in the Western Cape, the smaller Cape Town market fulfils a similar function. Both these wholesale markets source their produce from a wide range of local South African producers as well as a small volume of international (mainly African) suppliers. The Joburg Market (previously known as the Johannesburg Fresh Produce Market) assumes a central role in the supply chain for the luxury safari lodges in South Africa; 80% of produce from the market is South African in origin. One supplier of vegetables grown in Hazyview, close to the Kruger Park cluster, explained: "nothing is grown here for selling direct to the public. It is all sent to Johannesburg".

From detailed responses offered by ASL respondents, three influences are changing the patterns of food supply requirements. First is that South Africa now provides an increased level of variety, quality and service delivery of many kinds of food product. In addition, local suppliers have an increased understanding of gourmet cuisine and of necessary required ingredients. Second, in response to the international movement towards health conscious food choices, respondents noted a trend for changed menus and methods of food preparation to offer lighter meals with increased organic ingredients resulting in an increased demand for fresh organic produce. From one private game reserve in Sabi Sands, it was noted: "We now offer a healthier lighter menu including more home cooked and leaner foods." Third, a key factor driving increased local food procurement is the South African Fair Trade in Tourism certification process. By becoming Fair Trade certified, a lodge pledges to seek to source goods locally wherever quality and availability permits. At least two ASL interviewees stressed that because of their Fair Trade certification they had significantly increased the proportion of their goods that are sourced locally. As the next section shows, however, this willingness to increase local procurement and expand backward linkages is restricted by several constraints.

Constraints on backward linkages

From the international scholarship on tourism–agriculture linkages, many different demand-related, supply or intermediary factors can explain the difficulties or limitations upon developing stronger backward economic linkages (Meyer, 2006, 2007; Rueegg, 2009; Torres, 2002, 2003; Torres & Momsen, 2004, 2011). The 56 ASL interviewees were asked to rate certain factors which they perceived as of high importance, of low importance or of no importance for sourcing more local food products supplies. The overall results are presented in Figure 3.

In accounting for limited backward linkages to local food suppliers, the most important reason that was offered from ASL respondents relates to the inability of local producers to offer consistent and reliable amounts of the required food products. Typical replies from interviewees were that: "There is no guarantee that they [food goods] will be the same quality as the week before" (Sabi Sands), "Consistent supply is just not there" (Addo) or "Locals just don't have the ability to service our requirements" (Thornybush). Often the reason indicated for the low level of local procurement was that local communities could not

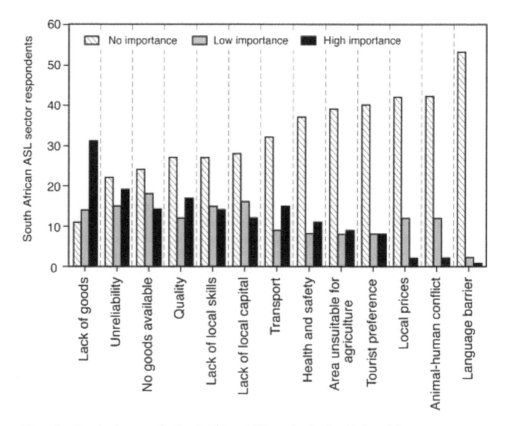

Figure 3.   Perceived reasons for South African ASL's not buying locally ($n = 56$).

Table 3. Responses from ASL interviewees on the unreliability of local suppliers.

Location	Response
Sabi Sands	"Locals are unfortunately not reliable enough to rely on. There is no guarantee of consistency."
Waterberg	"There is no reliability or consistency with local producers."
Makuleke	"We would rather buy locally but consistency and reliability is a problem."
Eastern Cape	"We have changed suppliers due to better service provision. Service provision is more important to us than price. And anyway prices differ little between suppliers. Locals don't provide reliable service."
Addo	"The quality of the produce is not the same as a commercial farmer, it is also not dependable at all."
Madikwe	"Our supplier is very expensive but is reliable and that is what's most important."
Sabi Sands	"Pick n Pay are reliable. We fax in the order on Tuesday and that afternoon they get back with information. The communication with local communities is not like that."

provide the goods that were demanded. In total, 14 respondents (or 25%) claimed even that there were no goods available to them locally. Further analysis revealed that goods could be obtained locally, albeit not necessarily of the variety, quality, quantity or consistency that the five-star ASL establishments demanded.

The critical issues of quality and reliability of suppliers highlight the mistrust between ASLs and local producers. As is evident from the qualitative responses made by interviewees, most food decision-makers at ASLs consider local producers as untrustworthy, inconsistent and unreliable, and complain of poor quality, lack of product consistency and unpredictable deliveries (Table 3).

Several incidents were recounted from different parts of South Africa of local farmers failing to meet promised standards, which caused general mistrust of small producers. Illustratively, the following comments were offered:

- "We had to double check everything from locals. Once a food bag arrived with rat pee on it which is highly dangerous" (Southern Kruger); and
- "Local producers are just not reliable, you think you're going to get a bag of carrots and you don't" (Private Game Reserve Eastern Cape).

The building of relationships of long-term trust between local producers and the lodges is constrained by the high level of staff turnover that was observed at the ASLs. It is evident from Figure 4 that high levels of staff turnover are recorded at ASLs throughout South Africa and that the majority of decision-makers have been occupying their current position for a period of less than four years. The possibilities for developing sustainable backward linkages are tenuous in circumstances when an individual lodge manager or chef is the only link for a local supplier to the ASL. Suppliers and linkages are often changed with the appointment of new personnel. Indeed, one interviewee claimed on taking up employment at an ASL that he had changed all existing suppliers to others that "he was more confident with". The challenge of establishing, building and sustaining business relationships beyond the working life of one individual decision-maker must be addressed to create stable patterns of procurement and backward economic linkages.

The question of the high cost of locally produced food was identified as a constraint by 25% of the survey respondents. The mass of smallholder farmers in South Africa lack the ability to compete with larger commercial farmers (Mmbengwa et al., 2011). Most

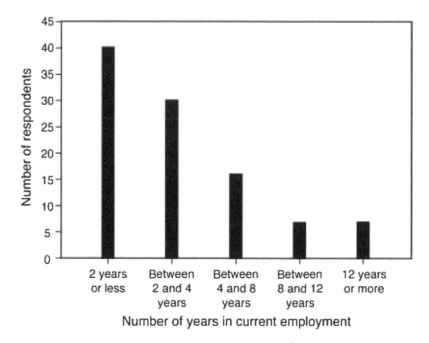

Figure 4.   The period in current employment of survey respondents ($n = 56$).

respondents, however, expressed the viewpoint that reliable service delivery was more important than price in making decisions on where to source goods. Often ASLs pay higher prices to intermediary suppliers in order to ensure that required produce arrives on time and to the quantity and consistency that is needed. One ASL in the Southern Kruger cluster responded: "I try to avoid sourcing locally as much as I can. It is too much hassle." This deep mistrust of local producers severely restricts the ability to form food supply partnerships between small-scale farmers and the ASL sector.

Questions of transport logistics were highlighted by 24 respondents (or 42.8%) as a constraint to sourcing goods locally in South Africa. Of these respondents, 15 (or 26.8%) claimed that this was a highly important barrier. As ASLs in South Africa are located on average 23.8 km from their nearest local community and 74 km from their nearest urban centre, transport logistics can be significant barriers to strengthening tourism–agriculture linkages. The majority of ASLs in the Southern Kruger, Cape Town, Addo Elephant Park and Madikwe clusters insist that suppliers deliver their goods directly to them. Hence, even the closest producers to the ASLs must transport goods directly to the lodges. As shown in the responses in Table 4, improvement and coordination of transport is essential to developing extended backward economic linkages.

One option for small producers is to go through central buying locations where inter-mediary suppliers can buy from them for subsequent delivery to the ASLs. Nevertheless, in relation to the provision of fresh fruit and vegetables, there are few central markets in South Africa that offer the quality, consistency and reliability of the Joburg Market. This situation results in unnecessary costs being added to produce. Citrus fruits and avocados grown outside the Orpen Gate of the Kruger National Park are picked and loaded onto trucks for the Joburg Market. From there, ASL suppliers buy these products which are then driven back to the Kruger Park area for distribution to the various lodges. This re-turn journey adds an estimated 1070 km to the distance travelled by these products. ASL

Table 4.   Responses from interviewees on transport logistics, South Africa.

Location	Response
Madikwe	"Deliveries are an issue as people can produce goods but they find it difficult to deliver them to us and that is a requirement."
Southern Kruger	"It's all about logistics. I make two phone calls and all my food and beverage needs are sorted. I do no buying or delivering myself it is all done by Lebamba and the butcher."
Northern KwaZulu-Natal	"Transport logistics are the most important issue. There is a tomato farm nearby but they have no transport to be able to deliver to us."
Supplier respondent Hazyview	"The major problem is that people don't think about how to logistically get a product out. It's all very well growing it, it's the selling and delivering part that is the problem."
Sabi Sands	"If people worked together as in some suppliers deliver to Matumi and they deliver to us-or our meat supplier delivers for the chocolate company, then it will work. If you can deliver we can buy."

interviewees did acknowledge that "buying local" would negate transport costs as well as being more environmentally friendly and supporting the goals of responsible tourism (cf. Gössling et al., 2011). But the difficulties of transport logistics and local purchasing mean that in the words of one interviewee: "we pay for our produce to have a nice trip to Joburg and back" (Timbavati Private Game Reserve).

Further barriers to linkages relate to lack of local farming skills and access to agricultural investment capital, issues which were raised by almost half of the survey respondents as contributing to the poor quality of local agricultural supplies. These findings confirm the major constraints identified by agricultural researchers concerning market access barriers faced by South African small-scale farmers (Magingxa, Alemu, & van Schalkwyk, 2009; Mmbengwa et al., 2011). Overall, 12 respondents (21%) considered lack of financial investment in local agriculture as of "high importance" and 14 respondents (25%) believed lack of skills was of high importance. As one respondent explained: "low education results in poor farming practices and lack of understanding of tourism and often a lack of initiative" (Waterberg). Associated with local technological skills was the issue of maintaining health and safety standards, which is a priority consideration for producers in South Africa. In total, 33.9% of the respondents mentioned (rising) health and safety considerations as either of "some" or of "high" importance when deciding whether to source goods locally. One interviewee stated that this was the main reason she could not procure goods locally. Likewise, another respondent explained that due to a voluntary monthly health and safety assessment conducted by an external private health and safety company, their local procurement efforts were severely restricted.

A significant finding was that 36% of the surveyed ASLs had been actively involved in either initiating or supporting projects with local communities in terms of galvanizing local food production for direct supply to the lodges. The majority of these projects, however, have been short-lived and currently less than half of projects still function. As is evident from the detailed interview responses captured in Table 5, the core reasons behind the collapse of projects relate to poor management, organizational difficulties of running community farming projects and lack of capacity within many local communities. It is significant that failures are recorded particularly in the surrounds of the Isimangaliso Wetlands Park, an area with favourable environmental conditions – in terms of adequate rainfall – for crop production. Environmental limitations in terms of lack of rainfall explain in part the difficulties of local food production in other areas such as the Southern Kruger. Around

Table 5.   The record of community food production projects.

Location	Response
Northern Kruger NP	"There was a community project that we bought from. A hydroponics business in Makuleke but with poor management it collapsed. We really tried to buy from them but had to give up after six months. They tried to do soft herbs but they just didn't get it right. They need someone with experience to know when to plant and how to grow and sell and package. A two year management plan might have helped."
Isimangaliso	"Many NGO's have tried to set up projects in this area but not continued them. We have approached communities and offered to regularly buy produce but it was never followed up by the community."
Isimangaliso	"We set up a vegetable garden for them, gave seeds and a guaranteed market. One guy tried to keep it working but the others pillaged it and he eventually gave up."
Grahamstown	"People have tried but there was no follow up and the project collapsed."
Thornybush	"Show me an example where a community project like this has worked, worked for 10 years, and we'll do it tomorrow. But I've lived on this continent too long and it won't work. You just end up getting your fingers burnt."
Sabi Sands	"We tried to start a project but the money was stolen and the locals just wouldn't work they have no interest and no training."
Sabi Sands	"A green house was donated to a school by Telkom, the village did not have the financial input or skill to co ordinate the project and there is no access to water in the village except for pumps and then only transported by wheelbarrows in containers."
Madikwe	"There are many good intentions to set up initiatives, we also get a lot of guests who would like to help but for some reason or another they all fall flat."
Waterberg	"A sustainable farm was set up but the people were not interested or motivated and it failed. People here prefer not to work. The only major player passed away and so the drive behind the project was lost."

the private game reserves in Sabi Sands, the climate is marginal for crop production and opportunities for irrigation are limited. Likewise, in parts of the Eastern Cape, one interviewee observed the transition taking place from agriculture to game farms as a consequence of the environmental limitations upon commercial agriculture. By contrast, the ASLs in the Western Cape and those around Addo are situated close to highly productive commercial agriculture, which facilitates their access to a wide range of quality local produce.

Finally, of note is the minor significance that was accorded by ASLs to the role of tourist preferences as a constraint upon the strengthening of tourism–agriculture linkages (cf. König, 2007; Rueegg, 2009; Torres, 2002). As noted earlier (Table 1), the choice of menu and foods to be prepared at ASLs is a decision made mainly by the local chef themselves or jointly with lodge management. Only a small number of these decisions are being made by non-South Africans; the survey disclosed that 82% of the respondents were South Africans. The vast majority of gourmet food prepared at ASLs represents a European style of cuisine. Interviewees stressed that distinctive South African cuisine was "limited" and that there were few "African" dishes that they might offer to visitors. Nonetheless, a growing trend is the emergence of "African fusion" cuisine as reflected in the preparation of dishes such as ostrich carpaccio or springbok loin cooked in local herbs.

Conclusion

Across the developing world, Telfer and Sharpley (2008) argue that a major contribution of tourism is its potential to stimulate backward linkages throughout a local economy. Strengthened tourism–agriculture linkages in the developing world can contribute potentially towards a more sustainable path of tourism development, promote pro-poor impacts as well as reduce the "foodprint" of tourist food consumption (Gössling et al., 2011; Mitchell & Ashley, 2010; Torres & Momsen, 2011). Improved understanding of the supply chains of tourism accommodation or lodging establishments is essential (Ashley & Haysom, 2008; Meyer, 2007; Timothy & Teye, 2009).

Torres and Momsen (2004, p. 311) emphasize that nurturing linkages between tourist food consumption and local agricultural production constitutes "an important potential mechanism through which to achieve pro-poor tourism objectives". Equally, Telfer and Wall (1996, p. 650) maintain that "if tourism is to contribute to the well-being of destination residents, it is important that careful consideration be given to enhancing backward economic linkages". Indeed, if local farmers can supply the tourism accommodation sector, the positive local development impacts will be that leakages are reduced, local multipliers enhanced and a greater share of the local economic benefits generated by the tourism industry captured by poor neighbouring communities (Meyer, 2006, 2007). Accordingly, for advancing the objective of maximizing local economic development impacts, there is "an urgent need to understand why such linkages rarely materialize and to identify the conditions necessary for them to do so" (Torres & Momsen, 2004, p. 296). This challenge is relevant especially in the region of southern Africa, which has been a laboratory and source of innovation for pro-poor tourism scholarship (Rogerson & Visser, 2011) and local economic development planning (Rogerson & Rogerson, 2010).

As a consequence of its location in peripheral rural areas of South Africa, the ASL sector is a key potential basis for pro-poor local economic development (Rogerson, 2006). Notwithstanding a supportive policy environment that promotes "responsible tourism" and the encouragement of local procurement, this "alternative" form of tourism has been shown to have evolved only limited linkages with local (especially small) food producers. The food supply chains of these luxury accommodation establishments are organized by a network of intermediary suppliers, which source the bulk of fresh fruit and vegetable produce from distant urban wholesale markets. Other more specialized food products demanded by these lodges are sourced almost exclusively from suppliers based either in Johannesburg or in Cape Town. Geographical variations in the patterns of local food sourcing were disclosed between the different ASL clusters that exist in South Africa. In relation to previous investigations of tourism–agriculture linkages, which have been completed in other parts of the developing world, common findings emerge and some contrasts. The major contrast is perhaps that the ASL sector in South Africa is owned mainly by domestic capital, and the enterprises are operated in the vast majority of cases by South African nationals. Accordingly, issues of foreign ownership or of the influence of the foreign nationality of decision-makers are not in evidence in rural South Africa. Nevertheless, in common with similar studies undertaken in the Caribbean, Mexico and Indonesia, several factors were highlighted that account for the limited development of local linkages. For example, the lack of capacity of local producers to offer the quality, consistency and volume of products required by the ASL sector in South Africa and patterns of long-distance sourcing mirror those of previous investigations.

In the final analysis, when examining the challenges faced by policymakers in building local tourism–agriculture linkages, it must be appreciated that as different barriers are identified in different parts of the developing world, local solutions are essential. In the

South African case, the issue of linking small producers to the supply chains of large tourism accommodation establishments can be considered as part of the wider challenge of catalysing the country's small enterprise economy as a whole. The evidence points to a need to potentially encourage small agricultural producers to organize themselves into groups, which might be able to better access market opportunities and supply the food requirements of accommodation establishments. Enhancing the awareness of local producers of the food supply needs and high-quality standards of these rural lodges is a further policy recommendation (Hunt, 2010). Other policy considerations relate to capacity building and enabling support for small-scale producers to enter the food supply chains, including credit. Above all, the findings from rural South Africa underline the fundamental need to transcend the existing poor levels of communication and corresponding deep mistrust that exists currently between food supply decision-makers, intermediary supplier organizations and local producers.

Acknowledgements

Thanks are due to the comments received from three anonymous referees on an earlier version of this paper. The considerable inputs of the research interviews conducted by Holly Hunt are acknowledged. Wendy Job of the School of Geography, Environment Management and Energy Studies, University of Johannesburg, prepared the accompanying figures. Research funding was from the National Research Foundation, Pretoria, and University of Johannesburg. Usual disclaimers apply.

References

Ashley, C., de Brine, P., Lehr, A., & Wilde, H. (2007). *The role of the tourism sector in expanding economic opportunity* (Corporate Social Responsibility Initiative Rep. No. 23). Cambridge, MA: Harvard University, Kennedy School of Government.

Ashley, C., & Haysom, G. (2008). The development impacts of tourism supply chains: Increasing impact on poverty and decreasing our ignorance. In A. Spenceley (Ed.), *Responsible tourism: Critical issues for conservation and development* (pp. 129–156). London: Earthscan.

Ashley, C., & Roe, D. (2002). Making tourism work for the poor: Strategies and challenges in southern Africa. *Development Southern Africa, 19*, 61–82.

Belisle, F.J. (1983). Tourism and food production in the Caribbean. *Annals of Tourism Research, 10*, 497–513.

Brown, R.L., Cox, L.J., & Fox, M. (1991). The interface between tourism and agriculture. *Journal of Tourism Studies, 2*(2), 43–54.

Cox, L.J., Fox, M., & Bowen, R.L. (1994). Does tourism destroy agriculture? *Annals of Tourism Research, 22*, 210–213.

Fleischer, A., & Tchetchik, A. (2005). Does rural tourism benefit from agriculture? *Tourism Management, 26*, 493–501.

Gössling, S., Garrod, B., Aall, C., Hille, J., & Peeters, P. (2011). Food management in tourism: Reducing tourism's carbon "foodprint". *Tourism Management, 32*, 534–543.

Hall, C.M., & Page, S.J. (2009). Progress in tourism management: From the geography of tourism to geographies of tourism – A review. *Tourism Management, 30*, 3–16.

Hermans, D. (1981). The encounter of agriculture and tourism: A Catalan case. *Annals of Tourism Research, 8*(3), 462–479.

Hunt, H. (2010). *African safari lodges food supply chains: The potential for establishing "pro-poor" linkages* (Unpublished master's dissertation). University of the Witwatersrand, Johannesburg, South Africa.

Kirsten, M., & Rogerson, C.M. (2002). Tourism, business linkages and small enterprise development in South Africa. *Development Southern Africa, 19*, 29–58.

Knowd, I. (2006). Tourism as a mechanism for farm survival. *Journal of Sustainable Tourism, 14*, 24–42.

König, D.A. (2007). *Linking agriculture to tourism in Sierra Leone – A preliminary research* (Unpublished master's thesis). University of Applied Sciences of Eberswalde, Germany.

Lacher, R.G., & Nepal, S.K. (2010). From leakages to linkages: Local-level strategies for capturing tourism revenue in Northern Thailand. *Tourism Geographies, 12*, 77–99.

Magingxa, L.L., Alemu, Z.G., & van Schalkwyk, H.D. (2009). Factors influencing access to produce markets for smallholder irrigators in South Africa. *Development Southern Africa, 26*, 47–58.

Massyn, P., & Koch, E. (2004). African game lodges and rural benefit in two Southern African countries. In C.M. Rogerson & G. Visser (Eds.), *Tourism and development issues in contemporary South Africa* (pp. 102–138). Pretoria: Africa Institute of South Africa.

Mbaiwa, J.E., & Darkoh, M.B.K. (2006). *Tourism and environment in the Okavango, Botswana.* Gaborone: Pula.

Meyer, D. (2006). *Caribbean tourism, local sourcing and enterprise development: Review of the literature.* Pro-Poor Tourism Working Paper No. 18. London: Pro-Poor Tourism Partnership.

Meyer, D. (2007). Pro-poor tourism: From leakages to linkages: A conceptual framework for creating linkages between the accommodation sector and "poor" neighbouring communities. *Current Issues in Tourism, 10*, 558–583.

Meyer, D. (2011). Changing power relations: Foreign direct investment in Zanzibar. In J. Mosedale (Ed.), *Political economy of tourism: A critical perspective* (pp. 157–174). Abingdon: Routledge.

Meyer, D., Ashley, C., & Poultney, C. (2004). *Boosting local inputs into the supply chain*. Pro-Poor Tourism in Practice Business Implementation of Pro-Poor Tourism Case Study Briefs No. 2. London: Department for International Development.

Mitchell, J., & Ashley, C. (2006). *Tourism business and the local economy: Increasing impact through a linkages approach.* Briefing Paper. London: Overseas Development Institute.

Mitchell, J., & Ashley, C. (2009). *Value chain analysis and poverty reduction at scale: Evidence from tourism is changing mindsets.* Briefing Paper No. 49. London: Overseas Development Institute.

Mitchell, J., & Ashley, C. (2010). *Tourism and poverty reduction: Pathways to prosperity.* London: Earthscan.

Mitchell, J., Ashley, C., & Mann, S. (2007). *Can tourism offer pro-poor pathways to prosperity?* Briefing Paper No. 22. London: Overseas Development Institute.

Mmbengwa, V.M., Ramukumba, T., Groenewald, J.A., van Schalkwyk, H.D., Gundidza, M.B., & Maiwashe, A.N. (2011). Evaluation of essential capacities required for the performance of farming small, micro and medium enterprise (SMMEs) in South Africa. *African Journal of Agricultural Research, 6*(6), 1500–1507.

Momsen, J. (1998). *Caribbean tourism and agriculture: Problems for the smaller Caribbean economies.* Seminar Paper No. 45. Newcastle: University of Newcastle.

Republic of South Africa. (2010). *South Africa's Department of Tourism.* Retrieved April 1, 2010, from http://www.tourism.gov.za

Republic of South Africa. (2011). *National tourism sector strategy.* Pretoria: Department of Tourism.

Rogerson, C.M. (2002). Tourism-led local economic development: The South African experience. *Urban Forum, 13*, 95–119.

Rogerson, C.M. (2006). Pro-poor local economic development in South Africa: The role of pro-poor tourism. *Local Environment, 11*, 37–60.

Rogerson, C.M. (2007). Reviewing Africa in the global tourism economy. *Development Southern Africa, 24*, 361–379.

Rogerson, C.M. (2009). Tourism development in Southern Africa: Patterns, issues and constraints. In J. Saarinen, F. Becker, H. Manwa, & D. Wilson (Eds.), *Sustainable tourism in Southern Africa: Local communities and natural resources in transition* (pp. 20–41). Bristol: Channel View Publications.

Rogerson, C.M., & Rogerson, J.M. (2010). Local economic development in Africa: Global context and research directions. *Development Southern Africa, 27*, 465–480.

Rogerson, C.M., & Rogerson, J.M. (2011). Tourism research within the Southern African Development Community: Production and consumption in academic journals, 2000–2010. *Tourism Review International, 15*, 213–222.

Rogerson, C.M., & Visser, G. (Eds.). (2004). *Tourism and development issues in contemporary South Africa*. Pretoria: Africa Institute of South Africa.

Rogerson, C.M., & Visser, G. (2006). International tourist flows and urban tourism in South Africa. *Urban Forum, 17*, 199–213.

Rogerson, C.M., & Visser, G. (2011). African tourism geographies: Existing paths and new directions. *Tijdschrift voor Economische en Sociale Geografie, 102*, 251–259.

Rueegg, M. (2009). *The impact of tourism on rural poverty through supply chain linkages to local food producers in the Bolivian Altiplano* (Unpublished master's dissertation). London School of Economics and Political Science, London.

Sims, D. (2009). Food, place and authenticity: Local food and the sustainable tourism experience. *Journal of Sustainable Tourism, 17*(3), 321–336.

Skuras, D., Dimara, E., & Petrou, A. (2006). Rural tourism and visitors' expenditures for local food products. *Regional Studies, 40*, 769–779.

Spenceley, A. (Ed.). (2008). *Responsible tourism: Critical issues for conservation and development*. London: Earthscan.

Spenceley, A., Relly, P., Keyser, H., Warmeant, P., McKenzie, M., Matboge, A., Norton, P., Mahlangu, S., & Seif, J. (2002). *Responsible tourism manual for South Africa*. Pretoria: Department of Environmental Affairs and Tourism.

Telfer, D.J. (2000). Tastes of Niagara: Building strategic alliances between tourism and agriculture. *International Journal of Hospitality and Tourism Administration, 1*(1), 71–88.

Telfer, D.J., & Sharpley, R. (2008). *Tourism and development in the developing world*. London: Routledge.

Telfer, D.J., & Wall, G. (1996). Linkages between tourism and food production. *Annals of Tourism Research, 23*, 635–653.

Telfer, D.J., & Wall, G. (2000). Strengthening backward economic linkages: Local food purchasing by three Indonesian hotels. *Tourism Geographies, 2*, 421–447.

Timms, B. (2006). Caribbean agriculture-tourism linkages in a neoliberal world: Problems and prospects for St Lucia. *International Development Planning Review, 28*, 35–56.

Timothy, D.J., & Teye, V.B. (2009). *Tourism and the lodging sector*. Oxford: Butterworth-Heinemann.

Torres, R. (2002). Toward a better understanding of tourism and agriculture linkages in the Yucatan: Tourist food consumption and preferences. *Tourism Geographies, 4*, 282–306.

Torres, R. (2003). Linkages between tourism and agriculture in Mexico. *Annals of Tourism Research, 30*, 546–566.

Torres, R., & Momsen, J.H. (2004). Challenges and potential for linking tourism and agriculture to achieve pro-poor tourism objectives. *Progress in Development Studies, 4*, 294–318.

Torres, R., & Momsen, J.H. (Eds.). (2011). *Tourism and agriculture: New geographies of consumption, production and rural restructuring*. London: Routledge.

Visser, G., & Hoogendoorn, G. (2011). Current paths in South African tourism research. *Tourism Review International, 15*(1–2), 5–20.

Social enterprises in tourism: an exploratory study of operational models and success factors

Janina von der Weppen and Janet Cochrane

School of Events, Tourism and Hospitality, Leeds Metropolitan University, UK

Organisations using market-based approaches to achieve social and/or environmental aims are increasingly appearing in tourism. These "social enterprises" express responsible tourism through contributing to poverty alleviation and environmental protection while being financially self-sustaining. This study uncovers the approach of such enterprises in balancing commercial and social/environmental objectives, and investigates the determinants of success. The paper applies Alter's 2006 seven-model framework of social enterprise models to a sample of successful enterprises, "success" being aligned with the broader aims of social enterprises. Overall, it was found that touristic social enterprises operate similarly to those in other sectors, although with a clear preference for three "Alter" models, depending on the type of activity, namely Service Subsidisation, Employment and the Market Intermediary Model. Success factors appear to be valid across all social enterprises in tourism, irrespective of primary business activity or operational model, and cannot be attributed to a single factor but to combinations of factors in the multiple dimensions of leadership, strategy and organisational culture. These guide the implementing mechanisms of processes and structure, human resources, financing, governance, performance measurement and marketing. The most likely success factors are strong leadership, clear market orientation and organisational culture, which balances financial with social/environmental aims.

Introduction

The last decade has seen social enterprises increasingly appearing in the tourism sector alongside private industry, government institutions and charities. The landscape of social enterprise covers a wide spectrum of institutions, but increasing academic scrutiny has resulted in a consensus that the primary goal of any social enterprise is the adoption of financially sustainable strategies to achieve social aims (Haugh, 2005, p. 1). This fundamental "double bottom line" characteristic, the imperative to achieve both financial and social returns on investment (Dart, 2004; Peredo & McLean, 2006; Wallace, 2005), has engendered many definitions of the movement, perhaps most succinctly encapsulated by Kerlin (2006, p. 247) as "the use of nongovernmental, market-based approaches to address social issues". The driving force is the organisation's mission, which – despite the term "social enterprise" – can be social or environmental and sometimes both (Pearce, 2003, p. 33).

In 2006, Nicholls called for research into case study examples that illustrate the range of social enterprises, and this study answers that call. The paper is concerned with the approach of touristic social enterprises in pursuing their objectives, the challenges they face and the key ingredients of success. The investigation is timely because of the growing importance of such enterprises in the responsible development of tourism. Tourism is a key revenue sector for many low- and middle-income countries and there is a constant search for ways of ensuring that a greater share of benefits reaches the poorest segments of the community in these countries (Mitchell & Ashley, 2010). One of these ways is through tourism-oriented social enterprises. As Nicholls and Young (2008, p. vii) comment: "Despite patchy empirical data, it seems clear that over the last four years there has been steady growth in the number of socially entrepreneurial organisations globally and that their interventions in institutional voids or suboptimal markets are making a significant difference". Tourism is a particularly apt arena for study because of its potential for stimulating both social and financial added value along the supply chain.

After a review of the emergence and development of the social enterprise and social entrepreneurship movement, we take a case-study approach to explore the characteristics of touristic social enterprises, with the features of 11 award-winning organisations active in tourism mapped against a business-oriented classification of social enterprises in order to ascertain the most frequent choice of organisational model. The literature revealed several attempts to typologise and classify social enterprises, and our choice of framework was deliberately chosen in order to understand the management models expressed by entrepreneurs and because it offered a way of uncovering pragmatic insights into the motives and behaviour of social entrepreneurs. We reach conclusions as to the most commonly expressed models for particular types of enterprise.

The study is not intended to expand the already large corpus of writing on conceptual aspects of social enterprise, but to shed light on a particular sub-sector of the genus and to provide practical guidance to neophytes – those new to the concept and its practices – and as such we make no apology for referring to practitioner as well as academic literature.

Social enterprise

A review of literature on social enterprise, social entrepreneurship and social entrepreneurs over the last decade reveals a gradual convergence of opinion as to the core characteristics of social enterprises and an increasing complexity of approach as these characteristics were discussed and refined. Early conceptualisations (Defourny, 2001; Laville & Nyssens, 2001) emphasised the roots of the movement in the third sector and its collective and community facets; we would argue that it emanated from the same altruistic stream as the participatory and sustainable livelihoods approaches to development advocated from the 1980s onwards, from a desire to address social and environmental injustices for reasons of morality and fairness and to counter the top-down neoliberal tools of economic manipulation.

At the same time, the movement can be seen as a marriage between altruism and capitalism in moving social interventions away from dependency by endeavouring to harness market forces for social aims. This shift has given rise to tension concerning exactly how far social enterprises can veer towards the profit-making end of the spectrum. Boschee and McClurg (2003, p. 3) make a useful distinction between social enterprises and traditional ones which act in a socially responsible way; the difference is that for social enterprises "their earned income strategies are tied *directly* to their mission". Later authors stress the shared characteristics of economic or social entrepreneurs in that each has to understand social and economic processes in order to create both types of value (Chell, 2007), while

Austin, Stevenson and Wci-Skillern (2006) use Sahlman's (1996) analytical model of enterprise management (a dynamic fit between People, Context, Deal and Opportunity) to identify the similarity between social and economic entrepreneurs, but conclude that for the former a social-value proposition should be included as a key integrative driver. Simms and Robinson (2008) use an identity-based analysis to assess the necessary characteristics of entrepreneurs, and recognise that an entrepreneurial identity has to be cultivated in order to maximise the profits needed to plough back into social aims. Later still, Nicholls (2010) reminds us of the two predominant discourse streams on social entrepreneurship: one focusing on "hero social entrepreneurs" who evidence individualistic characteristics such as leadership and ambition, and the other on collective settings and networks of actions (Nicholls, 2010, p. 21). Several authors (including Defourny & Nyssens, 2006) recognise that this dichotomy has been present since the early years of discussion of the social enterprise phenomenon, in that the US model was focused on commercial entrepreneurship at a much earlier stage than in Europe, where there was more reliance on the deeply rooted tradition of the cooperative movement.

Whether individually led or community-based, social enterprises "typically address areas of unmet social need or new social opportunity creation that the public or private sectors have failed to address" (Nicholls, 2006, p. 15). The central pillars of the businesses themselves are generally agreed as threefold: the production and sale of goods and/or services, the creation of social value rather than financial capital for stakeholders, and some form of social ownership (Allan, 2005; Austin et al., 2006). The spectrum of operational models of social enterprises is usefully typologised by Alter (2006) to explain "how social value and economic value are created within the different social enterprise models . . . [and] . . . how models can be combined and enhanced to achieve maximum value creation" (Alter, 2006, p. 214; Table 1).

Table 1. Operational models of social enterprise.

Operational model and level of integration	Model description
Entrepreneur Support Model	Sells business support and financial services to individuals/small firms, which then sell products/services on the open market.
Market Intermediary Model	Provides services to small producers to help them access markets, e.g. product development. Products are purchased at fair prices and sold on at a margin.
Employment Model	Provides employment opportunities/job training for people with high barriers to employment through enterprises that sell products or services on the open market.
Fee-for-Service Model	Commercialises its services, then sells them to individuals, firms, communities or a third party payer.
Market Linkage Model	Facilitates trading between small producers/local firms/cooperatives and external markets, e.g. through market information.
Service Subsidisation Model	Sells products/services externally. Business mandate is separate from social mission, but business activities are often mission-related. Income is used to subsidise/fund social programmes.
Organisational Support Model	Sells products/services externally. Business activities separate from social programmes and unrelated to the mission. Income is used to cover programme costs and operating expenses of parent organisation.

Source: Alter (2006, pp. 212–227). By permission of Oxford University Press.

In our study, these operational models were used to categorise touristic social enterprises, while key management areas identified in a study of social enterprises in Latin America were used to examine the management inputs and success (or failure) factors expressed by the enterprises studied. Austin, Gutiérrez, Ogliastri and Reficco (2006) grouped principal management areas into three "integrative drivers" that ensure organisational coherence with the mission – leadership, strategy and organisational culture – and five "implementing mechanisms" for strategy execution – processes and structure, human resources, financing, governance, and performance measurement. Some of these factors are common to any business venture while others reflect the pressures of accomplishing the twin objectives of income generation and mission fulfilment. Taking account of the need for a commercial outlook emphasised by some commentators (Boschee & McClurg, 2003), for market awareness in the highly competitive sector of tourism, and for marketing skills to effect behavioural change (London & Morfopoulos, 2010), a sixth implementing mechanism – market awareness – was added by the authors since this was also considered a significant implementing mechanism.

Selection of social enterprises studied

In order to identify suitable enterprises to examine, the finalists in 2008 and 2009 of three major responsible/sustainable tourism awards were listed. The competitions concerned were the Responsible Tourism Awards (sponsored by Virgin Holidays and responsibletravel.com), the Geotourism Challenge (National Geographic and Ashoka's Changemakers) and the Tourism for Tomorrow Awards (World Travel and Tourism Council, 2009). The criteria for selection and short-listing are similar in all three cases, centring on evidence of effective contributions to local livelihoods, cultural heritage and the environment through innovative responsible tourism experiences, with the Geotourism Challenge also emphasising the financial sustainability of the organisations (Ashoka Changemakers, 2009; Responsibletravel.com, 2009; World Travel and Tourism Council, 2009). The addition of financial criteria for the Geotourism Challenge is interesting since the awarding organisation is Ashoka, one of the leading bodies globally in promoting social entrepreneurship, which could thus be expected to emphasise the second pillar of social entrepreneurship, i.e. the creation of social rather than financial capital for stakeholders (see www.ashoka.org).

The population resulting from the 2008 and 2009 shortlists ($n = 50$) was stratified into four categories: accommodation providers ($n = 17$), tour operators ($n = 14$), tour operators specialising in volunteer trips ($n = 8$) and "other" organisations ($n = 11$). Businesses were randomly selected from each category to ensure representation of each. This resulted in a sample of three accommodation providers, four tour operators, two volunteer placement operators, a destination management organisation (DMO) for a national park and a visitor attraction. A brief outline of geographical location and enterprise sector is given in Table 2.

The key features of the enterprises were identified via desk research and exploration of endogenous and exogenous perspectives. The endogenous perspective consisted essentially of practitioners' views obtained through semi-structured interviews with the enterprise founders or senior representatives, with questions informed by desk research into responsible tourism practices and the organisations' self-stated aims and achievements. It is acknowledged that research participants are likely to present information on their organisation's achievements subjectively – especially since the interviewee was often the originator of the enterprise. Responses were triangulated against the exogenous views of expert outsiders and of tourists as expressed in blogs and discussion forums. Obtaining the views of

Table 2. Selection of tourism businesses in sample.

Name of business	Type of business	Geographical location
Guludo Beach Lodge	Ecolodge, activities	Mozambique
Misool Eco Resort	Ecolodge, diving	Indonesia
Yachana Lodge	Rainforest lodge	Ecuador
Adventure Alternative	Adventure tour operator (outbound)	UK-based (operates in East Africa, Russia, Nepal)
Andaman Discoveries	Community-based tour operator (inbound)	Thailand
PEPY Tours/PEPY Ride	Cycling tour operator (inbound)	Cambodia
Village Ways	Trekking tour operator (outbound)	UK and India-based (operates in India, Ethiopia)
People and Places	Volunteering placement operator	UK (operates in Africa, Asia, Latin America)
Way Out Experience (WOX)	Volunteering placement operator	UK (operates in Malaysia)
Scottish Seabird Centre	Wildlife visitor attraction	Scotland, UK
Rinjani Trek Ecotourism Programme/RTMB	Destination management organisation, national park	Indonesia

people external to the organisation was considered essential as it enabled the researchers to place the responses of practitioners in the context of learning and practice about social entrepreneurship in tourism, and a range of key informants was purposively selected based on their expertise in responsible tourism and ecotourism (2 people), organisational change and restructuring for social enterprise (1 person) and entrepreneurship (1 person). In each case, the experts had been involved in their respective fields for at least 20 years. These informants were asked questions on issues specific to social enterprises, for insights into social enterprise in tourism and possible success factors and challenges, and their responses were mapped against the responses from the practitioners.

Findings

Operational models

Mapping the case studies against the seven operational models identified above revealed that the organisations displayed characteristics of a variety of models – in several cases more than one. Taking the Entrepreneur Support Model (ESM) first, it was found that although minor elements of this were present in a few cases that provided business support to their partners, none of the partners continued on to sell these services on the open market. The Market Intermediary Model (MIM) was used by two of the tour operators and one of the volunteer placement operators, which helped their partners to "develop and sell their products in high-value markets" (Alter, 2006, p. 216).

In five cases, employment was a crucial element of the mission (the Employment Model – EM) as an attempt to address the peripherality effect on employment prospects (for instance, lack of formal education or discrimination on grounds of gender or ethnicity). All five used this model in combination with the Service Subsidisation Model (SSM), the most widely used model overall ($n = 9$; or Organisational Support Model – OSM – in some cases). SSM was illustrated by all the accommodation providers, three of the four tour operators and the visitor attraction, which used commercial activities both as a funding mechanism and as a way to "enlarge or enhance" the mission (Alter, 2006, p. 220). For example, an island eco-resort protects its "No Take Zone" by providing alternative income for villagers who otherwise might fish in the area. Although OSM was not exclusively expressed by any of the cases, three organisations were located mid-way between SSM and OSM, keeping business activities separate from social and environmental programmes but with substantial overlap in staff and other resources.

Only the DMO was looking to move towards Fee-for-Service Model (FSM) by charging a fee for its market linkage services, driven by the increasing difficulty of accessing donor support. Meanwhile, two of the cases operated entirely according to the Market Linkage Model (MLM). One of the volunteer placement operators linked clients directly to markets rather than acting as intermediary; the income generated covered operating expenses and profits were channelled to projects via an external charity. The DMO facilitated trade relationships for trekking centre cooperatives and promoted its host national park in exchange for a portion of the park entrance fee.

Integrative drivers

A key area of investigation was to examine how the social enterprises navigated around challenges and achieved success. The findings generated in case-by-case and comparative analyses of the 11 organisations are presented using the integrative drivers named above.

First, the drivers of leadership, strategy and organisational culture were analysed. The social enterprises studied were at different stages of business evolution, with almost equal numbers in the phases of institutionalisation ($n = 4$), decentralisation ($n = 3$) and diversification/expansion/consolidation ($n = 4$). Not surprisingly, given the proven success of the organisations, it was found that the leaders had successfully adapted their skills to move from developing to consolidating their business, performing tasks and drawing on skills normally associated with more than one phase, such as the charismatic leadership and entrepreneurial skills needed to establish and position the organisation and raise necessary resources in the start-up phase, coupled with the harmonising and motivating skills needed for the subsequent institutionalisation phase.

As predicted by the literature, all the senior representatives interviewed embodied the typical qualities of entrepreneurs such as identification of market opportunities, innovation and determination to succeed (Boschee & McClurg, 2003; Forbes, 2009; London & Morfopoulos, 2010), but with the additional characteristics of passion and belief in people's capacity to contribute to economic and social development. They saw their enterprise as a way to operationalise these beliefs in practical and innovative ways – sometimes spurred on by impatience or dissatisfaction with the government or voluntary sector. All the leaders were guided by strong principles, although it was less clear how many had devised their principles in conjunction with the management board and employees, as stipulated by "best practice" (Lynch & Walls, 2009, p. 31).

Many of the entrepreneurs consciously grappled with the pressures of simultaneously addressing social/environmental outcomes and earning an income, because "to fulfil the mission we need income and sometimes we don't have it" (D. McMeekin, personal communication, December 27, 2009), especially in times of recession (A. Mauthoor, personal communication, January 4, 2010).

They employed a range of strategies for achieving this delicate balance. Several had generated a virtuous positive feedback cycle through running business activities that supported the mission financially as well as through awareness-raising and in some cases through attracting volunteers, often considering their "ethical product" (A. Carter-James, personal communication, December 31, 2009), their "leading position in sustainable development"

(D. McMeekin, personal communication, December 27, 2009), or their involvement in community-based tourism (B. Garrett, personal communication, January 11, 2010) as a competitive advantage. Another balancing factor was the involvement of beneficiaries in analysing problems and implementing solutions. All the enterprises cooperated closely with their target populations, ranging from institutional structures that placed community members on the management board to informal approaches such as consulting village elders. In five cases the beneficiaries were also employees. In other cases, care was taken to ensure projects are "locally driven" (S. Grayson, personal communication, January 12, 2010), "bottom-up" (R. Hearn, personal communication, January 20, 2010) and that the beneficiaries' capacity was enhanced so that they could implement solutions themselves. The organisations also balanced their objectives by ensuring that business expansion was undertaken only to maximise beneficial impacts.

About half ($n = 5$) the entrepreneurs had previous experience in tourism, while less experienced leaders ($n = 4$) conducted research to learn about the market. In two cases, however, newcomers to tourism preferred to be guided solely by instinct. Generally, the cases studied only considered activities in areas of current operation; for instance, the tour operators diversified the range of destinations offered. Some had gone further, with varying success: one organisation had branched out briefly but unprofitably into a different sector (cocoa production), while the owners of a beach lodge were preparing to expand into other sectors because their entrepreneurship was never "just about tourism [but] using business for development" (A. Carter-James, personal communication, December 31, 2009).

A major part of strategy consists of careful planning. The enterprises all made strategic plans that reflected their long-term vision. In most cases this translated into professional business plans reviewed regularly, while they generally had a realistic appreciation of their capabilities, planning in accordance with available capacity and recognising that capacities needed to be developed in some areas (e.g. training hospitality staff). Only one entrepreneur admitted to being more of a "doer" than a "planner", with tours currently "still run in a very ad hoc, side-project kind of a way" (D.R. Papi, personal communication, December 23, 2009). All organisations allowed for the flexibility to rethink strategies when necessary.

As far as organisational culture was concerned, the enterprises had developed a culture in line with identified success factors. First, strong values related to the social or environmental mission such as "solidarity, ethics, trust, and mobilisation for action" (Austin et al., 2006, p. 96) helped to create internal cohesion. The founder of one of the tour operators explained how "the number one vision for the organisation was partnership with communities .... It is a social endeavour" (B. Garrett, personal communication, January 11, 2010). In order for the vision to inspire all employees and partners and to create a culture of shared responsibility for results, the central messages and objectives had to be communicated via a constant flow of communication between staff and partners (Austin et al., 2006). We found that to ensure shared goals, all the organisations had good internal communications and greatly valued the learning process, starting with the leaders themselves: they invested in training and coaching staff and project partners, with sharing of lessons and experience actively encouraged. However, while there was usually a shared passion for the social or environmental mission of the enterprise, challenges in the area of revenue-generation were evident: one representative mentioned the difficulty of immersing all staff in an income-earning culture (L. Dalgleish, personal communication, December 18, 2009), while some organisations based in developing countries struggled with basic issues such as training staff "in just what it means to be an employee" (M. Miners, personal communication, January 9, 2010). This aspect has implications for the "human resources" implementing mechanism discussed in the next section.

Despite occasional challenges in resolving the conflict in between mission-centric and enterprise-focused orientations, the organisations' internal communications strategies and shared vision resulted in cohorts of staff and partners who were loyal, took pride in their work, and expressed enthusiasm and ideas (G. Bate, personal communication, December 14, 2009; A. Mauthoor, personal communication, January 4, 2010). In line with the vision, passion and persistence in communication noted by London and Morfopoulos (2010) as characteristics of transformational leadership, one of the independent experts explained that "when you have everyone as committed and as involved as the original founder, you can make incredible changes" (W. Vaughan, personal communication, December 3, 2009). This was expressed by one of the business leaders as "the commitment … carries you through the tough times" (A. Mauthoor, personal communication, January 4, 2010).

Implementing mechanisms

As defined in practitioner literature (Austin et al., 2006; London & Morfopoulos, 2010; Lynch & Walls, 2009), the necessary implementing mechanisms for successful social enterprises fall into six categories: (1) processes and structure, (2) human resources, (3) financing, (4) governance, (5) performance measurement and (6) market awareness. We now review the enterprises' operations against each of these categories.

The organisations studied strove to achieve operational excellence in various ways. Most reviewed their operations frequently to optimise them, and the majority had created clear roles within the management team, with close cooperation between technical units implementing the social projects and administrative units. In terms of legal structure, all the organisations had at least one unit that was a commercial business, e.g. a limited company, although only one operated exclusively as a business (this one was in the process of obtaining charitable status). In three cases, the enterprises cooperated with a charity, transferring funds between the entities, but they did not fulfil their primary mission through these. One expert commented that the private sector model or "social business" is the best choice because it is more likely to be "financially auto-sustainable" (M. Epler Wood, personal communication, January 27, 2010); the remaining cases used a combination of a "for-profit" company with a legally separate charity, which implemented the social and environmental programmes. This was in order for non-revenue income streams of donor or charitable funding to be tapped as well as generating trading income through entrepreneurial activity. Since the company and charity were founded by the same entrepreneur, however, they tended to "see it as one model with two facets" (A. Carter-James, personal communication, December 31, 2009), and as we will note below, the close connection between the two sides of an enterprise could lead to poor financial accounting practices.

Human resources are crucial for any enterprise, and the organisations studied tackled the challenges of attracting and retaining good staff (or partners) in various ways. They all tried to match job candidates' values with organisational values, especially for more senior positions; one of the tour operators for example is very selective in its choice of project ambassadors (A. Mauthoor, personal communication, January 4, 2010). However, as discussed in the previous section, organisations in remote locations or those committed to hiring local staff sometimes had to overcome a differential in shared expectations of employment or had limited choice of personnel. Finding candidates endowed both with suitable values and experience was a common challenge, often resolved by hiring and training inexperienced people who seemed likely to develop into the "multi-tool" players most valuable to social enterprises (Lynch & Walls, 2009, p. 95). In some cases, skilled labour had to be brought in from further afield or abroad, although the development of the local population as a source of future workers was generally high on the agenda. The one organisation operating wholly in the UK was in a very different situation in that it experienced considerable competition for jobs.

In keeping with the roots of social enterprise in a participatory discourse and as discussed above in assessing the key integrative drivers, there were several examples of participative mechanisms and organisational learning in management, ranging from participation in decision-making to providing channels for staff feedback. Bornstein's 2004 study (as cited in London & Morfopoulos, 2010) in fact identified the institutionalisation of "listening" through various mechanisms as one of the four key practices of social entrepreneurs. The leader's two-way communication skills are essential to pass on the vision and listen to staff concerns: without it, there is unlikely to be long-term staff involvement, and, as one expert interviewee put it, "if there is no involvement, there is no commitment" (W. Vaughan, personal communication, December 3, 2009). Not surprisingly, it was found that staff participation in decisions was more likely in the organisations with good communication and close internal relationships.

The tension between mission and commercial activity was not always so successfully handled in terms of managing financial resources. Where enterprises had affiliated not-for-profit structures, all strove to achieve financial sustainability by combining funds generated by business activities with non-revenue funding streams, and generally the enterprises either paid the overheads of the affiliated charities or used operating surpluses to fund social/environmental work. The practice of many of the enterprises confirmed Pearce's (2003) comment that most social enterprises use a combination of income sources, including trading, contracts, public sector or foundation grants, volunteer labour and fundraising activities. To help generate external funds, some organisations required their customers to fundraise, while others built a donation for the beneficiary groups into the holiday price. Many also benefited from generous giving by current or past customers. However, although lack of good financial literacy was admitted by only one organisation and in most cases the founders' previous business experience had led to good practice, there were challenges in implementing the cost accounting practices recommended by practitioner guides (Lynch & Walls, 2009). This was especially the case in separating out the costs of the charity from enterprise operating costs, with earned revenue sometimes siphoned away from essential business investment in order to cover mission-related costs. One respondent commented on the negative feedback cycle created by this: the lack of investment resulted in even fewer volunteers and donations, which in turn affected the conservation programme (A. Mauthoor, personal communication, January 4, 2010). To avoid these scenarios, the majority of enterprise leaders aimed for business expansion because it created more social value. However, the approach was mostly cautious, with a preference for "slow organic growth" (G. Bate, personal communication, December 14, 2009) or a model that is "tried and tested" before scaling up (S. Grayson, personal communication, January 12, 2010).

For governance to be an enabler for social enterprise, "governance schemes, processes, and structures must be designed to respond to social initiatives' sustainability requirements" (Austin et al., 2006, p. 221). Although it proved impossible to obtain thorough evidence of this amongst the sampled organisations, the research did indicate that many had strategically appointed board members "because they are likely to add value" (B. Garrett, personal communication, January 11, 2010). One accommodation provider, for example, benefited from trustees with expertise in architecture and finance that would be locally scarce and costly (A. Carter-James, personal communication, December 31, 2009). Some boards included local representatives, thus conferring credibility before the community and public opinion.

A potential source of challenge to the long-term viability of the enterprises was the involvement of governance body members in operational issues, particularly in organisations that were private limited companies and where the board of directors naturally included the founder(s)/owner(s), or when trustees of the affiliated not-for-profit organisations were also responsible for strategy and operations. One key informant explained that founding entrepreneurs are often powerful individuals who may not introduce sufficient checks and balances to their own personality (G. Cox, personal communication, February 3, 2010), and it was certainly not clear in all cases how institutional and financial self-sustainability would be assured in the event that the founder was no longer present.

As far as performance management was concerned, at least four of the organisations had a formalised, comprehensive process involving a mix of indicators and methods designed to chart progress against mission aims and outcomes. However, several used a more informal approach, often consisting of the founder or senior management observing the situation and gathering feedback from stakeholders. While this approach can be thorough, some interviewees expressed a desire for improvement rather than being "dependent on anecdotal information" from volunteers and partners – although the weak reporting capacity of project beneficiaries was recognised as a barrier to better practice (S. Grayson, personal communication, January 12, 2010). Only one organisation set clear baselines and targets and undertook regular and comprehensive impact measurement. It is challenging in these circumstances to gauge "success", which is why the careful and objective assessment of the responsible tourism or sustainable tourism awards judging panels was used for the initial selection of case-study organisations.

The final implementing mechanism is market awareness, including the ability to harness market forces. The majority of the organisations understood that "central to everything is that you have to have a great product" (A. Carter-Jones, personal communication, December 31, 2009) and products "that will work" (A. Mauthoor, personal communication, January 4, 2010). Here, the accommodation providers and visitor attraction claimed (corroborated by travellers' reviews) to be located in beautiful places with diverse nature and wildlife, comfortable facilities, knowledgeable interpreters and instructors, while the ethical nature of their services and social/environmental activities were widely counted as competitive advantages. Some of the organisations built on these aspects by creating connections with customers and giving the mission a real face (as advocated by practitioners Lynch & Walls, 2009). A ground operator in Asia related her own first fundraising cycle trip on the organisation's website, while an eco-resort owner said, "before we even had names for our resort and the business, we already had a blog documenting the whole building concept. That got people already emotionally invested in what we were doing. That was one of our best marketing tools so far" (M. Miners, personal communication, January 9, 2010). As with the choice of operational model, however, these techniques tended to come about through instinctive or habitual practice rather than deliberate design.

In order to gauge the contextual forces surrounding their operations, research participants were also asked about the external challenges they faced. Most highlighted the economic environment, specifically the recession. Other challenges related to the political ecology of their operating environment or an unfavourable investment climate due to the political culture, for example corruption. Fears of global insecurity, the threat of disease outbreaks and natural disasters – all of which affect tourism generally – were also mentioned. A challenge more closely tied into the nexus of social and environmental activism with profit-making related to problems with communication technology and logistics in the remote places where some enterprises were located.

Discussion

While it is recognised that findings from case studies do not usually allow statistical generalisation, we believe that our investigation has resulted in a high level of real-world validity. The intention was to examine and understand how the investigated enterprises operate and fulfil their objectives, and despite the diversity of the organisations studied, emergent patterns indicate that some operational models predominate.

The most popular model overall was Service Subsidisation (SSM), probably due to its broad application to many different tourism organisations, irrespective of structure, external market or target population. An obvious further advantage is that while the enterprise is primarily a funding mechanism for social and environmental work, there is sufficient overlap between business activities and the social/environmental programmes to allow for a synergistic relationship. Some divergence was noted between social enterprise theory and its application in tourism, however. Alter's framework explains that SSM is activated when organisations "leverage assets as the basis of their activities", either by commercialising social services or by using available physical resources (Alter, 2006, p. 221), on the assumption that business activities are initiated by a not-for-profit parent organisation. In our study this was only the case with two organisations, while for the others business activities and social/environmental initiatives developed concurrently – or the situation was even reversed from the model, with the business established first and the charitable arm formalised at a later stage.

Accommodation providers were found to prefer EM in combination with SSM. EM is a natural fit for unilocal organisations, especially marginalised or peripheral ones, since they can make a real difference to local economic development through the multiplier effect. Local job creation can also be critical for synergies between business and the mission, as seen with an eco-resort that has become a vehicle for conservation (M. Miners, personal communication, January 9, 2010).

The most appealing model to tour operators was MIM, with holiday packages created from products and services provided by others. According to Alter (2006), the model has three main advantages: potential for scalability by reaching out to communities in various destinations; a guarantee of continuous focus on the mission; and the potential for self-financing – although in practice, while some organisations had achieved self-sufficiency, others were still struggling. Although she also states that "difficulties can arise in finding markets for client-made products due to market saturation [and] poor or inconsistent quality" (Alter, 2007, pp. 216–217), the enterprises in our study resolved this by tailoring their product offer to specific market segments and by supporting suppliers through business coaching, training, product development and, sometimes, loans.

The cases studied hardly used the ESM and FSM models because the target population assumed in these models – generally poor or otherwise disadvantaged people – was also the market, making it unlikely that financial viability could be achieved. Most touristic social enterprises sell to an external market, which is quite separate from the mission beneficiaries; indeed almost all the organisations studied targeted western tourists, in particular a high-end market.

As discussed earlier, the literature (e.g. Allan, 2005) suggests that social enterprises have three basic characteristics: an enterprise orientation, social aims and social ownership. However, while all the businesses in the study fulfilled the first two of these central pillars in that they all created and sold products or services in order to generate social and environmental value, the third aspect did not generally apply. While the guidance of the board of trustees or advisors was appreciated, in particular inputs into decision-making and because of the two-way communications facilitated, actual ownership of the enterprise tended to reside with the founder-entrepreneurs.

Factors critical to success

The study finding that the 11 organisations made extensive use of the "smart practices" conducive to strong performance was unsurprising in that all the organisations were winners or highly commended in business competitions. In the areas of leadership, strategy and organisational culture, the results were very much in line with the identified success factors, suggesting that strong "integrative drivers" are crucial, as with any high-performing business. In the key management area of "implementing mechanisms", the cases also displayed the majority of the success factors, although some slight exceptions were observed.

First, one organisation showed weaknesses in strategy (particularly planning) as well as in operational processes and structures (e.g. rethinking of work system design and clear role distribution). This may have been because its business activities were still developing, and it illustrates how performance across key management areas is interdependent. Secondly, the legal structures of the organisations were chosen strategically, but in two cases failed to "finance growth" (Lynch & Walls, 2009, p. 51): in one case the organisation was purely not-for-profit and relied mainly on donor funding, while the other worked exclusively through its for-profit company structure, with no external income except donations tied to the amount of business generated. This suggests that the most successful structures will support a combination of internally generated revenue from business activities and externally generated funds from grants or donations unrelated to customer numbers and confirms that a twin corporate or institutional structure – depending on the legal system in the base jurisdiction – is likely to be beneficial to social enterprises in allowing access to trading revenue and non-revenue sources and in enabling more effective harnessing of both social and commercial capital (Chell, 2007) to achieve their aims.

Finally, performance measurement was where results were the least consistent with "smart practice", in that several organisations measured impacts informally and irregularly, sometimes relying on anecdotal information gathered by untrained people. Generally, it is frequently the case that in the day-to-day pressure of business growth and management, detailed evaluation will be sidelined: the measures suggested by practitioner manuals such as London and Morfopoulos' (2010) "how to" guide are challenging to implement in practice. In mitigation, it can be argued that an over-emphasis on performance measurement can be counterproductive through reducing resources for core functions.

Conclusion

This study set out to shed light on social enterprises in the tourism sector, starting with an examination of how the movement has grown from a rather nebulous concept rooted in collective and participatory action to a well-accepted tool in the suite of development approaches. Indeed, Mukherjee Reed (2010, p. 255) concludes that while civil society actors have been critical of the role of business in development, "the reclamation of the human development agenda ... cannot be achieved without fully engaging the role of business, understood as corporate power".

Our paper aimed to explore social enterprise models in tourism and to identify critical success and challenge factors. It was found that the organisations' approaches to fulfilling the twin aims of generating economic and social/environmental values are generally consistent with Alter's (2006) operational models of social enterprise. Three of the seven models were more frequently used, suggesting that they have more relevance in tourism. In all cases, the target population (beneficiaries of the social/environmental programmes) was separate from the target market (customers for the tourism products), which allowed organisations to tap into the potentially high earning opportunities of tourism to support their mission. In practice, enterprises rarely slotted neatly into one of the models outlined. Rather, the operational models served as "building blocks", which social entrepreneurs arranged and combined to achieve their objectives, forming complex models. We emphasise, however, that there was no deliberate use of the models, since none of the entrepreneurs interviewed was aware of the typology in advance of this study – although one did actually alter the structure of his venture after the lead researcher gave him an explanation of the model he was using compared to others in the research study.

Although our investigation found that success cannot be attributed to any one factor (or even to a group of factors in one management area) but to a combination of these, it can be suggested that essential success factors concern awareness of market conditions, including the need for a good product (and, by extension, the need to match product to market), and for strong leadership to shape a coherent organisational culture that provides the context for different stages of enterprise growth, and to create a balance between financial and social/environmental aims. These factors appear to be valid for social enterprises in tourism regardless of the primary business activity or the model chosen. More specifically, success also lies in choosing one of the operational models in which paying customers are different from target beneficiaries of the social mission. Patterns emerging from the study showed that accommodation providers and tour operators (albeit unconsciously) implemented models that naturally fitted their business activities: SSM appears appropriate for organisations with an overlap between social programmes and business activities, while EM is more suitable for accommodation providers and MIM for tour operators.

Ultimately, the success of any social enterprise relies on maintaining a balance between mission and profit through the integrative drivers of leadership, strategy and organisational culture, and through successful implementation of the mechanisms that operationalise the strategy. Despite the external recognition of their achievements, however, several of the organisations struggled to balance financial viability with mission outcomes, and research into other organisations – for instance those that were long-listed for responsible or sustainable tourism awards but failed to progress further – might reveal even less success in dealing with this dilemma.

This investigation represents a "snapshot" of the organisations at a particular time when they have achieved external recognition for their contribution to social and economic development through tourism, but there is no guarantee that they will continue along the same path in the future. Nevertheless, while further research will undoubtedly reveal more insights, the findings of this study are considered sufficiently robust to inform management decisions concerning existing or aspiring social enterprises in tourism. They may even go some way towards bridging the gap between theory and practice, since the entrepreneurs concerned had all started their venture based on belief in the power of commerce to effect change and after identifying a gap in the market, rather than doing so after reading a manual. They represent the "transformational leaders" noted by London and Morfopoulos (2010, p. 64) and confirm the place of "inspirational ideas and individuals" (Green, 2008, p. 438) as significant agents in the complex and unpredictable dynamics of change.

Key characteristics that emerge are the eclecticism and pragmatism of these individuals: they are not themselves concerned with conceptualising their actions but simply engage with a variety of strategies and a range of tools as they consider will best achieve their aims, utilising different types of institutional structures and organisational models according to the national regulatory context, the funding mechanisms and the social and community capital resources available. As researchers we were always impressed with their enthusiasm and determination, and if we have any concerns it is that some are feeling their way ahead somewhat blindly, perhaps having heard of "social entrepreneurship" but having little knowledge of potentially helpful concepts and models. If our work is to have any application in the real world, it would be to provide some guidance to nascent philanthropic entrepreneurs as to possible courses of actions that would lead to swifter achievement of their goals.

References

Allan, B. (2005). Social enterprise: Through the eyes of the consumer. *Social Enterprise Journal, 1*, 57–77.

Alter, S.K. (2006). Social enterprise models and their mission and money relationships. In A. Nicholls (Ed.), *Social entrepreneurship: New models of sustainable change* (pp. 205–232). Oxford: Oxford University Press.

Alter, S.K. (2007). *Social enterprise typology*. Retrieved from http://www.virtueventures.com/resources/setypology

Ashoka Changemakers. (2009). *Geotourism challenge 2010*. Retrieved from http://www.changemakers.com/coasts

Austin, J., Stevenson, H., & Wei-Skillern, J. (2006). Social and commercial entrepreneurship: Same, different, or both? *Entrepreneurship Theory and Practice* (January), 1–22.

Austin, J.E., Gutiérrez, R., Ogliastri, E., & Reficco, E. (2006). *Effective management of social enterprises: Lessons from businesses and civil society organizations in Iberoamerica*. Cambridge: Harvard University Press.

Bornstein, D. (2004). *How to change the world: Social entrepreneurs and the power of new ideas*. New York: Oxford University Press.

Boschee, J., & McClurg, J. (2003). *Toward a better understanding of social entrepreneurship: Some important distinctions*. Retrieved from www.caledonia.org.uk/papers/social-Entrepreneurship.doc

Chell, E. (2007). Social enterprise and entrepreneurship: Towards a convergent theory of the entrepreneurial process. *International Small Business Journal, 25*, 5–26.

Dart, R. (2004). The legitimacy of social enterprise. *Nonprofit Management and Leadership, 14*, 411–424.

Defourny, J. (2001). From third sector to social enterprise. In C. Borzaga & J. Defourny (Eds.), *The emergence of social enterprise* (pp. 1–18). London: Routledge.

Defourny, J., & Nyssens, M. (2006). Defining social enterprise. In M. Nyssens (Ed.), *Social enterprise: At the crossroads of market, public policies and civil society* (pp. 3–26). London: Routledge.

Forbes, T. (2009). Entrepreneurs, institutions and institutional entrepreneurship: New light through old windows? In J. Ateljevic & S.J. Page (Eds.), *Tourism and entrepreneurship: International perspectives* (pp. 91–106). Oxford: Butterworth Heinemann.

Green, D. (2008). *From poverty to power: How active citizens and effective states can change the world*. Oxford: Oxfam.

Haugh, H. (2005). A research agenda for social entrepreneurship. *Social Enterprise Journal, 1*, 1–12.

Kerlin, J.A. (2006). Social enterprise in the United States and Europe: Understanding and learning from the differences. *Voluntas, 17*, 247–263.

Laville, J.-L., & Nyssens, M. (2001). The social enterprise: Towards a theoretical socio-economic approach. In C. Borzaga & J. Defourny (Eds.), *The emergence of social enterprise* (pp. 312–332). London: Routledge.

London, M., & Morfopoulos, R.G. (2010). *Social entrepreneurship: How to start successful corporate social responsibility and community-based initiatives for advocacy and change.* London: Routledge.

Lynch, K., & Walls, J., Jr. (2009). *Mission, Inc.: The practitioner's guide to social enterprise.* San Francisco, CA: Berrett-Koehler.

Mitchell, J., & Ashley, C. (2010). *Tourism and poverty reduction: Pathways to prosperity.* London: Earthscan.

Mukherjee Reed, A. (2010). Business, development, and inequality. In J. Clapp & R. Wilkinson (Eds.), *Global governance, poverty and inequality* (pp. 235–262). London: Routledge.

Nicholls, A. (2006). Introduction. In A. Nicholls (Ed.), *Social entrepreneurship: New models of sustainable change* (pp. 1–36). Oxford: Oxford University Press.

Nicholls, A. (2010). The legitimacy of social entrepreneurship: Reflexive isomorphism in a pre-paradigmatic field. *Entrepreneurship Theory and Practice* (July), 611–633.

Nicholls, A., & Young, R. (2008). Preface to the paperback edition. In A. Nicholls (Ed.), *Social entrepreneurship: New models of sustainable change* (pp. vii–xxiv). Oxford: Oxford University Press.

Pearce, J. (2003). *Social enterprise in any town.* London: Calouste Gulbenkian Foundation.

Peredo, A.M., & McLean, M. (2006). Social entrepreneurship: A critical review of the concept. *Journal of World Business, 41*, 56–65.

Responsibletravel.com. (2009). *Responsible Tourism awards.* Retrieved from http://www.responsibletravel.com/awards/winners/

Sahlman, W.A. (1996). Some thoughts on business plans. In W.A. Sahlman, H. Stevenson, M.J. Roberts & A.V. Bhide (Eds.), *The entrepreneurial venture* (pp. 138–176). Boston, MA: Harvard Business School Press.

Simms, S.V.K., & Robinson, J.A. (2008). Activist or entrepreneur: An identity-based model of social entrepreneurship. In J. Robinson, J. Mair & K. Hockerts (Eds.), *International perspectives on social entrepreneurship* (pp. 9–26). London: Palgrave Macmillan.

Wallace, B. (2005). Exploring the meaning(s) of sustainability for community-based social entrepreneurs. *Social Enterprise Journal, 1*, 78–89.

World Travel and Tourism Council. (2009). *Tourism for Tomorrow: Awards 2012.* Retrieved from http://www.tourismfortomorrow.com/The_Awards/

Index

Note: Page numbers in *italics* represent tables
Page numbers in **bold** represent figures
Page numbers followed by 'n' refer to notes

INDEX

For Product Safety Concerns and Information please contact our
EU representative GPSR@taylorandfrancis.com Taylor & Francis
Verlag GmbH, Kaufingerstraße 24, 80331 München, Germany